THE DECLINE AND FALL OF BRITISH CAPITALISM

THE
DECLINE & FALL
OF BRITISH
CAPITALISM

by

KEITH HUTCHISON

WITH A NEW FOREWORD BY
DAVID OWEN

ARCHON BOOKS
HAMDEN CONNECTICUT
1966

FIRST PUBLISHED 1951
REPRINTED 1966 WITH PERMISSION

WITH A FOREWORD BY DAVID OWEN
AND A NEW PREFACE BY THE AUTHOR

To
Mary Agnes Hamilton

FOREWORD

It is something of a black mark, I think, against the publishing world that, when this book went out of print a number of years ago, neither the British nor the American publishers—nor, indeed, any paper-back house—seemed to show interest in a reprinting. For teachers of recent English history this was an unhappy decision. Mr. Hutchison's was virtually the only book that set out to trace, within reasonable compass, the decline of Britain's free-market economy from the early 1880's and the building up of a mixed economy and a welfare society—in other words, to follow the transformation of the role of the State from "that of neutral policeman to social worker and economic planner." Not merely was this almost the only book on the subject but, more important, it was a good one and one which neither students nor general readers interested in the antecedents of British postwar society could well dispense with. Archon Books, I was happy to learn, has decided to make good the omission.

Readers may be inclined to boggle at Mr. Hutchison's title, *The Decline and Fall of British Capitalism*, as I have found myself tempted to do at various times. Obviously capitalism in the sense of a productive system under the immediate command of private individuals is not dead in Britain, nor is capitalism as a social system. Not all of industry, nor indeed most of it, is socialized. But Mr. Hutchison's meaning is more particular. What concerns him is the gradual weakening of the free-market system by planning—planned prices, planned manpower, planned investments, planned allocation of materials—and the redistribution of incomes that has taken place through steeply graduated taxation. So that today the British economy, although superficially it does not seem so much different from free-wheeling capitalism is, in fact, relying on controls other than the natural forces of the market. And, indeed, these forces had been so attenuated by six decades of legislative intervention, which included two World Wars, that the decisions of the Labour Government in the late '40's seemed no great shock. Sometimes the system has been operated through physical controls, more recently by economic management, which, as Professor S. H. Beer points out, has made traditional Socialism and more public owner-ship irrelevant. For, although this mixed economy by no means dis-cards private ownership and the profit motive, ultimate, if indirect, control remains firmly in public hands.

Mr. Hutchison has the twin advantages of having been born a Briton and having been trained as an economist. The former is, at the least, no handicap, and the latter is almost essential prepara-tion for dealing with this period of English history. For, through-out the seventy years that he covers, economic issues were crucial, though often under the surface. Just as mid-Victorian preëminence rested on British domination of world trade, so British decline marked the loss of that commercial hegemony, and the years from the early 1880's show a gradual recession of British power, from 1918 to 1939 only fitfully recognized but unmistakable after 1945. Throughout the book the economic issue emerges as crucial, and questions of trade and finance are canvassed with the expertise—but blessedly without the technical intricacies—of the professional. Mr. Hutchison points out, for example, that the Edwardian period, to which the upper classes look back nostalgically, from the work-ing class point of view was an age of retrogression. Apparent progress was mostly a trick of the price level. During the last quarter of the nineteenth century, the fact of working class advance was clouded by falling prices, while in the Edwardian period rising prices threw a false aura of prosperity around the society.

In 1914, we now recognize, capitalism's "slow decline turned to rapid decay." The British economic machine was never again the same, for the sheer cost of the war, the quasi-socialist expedients which the State had to fashion, and the whole disorganized credit mechanism, domestic and international, all these made a return to stability and prosperity not only difficult but impossible. What, in the United States, Harding termed "normalcy" was out of the ques-tion for Britain. Yet throughout the '20's governments pursued the fata morgana of Edwardian "prosperity," and the gold standard—more than that, the gold standard with the pound at pre-war parity with the dollar—was the prescription written by most financial experts. The pill, of course, proved disastrous, as Mr. Hutchison points out in one of his best chapters, "Procrustes' Bed of Gold."

FOREWORD

The consequence was that ministers who themselves were implacably hostile to socialism were left with no alternatives, given the range of social distress and the pressure of an organized working class now armed with the ballot. Repeatedly they found themselves bringing in measures that involved economic planning or that raised the income tax to new, punitive heights.

In other words, as Mr. Hutchison suggests, the collectivist current, once set in motion, proved irreversible. Just as mid-Victorian statesmen had customarily announced their hostility to democracy when introducing bills for broadening the franchise, so now their successors might profess an undying antipathy to socialism. But they still continued to encroach on the free market and to put the State more and more firmly in the business of social welfare. In the 1920's, for example, the Chamberlain Act of 1923, sponsored by a non-socialist, and the Wheatley Act of 1924, a Labour measure, together accounted for the building of about a million houses. Gradually the "Collectivist Coral Island" had been enlarged until on the eve of the Second World War it seemed clear that, if Britain survived at all, her governments would have to take even more decisive steps away from free-market capitalism.

I do not imply that this is an economic or fiscal history of Britain. The value of the book lies in the way that it deals with the interwoven economic, political, and social factors and shows how they interacted (in a wholly un-Marxian fashion, Mr. Hutchison notes) to destroy classic, free-market capitalism. This was, of course, a complex process, in which political, as well as economic, factors figured heavily. Plainly such developments as the coming of democracy, the political organization of Labour and its commitment to socialism, the disintegration of the Liberal Party, two World Wars, and countless other factors are involved, and these are seen in their relation to the main theme. Indeed, it is one of the merits of Mr. Hutchison's study that he never loses sight of his main thesis but selects his material in the light of its relevance to the central point.

For a book written sixteen years ago, this one has stood up remarkably well. There is little that I should wish to change, though more recent research has modified our interpretation of some matters, most of them not substantial. More to the point is to ask

FOREWORD

whether one can fairly take as optimistic a view of the British position as did Mr. Hutchison. In the early 1950's he finds Britain "enjoying a breather while its leaders checked their bearings." Now, after sixteen years of alternating spells of exhilaration and depression, the country is still facing what, in essentials, are the same problems that have been dogging it since the War. Leaders are not now "enjoying a breather" before undertaking further advance; they are struggling to keep the economy afloat, this in spite of the average tourist's impression of a country luxuriating in relative affluence. The plainest symptom of trouble is, of course, the persistent and heavy adverse balance in the nation's international account. The crisis in the autumn of 1964 was weathered by massive foreign credits, but no decisive steps have yet been taken to bring the account into balance. Granted that such measures are unattractive to contemplate and disagreeable for a government to administer. Granted, also, that they cannot be hastily improvised and put into effect. But the primary issue in Britain today is not, I think, that of more or less socialism but simply that of maintaining a viable economy. This would be the critical question with either a Tory or a Labour Government in power, and for both of them the options would be gravely limited in number and distressingly similar in character.

Harvard University,   David Owen
Cambridge, Massachusetts,
June, 1966.

PREFACE TO 1966 EDITION

When this book was first published, some critics suggested that the title was more provocative than accurate. Conceding that British capitalism had sustained many damaging blows in its prolonged fight against socialism, they were not ready to admit even a technical knock-out. I agreed then that this was an arguable view, for my own enthusiasm for the title had diminished since the book was conceived in 1947. The years since 1950 have in some ways strengthened my critics' case and, if I were now rewriting the book rather than re-issuing it, I would probably decide on a less challenging title.

This does not mean that I feel called upon to apologise for the book itself or to modify its main thesis. My purpose was to trace the antecedents of the Labour Party's victory in 1945 back to the widening of the suffrage by the Third Reform Act of 1884 and explain the economic and social effects of the advance of British democracy. That the result of this advance was a decline in the power of British capitalism is surely incontestable and although it may not have fallen, it has certainly been transformed.

In the new final chapter written for the English edition in 1950, when the second Attlee government with its thread-bare majority was visibly failing, I maintained that the massive reforms of the previous five years were the culmination of a long process and, by and large, were irreversible. This argument, I believe, has been fully sustained by subsequent events. Foreseeing the return of the Tory Party to power, I suggested it would not make a great deal of difference to the British social and economic system and this has proved to be the case. Apart from restoring most of the steel industry to private ownership (though under a system of stringent controls) the Tories did not interfere with the nationalisation schemes carried out by the Attlee government. Neither did they tamper seriously with the social security system nor repudiate the national obligation to maintain full employment. Moreover, under Tory rule significant, if still inadequate, steps were taken to expand opportunity for higher education, a development which, in the long run, must tend to modify the rigidities of the British class system.

The Tories in short accepted the fact that there could be no return to the good old days of Victorian or even Edwardian capitalism. The economy had become "mixed", combining large elements of socialism with still strong and important segments of private enterprise. The market was no longer king and the main directions of the economy were determined, not by the forces of supply and demand, but by the decisions of the government. It was a model that owed little to Adam Smith or Ricardo and much to J. M. Keynes, Sidney Webb, and Lord Beveridge.

It is necessary to add that British capitalism has adapted itself to changed conditions with a good deal more success than might have been anticipated. In the restricted but still large sphere open to it private enterprise has flourished in the past fifteen years. High taxation and a creeping inflation have squeezed the *rentier* class but active entrepreneurs, able to take advantage of tax-loopholes, and, until very recently, unhampered by any form of capital-gains tax, have in many cases added impressively to their fortunes.

At the same time British socialists have been rather lacking in resilience. After implementing its 1945 program, the Labour Party seemed uncertain about what steps to take next. During its long spell in opposition it devoted a great deal of time and energy to futile squabbles between its right and left wings. The thinking of the left was, in a sense, the more conservative: it seemed to be nostalgically looking back to Keir Hardie and the early days of the movement as it called for the nationalization of more and more industries. The Right Wingers, more aware of the economic realities of Britain's position, realized that nationalization was far from a panacea, but lacked striking new ideas on which to base a substitute program.

The Labour Party closed its ranks under the leadership of Harold Wilson, an aggressive, able, and thoroughly pragmatic politician who has moved from left of center well over to the right, without really resolving its doctrinal difficulties. Now returned to power with an ample working majority, it finds itself boxed in. The recurring crises of the pound sterling limit the Labour Government's freedom of action in many directions. It must postpone plans for the extension of social services, limit new investment unless it contributes to an improvement in the balance of payments, hold down wage increases and discourage consumption. All this is very frustrating to the back-bench left-wingers who are further irked by what they feel is Mr. Wilson's undue subservience to Washington, which in turn is closely related to the exchange problem.

It may be that Mr. Wilson's hopes of improving the efficiency and restoring the competitiveness of British industry will be fulfilled and sterling soundly established in time for his government to turn to more constructive policies before its mandate expires. But at this time it must be admitted that the future of Britain under any political regime is clouded. The Tories proved unable to retreat: Labour seems unable to advance. Neither party has found a solution for Britain's fundamental economic problems. It may be that the only way out of this impasse is adherence to the European Economic Community and the Wilson government does seem to be moving cautiously in this direction. Many British socialists fear that this development would give a new lease of life to capitalism. In view of the historical record, I doubt this. The economies of the present "Six" are as "mixed" as Britain's and are likely to remain so. There is, I suspect, little future in the western world for either pure capitalism or pure socialism.

Keith Hutchison

Durham, Connecticut
July 4, 1966

ACKNOWLEDGMENTS

A B O O K of this kind is necessarily, in some sense, a work of collaboration. As any writer of history must, I have drawn freely on the labours of others — the researches of scholars, the records of contemporary journalists, the diaries and recollections of statesmen. To them I owe a debt on which only token payment can be made in the list of books on page 273.

It is noteworthy that the most numerous entries on this list are under the name of Winston Spencer Churchill, whose span of years almost exactly coincides with the events described in this book, and who for two-thirds of the period has been writing history magnificently as well as making it. Mr. Churchill has dominated the British political scene during the first half of the twentieth century as Gladstone dominated it in the second half of the nineteenth. At times he has swung with the incoming tide of socialism; at others he has sought to stem it. Always a controversial figure, he has compelled admiration as easily as he has provoked disagreement. A critical admirer myself, I cannot resist this opportunity to salute him.

Among my friends, I am particularly grateful to Mary Agnes Hamilton, Professor Theresa Wolfson of Brooklyn College, and Professor H. L. Beales of The London School of Economics, who have read sections of this book in manuscript and have given me the benefit of their special knowledge of the period. They are, of course, in no way responsible for any of the opinions expressed, or for any errors.

I have to thank the staffs of the New York Society Library and the Library of the British Information Service in New York for much assistance and many courtesies while I was gathering material for this book.

What was in effect a summary of this book appeared in the Fall, 1949, issue of *The Antioch Review*. I am grateful to the Editors for permission to incorporate parts of this article in my text.

This book was originally finished in the autumn of 1949 and was published in New York in March 1950. Following the General Election of 1950, Part Five, Chapter II, was revised and some of its material incorporated in a new final chapter.

ACKNOWLEDGMENTS

My daughter, Kate, and my son, David, well trained by the teachers and librarians of the late-lamented Horace Mann-Lincoln School in New York, have both been most helpful in checking references for me. And I am more grateful to them than they know for their consideration in limiting their proper claims on my time and attention while I was engaged in writing.

Any attempt to say how much I owe to the constant encouragement and astute criticisms of my first wife, the late Betsy Hutchison, and to her skilled assistance in editing and proof reading, would call for expression of the inexpressible. It is her book as well as mine.

K. H.

CONTENTS

CONTENTS

INTRODUCTION:

REVOLUTION IN SLOW MOTION

N O one is likely to deny the decline of British capitalism in
this century, but the suggestion that it has actually fallen
may evoke protests from both left and right. Communists,
of course, will reject it with scorn, and there are also sincere
socialists who believe that the citadel of capitalism is yet intact
even if its outposts have been captured. A major part of British
industry, they will point out, remains in the hands of private
enterprise; wealth is still concentrated in the hands of a relatively
small class; the power of property is temporarily circumscribed
rather than permanently broken. Coinciding with such fears are
the hopes of a dwindling but doughty band of right-wingers
who, bloody but unbowed, insist that before long, when socialism
has proved an abject failure, capitalism will enjoy a glorious
revival.

The chief evidence contradicting these fears and hopes is not
the socialization of key industries since 1945. Much more important are two forces which began to gather strength long before
a Labour government seemed a practical possibility. The first is
the undermining of the free-market system; the second the trend
towards redistribution of incomes by way of steeply graduated
direct taxation and a comprehensive network of social services.

Under the Labour Government the potency of these forces has
of course been immensely increased. The free-market system, the
heart of the capitalist economy, has almost ceased functioning.
Supply and demand, which once determined the distribution of
resources, have yielded to planned prices, planned investments,
planned allocation of materials. Where their grandfathers relied
on the impersonal forces of the market to maintain a balanced
economy and to promote automatically wealth and welfare,
the British people now look to the State, acting as agent for the
community, to achieve consciously desired ends. Meanwhile
redistribution of incomes has brought the country a long way —
perhaps nearly as far as is practical — towards the ideal of equality.

Such steps are not readily reversed. A change in government

in Britain might mean a change in plans, but hardly abandonment of planning. Even more unlikely is a successful effort to widen appreciably the diminished gap between rich and poor. In a democracy, the few may for a time succeed in securing a dispro-portionate share of the national cake; but once they have been made to yield part of it for the benefit of the many, their prospects of restoring the original division are slim indeed.

The purpose of this book, however, is not to describe the changes in Britain's economic and social structure made in the past few years. It is rather to trace the development of the inter-woven economic and political factors that prepared the way for these changes.

The story opens in the early eighteen-eighties, the period in which extension of the franchise created a working-class majority in the electorate. It was a time, also, when British capitalism, after nearly a century of amazing advance, began to show signs of faltering. Henceforth it was to lose ground to competing capital-isms and to suffer more and more from those contradictions which Karl Marx had analysed not many years earlier. Recurring crises of overproduction sharpened the struggle for markets and even-tually led to war on a scale so gigantic that it left the capitalist economies of the old world permanently crippled.

But in Britain, at least, Marx's idea that as capitalism approached decay the class struggle would become progressively more acute was not realized. In the famous thirty-third chapter of *Das Kapital* he had written of capitalist accumulation as a canni-balistic process in which the large owners of productive property swallowed the small. With the growth of monopoly, he asserted, 'grows the mass of misery, oppression, slavery, degradation, exploitation: but with this too grows the revolt of the working class, a class always increasing in numbers, and disciplined, united, organized by the very mechanism of the process of capital-ist production itself'.

Marx saw no possibility of compromise between capital and labour, and was certain that the inevitable triumph of the workers would come only after a violent upheaval, although he once admitted that in Britain the issue might possibly be settled with-out revolution. He never anticipated, however, what has actually happened — a Fabian retreat of the British capitalist forces before the slowly advancing political and industrial armies of labour. The most ironic of the contradictions of capitalism was, in fact, overlooked by Marx, although the evidence lay beneath his nose during his long years of exile in London. It was the peaceful surrender by the British bourgeois of their political monopoly, the preliminary stages of which had occurred before the socialist prophet died in 1883.

The paradoxical mission of nineteenth-century liberalism was to create both the free-market economy and the democracy that was to destroy it. To gain the first objective, the political monopoly of the aristocracy had to be smashed, but, having accomplished this end in 1832, the liberal bourgeoisie could not stop. For, while they might defend as a temporary expedient a franchise based on property, philosophically they were committed to equality of civic rights. Thus, hesitatingly and somewhat fearfully, they advanced step by step towards manhood suffrage, and so to the transfer of ultimate sovereignty to the masses. Henceforth the few who exerted economic power through the ownership of property became subject to the political authority of the propertyless multitude.

Beatrice Webb in *Our Partnership* summed up the inevitable conflict of interests that ensued:

The rule of the capitalist and the landlord has proved to be hopelessly inconsistent with political democracy. There can be no permanence of social peace in a situation in which we abandon production to a tiny proportion of the population, who own the means of production, and yet give the workers the political power to enforce demands on the national income which capitalism has neither the ability nor the incentive to supply.[1]

The remarkable thing is that the British ruling classes were able for so long to retain a large, although gradually diminishing, measure of political and economic power. Their generals conducted the retreat with great skill, not infrequently delaying their adversaries by diversionary movements, sometimes winning useful periods of truce by modest concessions, occasionally staging temporarily effective counter-offensives. Nevertheless, over the years, they retired farther and farther from the spacious citadel which

[1] Longmans, Green (London, 1948), p. 489.

they occupied so confidently up to the last quarter of the nineteenth century. In the sixty-one years that separated the Third Reform Act from the advent of the Labour Government in 1945, the capitalist system was sensibly modified, and the free market partially paralysed. The role of the State was changed from that of neutral policeman to social worker and economic planner; it acquired specific responsibility for social security and welfare and became an agency for the redistribution of property and income. And most of the measures that wrought this change were written and steered through Parliament by ministers who were vehemently opposed to socialism.

Seen, then, in the perspective of history, the sweeping electoral victory of the Labour Party in 1945 appears not as a startling change of direction on the part of the British people but as a quickened step along a familiar path. It marked a new stage in that revolution in slow motion which, in the period covered by this book, has brought about the transfer of political power from a small ruling class to the mass of the workers by hand and brain, and the transformation of an individualistic economic system into one broadly socialist.

PART ONE

DIMINISHING RETURNS: 1880-1900

It was the end of an epoch. The long dominion of the Middle-classes, which had begun in 1832, had come to its close and with it the almost equal reign of Liberalism. The great victories had been won. All sorts of lumbering tyrannies had been toppled over. Authority was everywhere broken. Slaves were free. Conscience was free. Trade was free. But hunger and squalor and cold were also free; and the people demanded something more than liberty.

WINSTON S. CHURCHILL: *Lord Randolph Churchill*

CHAPTER I

LOST MONOPOLY

FOR six months in 1884, for eight the next year, Arthur Henderson together with thousands of fellow workers tramped the Tyneside vainly seeking work. The future master builder of the Labour Party, then in his twenty-first year, was a skilled iron-moulder who had been employed in one of the great engineering shops of the district which built locomotives and supplied the shipbuilding industry. For a few years trade had been good. After the disastrous slump of the mid-seventies, recovery had been marked by a railway boom in the United States and a shipping boom in Britain. There was a close connection between these two developments: as the steel network spread across America opening up the virgin lands of the west, huge quantities of cheap grain and meat were made available to the British market, creating a demand for new ocean tonnage. Speculative construction raised the carrying capacity of the British merchant marine by nearly 50 per cent between 1875 and 1883, when total launchings in British yards were no less than 1,250,000 tons. But demand suddenly dried up. In 1884 the output of British shipbuilders was only 750,000 tons and in 1886 it had slipped to under 500,000.

In those days there were no government unemployment returns, but statistics published by a number of trade unions showed an average of 10 per cent of their members out of work in 1885-86. The small fraction of the working classes covered by such figures were skilled men earning wages in good times which might permit the accumulation of modest savings. Moreover, some of them, like Henderson, were able to draw unemployment benefit from their union funds. The huge and unrecorded mass of the unskilled and unorganized labourers had no such resources. For them loss of work meant destitution mitigated by private charity or, when that failed, by the relief dispensed by the Guardians of the Poor on terms deliberately designed to deter all but the most desperate applicants.

Unemployment was among the ugly facts of life for the workers, but the comfortable classes hardly recognized its existence and the word itself was not dignified by admission to the *Oxford Dictionary* until 1888. Loss of a job, it was felt, was more often than not due to defects of character; mass dismissals, which could not be so simply explained, were ascribed to the inscrutable and, in the long run, benevolent forces which presided over the market. Since every precept of economic science forbade any attempt to interfere with these forces, nothing could be done to prevent unemployment or, except by way of philanthropy, to reduce the distress it caused.

Hungry workers, however, were not always as resigned to their lot as they should have been. Apostles of revolutionary doctrines were urging them to demand relief as a right. In February 1885, a young socialist, John Burns, led a deputation to the Local Government Board, the department which supervised administration of the Poor Law. He demanded action in strong language: unless relief was provided, he said, there would be deaths from starvation and the Board and the Government would be guilty of murder. Shocked civil servants listened coldly to this harangue: officially there was no unemployment problem with which the State could, or should, concern itself.

The agitation continued. In September 1885 a series of un-employed marches and demonstrations in London led to clashes with the police who sought to prevent street meetings and so raised the issue of free speech. The following February, after a great rally in Trafalgar Square under the auspices of the Social Democratic Federation, an angry mob marched via Pall Mall and Piccadilly to Hyde Park, shattering on its way hundreds of windows of clubs, houses, and shops. Four of the leaders were arrested on charges of sedition but were later acquitted after a trial which they contrived to turn into a socialist demonstration. Meanwhile the broken glass cut many purse strings, and contributions poured into a relief fund opened by the Lord Mayor. They were needed. That winter, one-fifth of the population of White-chapel, nearly one-third of that of the parish of St. George's East, applied to this fund for assistance.

Poverty was an old story; so was the syncopated rhythm of trade and the ebb and flow of employment. But discerning contemporary eyes saw new elements in the cyclical pattern that was unfolding during the last quarter of the nineteenth century. The British economy appeared to have lost some of the resilience which it had exhibited since the beginning of the industrial revolution; there was no longer the same assurance that each new wave of prosperity would reach a higher point than the last. Since 1872, when the value of British exports touched a peak not to be sighted again until the 'nineties, British manufacturers had been confronted by rising tariff walls in the United States, Austria, Russia, Germany, France and Italy. And in all foreign markets they were meeting more and more intensive competition from the rapidly expanding industries of the United States, France and, in particular, Germany. A Royal Commission appointed to inquire into the depression of trade and industry reported in 1886:

We are beginning to feel the effects of foreign competition in quarters where our trade formerly enjoyed a practical monopoly . . . In every quarter of the world the perseverance and enterprise of the Germans are making themselves felt. In the actual production of commodities we have now few, if any, advantages over them; and in a knowledge of the markets of the world . . . a determination to obtain a footing wherever they can, and a tenacity in maintaining it, they appear to be gaining ground on us.

Nor was it only abroad that British industry found its one-time supremacy challenged. In the unprotected home market increased quantities of foreign goods were being sold. Complaints were heard that American trusts and German cartels were abusing the hospitality of free-trade Britain by 'dumping' surplus goods which they could not sell at monopoly prices to domestic consumers. 'Made in Germany', originally an expression of contempt, was becoming 'a catchword of alarm'.[1] In 1881, the organization of the Fair Trade League emphasized the growing fear of foreign competition. Free trade, its sponsors claimed, was 'unfair trade' unless it was reciprocal. Britain, they urged, should deny duty-free entry to imports from countries that raised barriers against her goods.

The case of the 'Fair Traders' was put very forcibly in 1884

[1] J. H. CLAPHAM, *An Economic History of Modern Britain*. Cambridge University Press (1938), vol. III, p. 38.

DIMINISHING RETURNS: 1880-1900

by Lord Randolph Churchill, then nearing the zenith of his meteoric career. Speaking at Blackpool, he said:

We are suffering from a depression of trade extending as far back as 1874 . . . and the most hopeful among either our capitalists or our artisans can discover no signs of a revival. Your iron industry is dead, dead as mutton; your coal industries, which depend greatly on the iron industries, are languishing. Your silk industry is dead, assassinated by the foreigner. Your wool industry is *in articulo mortis*, gasping, struggling. Your cotton industry is seriously sick. The shipbuilding industry, which held out longest of all, is come to a standstill . . . Well, but with this state of British industry what do you find going on? You find foreign iron, foreign wool, foreign silk and cotton pouring into the country, flooding you, drowning you, sinking you, swamping you: your labour market is congested; wages have sunk below the level of life; the misery in our large towns is too frightful to contemplate, and emigration or starvation is the remedy which the Radicals offer you with the most undisturbed complacency. But what produced this state of things? Free imports? I am not sure; I should like inquiry; but I suspect free imports of the murder of our industries much in the same way as if I found a man standing over a corpse and plunging his knife into it I should suspect that man of homicide, and I should recommend a coroner's inquest, and a trial by jury.[1]

This rhetorical picture was far too highly coloured. Actually, the period 1875 to 1900, despite many ups and downs, was one of economic progress in Britain. Although the absolute rate of home capital accumulation did not again match that of the decade ending in 1875, there was a steady rise in productivity, with output per occupied person (at constant prices) advancing from an average of £69.3 in 1870-76 to an average of £105.4 in 1894-1903.[2] Nor was the fate of British exports nearly as grim as the trade returns suggested: a gradual expansion in volume was masked by a fall in prices. True, there was no longer growth at

[1] Politically, Fair Trade attracted very little support, and the League's candidates were soundly beaten in the General Election of 1885. Randolph Churchill's flirtation with the movement proved short-lived. In a speech at Sunderland in October 1887, he finally repudiated protectionism, arguing that to safeguard agriculture equally with industry huge rates of duty would be necessary. 'Low prices in the necessaries of life and political stability in a democratic constitution are,' he said, 'practically inseparable.'
[2] COLIN CLARK, *National Income and Outlay.* Macmillan (London, 1937), pp. 232, 273.

20

the phenomenal rate witnessed between 1824 and 1872, when British exports expanded at a cumulative annual rate of 4.7 per cent.[1] But this was hardly to be expected. As other nations industrialized — a process assisted by British exports of capital goods — one small island, rather meagrely blessed with raw materials apart from coal, could not hope to enjoy indefinitely 38 per cent of world trade in manufactured goods as it had in the quinquennium 1876-80.

What alarmed many contemporaries was the fact that, while exports lagged, imports expanded and the apparent adverse balance of trade steadily increased. Was Britain then growing poorer, living on the accumulated capital of the past? Some observers viewed this possibility with despondency and alarm. In *England, Its People, Polity, and Pursuits*, published in 1879, T. H. S. Escott, who was shortly to succeed John Morley as editor of the *Fortnightly Review*, expressed grave concern about the 'tremendous drafts' on British wealth 'represented by adverse trade balances of hundreds of millions sterling'. Although he deprecated 'theories of "definitive crises" such as are bruited abroad on the continent', he concluded 'that with our growing tastes for luxuries as a people, and the enormous additions to our national expenditure in consequence, we have come to occupy a position in which we are no longer progressing, but rather appear to be standing still, if we are not even falling back'.[2]

This gloomy interpretation of trade statistics underestimated the growth of income from invisible exports and overlooked the steady improvement in British 'terms of trade'. It is possible that for a few years in the late 'seventies an actual deficit in the international balance of payments compelled some liquidation of foreign assets. But according to C. K. Hobson's estimates, the surplus available for overseas investment averaged £30 million per annum in 1881-85, £50 million in 1886-90 and £30 million in 1891-1904.[3] This surplus was created by a steady growth in payments for services and in receipts of interest and dividends from abroad. In whatever other fields Britain might be challenged, it remained supreme in the ocean-carrying trade, owning five-

---

[1] W. ARTHUR LEWIS, in *The Manchester School*, May 1948, p. 145.
[2] T. H. S. ESCOTT, *England, Its People, Polity, and Pursuits*. Cassell (London, 1879), vol. I, p. 216.
[3] C. K. HOBSON, *The Export of Capital*. Constable (London, 1914), p. 219.

eighths of the world's steamer tonnage in 1887, and in international finance. Thus the enlargement of world trade assured an increasing income to the shipping industry and to London banks, brokers and insurance institutions.

From the mid-'seventies until almost the end of the century the trend of world prices was downward. The cause appears to have been a coincidence between a relative decline in money supplies and a great expansion in world production. After the Californian and Australian discoveries around 1850, the output of gold had fallen off while adherence of one country after another to the gold standard had multiplied demand for the precious metal. At the same time, improvements in communications had opened up vast areas, which began to pour primary commodities into the international market, and the spread of industrialization had swollen the supply of manufactured products. The result was 'a buyers' market' in which goods ardently chased money.

Prolonged deflation proved disastrous to British agriculture, permanently changing its character. And, as deflation always does, it served as a psychological depressant of business confidence. But its effects, on balance, may have been positively advantageous to the British economy. As the world's chief buyer of food and raw materials and principal seller of manufactures, Britain reaped a profit because prices of the former were far more drastically reduced than those of the latter. In terms of wheat or meat or sugar or wool, the exchange value of a steel plough or a bolt of cotton cloth was enhanced. The consequent fall in the cost of living turned a gradual increase in money wages between 1880 and 1900 into a marked advance in real wages.[1] Many industries also profited. The dumping of cheap raw steel might be distressing to British steel masters but it was a boon to the engineering trades; colonial planters and domestic refiners could rightfully complain they were being throttled by the competition of subsidized European beet sugar, but biscuit and preserve manufacturers gained thereby an advantage enabling them to build up a world-wide trade.

[1] Striking evidence of this fact is provided by consumption figures. 'Per head of population, the consumption of bread stood practically still; but meat consumption rose from about 110 pounds a year in the middle 'seventies to nearly 130 pounds twenty years later. The consumption of tea increased from 4½ pounds to nearly 6 pounds, and that of sugar from about 60 pounds to well over 80 pounds.' G. D. H. COLE and RAYMOND POSTGATE, *The Common People, 1746-1946.* Methuen (London, 1947), p. 442.

Ignoring the favourable 'invisible' items in Britain's international accounts, Henry Adams wrote from London to his brother Brooks in 1898: 'The secret of all lies in the returns of the Board of Trade, which show that this year at last settles the fact that British industry is quite ruined and that its decline has at last become a débâcle.'

Obviously, the complete statistical evidence did not support this conclusion, but the intuition of the American historian was not at fault when he added: 'The world has entered a new phase of far-reaching revolution.' He thought he perceived an absolute decline in Britain's economic strength: the real pointer to a tempestuous twentieth century was a relative loss of power. While Britain had been progressing at a sedate trot, other nations were coming up at the gallop. In 1880 the British output of steel was 1,020,000 tons — one-third of the world total; by 1902 it had increased nearly fivefold but was only one-seventh of the world total. In those twenty-two years the United States and Germany had jumped to first and second place respectively in the production of this key commodity. Again, while Britain remained the world's leading exporter, these same nations were gaining on it. In money values, Britain's exports of domestic produce increased only 6.4 per cent between 1880-84 and 1894-1900. In the same period the United States showed a 42.8 per cent gain and Germany one of 23 per cent.

Such comparisons were not necessarily a cause for alarm. It was inevitable that, as they industrialized, countries with larger populations than Britain should overtake it in certain respects. What could legitimately inspire concern was the greater technical progress of America and Germany in some of the old staple industries and their greater readiness to develop and exploit new ones. Reluctance on the part of British capitalists to change time-honoured methods was frequently the subject of comment in the late nineteenth century. 'Basic steel' had been a British invention, but the process, though designed for the phosphoric ores of which Britain had large reserves, had been neglected. In 1884, Lowthian Bell, the famous ironmaster, was complaining that 'until very recently no kind of progress had been made for fifty years' in the manufacture of coke. His firm was one of the few that sought to lower costs by utilizing the waste heat and by-products which were lost when coke was produced in the common 'beehive oven'. But even in 1902 only 10 per cent of the British coke output came from by-product ovens, mostly of foreign design.[1]

The inventive genius of Britain, which had blossomed so amazingly in the early years of the industrial revolution, was now frequently discouraged by the conservatism of captains of industry. The notorious failure to exploit Perkin's discovery of coal-tar dyes was but one example of domestic neglect of the work of British scientists. Another was a lag in electrical development despite the pioneer experimental triumphs of Faraday and his successors. In 1886-88, when few American towns of 20,000 inhabitants lacked electric light, central power stations were still a rarity in Britain. As late as 1894, the then President of the Institute of Mechanical Engineers believed that the chief business of public generating stations 'was, and probably always would be, to supply energy for lighting purposes'. Under these circumstances it was hardly surprising that electrical engineering developed rather slowly in Britain, or that some of the earliest plants in the field were offshoots of American companies. This was by no means the only example of transatlantic technical leadership. When in the last decade of the century boot and shoe making was transformed from a semi-handicraft to a mass-production industry, the change was brought about by American machinery. So, too, was the development of steam laundries and the great expansion of the hosiery industry.

There were several reasons for this technical lag. British industrialists were set in their ways. Overconscious of their role in the development of machine industry, they were inclined to regard the panting efforts of competitors with the tired complacency that the old so often exhibit towards the young. With a heavy investment in tried and trusted processes, they were cautious in risking their money on innovations. Some new industries had to overcome the stubborn opposition of vested interests which were more strongly entrenched than in recently industrialized countries. For instance, many cities in the United States jumped directly from oil lamps and candles to electric light: in Britain a firmly established gas industry, which had long supplied all urban centres, was in

[1] J. H. CLAPHAM, op. cit., vol. III, p. 147.

a position to delay the advent of a rival form of illumination.

Another of Britain's handicaps was backwardness in education. It had incomparable craftsmen but lacked the skilled technicians who were the backbone of the German chemical industry. And its workers, mewed up in class compartments and taught to 'keep their place', had little of the independent, experimental spirit which was such an important element in American 'know-how'. Moreover, in Britain labour was too plentiful and too cheap. Employers had not the same incentive as in the United States to cut costs by saving labour: too often the hand seemed less expensive than the machine.

There was, as already noted, a rise both in money wages and real wages between 1880 and 1900. But while standards of living improved, they were still, taking the working classes as a whole, extremely low, and, among the unskilled, the extent of poverty remained appalling.[1] Higher earnings had also, to some extent, been accompanied by greater insecurity. The swings of the trade cycle were becoming more frequent and more violent. From 1870 to 1876 the unemployment rate had averaged 1.5 per cent; from 1877 to 1885 it was 5.6 per cent, and from 1886 to 1893, a period which included some very prosperous years, 5.3 per cent.[2] Yet the country was clearly growing wealthier. Depressions had once been associated with harvest failures and scarcity: now they seemed to spring from overabundance.

Why was 'the invisible hand', which through the free-market mechanism was supposed to maintain economic stability, proving so clumsy? Was it true, as Karl Marx had declared, that the capitalist system was involved in insoluble contradictions, that the owners of industry, unable to consume all their profits, were forced to invest in new productive capacity which continually tended to exceed effective demand for goods — demand limited by the low purchasing power of the masses? Recurrent crises of overproduction seemed to lend weight to such theories. So did the steady increase in foreign investment, a development which, to Marxian eyes, represented an attempt by capitalists to escape from their dilemma by dumping surplus commodities into overseas markets.

Shortly before Marx died in 1883, the hunt for new markets

[1] See Part One, Chapter V.   [2] COLIN CLARK, op. cit., p. 232.

had helped to reawaken interest in the Empire. During the *laissez-faire* era the colonies had languished, half-forgotten: many British statesmen regarded them as expensive encumbrances and looked forward to the day when they could be gently detached from the mother country. Even Queen Victoria, whose Diamond Jubilee was to be celebrated as an apotheosis of Empire, at one time looked upon the colonies 'much as the Tudors looked upon the block: as a convenient way of being rid of disturbing people. As late as 1872 she wrote of an official who had been "rude and tactless", that it might be best to find him a post "in the colonies"'.[1] But now the views of Queen and subjects alike were undergoing a change. The old absent-mindedness with which Britain had collected scattered pieces of territory in all parts of the globe was being replaced by a conscious effort to develop the Empire as a source of raw materials and an outlet for surplus goods, surplus capital and surplus people.

'Among the chief wants of domestic England,' wrote T. H. S. Escott in 1879, 'is that of careers and professions for her sons.' In 1876, he pointed out, the population had reached nearly 34 million and it was increasing at the rate of 2 million every decade. This was too 'vast a multitude' to find employment and subsistence within the United Kingdon. Even though nearly 250,000 persons had emigrated in 1877, 'a larger number could well have been spared'.[2] Not all these seekers after fortune had gone to the British colonies: many of them considered the United States a more hopeful destination and were therefore lost as potential consumers of British goods.

The United States, as we have already noted, was growing rapidly as an industrial power and its intake of British manufactures was diminishing. That made it important, Escott suggested, 'to cement commercial union between Great Britain and her colonies', which at the time supplied only 11 per cent of British imports and bought only 12½ per cent of British exports. Unfortunately, the English-speaking sections of the Empire were all self-governing and had become extremely independent. They were anxious to foster industry within their own borders and to this end imposed import duties on many articles, sometimes at prohibitive

---

[1] HECTOR BOLITHO, *The Reign of Queen Victoria*. Collins (London, 1949), p. 254.
[2] T. H. S. ESCOTT, op. cit., vol. II, p. 482.

rates. Thoughout the 'eighties and 'nineties there was much talk in Britain of an 'imperial *Zollverein*' — free trade within an empire protected from foreign goods by a common tariff. This was Joseph Chamberlain's original ideal, but when, as Colonial Secretary, he placed the proposal before the Empire Conference, which assembled in London on the occasion of the Diamond Jubilee in 1897, he found the Dominion statesmen very unresponsive.

There remained for economic exploitation, however, the crown colonies and protectorates inhabited by 'the lesser breeds without the law'. Into this category fell most of the vast areas, totalling 2,854,000 square miles, added to the Empire between 1871 and 1899. A large part of the increase was accounted for by Britain's share in 'the partition of Africa' — the chief preoccupation of the European powers during these years. Until this scramble began, most of Africa was free from even nominal European rule. France was in possession of Algeria in the north, while the British and the Boers shared uneasily the extreme south. Portugal had its old but little developed colonies on the east and west coasts. Outside these settlements there were a few small colonies and a number of scattered trading posts, mostly in West Africa and mostly under the British flag. Explaining the changed situation to the House of Lords in July 1890, Lord Salisbury pointed out that, until ten years earlier, naval supremacy and 'considerable experience in dealing with native races' had enabled Britain to control Africa 'without being put to the inconvenience of protectorates or anything of that sort'. 'Enormous stretches of coast' had been left to native rulers 'in the hope that they would gradually acquire their own proper civilization without any interference on our part.' But control without formal occupation was unsanctioned by international law and 'suddenly we found . . . we had no rights over all those vast stretches of coast — we had no power to prevent any other nation from coming in and seizing any part of them'.

The story of Livingstone's missionary journeys had excited the world's interest; tales of explorers, ivory hunters and traders, of many nationalities, who were beginning to penetrate the interior of the continent, aroused its greed. About 1870, discovery of the Kimberley diamond field revived old myths of African wealth and attracted a host of speculators and adventurers. Concession hunters were beginning to persuade native chiefs to sign away lands and mineral rights and, when they encountered trouble, whether from the despoiled Negroes or from European rivals, they looked for backing from their home governments. In Europe, Germany and Italy, flexing their new national muscles, were anxious to prove their fitness for imperial rule. France, humiliated by Germany in the war of 1870, was seeking colonial plasters for its hurt pride. 'When I left the Foreign Office in 1880,' Lord Salisbury told a Glasgow audience in May 1891, 'nobody thought about Africa. When I returned to it in 1885, the nations of Europe were almost quarrelling with each other as to the various portions of Africa which they could obtain. I do not exactly know the cause of this sudden revolution. But there it is. It is a great force — a great civilizing, Christianizing force.'

All the European powers liked to stress the benefits they were conferring on the wretched African by putting down the slave trade, by suppressing tribal warfare, and by introducing Western religion, medicine and piece goods. But none of them, in fact, was prepared to spend large sums on education, health, soil conservation, and similar long-term projects which might in time have brought enough of the blessings of civilization to compensate for its drawbacks. They were looking rather for investments which promised quick returns and they were not overscrupulous in their treatment of the natives, whose cheap labour was the chief contributor to their profits. The Arab slavers were indeed banished in time, but had their whips bitten any deeper than those of the overseers in King Leopold's Congo plantations? Had their raids done any more to destroy tribal organization than alienation of great areas of fertile land for the benefit of white settlers in such colonies as Rhodesia and Kenya, or the labour recruiting methods of the gold and copper companies?

The chief concern of the European statesmen who presided over the division of Africa was to grab as much as possible with the minimum of risk. That in the process they did not come to blows, was due in large measure to the efforts of Lord Salisbury. To the disgust of some 'men on the spot' like Cecil Rhodes, he made no effort to claim a British monopoly, but by skilled diplomacy contrived to keep both the peace and a generous slice of the cake. His biggest coup was in 1890, when in return for Heligoland, coveted by the young Emperor William II because of his naval ambitions, he secured abandonment of all German claims in the Central African lake region and German consent to a British protectorate over Zanzibar. He then pacified the French, who had been infuriated by this deal, by recognizing their protectorate in Madagascar and their 'sphere of influence' in the vast Algerian hinterland.

Africa made some men rich, but its wealth proved hardly commensurate with the hopes it had inspired. The biggest prize was the Rand goldfield, from which bullion began to flow in 1887. A few years later, discovery of the cyanide process for separating the metal made exploitation of huge beds of low-grade ore profitable and saved Johannesburg from becoming a ghost town like so many of the mining centres in western America. But it also insured conflict between the British and the Boer. Meanwhile the mounting flood of new gold from the Rand swelled world monetary supplies and put an end to the long decline in prices. Business confidence revived in a mildly inflationary atmosphere and a new era of world-wide commercial expansion opened.

Richard Cobden had dreamt of the growth of international trade as the cement of friendship between nations and a guarantee of peace.[1] Marx saw it taking the form of intensified competition between rival national groups, a competition bound to move from an economic to a political plane and finally to a military one. The march of events as the nineteenth century drew to its close was clearly more in accord with the apocalyptic vision of the international socialist than with the Utopian hopes of the liberal internationalist. Multiplication of trade barriers was dissipating the benefits that might have been gained by the fullest possible international division of labour. Competition at home and abroad was taking the form of attempts to corner markets and monopolize raw materials. International economic co-operation was to be found mainly in sinister combinations to fix prices and limit production.

---

[1] 'Free trade! What is it? Why, breaking down the barriers that separate nations; those barriers behind which nestle the feelings of pride, revenge, hatred, and jealousy, which every now and then burst their bounds and deluge whole countries with blood.' RICHARD COBDEN, *Speeches on Questions of Public Policy.* Macmillan (London, 1870), vol. I, p. 79.

Omens for long-continued peace were inauspicious. The great European powers were gloating over British difficulties in subjugating the Boers in a war precipitated by economic imperialism. Anglo-French relations were still strained owing to soreness left by the Fashoda incident. In Asia, Britain was encouraging Japan to counteract the steady eastward advance of Russia, and all the powers were eyeing greedily the crumbling Chinese empire and squabbling over concessions. Finally, the naval ambitions of the German Emperor were causing apprehension in London and stirring preparations for an armament race. The increasing chill of the international atmosphere gave warning that the long, golden summer of British capitalism was over and that a stormy autumn lay ahead.

CHAPTER II

STIRRING UP THE PEOPLE

I am sure it is right, whatever the apparent consequences may be, to stir up the lower classes (damn the word) to demand a higher standard of life for themselves, not merely . . . for the sake of the material comfort it will bring, but for the good of the whole world and the regeneration of the conscience of man; and this stirring up is part of the necessary education which must in good truth go before the reconstruction of society.—Letter of William Morris to Lady Burne-Jones[1]

IN the broad stream of history, material, ideological and spiritual currents mingle and interact. Capitalism had transformed society and vastly increased economic efficiency measured in terms of the production of goods and services. On the other hand, its ugly social consequences provoked moral revulsion and intellectual criticism which in due course was reflected in political action modifying and eventually transforming the economic system. Before that could happen, the people, as William Morris said, had to be stirred up and convinced that there were remedies for their ills which they had the power to apply. This process was the work of many different hands, and the resulting ferment was composed of very varied ideas and emotions.

One of the ingredients, though not perhaps the most important, was the 'scientific socialism' of Karl Marx. When he died in London in March 1883, his theories were already influential on the continent, but in the land where he had lived as a political exile for over thirty years he was a prophet held in little honour. The first English translation of *Das Kapital* did not appear until 1886 and was by no means a best seller. The force it undoubtedly exerted in the long run was mostly indirect, through interpretations that diluted and modified the pure doctrine to suit British ways.

A more immediate stimulus to socialist thinking was *Progress and Poverty*, the work of an American publicist, Henry George.

[1] J. W. MACKAIL, *Life of William Morris*. Longmans, Green (London, 1899), vol. II, p. 112.

This denunciation of land monopoly, published in America in 1879, appeared in a cheap English edition at the end of 1881. It was an opportune moment. The land question was one of the main roots of Ireland's troubles, which were absorbing increasingly the attention of the British Parliament. It was also a matter for popular concern in England and Scotland, for the monopolistic grip of a few thousand landowners was regarded as a major obstacle to social and political progress. One-fifth of the total area of Great Britain was owned by 600 noblemen, one-half by 7400 individuals.[1] At that time the urban masses were closer to the soil than they are today. Throughout the century there had been a steady movement of population from the countryside to the towns and now the agricultural crisis which had begun in the mid-'seventies was swelling that exodus. Many a newly cooped-up slum-dweller, alienated from soil on which he had been born, was ready to listen to those who told him his fate was due to private monopoly of what should be the heritage of all.

George's book had an immense success, selling as no work on economics had ever sold before. When its author came over on a lecture tour in 1884, he attracted great audiences and thoroughly frightened the men of property. They used their influence to prevent his sponsors from hiring halls but only succeeded in giving him more publicity. They organized a Liberty and Property Defence League with the slogan 'Individualism versus Socialism' for the purposes of combating his pernicious teaching.

Henry George, of course, was not a socialist at all, and was always quarrelling with socialists who wanted to use his attack on the landlords as a jumping-off point for assaults on the owners of the other means of production. He was a defender of private property and private enterprise. He believed that if the land were returned to the people, through the instrument of a 'single tax' which secured to the community the whole of its economic rents, other social and industrial problems would be solved almost automatically. Nevertheless, George helped to undermine the doctrines of *laissez-faire*, and so prepare the way for socialism, by driving home with immense force and sincerity the lesson that poverty was an evil that could be eradicated by political action. If his influence waned rapidly after a few years, it was because his programme was

[1] T. H. S. Escott, op. cit., vol. I, p. 327.

too circumscribed: the problems of a highly industrialized country could not be solved by eliminating just one form of monopoly.

In support of his claims, George used to quote extensively from the Old Testament. He was not the only reformer who linked social problems to religion and used the Bible as a textbook. In the 1880's there was an organized group of Christian Socialists, The Guild of St. Matthew, but its influence was never very great. A much more important factor in the 'stirring up' process was that formidable instrument, the nonconformist conscience. Earlier, chapel and church alike had usually held aloof from political and economic controversies and been content to console the poor for their sufferings in this world by offering hope of future bliss. That seemed an inadequate interpretation of Christian duty to men like the Reverend Andrew Mearns, Secretary of the Congregational Union, whose pamphlet *The Bitter Cry of Outcast London*, published in 1883, attracted wide notice. 'The flood of sin and misery,' he wrote, 'is gaining on us.' It could not be stemmed by purely spiritual means. 'The State must interfere and give people the right to live before the Church can have much chance with them.' The same attitude was taken by another Congregationalist minister, the Reverend R. W. Dale of Birmingham, who steadfastly repudiated the idea of religious neutrality in politics and did much to inspire Joseph Chamberlain's early radicalism. Cruder in his thinking and methods of attack, but still more successful in forcing public recognition of the degrading facts of poverty, was General William Booth, founder of the Salvation Army. His book, *In Darkest England, and the Way Out*, which hammered on the theme that it was necessary to succour bodies as well as souls, shocked the complacency of many of the comfortably off classes.

Education for the same purpose was carried on more quietly by the university settlements, the first of which, Toynbee Hall in Whitechapel, was founded in 1884. The university settlement was both a social and cultural centre and a residential club for young men of the upper and middle classes who were prepared to give part of their time to working for the local community and getting to know their less privileged neighbours. Its importance lay not so much in its actual social work as in its influence on the men it introduced to working-class problems. Many future politicians

C B.C. 33

and administrators acquired in the university settlements a lasting interest in social reform; not a few, including one Clement Attlee, became socialists.

Among the workers of the great industrial centres and the coalfields, the religion of John Wesley, Methodism, was the outstanding creed. In the 'eighties, under the leadership of men like Hugh Price Hughes, it too was subjecting the existing economic system to Christian tests and finding it wanting. Several hundred Methodist missions were founded to combine social service with spreading the gospel. Above all, the Methodist Church in these years served as a training-school for working-class leaders. Literally hundreds of trade union officials and Labour politicians prominent in the last sixty years started public life as Methodist lay preachers. That was no accident. As the biographer of one of them, the late Arthur Henderson, has written:

The core of Wesleyanism, and its distinctive feature, is that it is a religion of conduct and fellowship. The social fact is stressed. No saving of the solitary soul will serve . . . The sense of belonging to a community is pervasive: so is the share in responsibility.[1]

By building up the sense of social responsibility, the churches, together with various organizations directed at the removal of particular evils — slums, sweating, and so forth — helped to create a climate of opinion favourable to the growth of socialist ideas. Actual propagation of such ideas in the 'eighties was the work of two small groups, the Social Democratic Federation and the Fabian Society.

The first of these was launched in 1881 as the Democratic Federation. Its original sponsors were a mixed lot of radicals, freethinkers, Irish Nationalists, positivists, anarchists, land reformers and republicans, whose chief common bond was a sturdy hatred of Mr. Gladstone, Prime Minister and idol of the masses. Their intention was to form a Federation of Radical Clubs to agitate for such measures as land reform and abolition of the House of Lords. A few among them, however, were thinking in terms of a definitely socialist party. The leader of this group was H. M. Hyndman, one of those ideological 'sports' whose rather frequent appearance enlivens the English upper-class pattern. He was in a sense a

[1] MARY AGNES HAMILTON, *Arthur Henderson*. Heinemann (London, 1938), p. 35.

double eccentric. A man of some means, educated at Eton and Cambridge, he outraged good society by spouting revolution and consorting with the 'great unwashed'. But in his appeals to the proletariat he emphasized his own bourgeois origin and habits, speaking from soapboxes, and selling literature at street corners, arrayed in immaculate frock coat and glossy top hat.

In 1880 Hyndman read *Das Kapital* in a French edition and sought out Marx and Engels, with whom he had many discussions. Converted, he dashed off a popularization of Marxist socialism, *A Textbook of Democracy: England for All*, and presented a copy to every delegate at the first full conference of the Democratic Federation in June 1881. This led to a withdrawal of those members not prepared to back a collectivist programme. It also caused a breach between Marx and Hyndman, which the latter, in his autobiography, attributes to the malice and jealousy of Engels. The real trouble was that the author of *England for All* had omitted to give credit to Marx, referring merely to 'the work of a great thinker and original writer . . . inaccessible to the majority of my countrymen'. Furious, the touchy old prophet promptly excommunicated the first Marxist organization in Britain.

A Liberal government with a powerful majority had been in office since 1880. But it was immersed in the problems of Ireland and Egypt and, despite Joseph Chamberlain's presence in the Cabinet, was making a meagre record in social reform. Moreover, it was proving totally unable to grapple with the trade depression which became acute in 1884. This gave the Democratic Federation, which was preaching that unemployment was the inevitable consequence of capitalism, an opportunity to wean some of the younger trade unionists from the Liberal faith to which the mass of organized workers then adhered. Among them were two young engineers, Tom Mann and John Burns, soon to become famous as organizers of the unskilled. Most of the other notable figures in the new movement were, however, middle class. They included the poet and artist William Morris, and Edward Carpenter, the writer; J. L. Joynes and E. S. Salt, both former masters at Eton; and H. H. Champion, an ex-army officer who spent months drilling the unemployed in readiness for the international revolution which Hyndman expected in 1889, the centenary of the fall of the Bastille.

While preparing for revolution, the organization dabbled in politics. In 1884, after changing its name to the Social Democratic Federation and so aligning itself with the continental Marxist parties, it decided to put forward three candidates at the general election which was to take place the following January. As funds were low, Hyndman, according to some authorities, accepted a subvention from the Tories, who hoped to benefit from a split in the progressive vote. But if 'Tory Gold' was received, the donors made a bad bargain. The S.D.F. candidates at Hampstead and Kennington polled 27 and 32 votes respectively. John Burns at Nottingham made a rather better showing, but his 598 supporters were swamped by the Liberal's 6639 and the Tory's 3797.

This political excursion produced a schism in which William Morris and about half the membership of the S.D.F. broke away to form the Socialist League. Morris disapproved of Hyndman's opportunistic tactics and considered attempts at Parliamentary action ridiculous so long as the people had hardly any notion of the meaning of socialism: he wanted to concentrate on propaganda and education. In addition, there was an inevitable clash of temperaments between the 'scientific' socialist with his bourgeois habits and the unconventional artist who could explode: 'I do not know what Marx's theory of value is, and I'm damned if I want to know'.[1]

The Socialist League launched its own weekly paper, *The Commonweal*, in which many of Morris's finest songs and stories first appeared. But Morris soon found his leadership challenged by an anarchist faction. Although something of a philosophic anarchist himself, as *News from Nowhere* indicates, he vigorously denounced their theory that any kind of social authority was a bar to freedom. The inner struggle continued till 1889, when the anarchists captured the League and splintered it into oblivion.

Meanwhile, the S.D.F. had staged a comeback by putting itself at the head of the unemployed. The West End riot following one of its meetings, which led to the prosecution and triumphant acquittal of Hyndman, Burns, Champion and Jack Williams, has already been mentioned.[2] Thus encouraged and advertised, the

[1] See J. BRUCE GLASIER's *William Morris and the Early Days of the Socialist Movement*. Longmans, Green (London, 1921). Glasier, later a stalwart of the Independent Labour Party, was one of those who followed Morris into the Socialist League.
[2] See Part One, Chapter I, p. 18.

agitation continued on such a scale that in November 1887 the Chief Commissioner of the Metropolitan Police prohibited further meetings in Trafalgar Square. The socialists took up the challenge and the following Sunday marched on the Square and sought to break through the barriers that guarded it from the perils of Free Speech. In the riot that followed, batons were used freely and forcibly and the embattled constabulary sent for military reinforcements. One socialist died of his injuries; John Burns and that quixotic Scotch laird, R. B. Cunninghame Graham, leaders of the procession, were arrested and later sentenced to terms of imprisonment.

During the next few years, the S.D.F. reached it greatest influence. It attained larger numbers later, but after 1893 it was overshadowed as a socialist force by the Independent Labour Party, a body better adapted, both in methods and principles, to the British political tradition and the innate conservatism of the great mass of the working class. But Hyndman by his popularization of Marxian economics, Morris by his protests against the physical and moral ugliness of capitalist industrialism and his appeals for a fuller and more beautiful life for the workers, left their mark. As a pioneer movement, which introduced socialism to the streets and to the stuffy precincts of the Trades Union Congress, the S.D.F. has a significant place in the history of British Labour.

The Social Democrats may be regarded as the advance skirmishers of a labour movement not yet ready to deploy its forces in political warfare. The Fabians have been described by G. M. Trevelyan as 'intelligence officers without an army' who 'influenced the strategy and even the direction of the great hosts moving under other banners'.[1] Their chosen role was the collection and dissemination of facts and the preparation of plans for change in a generally socialist direction. The Fabian Society was opposed to revolutionary agitation, uninterested in mass propaganda, unconcerned with attracting a large membership or building a political machine. Rather it devoted itself, in the words of Beatrice and Sidney Webb, 'to impregnating all the existing forces of society with Collectivist ideals and Collectivist principles'.[2] Seek-

[1] G. M. TREVELYAN, *British History in the Nineteenth Century*. Longmans, Green (London, 1931), p. 403.
[2] SIDNEY and BEATRICE WEBB, *The History of Trade Unionism*. Longmans, Green (Revised Ed.; London, 1920), p. 414.

37

ing to permeate rather than supplant the organized forces of capitalism, it was inclined to look upon itself as a select leaven in the midst of the political dough — an attitude which betrayed some degree of intellectual arrogance and was apt to irritate the unselect.

This first of the 'brains trusts' began rather quaintly as an offshoot of a little society called The Fellowship of the New Life, the ruling principle of which was subordination of the material things of life to the spiritual, with the object of cultivating 'a perfect character in each and all'.[1] A majority of the members rapidly came to the conclusion that, before attempting the arduous task of perfecting human nature, they should do something to improve the human environment. Early in 1884, they broke away to form the Fabian Society with the aim of reconstructing the economic system on a non-competitive basis. Their approach to this undertaking was indicated by the name they chose and the text they adopted. 'For the right moment you must wait, as Fabius did most patiently when warring against Hannibal, though many censured his delays; but when the time comes you must strike hard as Fabius did, or your waiting will be in vain and fruitless.'

The roster of the Fabian Society during the past sixty-five years has included the names of hundreds of able men and women. But it will always be associated particularly with the two Webbs and George Bernard Shaw. They made a wonderful combination as the wit of G. B. S. served to illuminate and enliven the solid, but sometimes dreary scholarship of Beatrice and Sidney. None of these three was among the founders of the Society. Shaw joined in the autumn of 1884, Webb the following year, and his wife after their marriage in 1893.

Before the Fabians settled down to real work, they indulged in a certain amount of intellectual skittishness, for much of which G. B. S. was undoubtedly responsible. He represented the Society in January 1885 at the Industrial Remuneration Conference, a gathering of philanthropists, economists and captains of industry, at whom he fired a speech lumping together, as the similar enemies of society, the landlord, the capitalist and the burglar.

[1] E. R. PEASE, *History of the Fabian Society*. Allen & Unwin (2nd edn., London, 1925), p. 32.

He was unmistakably the author of *Fabian Tract No. 3* (1885) which warned landlords with mock solemnity that, if they wished to avoid the horrors of socialism, including the necessity of working for their living, they had better turn over some of their property to smallholders who would 'have a common interest with the landlord in resisting revolutionary proposals'.

By 1888, however, the Society had outgrown its youthful follies and established itself as a force to be reckoned with. In that year it published *Fabian Essays*, an exposition of the basis and prospects of socialism by seven leading members, which had a surprisingly large sale. About the same time, the Society, then comprising only some 150 members, successfully infiltrated the Liberal press. This manœuvre deserves a quotation from Bernard Shaw:

We collared the *Star* by a stage army stratagem, and before the year was out had the assistant editor, Mr. H. W. Massingham, writing as extreme articles as Hyndman had ever written in *Justice*. Before the capitalist proprietors woke to our game and cleared us out, the competition of the *Star*, which was immensely popular under what I may call the Fabian regime, encouraged a morning daily, the *Chronicle*, to take up the running; and the *Star*, when it tried to go back, found that it could not do so further than to Gladstonize its party politics. On other questions it remained and remains far more advanced than the wildest Socialist three years before ever hoped to see a capitalist paper.[1]

We must allow for Shavian exuberance in this account, but undoubtedly the Fabian invasion of Fleet Street did introduce some fresh currents into the then stagnant pools of Liberalism. Fabian planning of both tactics and strategy was a definite factor in the victory of the Progressives in the first London County Council election in January 1889. This triumph was repeated three years later when the Progressives adopted a programme stressing municipal socialism, which Sidney Webb, himself a winning candidate, had drafted. Nationally, Fabian 'permeation' proved less successful. The Society claimed partial credit for the 'Newcastle Programme' on which the Liberal Party fought and won the General Election of 1892. But while this included some

[1] GEORGE BERNARD SHAW, *The Early History of the Fabian Society*. Fabian Society (London, 1891).

39

radical political planks, such as 'ending or mending' of the House of Lords, its social reform proposals were timid and vague, and the new administration — Gladstone's last — ignored them.

Fabian disillusionment was expressed in November 1893 by a manifesto entitle *To Your Tents, O Israel!* which asserted that the left-wing Liberals had been 'hampered, blocked, and eventually overborne ... by Mr. Gladstone's complete absorption in Home Rule ... by the active hostility of such seasoned Whigs as Sir William Harcourt ... by the doctrinaire *Manchesterism* and pettish temper of Mr. John Morley ... by the ignorance, indifference, and inertia of the Whig peers'. If the interests of labour were to be attended to, the manifesto continued, the workers must get their own people into Parliament. At the next election there should be at least fifty labour candidates backed with adequate funds and a vigorous campaign.

The question is, who is to do it? There is, unfortunately, no such thing as a completely effective and general organization of the working-classes in this or in any other country. But there is one organizing agency, which is so much more effective and advanced than any other, that its superior fitness for the political work in hand is beyond all question; and that is the trade union organization ... Neither the Fabian Society nor the Social Democratic Federation, neither the Labour Electoral Association nor the Society known as the Independent Labour Party, has the slightest prospect of mustering enough money to carry through three serious candidatures, much less fifty. Their part will be to provide the agitation which will enable the trade union leaders to obtain the support of the rank and file in rising to the occasion.

Seven years were to pass before the Labour Party was organized as a federation of trade unions and socialist societies very much along the lines proposed in this manifesto. But in the tough battle to convince the Trades Union Congress that independent political action was vital, the Fabian Society took little part. Content to sow the seeds, it left their cultivation to the Independent Labour Party. That story will be told later. Meanwhile we must give some consideration to the ruling classes and see how economic change and the 'stirring up' of the people were affecting their ideas and activities.

CHAPTER III

THE CLASSES AND THE MASSES

THE *Radical Programme*, a manifesto representing the views of Joseph Chamberlain, John Morley and Sir Charles Dilke, issued in the spring of 1885, opened with the statement: The Parliament of 1880 was elected by three millions of electors, of whom it was estimated one third were of the working-class. The next House of Commons will be elected by five millions of men, of whom three fifths belong to the labouring population.

This dramatic shift of ultimate political power was the fruit of the County Franchise Act of 1884, the third of the great reform measures that transformed Britain from an oligarchy to a popular democracy. It had ended the anomaly left by the Reform Act of 1867, which abolished property qualifications only for voters in the boroughs, by extending the suffrage to all householders in the county constituencies. The former arbitrary determination of voting rights by place of residence had excluded practically all the agricultural workers, a large number of miners who lived in unincorporated towns and villages, and many industrial workers. A Glasgow boilermaker with a home inside city limits was a full citizen: if he moved across the Clyde to one of the suburbs in nominally rural Renfrew, he automatically became a political untouchable. Moreover, the restricted county vote had a much higher political value than that in the boroughs. The Redistribution Act of 1868 had left the rural areas greatly over-represented in Parliament. A voter in the sparsely inhabited Lake District, for instance, carried six times the weight of one in the populous, industrial north-east.

Both the distribution of seats and exclusion of rural workers from the franchise had been designed, of course, to prevent the Tory Party,[1] which was dominant in the countryside, from being

---

[1] In the period covered by this book, the chief right-wing British political party has been variously denominated – Tory, Tory-Unionist, Unionist and Conservative. This book for the sake of continuity and to avoid confusion uses the first of these descriptions throughout. Nothing derogatory is intended. The author has, in fact, been told by some of the younger Tories that they regard the title 'Conservative Party' as a little 'stuffy' and would like an official return to the old name with its Disraelian overtones.

41

swamped by rapidly expanding, normally Liberal, urban masses. Not surprisingly, therefore, efforts to persuade Parliament to take up the franchise question between 1874 and 1880, when the Tories were in office, proved futile. But after the great Liberal triumph of 1880, it was clear to Mr. Gladstone that reform could not long be delayed, although, according to his biographer, he himself was 'not naturally any more ardent for change in political machinery than Burke or Canning had been'.[1]

The Liberal Prime Minister was in no great hurry, therefore, and it was not until the spring of 1884, at a time when his battered administration badly needed to repair its popularity, that the County Franchise Bill came before the Commons. 'Never was there a bill', said Gladstone in his introductory speech, 'so large in respect of the numbers to have votes; so innocent in point of principle.' From the Tory point of view that was only too embarrassingly true. It was their leader and dead hero, Disraeli, who, in his zeal to 'dish the Whigs', had created the urban householder franchise in 1867. They could not oppose the new bill on any point of principle but they feared — was it guilty consciences? — that farm labourers would use their votes as a weapon against the landed interest. The Tory future looked extremely dim, particularly if the bill was followed by a redistribution of seats based on the old radical principle — included among the Chartists' famous 'Six Points' — of equal electoral districts.

The Government had decided against dealing with redistribution and extension of the franchise in one measure, believing that the progress of an omnibus bill would be impeded by interminable squabbles over the boundaries of particular constituencies. Tory tactics were to force simultaneous consideration of both measures. An amendment to this effect was decisively rejected in the Commons, and the opposition then left the defence of its interests to the permanent Tory majority in the House of Lords.

When the bill met its expected death at the hands of the peers, whose natural instincts were uninhibited by vote-catching considerations, a violent controversy broke out. To the Liberal left-wingers this thwarting of the popular will by an unrepresentative Chamber appeared as a splendid opportunity to 'end or mend' the House of Lords, and they strongly urged Gladstone to

[1] JOHN MORLEY, *Life of Gladstone*. Macmillan (London, 1903), vol. III, p. 125.

go to the country on the issue of 'the peers versus the people'. In a speech at Birmingham, Joseph Chamberlain accused the House of Lords of being 'irresponsible without independence, obstinate without courage, arbitrary without judgment, and arrogant without knowledge'. A few weeks later, he denied a desire 'to deface' these 'ancient monuments'; but added: 'I cannot admit that we can build upon these interesting ruins the foundations of our government.'

The Prime Minister, however, was cautious. Although his opponents liked to denounce him as a firebrand, he was most reluctant to start a conflagration at this time. As a political tactician, too, he may have considered the electoral prospects of his party less promising than some of his supporters believed. He was no doubt aware that the Tories also were anxious for a dissolution so that the next election could be fought on the old franchise. Under such circumstances, they thought, they would be able to campaign on the unpopular foreign policies of the Government with good hopes of success.

At any rate, Gladstone laboured to bring about a compromise and to this end sought the assistance of the Queen, who, much exercised about 'those dreadful Socialists, Mr. Chamberlain and others', was more than willing to urge the Tories to modify their stand. She helped to bring the party leaders together, and, after 'weeks of haggling, expostulations, menace and intrigue' — to quote Winston Churchill's account of the controversy[1] — a bargain was struck. Details of the Redistribution Bill, which the Government proposed to introduce in the Commons as soon as the Franchise Bill passed its second reading stage in the Lords, were communicated to Lord Salisbury, the Tory leader. And with the reassurance these offered, the Tory peers withdrew their opposition and claimed a moral victory. In fact, while the Redistribution Bill did not wholly follow the principle of equal electoral districts, it went a long way in that direction. Boroughs with less than 15,000 inhabitants lost their special representation and were merged with county areas; those with under 50,000 were allotted one member only; other electoral districts were roughly equalized. For the first time, London and the major

[1] WINSTON S. CHURCHILL, *Lord Randolph Churchill*. Macmillan (London, 1906), vol. I, p. 360.

cities obtained representation in Parliament proportionate to their populations.

The immediate results of the Third Reform Act had been anticipated by neither friends nor foes. So far from proving the beneficiary of the enlarged franchise, the old Liberal Party was the chief victim. Within its ranks, men who wished to woo the emancipated proletariat with more and more radical measures fought bitterly against those who stood firm on time-honoured Whig principles. Torn by the conflict, the party found itself after the election of November 1885 without a working majority. The Liberals had won 82 more seats than the Tories, but the balance of power was held by a solid block of 86 Irish Nationalists. Gladstone had three choices: he could seek a coalition with the Tories: he could attempt to carry on without appeasing the Nationalists, which meant defeat the first time they chose to vote with the opposition; he could win Irish support by introducing a Home Rule Bill. He decided on the third course and was soon deserted by most of the Whigs and some of the radicals. This split put the Tories into office and kept them there for twenty years, except for a short interlude of weak Liberal government in the 'nineties.

In 1880 no one could have believed such a turn of events was possible. The election of that year had given the Liberals an over-all majority of more than fifty and left the Tories deeply despondent about their future. But the fact was that the Liberal Party, for all its seeming strength, had become an uneasy coalition of disparate forces. It had been built as an alliance between the Whig aristocracy, whose historic mission had been to reduce the power of the Crown, and the new business class. Both groups believed in a strict limitation of the sphere of the State. They had acquired from the classical economists, whose theories rationalized the needs of dynamic industrialism, a philosophy emphasizing a 'natural' economic order to be achieved by releasing private enterprise from all restraints. Their political aim, therefore, was to remove every possible impediment to a free market in goods, labour and money. This done, they believed, competition would remedy economic abuses and insure the 'greatest good of the greatest number'.

The Liberal Party had proved to be a great iconoclastic and purging force. It had swept away innumerable archaic nuisances;

abolished the rotten boroughs; cleaned up the eighteenth-century system of patronage and sinecures; reformed the Civil Service and the Army; ended religious tests and broken the educational monopoly of the Established Church; routed the mercantilist system with all its restrictions on trade and business; and much else. But in carrying the constitutional reforms from which it sprang to their logical conclusion — a democratic franchise — it sealed its own doom. The emancipated middle class had used its political power to create an economic system suited to its interests; there was every reason to suppose that, in the long run, an emancipated working class would insist on reshaping that system to conform with its own needs.

After the Reform Act of 1867, Liberal propaganda had to appeal to a growing number of working-class voters, and while at the Parliamentary level the party remained a Whig-business alliance, in the constituencies it was becoming a labour-middle-class combination. To labour, at least, the doctrines of *laissez-faire* were proving less and less satisfying. The enlarged scale of industry was diminishing opportunities for workers to rise from the ranks; the increasing number of businesses organized as limited liability companies was widening the gap between master and men, and unrestricted private enterprise, so far from proving a social panacea, was rapidly breeding new abuses and creating new problems. Willy-nilly, governments found themselves compelled to interfere with it in the interests of health and safety. Within the ranks of the Liberal Party there was a growing and vocal radical group with a social programme it did not fear to call collectivist and a political programme which included reform of the House of Lords and disestablishment of the Church of England. Such proposals were anathema to the still powerful Whigs, who had come to rest on their reforming laurels and were exhibiting increasingly conservative tendencies.

It was the political genius and personality of Gladstone that held the party together. In 1880, the 'Grand Old Man' had passed his seventieth birthday but showed no sign of diminished powers. His long career had been moulded by the pressures of his age and he had become the archetype of the emancipated bourgeois. He himself had sprung from that class as the son of a man who had emerged from a family of small traders to become a merchant prince of Liverpool, a proprietor of West Indian plantations, and the owner of numerous slaves. Sent to Eton, the young Gladstone had there been flogged by the famous John Keate, and so received the accolade that marks, and makes, the English gentleman.[1] At Oxford he shone at Union debates as an exponent of deep-blue Toryism. One of his speeches opposing electoral reform made such an impression that shortly after receiving his degree he was offered Parliamentary patronage by the Duke of Newcastle and, at the age of twenty-three, entered the House of Commons. His first major speech was on a bill for the gradual abolition of slavery. It was a strong defence of the plantation interests coupled with a plea for the better religious education of their human property.

From such beginnings Gladstone had grown to become the unchallenged leader of the Liberal Party, the champion of the oppressed in all lands, the keeper of the nonconformist conscience, the hero of the working classes, and the terror of his opponents.

The most exalted of these last, Queen Victoria, was almost hysterical in 1880 at the thought of his replacing her beloved Dizzy. 'The Queen', she wrote in her habitual third person, 'will sooner *abdicate* than send for or have any *communication* with that *half-mad firebrand* who wd. soon ruin everything and be a dictator. Others but herself *may submit* to his democratic rule, but *not the Queen.*'[2]

Actually, Gladstone was anything but a revolutionary and was, indeed, quite out of sympathy with the socialist tendencies that were gathering momentum in the last years of his life. 'I am thankful', he wrote to a friend after his final retirement, 'to have borne a great part in the emancipating labours of the last sixty years, but entirely uncertain how, had I now to begin my life, I could face the very different problems of the next sixty years. Of one thing I am, and always have been, convinced — it is not by the State that man can be regenerated and the terrible woes of this darkened world effectually dealt with.'[3] In the 'eighties he

---

[1] ARTHUR PONSONBY, *Henry Ponsonby, Queen Victoria's Private Secretary*. Macmillan (London, 1942), p. 259. The victim's memory of the episode was still vivid when, at the age of seventy-five, he told the story at a dinner attended by Ponsonby. He insisted that he was flogged only once and not for any real sin but for 'good nature in not reminding Keate as I ought to have done that there were three friends of mine awaiting punishment'.

[2] ARTHUR PONSONBY, op. cit., p. 184.

[3] G. W. E. RUSSELL, *One Look Back*. Doubleday Page (New York, 1912), p. 265.

regarded himself, correctly, as a conservative influence. 'Some of those you live with,' he said to Henry Ponsonby in March 1881, 'probably accuse me of being a radical. I am not. But I believe that I have the confidence far more than I deserve of those that are extreme radicals but who, as long as I am here, pay me that respect of following me in most of what I do . . . But when I am gone younger men who will take my place will either be far more advanced that I have ever been, or will be forced on by the extreme liberalism of the masses.'[1]

Dread of 'the extreme liberalism of the masses' was a dominant motif in the political thought of the time. Speaking in opposition to the County Franchise Bill, that timorous and class-conscious Whig, G. J. Goschen, had asked rhetorically: 'Do we not see that democracy at every turn is clutching at the arm of the executive power?' Events were to prove that the emancipated masses, so far from greedily clutching at power, were for long to be content to pluck gently at its sleeve. Yet Goschen was right in stressing the revolutionary potential of an electorate with a large majority of workers who had no real stake in the existing economic system. If their votes were to decide who should govern, and on what principles, what hope had the upper classes of maintaining their grip on the State and so safeguarding the rights and privileges of property?

Walter Bagehot, in the introduction to his classic treatise, *The English Constitution*, had pointed out that the interests of 'the aristocracy' and 'the plutocracy' had become identical. Both were concerned 'to prevent or mitigate the rule of uneducated members' and to succeed 'they must not bid one against the other for the aid of their common opponent'. Since the Tory Party broadly represented the aristocracy and the Liberal Party the plutocracy, a merger might have been logical. But political organizations, however similar their objectives, do not easily coalesce. Moreover, a naked alliance of the forces of property would be likely to provoke a united front of the workers. In politics, as in business, the strongest monopolies are those that maintain a convincing façade of competition.

Wise intuition persuaded the British upper classes to keep two armies in the field while gradually concentrating their

[1] ARTHUR PONSONBY, op. cit., p. 256.

47

strength in the Tory camp. Apart from the fact that the Liberal Party had been infiltrated by democratic elements, the Tory banner was the natural rallying point for a plutocracy which, having secured the economic order most consonant with its interests, had passed from the offensive to the defensive. In addition, it now shared with the aristocracy a stake in that 'natural' social order exemplified by a popular Victorian hymn:

> The rich man in his castle,
>   The poor man at his gate,
> God made them high and lowly
>   And ordered their estate.

Tory philosophy had always emphasized this providential dispensation of class distinctions, and the aim of Tory politics was to keep inviolate those earthly institutions which expressed it — the Throne, the Established Church, the House of Lords and Property. Originally a party of landowners, the Tories had once regarded real estate as particularly sacred, but now that both the upper classes and their sources of wealth had become diversified, they stood ready to defend the rights of all property.

The aristocracy, the mainstay of the Tory Party, had, by welcoming recruits from below, recovered much of the strength it had lost in 1832. In the words of a warm champion, it had 'curbed the insolence of wealth in the most effective manner by frankly recognizing its reasonable pretensions and just claims'.[1] The manufacturer, merchant, or banker who acquired sufficient wealth was not likely to lack social recognition. His sons could share the privileges of public-school education with the scions of old families; his daughters could hope to marry peers, or at least their younger brothers. He might even acquire a title himself, though until the twentieth century this was the exception rather than the rule. While in the most select circles birth and breeding still commanded a premium, absence of these qualifications was not, in itself, an impassable social barrier. 'But deep down in the unconscious herd instinct of the British governing class there *was* a test of fitness for membership of this most gigantic of all social clubs . . . *the possession of some form of power over other people.* The

[1] WILLIAM CHARTERIS MACPHERSON, *The Baronage and the Senate.* J. Murray (London, 1893), p. 95.

most obvious form of power, and the most easily measurable, was the power of wealth.'[1]

During the nineteenth century the commingling of aristocracy and plutocracy proceeded apace stimulating, and stimulated by, a commingling of material interests. Successful businessmen bought themselves country estates while hereditary landowners shared in business prosperity. Many of the great territorial magnates enormously enhanced their wealth through the spread of industry, and were more than compensated for the fall in farm rents after 1875 by a steady rise in the value of their urban property. Thus the Dukes of Northumberland, owning thousands of acres along the Tyne, were enriched by the lease or sale of industrial and housing sites and, in addition, enjoyed an ever-increasing income from mineral rights.

Less fortunate landowners, hard hit by the agricultural depression, turned to business to recoup their losses. 'There is a rush just now equally on the part of patrician and plebeian parents to get their sons into business,' wrote T. H. S. Escott in 1879, 'and noblemen with the most illustrious titles . . . eagerly embrace any good opening in the City which may present itself for their sons.'[2] There were, indeed, openings for the fathers too as old family businesses were turned into limited liability companies. Promoters welcomed men of title who as 'guinea pig' directors lent an air of distinction to their prospectuses. Speculation in stocks, particularly after the discovery of the Rand goldfields, became a fashionable pursuit, and ability to provide 'inside information' a useful social asset.

As a result of this union between the aristocracy and plutocracy, the Tory Party in Parliament began to respresent the moneyed as well as the landed interest. The change in the composition of the party had been 'simply marvellous', Gladstone said in 1896: to the best of his recollection there had been no more than five Tory M.P.s, in 1835 associated with trade and industry.[3] In 1895, 244 M.P.s the majority of them Tory or

---

[1] BEATRICE WEBB, *My Apprenticeship*. Longmans, Green (London, 1926), p. 50. Mrs. Webb spoke with authority as a member of a family of middle-class origin which had been admitted to the 'club'.

[2] Op. cit., vol. II, p. 24.

[3] T. H. S. ESCOTT, *Social Transformations of the Victorian Age*. Seeley (London, 1897), p. 260.

Unionist, were identified with business. All the bankers in the House of Commons and a large majority of the brewers were of Tory persuasion.[1]

It was this consolidation of the upper classes that foredoomed Lord Randolph Churchill's effort to create a 'Tory Democracy' based on an alliance between the aristocracy and the workers. Addressing the National Union of Conservative Associations in October 1883, he had argued:

The Conservative Party will never exercise power until it has gained the confidence of the working classes; and the working classes are quite determined to govern themselves, and will not be driven or hoodwinked by any class or class interests . . . If you want to gain the confidence of the workers, let them have a share and a large share — a real share and not a sham share — in your party councils and your party government.

A younger son of the 7th Duke of Marlborough, Lord Randolph Churchill had entered Parliament in 1874 but made little impression on it before the advent of the Liberal Government in 1880. Then, in company with Sir Henry Wolff, John Gorst and A. J. Balfour, he began a sustained guerrilla campaign directed not only against the formidable Gladstone, but against his own leader, Sir Stafford Northcote, whom he considered far too unaggressive. The little group, which jestingly claimed to be 'The Fourth Party' — as Irish Nationalists were the third — thoroughly believed that 'the duty of an opposition is to oppose' and they did their duty with zest. Their special joy was to create trouble between the Government and its radical following. Thus they attacked an Employers' Liability Bill for falling short of the workers' demands and damned the Government's intervention in Egypt, on the occasion of the Arabist revolt, as 'a bondholders' war'. A resourceful, witty and sometimes savage debater, Lord Randolph rapidly became an outstanding figure at Westminister. He was equally successful as a platform speaker, attracting large crowds in cities not usually favourable to his party.

Many of Lord Randolph's fellow Tories regarded him with mixed feelings. He offended the official element by attacking the party machine as undemocratic and obsolete; he voiced views on

[1] ÉLIE HALÉVY, *History of the English People, Epilogue.* Benn (London, 1929), vol. I, p. 16 (n).

social reform which appeared downright radical. Nevertheless, most Tories 'could not overlook the commotion which Lord Randolph Churchill's denunciations wrought in the Liberal ranks. ... They loved their country much, but they hated Gladstone more: and they consoled themselves with the belief (which did Lord Randolph Churchill less justice than he deserved) that he didn't really mean all he said; that it was only his way of beating the G.O.M.; and that, after all, he was Jingo and True-Blue at heart'.[1]

One of the few lasting fruits of Tory Democracy, though one whose flavour never justified his hopes, was the Primrose League, so named because the primrose was supposed to be Disraeli's 'favourite flower'. This organization was sponsored by Lord Randolph and his friends as a means of mobilizing popular support for the Tory Party. It was to 'embrace all classes and creeds except atheists and enemies of the British Empire' and it hoped 'to instruct working men and women how to answer the arguments of the Radicals and Socialists'. In the beginning, however, membership was confined to 'Knights' and 'Dames' and the annual subscription set at twenty-one shillings — an average week's wage. After six months, a class of associate members, paying much lower dues, was created and some large 'habitations' mainly composed of workers were organized. But it is doubtful whether the League ever attracted mass support in the industrial areas, though feudal influences combined with the lure of lantern lectures (it was the pre-movie era) brought in a good many farm labourers.

A stated purpose of the Primrose League was to encourage social mingling of the classes, but rigid class lines inhibited anything like genuine comradeship. The taint of patronage pervaded the whole organization and was only emphasized by the pathetic attempts of its upper class managers to get a few genuine working men elected to local committees. Both the strength and weakness of the League depended on its snob appeal: that won large numbers of middle-class recruits but it repelled most workers who, while they might accept class distinctions as among the facts of life, were not given to snobbery. As a propaganda and canvassing auxiliary, the Primrose League undoubtedly proved

---

[1] WINSTON S. CHURCHILL, *Lord Randolph Churchill*, vol. I, p. 273.

valuable to the Tory Party. It never became, however, an organization transcending class lines.[1]

The first test of the League's political usefulness came in the General Election of November 1885. In the campaign, Lord Randolph, who had been appointed Secretary of State for India in Lord Salisbury's 'Caretaker Government' that succeeded the Gladstone administration in June, played an extremely prominent part. This was the year when another political gadfly, Joseph Chamberlain, was making a bold bid for Liberal leadership, rousing the country and badly upsetting old-fashioned colleagues with his 'Unauthorized Programme'. He demanded 'free land, free church, and free schools', the breaking up of large estates, 'three acres and a cow' for farm labourers, a graduated income tax, and authority for local governments to impose levies on the unearned increment of urban property. Chamberlain's main target was the landowner, who still seemed to many workers more the symbol of oppression than the capitalist. 'What ransom will property pay for the security it enjoys?' he thundered in one speech that shivered Whig and Tory spines alike. 'What,' he asked his Birmingham constituents, 'are the rights of property?'

Are the game laws a right of property? Is it a right of property that sailors should be sent to sea . . . without sufficient regard for their security? Is it an essential condition of private ownership of land that the agricultural labourers of this country . . . should be entirely divorced from the land they till, that they should be driven into the towns, to compete with you for work and to lower the rate of wages, and that, alike in town and country, the labouring population should be huddled into dwellings unfit for man or beast?

In making his counterbid for the workers' vote, Lord Randolph advocated many of the reforms his rival was urging. He stressed housing improvements, compulsory national insurance, temperance reform, provision of parks, museums and libraries, better education. His target, however, was the bourgeois employer, and he tried to persuade the electorate that the Tory Party com-

[1] JANET HENDERSON ROBB, from whose thorough and lively monograph, *The Primrose League, 1883-1906*, Columbia University Press (New York, 1942), most of these particulars are derived, tells an illuminating story about a garden party given by Lady Shelley for the Bournemouth Habitation. On this occasion, probably not unique, the 'Knights' and 'Dames' present were served tea in the manor house while mere associates were accommodated in a large tent on the lawn; p. 149 (n).

prised a 'free aristocracy in historical and natural alliance' against 'a party of and for the new middle class whose interests were diametrically opposed to those of the workers'.

In 1885, this contest between Chamberlain and Churchill, who, politics apart, were good friends, ended in a stalemate very satisfactory to property owners of all types. The working-class vote was fairly evenly split, with the Tories making big gains in the urban constituencies, in part owing to the efforts of Churchill and his Primrose League cohorts, while the Liberals carried the countryside. Subsequent events were even more reassuring. The following summer Chamberlain's break with his party over Home Rule sterilized him for ever as a radical influence, and less than six months later Churchill committed political suicide.

Until the end of 1886, however, the star of the Tory Democrat still seemed to be in the ascendant. He had earlier forced the retirement to the Lords of his old opponent, Sir Stafford Northcote, and when, following the defeat of the Home Rule Bill, Lord Salisbury formed his second administration, he became Chancellor of the Exchequer and Leader of the House of Commons. Still young, he had nearly reached the top of the ladder and seemed certain to attain the premiership. Lord Randolph soon discovered, however, that while his colleagues might tolerate a reformer on election platforms they had no intention of giving him freedom to legislate. In the Cabinet his schemes were blocked and, on November 6th, 1886, he was expressing his growing disillusion in a letter to his chief:

The Land Bill is rotten. I am afraid it is an idle schoolboy's dream to suppose that the Tories can legislate — as I did, stupidly. They can govern and make war and increase taxation and expenditure *à merveille*, but legislation is not their province in a democratic constitution.

Salisbury's reply the following day was revealing, and crushing:

The Tory party is composed of very varying elements, and there is merely trouble and vexation of spirit in trying to make them work together, I think the 'classes and the dependants of class' are the strongest ingredients in our composition, but we have so to conduct our legislation that we shall give some satisfaction to both classes and masses. This is especially difficult with the classes — because all legislation is rather unwelcome to them,

as tending to disturb a state of things with which they are satisfied.[1]

The rosy visions of Tory Democracy were dissolving in the
harsh light of class realities; the attempt to ally a party based on
property and social superiority with the proletariat was failing, as
it had been bound to fail. There was no permanent bridge to join
the 'two nations' of which Disraeli had written — 'the Privileged
and the People'. On December 23rd, Lord Randolph resigned. The
actual break came on his inability to secure backing in the Cabinet
for a reduction in the estimates of the War Department. A cut was
necessary, he felt, as part of the 'popular' budget he was drafting
— a budget which was to reconstruct taxation on the basis of ability to pay. His plans included increased death duties and house
duties and extension of the corporation tax. Excises on certain
luxuries were to be raised; tea and tobacco duties, which bore
heavily on low incomes, reduced. It would have been a most
unpopular budget in Tory circles, 'prejudicially' affecting 'the
estate of nearly every member of the House of Lords'.[2]

Possibly, when Lord Randolph jumped overboard, he expected that the captain of the ship would be forced to stop and
pick him up. He may have thought he was indispensable to a
government partially dependent on ex-radical votes. If so, he
failed to realize that Chamberlain and the other Liberal Unionists
had become prisoners of the Tory Party. Having made defeat of
Home Rule the criterion of their political action, they could not
turn back to Gladstone however much their new associates might
displease them on other matters.

Salisbury, accepting his resignation with polite regret and,
probably, a sigh of relief, seized the opportunity to cement his
alliance with the Whigs by appointing Goschen as Chancellor.
Some Tories were dismayed at the loss of their most popular
orator, but no strong agitation for his return developed inside the
party. After all, Tory Democracy had served its purpose and outlived its usefulness. It had checked the Liberal drive to capture
the new voters, and, now that the Liberals were split, the Tory
Party looked safe for a comfortable spell. Indications that the discontent of the masses was seeking new vehicles of expression were

[1] WINSTON S. CHURCHILL, *Lord Randolph Churchill*, vol. II, pp. 223-4.
[2] Ibid., p. 197.

viewed with complacency. 'Everything is very quiet in Europe,' Lord Salisbury was to report three years later to a British diplomat in Teheran, 'and so we are wholly given over to strikes and Socialist schemes. There is a strong current of this kind of feeling which may affect the general politics of the country, though I think the better opinion is that it will not last very long.'[1]

[1] LADY GWENDOLEN CECIL, *Life of Robert, Marquis of Salisbury.* Hodder & Stoughton (London, 1932), vol. IV, p. 206.

CHAPTER IV

THE AWAKENING OF LABOUR

All we ask for is that the men who stand on the platform as leaders of Trade Unionism should know no party but the party to which they belong — the Party of Labour in this country — concerning which Whigs and Tories were agreed in seeking to oppress and keep down and trample under foot, to prevent it coming into its own.

KEIR HARDIE, at the Trades Union Congress, Dundee, 1889

'THE politics of the future are social politics,' Joseph Chamberlain had said in 1883, and at that time 'the future' no doubt seemed to him and many of his followers to be just around the corner. But from 1886 to 1900, 'social politics' were to be pushed well to the rear of the Westminster stage. Parliament devoted a certain amount of its time to questions of local government reform, housing and labour, but these were not the issues that really excited it. The main political drama of the time was based on the interwoven themes of Ireland and the Empire. Chamberlain himself, having sacrificed his radical programme to the first, was to become increasingly absorbed in the second.

From the point of view of defenders of the political and economic *status quo*, these issues shared two great advantages: they diverted attention from social and economic problems, and they tended to divide the masses. On the whole, the most politically conscious workers, apart from a minority turning towards socialism, held to their old Liberal allegiance and backed Gladstone and Home Rule. But there were many others in whom belligerent protestantism was aroused by fears that the end of the union with Ireland would see a Papal legate supplanting the Queen's Lord-Lieutenant in Dublin Castle. Large sections of the masses were also an easy prey to the emotions of a flag-waving imperialism. The Boer War, at any rate in its early stages, was thoroughly popular, and the handful of radical and labour pacifists that denounced it — among them Lloyd George and Keir Hardie — were more than once threatened with mob violence. Even some socialists in these years were affected by the imperialist virus.

THE AWAKENING OF LABOUR

Robert Blatchford, ex-sergeant of the Dublin Fusiliers and journalist of genius, whose weekly paper, *The Clarion*, and whose book, *Merrie England*, had done much to spread socialist ideas, shocked many of his followers by jingoistic articles on the South African conflict. Among the Fabians, the Webbs and Shaw were pro-war, and the latter, in a speech in February 1900, scornfully dismissed self-determination for small countries. 'The world,' he maintained, 'is to the big and powerful states by necessity.'

At times the imperial brass nearly drowned out the voices of that small but growing band of socialists who sought to wean the working classes from their old allegiances and so bring about the overthrow of the existing economic system. Nevertheless, the stirring up of the people continued with new organizations coming forward to reinforce the Social Democratic Federation and the Fabian Society. Well below the level at which professional politicians operated, at street corners and in small dingy halls, at factory gates and pit-heads, men and women who felt they had seen a great light were spreading their social gospel with missionary zeal.

The vineyard in which they laboured the most earnestly was the trade-union movement, for without the co-operation of the one great body representing organized labour there was little hope of effective political action. It proved stony ground for socialist spades. The trade unions of the 'eighties comprised the aristocracy of labour. They were mainly organized on a craft basis, and their members were skilled men, relatively well paid and with no great sense of class solidarity with the submerged third of slum-dwellers and casual labourers who, as the investigations of Charles Booth were revealing, lived always on the edge of destitution. Trade unionism had made the most headway in the iron and steel, engineering and shipbuilding, textile, printing and building industries. Some coalfields had strong local unions, others were almost unorganized. Railway workers had, as yet, been unable to combine effectively in the face of fierce opposition to unionism by the companies.[1]

[1] SIR AUSTEN CHAMBERLAIN in his memoirs, *Down the Years*, Cassell (London, 1935), relates an anecdote illustrating the attitude of railway directors to their employees at that time. A stationmaster on the Cambrian Railway had been a witness in 1892 before a Select Committee of the Commons inquiring into hours of work on the railways. He was afterwards questioned about his evidence by the general manager and

The well-established craft unions had consolidated their position a generation earlier after a hard struggle, first to obtain collective bargaining, and then to secure legal safeguards for their funds and the right of peaceful picketing. They had built up their strength by developing mutual benefit activities and, in the process, had become respectable and cautious. Politically their members were inclined to the Liberal Party, sharing its faith in many of the shibboleths of *laissez-faire*. They favoured regulation of conditions of labour for women and children, but were chary of evoking the aid of the State on their own behalf. Trade unions had played some part in the agitation for extension of the franchise and, after 1868, had shown an intermittent interest in securing the election of working men to Parliament. In this endeavour they received little encouragement from the Liberal Party, which only belatedly and grudgingly took John Stuart Mill's advice to make room for representatives of labour.

The first trade unionists to enter Parliament were Thomas Burt and Alexander Macdonald, both miners, who secured election in 1874. Six years later they were joined by Henry Broadhurst, a stonemason, and in 1885 no less than eleven 'Labour' men were returned. But while their origins entitled them to that label, they had no distinctively labour programme; they regarded themselves as a section of the Liberal Party, which they fairly consistently supported. The bond was cemented in 1886 when Gladstone appointed Broadhurst as Under-Secretary to the Home Office — the department responsible for inspection of factories and mines.

Most leading trade unionists in the late 'eighties were quite content to accept Liberal patronage and warmly resented socialist efforts to persuade the Trades Union Congress to endorse the principle of independent political action. Year after year, resolutions to this effect were brought forward together with proposals for the adoption of a distinctive political programme. In 1887, the Congress sought to sidetrack these perennial issues by approving

three directors of the company, who then sacked him, nominally for some irregularity in accounts. The Committee reported the case as a breach of privilege, and the House ordered the officials, one of them himself an M.P., to appear at the Bar and be admonished by Mr. Speaker. This was done so forcefully that, according to Chamberlain, they 'wilted' and 'crept away like whipped hounds'. But they refused to reinstate the stationmaster and the House did not insist on their doing so, thus presenting another argument to advocates of an independent labour party.

formation of a Labour Electoral Association to act in liaison with the Parliamentary Committee of the T.U.C., though not under its actual direction. This move implied no real change in policy. The aim of the Association was to promote Parliamentary and municipal candidatures of trade unionists under the general auspices of the Liberal Party, which was inclined to treat them with the chilly familiarity reserved for poor relations and use them mainly to contest Tory strongholds. Nevertheless, the Association flourished for a few years and won some striking successes in local elections. In the General Election of 1892, fourteen members were returned — high water mark for this transitional form of labour politics. Three years later the Association was dissolved.

Meanwhile, in 1888 the forward group in the T.U.C. had been reinforced by the newly formed Miners' Federation, an aggressive body prepared to co-operate in seeking two socialist objectives — the eight-hour day and a legally enforced minimum wage. Among its leaders was Keir Hardie, who had spent years working to build miners' unions in Scotland. Long a left-wing Liberal, he had finally been convinced that party would never fulfil the worker's hopes and was now turning towards socialism and independent political action.

The 1889 meeting of the T.U.C., held at Dundee, was distinguished by a violent controversy between Hardie and Broadhurst, Secretary of the Parliamentary Committee and leader of the conservative element. A debate on the Annual Report, which included a sharp attack on the militants, opened the battle. Hardie retorted by a personal onslaught on Broadhurst, whom he accused of betraying labour by assisting the candidacy of a Liberal with a bad reputation as an employer. The secretary, he asserted, was not 'a fit and proper person' to hold office; but when he moved a vote of no-confidence he was defeated by 177 to 11 — a vote which reflected not so much the comparative strength of the two factions as resentment at Hardie's tactics. For the moment the left wing appeared crushed, but while the 'old guard' rejoiced in their victory on the banks of Tay, John Burns and Tom Mann, young engineers and agitators-at-large, were recruiting on the Thames a new army which was to make the triumph short-lived.

In May 1889 this pair, together with Will Thorne, had organized the gas-workers into the first unskilled union and gained for them an eight-hour day without a strike. They then turned their attention to the London dockers, among the worst paid and most downtrodden of workers. A year or two earlier, Mrs. Webb, as one of Charles Booth's investigators, had found that the chief London docks employed about 2188 regular hands and had work sufficient, if it could have been spread evenly through the year, for some 3000 others. For these additional jobs, the number of which fluctuated sharply from day to day, 10,000 casual labourers anxiously competed in Stepney alone; whenever times were bad, their ranks were swollen by unemployed workers from other trades. Wages were extremely low: even professional dockers earned on the average only 12 to 15 shillings a week.[1]

In no field was a trade union more badly needed: in none did its organization present greater difficulties. But in the August heat of 1889, a trivial dispute led to a walk-out at one dock. The opportunity was seized, and the strike spread all along the waterfront from Tilbury to London Bridge. Burns and Mann joined Ben Tillett, organizer of a small 'Tea Workers' and General Labourers' Union', in directing strategy. Burns addressed the strikers daily on Tower Hill and led them in ragged procession through the City and West End. Public sympathy was aroused, contributions, including large sums cabled from Australia, poured into the strike fund. Under fire from unexpected quarters, the dock employers reluctantly gave way, conceding nearly all the men's demands, including 'the Docker's Tanner' — i.e. a minimum wage of sixpence an hour.

This victory gave a tremendous impetus to trade unionism among the skilled workers as well as the unskilled. An energy was released which was not dissipated, as it was under somewhat similar circumstances in the United States in the 1930's, by efforts of the old unions to exclude the new. The struggle between the socialists, whose prestige had been much enhanced, and the old leaders continued, but it was a struggle inside the T.U.C. and not between rival national groups. At the 1890 conference the left wing pushed through an Eight Hour Bill resolution and two years later they carried by a majority of one an instruction to the Parliamentary Committee to draft a scheme for an electoral fund.

---

[1] CHARLES BOOTH, *Life and Labour of the People of London*. Macmillan (London, 1892), vol. IV, chap. II.

THE AWAKENING OF LABOUR

Before the T.U.C. met again, the proponents of political action had been strengthened by the advent of the Independent Labour Party (I.L.P.), founded in January 1893 at a conference at Bradford. The 115 delegates who attended came mostly from local groups variously denominated — Independent Labour Parties, Labour Unions, Labour Churches, Labour Armies and so forth — which had sprung up spontaneously all over the country during the past few years. Also present were representatives of the Social Democratic Federation and the Fabian Society. The object of the new party, the conference decided, was 'to assure the collective and communal ownership of all the means of production, distribution, and exchange'. But the programme adopted stressed equally such aims as abolition of overtime, piecework and child labour; the eight-hour day; national provision for the sick, disabled, aged, widows and orphans; free education up to the university level; provision of properly remunerated work for the unemployed.

The chosen method of the I.L.P. was propaganda and political action both in Parliamentary and local elections. It shunned the theory and practice of revolution, and for this reason the S.D.F. refused to collaborate with it. The Fabian Society encouraged its members to join but, as an organization, held a little aloof, believing that it would thus be in a better position to influence the new party without hampering its own efforts to permeate the political strongholds of capitalism. Moreover, the Webbs, whose plans for social democracy emphasized leadership by an intellectual élite, disapproved of Hardie and many of his followers. 'The Independent Labour Party', Beatrice Webb confided to her diary on March 12th, 1894, 'with its lack of money, brains, and, to some extent, moral characteristics, is as yet more a thorn in the side of the Liberals than an effective force on our side.'[1]

Certainly money was not plentiful in the I.L.P. and it attracted few intellectuals. As to 'moral characteristics', that is a matter of definition. Like the Fabian Society, the I.L.P. was opportunistic in its approach to politics and pragmatic in philosophy, refusing to insist on conformity to a narrow creed. What gave it an advantage over older socialist groups was an intuitive understanding of working-class psychology. The ethical and

[1] BEATRICE WEBB, *Our Partnership.* Longmans, Green (London, 1948), p. 117.

inspirational tone of its propaganda and the atmosphere of warm comradeship in which it operated appealed directly to trade unionists brought up in the evangelical tradition. In significant contrast to the S.D.F. and the Fabian Society, both centred in London, it found its main following in the industrial districts. An able observer has described the typical member of the early I.L.P. in the following terms:

With the addition of faith in Socialism, the Independent Labour man generally shared all the virtues and limitations of his fellows ... Quite possibly ... he took 'a drop too much' occasionally, but he was even more likely to be a Methodist local preacher, or perhaps a bigoted 'Rechabite'. His views on marriage and the family did not differ from those of other workmen of his class, and he was even less likely than other men to do anything unconventional or shocking to British respectability. He was generally far too busy. Altogether the new type of Socialist developed by I.L.P. influence was just the sort of person his fellow-workmen found it easy to associate with and trust. When he was 'religious' he filled the chapels of the district with a quaint mixture of Socialist aspiration and evangelical doctrine; if he had finally severed himself from orthodoxy, he joined a 'Labour Church' where they sang hymns and offered prayers in the most approved fashion of British nonconformity. It was a socialism racy of the soil.[1]

The moving spirit and first chairmain of the I.L.P. was Keir Hardie, now a kind of patron saint of the British Labour movement. He was a crusader for social justice, a man with a mission to unite the workers in a fight against poverty and exploitation. Those were matters of which he had intimate knowledge. Brought up in the Glasgow slums, he had started work as an errand boy at the age of seven and at ten and a half had become a 'trapper' in a coal mine. Somehow he educated himself and, forming his style on Robert Burns and the Bible, became an excellent writer. He learned public speaking as a lay preacher for the Evangelical Union and at gatherings of the Good Templars — an organization of teetotalers. Soon his fellow workers were asking him to take the chair at meetings and to lead deputations to management. At the age of twenty-three his reputation as 'an agitator' not only cost him his job but led to his being black-listed throughout the Lanarkshire coalfield.

[1] BROUGHAM VILLIERS, *The Socialist Movement in England.* Unwin (London, 1910).

Hardie continued to work for the miners as an organizer (mostly unpaid) while he supported his family as a journalist. In 1888, when a by-election occurred in Lanarkshire, he sought the Liberal nomination on a radical programme but was thrust aside in favour of a 'respectable' candidate. He went to the polls, nevertheless, as in independent and was heavily defeated. Four years later, shortly before the I.L.P. was launched, he was asked to contest West Ham by an independent local group and was elected.

The new M.P. shocked Westminster from the start. At a time when the correct Parliamentary uniform included top hat and frock coat, he appeared in his natural garb — rough tweeds and a miner's cloth cap. Etiquette was further disturbed when he moved an amendment to the address in reply to the Queen's speech in order to call attention to widespread unemployment — an effort in which he could gain no support from the well-behaved 'Liberal-Labour' trade unionists in the House. But his worst offence, and one that caused his colleagues to howl him down, followed an explosion at the Albion Colliery, Cilfyndd, South Wales, on June 23rd, 1894, which cost 260 lives.

Hardie knew that the mine had long been reported as unsafe but that no remedial measures had been taken. He therefore seized the first opportunity to expose in the Commons what he felt to be a typical example of 'capitalist exploitation'. It happened that on June 24th, President Carnot of France was assassinated. The next day, Sir Willian Harcourt, Leader of the House, moved a vote of condolence with the French people. Could not a similar message be sent to the relatives of the dead miners? asked Hardie. When this suggestion was dismissed by Harcourt with an offhand expression of sympathy, the member for West Ham offered an amendment to the motion asking that the Queen condole with the bereaved families in South Wales and that the House declare its abhorrence of a system that made such tragedies inevitable. He was ruled out of order. Then on June 28th, Harcourt proposed an address of congratulation to the Queen on the birth of a great-grandson, the future Edward VIII, now Duke of Windsor. Hardie rose to oppose the motion as 'a protest against the Leader of the House declining to take official cognizance of the terrible colliery accident in South

Wales' — an unprecedented action in which he stood completely alone. To loyal Liberals and Tories alike this was an insult to the Throne and they vented their feelings in a scene described by a reporter present as 'worse than a wild beast show at feeding time'.

It was not exhibitionism, or pleasure in baiting the bourgeoisie, that led Hardie to stage such solitary demonstrations: he was a sensitive man and probably felt his isolation at Westminster deeply. But burning conviction moved him to attack 'the system' whenever a chance offered; he hoped thereby to arouse the class consciousness of the workers, to show them they could never depend on the capitalist parties to guard their interests, and to drive home the necessity of a party which owed allegiance only to labour. Conversion of the T.U.C. to political action on these lines remained his primary objective. The I.L.P. was a promising spearhead, but to become a fully effective weapon it needed to be fastened to the heavy shaft of trade unionism.

That seemed to be the lesson of the General Election of 1895, when the I.L.P. with more courage than discretion strained its resources to contest twenty-eight seats. Among the candidates it sponsored were men who later became very prominent in the Labour movement — Robert Smillie, J. Ramsay MacDonald, Ben Tillett, James Sexton and Tom Mann. The party polled a total of 45,000 votes and in some cases contributed to Liberal defeats. But Hardie himself was beaten, and none of the others approached success.

One result of the election was a bitter fight at the next T.U.C. Failure at the polls of four prominent Liberal-Labour M.P.s was ascribed by John Jenkins, President of the Congress, to the I.L.P., which had advised its members to abstain from voting in constituencies where there was no socialist candidate. He accused Hardie and his friends of making the term Labour candidates into 'a byword of reproach and distrust' and hinted darkly they had been bought by Tory gold.[1] The 'old guard' took its revenge by pushing through an amendment to 'standing orders' which excluded as Congress delegates all but actual workers at a trade and

---

[1] A gross libel. Hardie was the most incorruptible of men: in 1892 he had refused an offer of financial assistance from Andrew Carnegie although, apparently, it was offered on a 'Scot to Scot' basis with no strings attached.

salaried officials of a union. This was aimed at Hardie and Tom Mann, neither of whom could qualify, but it also hit Broadhurst, so that the two old opponents found themselves in the same camp. Stranger still, according to Beatrice Webb, the instigator of the plot was John Burns, who was moved to join forces with the conservatives by 'virulent hatred of Keir Hardie and Tom Mann'; his 'egregious vanity' had been badly hurt by the greater popularity of the I.L.P. leaders.[1]

Even more important than the personal aspects of this intrigue was the fact that it produced another change in the 'standing orders' which ever since has saddled the T.U.C. with the incubus of the 'card' or 'block' vote. Before this time, the representative system had been followed: each constituent union was entitled to one or more delegates, in proportion to its membership, and each delegate voted as a person. Under the new rule, each union voted its aggregate membership, with the result that the Congress tended to be dominated by a few large unions and their permanent officials who, in effect, exercised proxies on their behalf. This system was foisted on the T.U.C., as Beatrice Webb puts it, by 'a *coup d'état*'; when critics had a chance to challenge it, they were defeated by the block vote, which was already in operation. The result, undoubtedly, was to dilute the democracy of the trade union movement and, in due course, that of the Labour Party too, since the big unions were able to enforce the same voting method there. In both organizations it has served, on many occasions, to impede freedom of discussion and decision.

Neither this factor, however, nor the exclusion of Hardie, could for long delay the political organization of labour. For at this stage in the battle, the efforts of those seeking to arouse the class consciousness of the workers were unwittingly seconded by the forces of capitalism. After the dockers' strike, increased trade-union activity had induced employers to co-operate more closely themselves, and now some of their organizations, perhaps seeing the temporary ascendancy of the T.U.C. conservatives as a sign of weakness, opened a counter-offensive. In 1897, the Federation of Engineering Employers declared a lockout following strikes for an eight-hour day in five London plants. The Amalgamated Society of Engineers thereupon proclaimed a general strike, and the

[1] *Our Partnership*, pp. 48-51.

dispute turned into a new battle over the principle of collective bargaining. After thirty weeks, the men were forced to go back on terms that constituted the most serious union defeat in many years. 'The employers have, as regards immediate victory, played their cards with remarkable astuteness,' Beatrice Webb wrote in her diary when, towards the end of the strike, G. N. Barnes, Secretary of the union, sought the advice of Sidney and herself. 'But they are overreaching themselves . . . It is childish to expect good results from a consent wrung from thousands of men by threats of absolute starvation . . . And they forget the polling booth!'[1]

So did the South Wales mine owners who, a few months later, became engaged in an equally bitter struggle — termed a lockout by the men, a strike by the employers — following a request by the union for revision of an old-established sliding-scale wage agreement. Although there was no violence or sabotage, the Tory Government responded readily to a request by the owners for troops to protect their property and so provided the I.L.P., which was very active in assisting the miners, with a new illustration of the class nature of the old parties. Again, the immediate result was victory for the employers. Poorly organized, the miners eventually returned to work on essentially the old terms: indeed, worse, for they lost a long-cherished monthly holiday. But the strike led to a reorganization of the union and helped to convert the South Wales coalfield into a 'red' stronghold. At the 'Khaki Election' of 1900, at a moment when Hardie was generally unpopular because of his opposition to the South African war, the miners rallied to make him M.P. for Merthyr Tydfil. He was to hold that seat until he died in 1915.

The history of British labour shows a long series of swings from industrial to political action and back again. When the one weapon proved temporarily blunted, the other was brought into play. So it was at the end of the nineteenth century. A number of unsuccessful strikes provoked renewed interest in political organization and, in 1899, the T.U.C. took the plunge which the socialists had so long been urging. The fateful resolution, drafted in the office of the *Labour Leader*, organ of the I.L.P., read as follows:

That this Congress, having regard to the decisions of former years,

[1] *Our Partnership*, p. 55.

and with a view to securing a better representation of the interests of Labour in the House of Commons, hereby instructs the Parliamentary Committee to invite the co-operation of all Co-operative, Socialistic, Trade Union and other working-class organizations to jointly co-operate in convening a special Congress from such of the above-named organizations as may be willing to take part, to devise ways and means for the securing of an increased number of Labour members in the next Parliament.

This clumsy and vaguely worded resolution was carried, on a card vote, by 546,000 to 434,000 — a relatively narrow margin. Whether all who favoured it realized the full implications of their action, is more than doubtful. Nevertheless, a decisive step had been taken. Hardie and his supporters had achieved their first aim — an alliance between the socialist groups and the trade unions on which a Labour Party, free of all ties to other parties, could be founded.

CHAPTER V

THE COLLECTIVIST CORAL ISLAND

> My studies among the recent speeches evolve the fact that
> 'Socialism' is the theme most of them deal with. I don't
> know exactly what it means. It don't mean the Socialism
> of the German Revolutionists but means I suppose Associa-
> tionalism as opposed to Individualism . . . I quite agree with
> those who say that to oppose its advance is madness . . . but I
> also think that Statesmen can direct the current of the
> advancing tide and use it beneficially instead of allowing it
> to overflow and destroy everything.—Letter from Sir Henry
> Ponsonby to his wife, November 18th, 1883[1]

SIXTY or seventy years ago, as this quotation suggests, the
word 'socialism' had a broader connotation than it does
now. Joseph Chamberlain, a mild radical by our standards,
and Herbert Spencer, a fervent individualist, agreed on little
except in using the term to cover almost any form of state intervention in social and economic matters. Even the stoutest exponents of 'economic freedom' today do not denounce public
sewers or the imposition of safety standards on industry as
improper and pernicious forms of state activity. But to Herbert
Spencer sanitary and safety legislation together with compulsory
education, the appointment of public analysts of food and drink,
the regulation of hours of labour for women and children, the
inspection of gasworks, the ban on payment of wages in public
houses, were just as much 'socialism' as state monopoly of the
telegraph system.

This apostle of 'liberalism' did not deny that many social evils
needed correction, but he insisted that the 'popular good' must
be sought indirectly by 'relaxation of restraints' and not directly
through 'coercive legislation'. If shipowners sent 'coffin ships'
to sea, they would eventually lose their business to competitors
with higher standards. If grocers sanded their sugar and adul-
terated their flour, as many did in working-class districts in mid-
Victorian days, their customers would desert them. If there was

---

[1] ARTHUR PONSONBY, *Henry Ponsonby, Queen Victoria's Private Secretary*. Macmillan
(London, 1942), p. 379.

really a demand for pure water in any town, some entrepreneur would find it worth while to supply it.

In *The Man versus the State*, published in 1884, Spencer accused the Liberal Party of betraying liberalism and substituting for it 'a new Toryism' which was the equivalent of socialism. 'Interferences with supply and demand,' he wrote, 'which a generation ago were admitted to be habitually mischievous, are now being daily made by Acts of Parliament in new fields; and ... they are in these fields increasing the evils to be cured and producing fresh ones.' But with workers, made discontented by education, receiving the franchise, and with politicians competing for their favour by promising new benefits, there seemed to Spencer little hope of preventing 'the coming slavery'. 'The numerous socialistic changes made by Acts of Parliament, joined with numerous others presently to be made, will by and by be all merged in State Socialism — swallowed in the vast wave which they little by little raised.'

Nowadays Spencer's views appear extreme to the point of quaintness, but in his own time they were treated with a good deal of respect. In theory, both Gladstone and Salisbury seem to have been in broad agreement with him; in practice, since they were not professional philosophers, but leaders of political parties, they often found themselves impelled to move in a contrary direction. They could not ignore public opinion which, when confronted by specific evils, was apt to revolt against over-reverence for the doctrine that the State could never be a positive force for good. As Karl Polanyi has demonstrated in *The Great Transformation*, human nature would not submit absolutely to the stark mechanisms of the market. Men refused to abandon altogether the customs and institutions that conflicted with it; they were unwilling to regard themselves as isolated bargaining units; they would not reduce their relationships completely to what Carlyle called 'the cash nexus'. Consequently, even during those years when capitalist interests almost dominated the State, the passionate individualists, who sought to purge the economic system of every vestige of social control, never quite achieved their aim.

Towards the end of the century, two pressures combined to enlarge the economic and social role of the State. On the one side were the enfranchised masses, slow to understand and endorse the full programme of the socialists, but demanding from their representatives in Parliament definite reforms — protection against the hazards of industry, better housing, free elementary education, land for allotments, space for recreation, more security of employment and income. Reinforcing these demands was the growth of social conscience among the upper classes, leading to investigation of, and publicity for, conditions in working-class areas which had for long been *terra incognita*. As the *Economist* complained in an editorial, 'The Advance to State Socialism', workers had come to regard the State 'as the biggest and, on the whole, most trustworthy Trade Union obtainable . . . and as at the same time, the directing classes happened to be full of pity, and the State itself rich', it had 'assumed the character of universal intervener'.[1]

Spencer had recognized 'pity' as one of the forces making for state interference and had deplored that fact that 'the miseries of the poor are depicted . . . as the miseries of the deserving poor, instead of being thought of, as in large measure they should be, as the miseries of the undeserving poor'.[2] He was not alone in that opinion, for while humanitarianism was spreading it had not infected all the prosperous. Plenty of them still considered 'the poor' to be a race apart and agreed with Tennyson's *Northern Farmer* that 'in a loomp' they were bad — improvident, lazy, dissolute. Books like General William Booth's *Darkest England* stirred the sympathies of many of the well to do, but they also produced such reactions as the following letter from General Lynedoch Gardner to Sir Henry Ponsonby:

20 November, 1890 . . . The inhabitants of Darkest England may want money — but to *give* them money is the most demoralizing thing you can do — most of it will be found next day in the tills of the nearest public houses: they may want better dwellings but if these are supplied tomorrow (unless worked on Miss Octavia Hill's plan) you will find them pigsties in a few weeks' time; they may want clothes, but if you supply them you will recognize them a few days later at the three balls.[3]

Men and women with more intimate knowledge of working-class conditions, while rejecting such trite generalizations, were

[1] April 7th, 1894.
[2] HERBERT SPENCER, *The Man versus the State*. Williams & Norgate (London, 1884), p. 18.
[3] ARTHUR PONSONBY, op. cit., p. 365.

also losing faith in the efficacy of charity. It might alleviate poverty; it could not cure it: that, some were beginning to suspect, would require drastic change in the economic system. 'No theory of progress,' said Canon Samuel Barnett, founder of Toynbee Hall, 'no proof that many individuals among the poor have become rich, will make them [those concerned about social welfare] satisfied with the doctrine of *laissez-faire*; they simply face the fact that, in the richest country of the world, the great mass of their countrymen live without the knowledge, the character, and the fullness of life which are the best gift to this age.'[1]

The story of Charles Booth's classic investigation of London poverty provides the best example of the crumbling of established economic theory under the impact of hard facts. Booth, a wealthy shipowner, was a conservative in politics and, when he began his laborious task, almost as staunch a believer in individualism as Spencer. His original purpose, in fact, was to refute the conclusion of a study sponsored by the Social Democratic Federation — that one-quarter of the population of London earned incomes too small to maintain their families in the barest decency. The often-quoted summary of Booth's own findings showed that actually the socialists had understated their case.

The result of all our inquiries makes it reasonably sure that one third of the population are on or about the line of poverty, or are below it, having at most an income which, one time with another, averages 21 or 22 shillings for a small family (or up to 25 or 26 shillings for one of larger size), and in many cases falling much below this level. There may be another third who have, perhaps, 10 shillings more or, taking the year around, from 25 to 35 shillings a week, among whom would be counted, in addition to wage-earners, many retail tradesmen and small masters; and the last third would include all who are better off. The first group are practically those who are living two or more persons to each room occupied. The next has, on the average, nearly one room to each person; while the final group includes all those who employ servants as well as some of those who do not. Of the first, many are pinched by want, and all live in poverty, if poverty be defined as having no surplus.[2]

[1] Quoted by G. H. Perris, *The Industrial History of Modern England*. Kegan Paul (London, 1914), p. 420.
[2] Charles Booth, *Life and Labour of the People of London*. Macmillan (London, 1892), vol. IX, p. 427.

It was a soberly worded statement but backed, as it was, by a wealth of statistical and other detail, it provided a real shock to upper-class complacency. One immediate result was the beginning of a movement to secure old-age pensions, a movement which, partly thanks to Booth's own unremitting efforts, was eventually to prove successful. But beyond that, in the words of Beatrice Webb, who served her apprenticeship as a social investigator under Booth, this great report 'was to give an entirely fresh impetus to the general adoption by the British people of . . . the policy of securing to every individual, as the very basis of his life and work, a prescribed national minimum of the requisites for efficient parenthood and citizenship. This policy may, or may not, be Socialism, but it is assuredly a decisive denial of the economic individualism of the 'eighties'.[1]

Called upon with increasing insistence to produce political remedies for social evils, Tory and Liberal statesmen sought to steer a course between the Scylla of Herbert Spencer and the Charybdis of Karl Marx. They had to appease the voting masses and assuage upper-class consciences; but they had also to be mindful of the sensitivity to new burdens of the propertied backbones of their parties. Pragmatically they attempted to solve their dilemma by doling out collectivist legislation in homeopathic doses and making a reassuring distinction between 'socialism' and 'social reform'. The delicacy of the task is illustrated by a letter which Lord Salisbury wrote to Joseph Chamberlain in June 1892 protesting his over-enthusiasm about the 'acceptable quality' of Tory social legislation. Trying to convince the Birmingham faithful — and, perhaps, himself — that he remained a genuine radical, Chamberlain had conveyed the impression he had converted the Tories to his former programme. His *de facto* chief objected strongly.

To say that the Tories have supported measures whose Liberalism you approve, will only be interpreted by them as showing that, knowing them better, you do them more justice. But if you say they have given in on all points on which you differed from them in 1885, you give them an uncomfortable feeling that they have deserted their colours and changed their coats.[2]

[1] *My Apprenticeship*, p. 256.
[2] LADY GWENDOLEN CECIL, *Life of Robert, Marquis of Salisbury*. Hodder & Stoughton (London, 1932), vol. IV, pp. 402-3.

Salisbury, his biographer tells us, was, in fact, doubtful of even the 'electoral arithmetic' of reform; saved by his peerage from direct contact with the electors, he persuaded himself that the votes gained by popular legislation were offset by the resultant apathy, if not hostility, of the party stalwarts. His nephew and political heir-apparent, A. J. Balfour, who had to fight for his place in Parliament, sought to overcome the opposition of the die-hards by approaching reform as a species of insurance:

Social legislation, as I conceive it, is not merely to be distinguished from Socialist legislation but it is . . . its most effective antidote. Socialism will never get possession of the great body of public opinion . . . if those who wield the collective forces of the community show themselves desirous . . . to ameliorate every legitimate grievance and to put society on a proper and more solid basis.[1]

The same idea had been more cynically expressed a few years earlier by Lady Dorothy Nevill in a conversation with Mr. H. M. Hyndman, the socialist leader:

The turn of the people will come some day. I see that quite as clearly as you do. But not yet, not yet. You will educate some of the working class . . . And when you have educated them we shall buy them, or, if we don't, the Liberals will . . . Besides we shall never offer any obstinate or bitter resistance to what is asked for. When your agitation becomes really serious we shall give way a little, and grant something of no great importance . . . Our object is to avoid any direct conflict in order to gain time.[2]

While labour remained without a satisfactory political vehicle for its aspirations, there was hope for such tactics. But even so, the difficulty of applying them was greater than Lady Dorothy realized. Social legislation innocuous enough to be acceptable to an overwhelmingly upper-class Parliament, too often only whetted the appetites of working-class Oliver Twists. Consequently, there was never any finality about social reforms. As soon as an Act had been passed and its shortcomings revealed, pressure for its amendment began to mount and, in a few years, the question had to be reopened. For example, between 1886 and 1899, Parliament was called upon four times to legislate on the hours and conditions of labour of children and young persons in the retail trade. It is true

[1] Speech at Manchester, January 16th, 1895.
[2] H. M. HYNDMAN, *Record of an Adventurous Life*. Macmillan (London, 1911), p. 385.

that, judged by the standards of recent years, the sum total of reform from 1880 to 1900 was not enormously impressive. But, as the *Economist* pointed out in May 1895, the effects, and the cost, were cumulative. 'Little by little, and year by year, the fabric of State expenditure and State responsibility is built up like a coral island, cell on cell.'

Any detailed account of the formation of the collectivist 'coral island' is beyond the scope of this book, but it is worth while to touch on some stages in its evolution. In the field of public ownership, the outstanding feature was the spread of 'gas and water socialism' in the towns. This had begun much earlier in the century, following organization of municipal government on a democratic basis, but it received a strong new impetus from low interest rates after the mid-'seventies. The city fathers who fostered public ownership of local utilities were certainly not socialists, nor did many of them regard their actions as in any way socialistic. They were drawn almost exclusively from the upper classes and were inspired partly by civic pride, partly by a desire to keep down the rates on property by adding earnings from profitable monopolies to their local treasuries. Moreover, many cities had been badly served by private enterprise. In Birmingham, for instance, when Joseph Chamberlain became its reforming Mayor in 1873, half the population of 300,000 received piped company water, but only for three days a week! The remaining citizens drew drinking water from surface wells, mostly polluted, or purchased it from perambulating carts. One of Chamberlain's first moves was to buy out the water company and to start operations which eventually gave the city an ample supply from the Welsh mountains. He also persuaded the Council to acquire the two local gas companies and to purchase a large area in the centre of the city, which was cleared of slums and turned into a valuable property.

A good deal of 'enabling' legislation was passed by Parliament in these years — acts which empowered local authorities to undertake all kinds of enterprises but did not compel them to do so. Consequently, there was no uniformity in development but a great many towns and cities made use of these general powers and often supplemented them by sponsoring in Parliament special local acts giving them authority to undertake particular schemes.

Toward the end of the century, municipal tramway and electricity departments became common, and a few cities started local telephone exchanges during the twilight period of mixed State and private enterprise before the Post Office took over the whole telephone system. Other common forms of municipal trading included docks, markets, slaughter-houses and concert halls, and the more enterprising cities multiplied opportunities for collective consumption with uncommercial amenities such as museums, libraries, parks and public baths.

From 1875 on, housing became a matter of increasing concern to both the national and local authorities, though for long there was more discussion and investigation than action. The jerry-built urban districts which had been flung together by speculative builders in the earlier stages of the industrial revolution were falling into a state of horrible decay, and a large fraction of the working class inhabited unspeakably overcrowded, badly ventilated, dilapidated and unsanitary dwellings. The census of 1891 showed that 11.2 per cent of the population of England and Wales were living two or more to a room. For the whole of London the percentage was 19.7, and in the worst districts almost 40. For Plymouth it was 26.2 and for Newcastle 35.1, but even these figures appeared good in comparison with conditions in Scotland, where nearly half the population was living more than two persons to a room. B. Seebohm Rowntree, in his investigation of poverty in York (1899), where actual overcrowding was below the average, found that 20 per cent of all the houses in the city were without separate privies, 15 per cent without a separate water supply, and 12 per cent of those occupied by the working class were 'back-to-backs' lacking through ventilation. This was the kind of shelter that profit-making private enterprise supplied in the richest country in the world. No wonder that John Morley, a far more cautious radical than his friend Joseph Chamberlain, said in a speech on housing at Newcastle in 1883:

I am beginning to doubt whether it is possible to grapple with this enormous mass of evil in our society by merely private, voluntary, and philanthropic effort. I believe we shall have to bring to bear the collective forces of the whole community, shortly called the State, in order to remedy things against which our social conscience is at last beginning to revolt.

DIMINISHING RETURNS: 1880-1900

In 1875, Disraeli's government had carried an Artisan's Dwellings Act, which proved helpful to Chamberlain in his slum-clearance projects, and from that time on statutes adding to the housing powers of local authorities appeared at fairly frequent intervals. But for years it was a losing battle: scattered improvements were swallowed up in an advancing jungle of decay. The contribution of urban congestion to disease is suggested by the fact that in 1891 the death rate per 10,000 in seven factory towns was 244, but only 164 in three agricultural counties.[1] Probably housing conditions did a great deal to offset all the advances made during Queen Victoria's reign in medical science and public health techniques, which, until the very end of the century, were barely reflected in the vital statistics. Discussing the progress of civilization on the occasion of the 1887 Jubilee, Sir Lyon Playfair, the scientist, noted with satisfaction that 'a child born today has three years more of life than if born in 1837.'[2] That is not very impressive in the light of the roughly 50 per cent increase in the expectation of life registered after another fifty years. Actually, between 1850 and 1900 the death rate was practically stationary, mainly owing to persistence of a high infantile-mortality rate. In 1850, described as 'a healthy year', it had been 146 per 1000 births; in 1898 (the healthiest year of the late 'nineties) it was 162. Thereafter it began to drop with dramatic rapidity.[3]

The oldest sector of the coral island, and the one in which cell-building had proceeded most rapidly, was State intervention for the protection of industrial labour. Beginning with the Factory Acts of the 'forties, there had been a steady accretion of statutes directed towards this end. Most were limited in scope, applicable to particular trades, but at intervals there were amending and consolidating measures such as the Factory and Workshops Act of 1891 which, in addition to revising existing law in many details, empowered the Home Secretary to make and enforce special rules in any factory-industry he had certified as involving dangers to health or to life or limb. H. H. Asquith, the future Prime Minister, who held this office from August 1892 to June 1895, administered the Act with considerable energy, and during his term sixteen

[1] G. H. PERRIS, op. cit., p. 396.
[2] ARTHUR PONSONBY, op. cit., p. 356.
[3] J. H. CLAPHAM, *An Economic History of Modern Britain.* Cambridge University Press (1938), vol. III, p. 452.

76

trades, including match manufacture, flax spinning and quarrying were certified and given special safety codes.

State inspection and regulation helped to raise health and safety standards, but a more positive incentive to the same end was provided by the slow — very slow — extension of the principle of employers' liability. Under the common law, the position of, say, a railway guard injured in a train accident, was greatly inferior to that of a passenger. To secure compensation he would have to prove that his employer was personally negligent and also that the injury did not arise in the course of 'common employment' through the negligence of a fellow employee. An Act of 1880 made a beginning in changing the law on these points but it remained full of holes through which employers frequently escaped liability. An attempt to stop up some of them made by Asquith in 1893-94 was thwarted by insistence of the House of Lords on a contracting-out clause. Three years later, the Tories, spurred on by Chamberlain, reopened the question with a much improved Act which abandoned the conception of negligence, a begetter of tortuous legal arguments, and established the plain principle that a workman or his heirs are entitled to compensation for injuries or death arising from his employment. However, seamen, agricultural labourers and domestic servants were excluded from the benefits of the Act, and industrial diseases were not placed in the same category as accidents.

Labour legislation of this kind, while collectivist in the sense that it involved State interference with private enterprise, put little strain on what the *Economist* called 'the fabric of State expenditure'. Administrative costs and inspectors' salaries were a minor item even in those days of small budgets. Nor was the Treasury seriously burdened by social reforms in the fields of health and housing; their cost was met largely from local taxation and, to a considerable extent, offset by rising urban property values. Up to 1900, the one extension of the sphere of the State giving concern to the Chancellor of the Exchequer was public education, which was financed partly from national and partly from local funds.

The first Treasury grant for educational purposes was a few thousand pounds given to religious organizations for school building in 1833. For nearly forty more years, educational responsibility was left to voluntary agencies subsidized on a gradually increasing scale by the State. The famous Act of 1870 — a Liberal measure — authorized School Boards, elected by local taxpayers, to provide schools in districts where the voluntary institutions were inadequate. Since at the time considerably less than 50 per cent of all working-class children were receiving any instruction, there was plenty of scope for the new boards. But it was not until 1876 that attendance was made compulsory for children up to the age of twelve, and yet another fifteen years were to pass before free elementary education was made available by a government grant equal to the average school fee.

Upper-class opinion about education for the masses was decidedly mixed. On the one hand, it was becoming increasingly evident that illiteracy was a handicap to a complex industrial society. Recruits were needed for the growing army of clerical labour, and much factory employment called for workers able to read, write and understand arithmetic. On the other hand, it was widely feared that education would make the lower classes 'uppish' and discontented and put dangerous ideas in their heads. A witness before a Royal Commission on Education in 1887 suggested that board schools were likely to foster socialism. Asked what he meant by socialism, he replied: 'The state of things in which there is not the respect for the classes above the children that I think there ought to be.'

One way of solving the dilemma was to confine State education as far as possible to dissemination of the three Rs. English board schools, unlike American public schools, had a definitely class character. As H. G. Wells said in his autobiography: 'The Education Act of 1871 [*sic*] was not an Act for a common, universal education; it was an Act to educate the lower classes for employment on lower class lines, with specially trained inferior teachers who had no university quality.'[1] While school boards were given some latitude in defining 'elementary education', those that departed far from the idea that it should be a cheap utility were likely to encounter the wrath of the large ratepayers. Thus in 1890, when the London School Board bought pianos for the use of schoolgirls, it was accused of gross extravagance.

Even with such trimmings, the cost of education was hardly

[1] H. G. WELLS, *Experiment in Autobiography*. Gollancz & Cresset (London, 1934), p. 93.

excessive. Before 1870, the annual charge on the Exchequer had been around £1½ million: by 1887-88 it accounted for nearly £5 million of a budget of £87 million and ten years later had reached £10.4 million, or roughly one-eleventh of total expenditure. This increase was not in itself of an order compelling extraordinary measures to swell revenue. But it was part of a rising tide of expenditure which no administration appeared able to stem though every Chanchellor of the Exchequer harped on the theme of retrenchment. At the same time, Parliament was reluctant to face the fact that the enlarged needs of the State demanded an overhaul of the existing revenue system. Hitherto, chief reliance had been placed on indirect taxation of a small number of commodities of popular consumption. This was all very well as long as most taxpayers were without votes, but with the wide extension of the franchise Chancellors became reluctant to add to tea or tobacco duties.

Direct taxes, mainly on incomes and estates, accounted for less than half the total revenue. Rates were low — sixpence in the pound income tax (2½ per cent) was normal in the 'eighties — and there was no differentiation according to size or character of income. Randolph Churchill, during his brief occupation of the Treasury, had plans for reform, particularly of the estate duties, but, as we saw in Part One, Chapter III, his Tory colleagues would not back him. His successor, Goschen, introduced in 1889 a rudimentary form of graduated direct taxation with a new estate duty of 1 per cent applying only to estates exceeding £10,000 in value. It was his one real innovation in five budgets. For the most part, Goschen, though often lamenting the inelastic nature of revenue in relation to 'very elastic' expenditure, was content to rely on expedients — raids on the sinking fund and small additions to existing taxes. Such measures sufficed, thanks partly to rising national income which automatically increased the yields of income and excise taxes, partly to a decline in interest rates which reduced debt charges and facilitated a large conversion scheme — Goschen's chief claim to fiscal fame.

The evil day for the well-to-do could not be long postponed, however. By the early 'nineties, the annual bill for defending an expanding empire and maintaining British supremacy on the seven seas was growing rapidly. It was this, rather than the cost of reform, that led a Liberal Chancellor, Sir William Harcourt, to introduce his 'Death Duties Budget' in 1894. Accounts for the previous year had closed with a small deficit, and Harcourt was called upon to provide for new expenditure of almost £4 million, most of which was earmarked for a programme of naval expansion and modernization. Refusing 'to peddle with' small taxes, the Chancellor brought forward a double-barrelled scheme for reforming the death duties and making them more remunerative. His first proposal was to change the method of assessment on real property so that it would no longer escape more lightly than personal property. Secondly, he adopted a graduated scale starting with a 1 per cent tax on estates over £100 but not exceeding £500 and rising to 8 per cent on those over £1,000,000. In addition, he made a move towards a fully graduated income tax by raising the exemption limit slightly and permitting abatements on incomes below £500.

Harcourt's budget was hotly attacked by such exponents of *laissez-faire* economics as Goschen, who argued prophetically that in applying the principle of graduation there was no point 'where you can say you ought to stop'; it was denounced by big property owners as confiscation. The Duke of Devonshire, addressing his Derbyshire tenants, warned them solemnly that 'the inexorable necessities of democratic finance' might force him to close some of his great houses and reduce his contributions to local charities. However, when the Finance Bill reached the House of Lords, Salisbury did not encourage the massed representatives of real property there to reject it. Instead he pointed to the constitutional dangers of violating the 'accepted practice' that the Upper House should not interfere with finance bills. Nor would he promise to undo Harcourt's work when the Tories returned to power. It was fortunate indeed for his party that he was so cautious. Only a few years later a Tory government had to finance the Boer War, and its chancellor, Sir Michael Hicks-Beach, had good reason to be thankful for the productivity of the reformed death duties and the increased flexibility of the income tax.[1]

[1] It is worth noting, however, that at the first opportunity, in 1896, Hicks-Beach solaced the landowners by relieving agricultural land of half local rates at a cost of £2 million a year paid by the Exchequer in compensation to the local authorities. This concession to property was hotly attacked by opposition speakers as a thoroughly unjustified 'dole'.

When Harcourt is remembered today it is usually as the man who said: 'We are all Socialists now.' Certainly, he was not a socialist himself; not even a radical, except when his combativeness was aroused by ultra-conservatives. On the other hand, it was hardly fair to call him, as Beatrice Webb did in *Our Partnership*, 'a reactionist'. His historic budget was a blow against privilege, and even though, as his biographer, A. G. Gardiner, has written, he 'probably did not realize the magnitude of the work he was doing', he launched a fiscal revolution. By firmly establishing the principle of taxation in accordance with ability to pay, he did as much as any man of his time to breach the bastions of capitalism and prepare the way for the assault forces of twentieth-century social democracy.

PART TWO

THE INDIAN SUMMER
OF
BRITISH CAPITALISM:
1900-1914

CHAPTER I

THE PARADOX
OF
EDWARDIAN PROSPERITY

THE British Story during the first fourteen years of the twentieth century abounds in paradox. It was at least on the surface an age of great economic activity. External trade leapt forward and year by year the surplus available for overseas investment mounted. Yet year by year also cries of 'ruinous' foreign competition grew louder and, for the first time since the 1840's, tariffs became a live political issue. The external signs of wealth multiplied and the leisured classes lived more splendidly than ever before. But sober statistics proved that by comparison with the years of 'the great depression' of the late nineteenth century, the rate of economic progress had been retarded. It was an age when labour, through industrial and political organization, was advancing to the position of a new estate of the realm, although, up to 1910, at any rate, the material condition of the workers was deteriorating in many respects. These were years in which the supposedly gentle sex developed a new technique of violent agitation; in which the constitution was rocked by the party claiming to be its peculiar guardian; in which the most conservative upholders of law and order turned to gun-running and threats of armed revolt. Finally, it was an era when to the man-in-the-street a world war seemed more and more unthinkable while insiders in diplomacy and the armed services saw it as more and more inevitable.

Many surviving Edwardians and early Georgians look back on this age of contradictions as a vanished utopia. A book published in 1948 bears the title, *Twenty Shillings in the Pound; A Lost Age of Plenty 1890-1914*. It voices the upper- and middle-class nostalgia for a time when income tax was seldom higher than a shilling in the pound, when Scotch cost four shillings or less a bottle; when a good flat in Mayfair might be rented for one hundred and fifty pounds a year, and a first-rate cook could be had for a pound a week. Insulated from revolutionary rumblings in the industrial districts, the fraction of one per cent of the population known as 'society' was enjoying a last fling. Mild inflation produced an atmosphere of bustling prosperity and money was plentiful. Social life quickened when the pleasure-loving Edward VII succeeded his retiring and strait-laced mother. The London season saw a succession of magnificent parties at the great West End houses, which had not yet been displaced by offices and flats: from August on, the old county families and the new rich provided abundant country hospitality, including prodigious numbers of carefully nurtured birds for their guests to slaughter. Few of those who followed this way of life seem to have had premonitions of its approaching end. As one of them wrote a good many years later:

I doubt whether in any period of history of the modern world, except perhaps that immediately preceding the French Revolution, has there been such a display of wealth and luxury as during King Edward's reign. Not even the death duties brought in by Sir William Harcourt a few years previously, or Mr. Lloyd George's rabid anti-wealth speeches at Limehouse and elsewhere, acted as a deterrent to extravagance. If Socialism was in the air, no one, in the class I refer to, bothered to think about it. The possibility of a Socialist Government was the last thing that entered into anyone's mind.[1]

But while this Indian summer of British capitalism brought carefree plenty to the well-to-do, it proved for the workers a winter of discontent, a time of deep frustration. Their pounds were worth considerably less than twenty shillings. Between 1896 and 1900, according to the Labour Department of the Board of Trade, the purchasing power of the pound, in terms of 23 selected articles of food, fell from 20 shillings to 18s. 5d., and by 1912 it was down to 16s. 3d. And there was no commensurate rise in wages. Real wages, in fact, declined steadily from 1900 to 1904, rose slowly for the next three years, and then receded sharply. Only after 1910 did they begin to advance, but even in 1914 they had not regained the level of 1896.

[1] George F. M. Cornwallis-West, *Edwardian Hey-Days.* Putnam (London, 1930) p. 131. Cornwallis-West retired as an officer in the Guards after the South African War and became a professional company director and dealer in stocks. His first wife was Lady Randolph Churchill; his second, Mrs. Pat Campbell, the famous actress

Other facts indicate that, from a working-class point of view, this was a period of retrogression. Unemployment, as measured by trade union returns, had been low in 1900, but thereafter it rose to 6.40 per cent in 1904. The next three years brought some improvement, but the depression which started in 1907 led to a rise to 8.70 per cent – the highest point since 1886. After 1910 the demand for labour became more insistent, and by 1913 the rate fell below the 1900 figure. Poor-law statistics tell a similar story with the proportion of the population forced to seek relief in the work-houses touching a fifty-year peak in 1910. Finally, during the first decade of the century, there was a perceptible slackening in the growth of deposits in the Post Office and trustee savings banks: their chief clients found it harder to make ends meet.

As we saw in Part One, Chapter 1, the extent of economic progress during the last quarter of the nineteenth century was obscured by falling prices. Now rising prices were lending a false air of prosperity. From 1900 to 1910, national income increased at an average annual rate of 1.75 per cent, compared to 2.55 per cent during the previous decade.[1] But while the size of the cake grew more slowly, those groups favoured by inflation — traders, speculators, entrepreneurs, owners of common stocks — were in a position to help themselves to larger slices. The combination of rising prices and stationary labour costs meant wider profit-margins. Moreover, a pound out of a high income held its value better than one out of a low income. A much smaller proportion of it had to be spent on food and other commodities affected by inflation; an important fraction went for personal service — always a leading item in the English middle- and upper-class standard of living — and wages remained low.[2]

According to a book much quoted during the Lloyd George Budget controversy of 1909-10, almost half the net national income accrued to those assessed for income tax, which then began

---

[1] A. R. PREST, *Economic Journal*, March 1948.

[2] The author's mother, a widow with an unearned income of around £300 a year, paid at this period about £20 a year for a 'general' and 2s. 6d. a day for an elderly gardener. At this rate, the family with £1000 a year could, and did, afford from three to five servants. The really wealthy employed unbelievable numbers. BEATRICE WEBB, in *Our Partnership*, p. 413, writes of Luton Hoo House, occupied by the owner, Sir Julius Wernher, the South African millionaire, only for occasional week-ends, and a few autumn months: 'The rest of the 365 days the big machine goes grinding on, with its 54 gardeners, 10 electricians, 20 or 30 house servants and endless labourers.'

at £160 per annum. Rather more than one-third of the total was received by those with over £700 a year (with their families, 1,400,000 persons); rather less than one-third by those with £160 to £700 (4,100,000 persons); the balance was divided among those with less than £160 per annum, representing a population of 39,000,000.[1] In his 1912 budget statement, Lloyd George mentioned that in the previous fiscal year, property passing at death, coming within the purview of the authorities, had totalled £276 million. One-third of this amount had belonged to 292 persons, one-half to 1300 persons, two-thirds to 4000 persons. But 335,000 of the 425,000 adults who had died during the year had left no property, or at least too little to make it worth while for anyone to pay the ten shilling fee required for its legal disposal.

It must be acknowledged that this picture of extreme inequality was slowly being modified and that the working classes during this period received some indirect compensation for the decline in real wages. State intervention for their protection was extended in a number of ways, particularly after 1906 when a powerful Liberal government took office. Conditions of the most helpless sections were improved through the institution of minimum wages in the sweated trades; old-age pensions made it possible for more workers to retire without falling into the clutches of the Poor Law; health insurance and a limited system of unemployment insurance provided for more social security. But the total wealth redistributed by such methods was not very large. Between 1897-98 and 1912-13, the cost of social services to the Exchequer rose by some £25 million, or 1¼ per cent of the national income. A generous allowance for redistribution through local taxation would increase the total to £40 million. Assuming that the whole sum accrued to wage earners in the form either of cash or services, it meant an addition of 6 per cent to their collective income.

There was a direct connection between the adverse conditions of British labour and the business boom which was based on expansion of exports, both of goods and capital, rather than on rising domestic consumption and investment. The world economy was in one of its expansionist phases. A flow of bullion from the Rand, supplemented by important gold discoveries in Canada,

[1] L. CHIOZZA MONEY, *Riches and Poverty*. Methuen (10th edn., London, 1911), p. 50.

Alaska, Australia and Siberia, doubled monetary gold stocks between 1896 and 1912 and killed the bimetallist agitation that had for long disturbed the United States and even infected some staunch British conservatives. Rising prices, due in part to an enlarged money supply, made speculation and investment more attractive at a moment when the growth of old industries and the emergence of new were creating new demands for raw materials and new outlets for capital. Motor-cars required the development of rubber plantations and oil fields; electrification speeded the search for additional copper supplies; the increasing popularity of canned foods stimulated tin mining.

For those seeking venture capital, London was still the financial Mecca. Although the United States had begun to invest abroad, exploitation of domestic resources absorbed nearly all its surplus. France was a creditor country of long standing but, outside its own colonies its investments were mainly shaped by political considerations; in particular, it was trying to strengthen its Russian ally by large infusions of capital. Germany's foreign investments were relatively small — it was expanding its own industrial equipment at a great rate — and were usually directed towards fostering political and trade relations with south-eastern Europe. British investment bankers, by contrast, were willing to cater to every variety of customer. They could find the funds for a large gilt-edged Dominion loan or for a small and extremely speculative lead mine in Peru or a coconut plantation in the Solomon Islands. And year by year, once the strain of financing the Boer War was over the British surplus available for overseas investment mounted steadily. From 1900 to 1904 it averaged £21.3 million, from 1905 to 1909, £109.5 million, and from 1910 to 1913, £185 million.

One reason for this extraordinary growth was that exports were expanding much more rapidly than imports. In 1900, the excess of imports over exports was £169 million; in 1913, on a much larger trade turnover, it was only £134 million. The deficit was nearly, if not quite, offset in most years by overseas income from services — shipping, banking, insurance — so that practically all receipts from interest and dividends on foreign holdings were available for reinvestment. Such receipts, it has been estimated, amounted in 1913 to some £200 million, representing an average return of about 5 per cent on aggregate foreign investments of around £4 billion. In 1895, the comparable figure had been £1.6 billion.[1]

These vast holdings were to prove a valuable foreign exchange reserve for Britain during two wars, when, in large part, they were taken over by the Government and liquidated to pay for food and munitions. Nevertheless, the rapidity of their accumulation during the Edwardian era can hardly be regarded as the result of a healthy national economy. The savings which were placed abroad accrued to the propertied classes but they represented the unrewarded abstinence of the workers, whose lower standard of living made the surplus possible. For it was reduced mass purchasing power that reversed the trade trend of the previous quarter century, when imports had ·grown faster than exports. Between 1900 and 1913, exports per head of population rose 62.4 per cent, imports only 28.9 per cent. Since these increases refer to values, not to quantities, they were in part due to inflation, but import prices rose rather more steeply than export prices, so that the actual growth of imports was even less than the percentage suggests. Had real wages continued to advance after 1900, had they even remained stable, the workers' greater consumption would have been reflected in greater imports. The favourable balance of payments would have been reduced and the surplus for overseas investment would have been smaller. On the other hand, more expenditure by the workers would have strengthened the demand for home-produced goods and encouraged investment in domestic industry.

As it was, while the foreign market boomed the home market tended to stagnate. From 1910 to 1913, more than three-quarters of the capital raised by public issues was for overseas account. British savings were building railroads in Canada and the Argentine, docks in West Africa, oil refineries in Persia, office buildings in Shanghai, tin-smelters in Malaya; they were not available in adequate volume for the re-equipment and expansion of British factories or for the building of British homes. And, as capital moved abroad, the workers were constrained to follow it. Emigration, which had declined during the 'nineties, was now rising

[1] Royal Institute of International Affairs, *The Problem of International Investment.* Oxford University Press (London, 1937), pp. 115-26.

rapidly. In the twelve years 1902-13, 2,181,000 Britons moved to countries outside Europe, an average of 181,750 yearly.[1] The country seemed to be moving towards that destiny foreseen in 1891 by the economist, J. A. Hobson:

Another century may see England the retreat for the old age of a small aristocracy of millionaires, who will have made their money where labour was cheapest, and return to spend it where life is pleasantest. No productive work will be possible in England but such labour as is required for personal service will be procurable at a cheap rate, owing to the reluctance of labour to keep pace with the migration of capital.[2]

Sir William (now Lord) Beveridge has suggested that one reason for the setback in wages after 1900 was a temporary bulge in the labour supply.[3] The natural rate of population increase in Britain had reached its maximum in the early 'eighties: thereafter the birth rate began to fall more rapidly than the death rate. But extension of education held back the entry into industry of children born during the peak period, so that around the turn of the century the labour market was flooded with young workers. Coincidentally, the cost of the South African war reduced the volume of savings available for investment in industry, strengthening the bargaining power of capital in relation to that of labour. Another factor, not mentioned by Beveridge, was the Taff Vale Decision, which put in jeopardy the funds of any union conducting a strike. Since this will be discussed in detail in Part Two, Chapter III, it is sufficient to state here that the effect was to paralyse trade union action from 1900 to 1906. Shortly after the situation was remedied, attempts by the unions to take advantage of their regained freedom were checked by a period of depression and unemployment. It was only after 1910, when the economic tide turned again, that vigorous industrial action by the workers began to show results in a gradual improvement in real wages.

Cheap labour was, of course, of assistance to the successful

---

[1] Statistical Abstract for the United Kingdom (1902-16). There is no actual record of the number of emigrants, but this figure was obtained by deducting the number of inward-bound passengers of British nationality from overseas destinations from the number outward bound.
[2] National Review, vol. XVII, 1891.
[3] W. H. BEVERIDGE, Unemployment: A Problem of Industry. Longmans, Green (London, 1930), chap. XVII.

British export drive, but it continued to act as a brake on technical progress in a number of leading industries. One particularly serious portent was a steady decline of productivity in coal mining which, in addition to providing the sinews of home industry, accounted in 1913 for one-tenth of the value of all exports. In 1881, output per man per year had been 403 tons; by 1901 it had fallen to 340 tons, and ten years later to 309 tons. In part the decline was due to shorter hours, but an equally important cause, perhaps, was the failure of management to compensate by greater efficiency for the growing average age of the mines. Much of the most accessible coal had been cut; now it was necessary to sink deeper shafts and construct longer underground galleries. As a result workers at the face, the actual hewers of coal, needed to be supported by an increasing number of men engaged in haulage, maintenance and other auxiliary tasks. Mineowners as a group seem to have been blinded to the significance of this trend by their ability to attract new recruits to the industry despite low wages and unfavourable conditions, and so to raise total production. Moreover, higher unit costs were offset by the tremendous foreign demand for coal (more than one-third of the output was exported in 1913), which kept prices up. There was, therefore, no very compelling incentive to economize manpower by introducing improved machinery.

Technical stagnation was also apparent in cotton textiles, which remained the foremost British export industry. A boom began in Lancashire in 1905, partly thanks to a succession of good harvests in India, and in two years ninety-five mills were erected and the number of spindles in operation increased by nearly one-fifth. The new plants were bigger and lighter than the old and their layouts more efficient but there was little change in the machinery they housed. In 1914 the weaving section of the industry had installed only 15,000 automatic looms compared to 400,000 in the United States. Here again a sudden spurt in foreign demand induced complacency though it should have been clear that, before long, Lancashire cotton would be faced by severe competition since new mills, many financed by British capital and supplied with British machinery, were springing up in all parts of the world.

Industries dependent on the home market were hindered by the slow growth of mass purchasing power. As a result, their owners and managers tended to emphasize security more than expansion: instead of attempting to create new demand by investment in cost-reducing machinery, they looked for means of easing competitive pressures. It was an age when the speculative spirit became the handmaiden of manipulation rather than of enterprise; when the old-fashioned captains of industry were to some extent displaced by promoters, financiers and company lawyers; when business organizers were increasingly concerned with the construction of mergers, trusts and trade associations.

The attitude of businessmen towards the ideal free market of the economists had always, of course, been somewhat ambivalent. They might agree that the philosophical justification of capitalism required the maintenance of as nearly perfect competition as possible and, when it was a matter of buying manpower, they resented any interference with the forces of supply and demand, whether by trade unions or the State. On the other hand, as sellers of goods, they found that too free a market tended to squeeze profit-margins and to maintain a high bankruptcy rate. In the eyes of the classical economists these rigorous consequences of perfect competition were wholly desirable; they assured the constant elimination of the less efficient. But practical businessmen, however much they approved of the theory of free enterprise, were not anxious to sacrifice themselves on its altar.

Adam Smith had remarked that whenever merchants gathered together they were apt to concoct schemes for raising prices, and this tendency had become more pronounced as trade and industry were organized in larger and larger units and the average amount of capital at risk in any one enterprise had increased. Attempts to limit competition had been common throughout the nineteenth century, but, where an industry was divided among many small firms, it was almost impossible to achieve a watertight agreement. In the late 'eighties, however, a more serious threat of monopoly arose from the physical merger of competitors. Some of the trusts founded about this time — J. and P. Coats, the makers of sewing cottons, are an example — depended more on improved efficiency than on artifical price-raising. Others, like Salt Union Ltd., which claimed control of 91 per cent of British production, took full advantage of their monopoly only to find they were conjuring up new competition both from domestic and foreign sources.

Lever Brothers, incorporated about the turn of the century, rapidly assumed a predominant position, partly by absorbing other soap-makers, partly by building up raw-material subsidiaries. In 1906 it sought to organize a cartel in company with ten other firms with the object of raising soap prices and curbing competitive advertising. This project, not suprisingly, had an exceptionally bad press, and was quickly abandoned.

Since open trustification invited public criticism and questions in Parliament, many industrialists preferred the less ostentatious methods of the trade association. According to a government committee on trusts which reported in 1919, most of the then existing trade associations, numbering many hundreds, had been formed since 1900. Some of these organizations, which were particularly prevalent in the iron and steel and building-material industries, were legitimately concerned with standardization, statistics and research; others were frankly restrictive in their aims, making use of such devices as agreed price lists, production quotas, and deferred rebates to those customers who undertook to deal only with members. The Steel Sheet Makers Association, for example, assigned each participating firm a quota which it was free to expand or contract. But those expanding bound themselves to pay fines to a fund from which members reducing output were compensated. This arrangement was defended as an economical and painless method of pensioning off the inefficient.[1]

One obstacle to monopoly in Britain was the absence of tariff barriers to competitive imports. Thus, a combine of Thames and Medway cement firms organized in 1901 soon found their price-raising plans disrupted by shipments from German and Belgian sources. On occasion, however, difficulties of this kind could be overcome by 'treaties' between national groups. In 1901, a much-advertised 'invasion' of the British market by J. B. Duke's American tobacco trust was repelled by mobilization of a number of British firms which merged to form The Imperial Tobacco Company. An unprofitable trade war was subsequently brought to a conclusion through an agreement·by the high contracting parties to stay out of each other's territories, and to join forces in The British-American Tobacco Company for the exploitation of neutral markets. Another international trade treaty was that

[1] J. H. CLAPHAM, op. cit., vol. III, p. 305.

signed in 1904 by British, French, German and Belgian makers of steel rails for the purpose of establishing export quotas for each group. There were also 'shipping conferences', some of them dating back to 1875, which fixed freight rates. By 1908, according to the Royal Commission on Shipping Rings (1909), the system applied to 'practically all the cargo except coal and special shipments, shipped outwards', from Britain.

Only one route, the North Atlantic, was not organized in this fashion, and here a more ambitious form of regulation had been attempted. In 1902, J. P. Morgan & Company, the Wall Street bankers, succeeded in gaining control of several leading Atlantic shipping firms, mostly British in origin. These were combined in the International Mercantile Marine Corporation, which entered into a traffic agreement with the two great German lines, the Hamburg-America and the North German Lloyd. In Germany there was an inclination to treat this deal as a blow to British shipping, while some British commentators saw it as a subtle German scheme to open a breach in 'the very stronghold of Anglo-American friendship — namely the world of business'.[1] This seems far-fetched. There was probably no more sinister intention behind this project than a banker's dream of turning a fiercely competitive trade route into a profitable monopoly. An invitation to join the combine was extended to the Cunard Company, but it preferred to accept a loan from the British Treasury for the construction of two fast liners and a special subsidy contingent on the preservation of British control. This is an interesting example of the way in which attempts at monopoly inspire State intervention.

In the United States, the passionate public resentment aroused by the great trusts led to remedial legislation which served as a check on monopoly even though it proved far from wholly effective. In Britain, perhaps because its industrialists were rather less blatant in their methods than their American counterparts, restrictive practices were subjected only to the mild curb of occasional public inquiry and criticism. Thus, British capitalism was permitted to become increasingly dependent on monopoly, a soothing drug but one that is both habit-forming and debilitating. In those years before World War I, in that age of glorious 'normalcy', private enterprise which to the outward eye was never

[1] *The Times*, May 27th, 1902.

more flourishing, was actually in many cases ceasing to be enterprising and thereby depriving itself of its economic *raison d'être*.
All unwittingly, company directors in their board-rooms, seeking
hot-house shelter from the cold winds of competition, were preparing a favourable seed-bed for socialism.

CHAPTER II

TARIFFS, TREATIES AND ARMAMENTS

THE political counterpart of the business trend towards monopoly was the campaign for tariff reform. Manufacturers concerned with blunting the edge of competition naturally looked askance at free trade. So long as the British market was an open one, any price-fixing arrangement could be undermined by an increased flow of foreign goods. Moreover, British industrialists felt at a disadvantage in international cartel negotiations: their opposite numbers in protectionist countries had always more bargaining power since they could maintain home prices at a high level and so afford to cut export prices, or, in other words, to use 'dumping' as a competitive weapon.

It was not suprising, therefore, that when Joseph Chamberlain launched his tariff crusade, his most eager backers were found in business circles. His original purpose, of course, was not so much to offer protection to home industry as to strengthen and unify the Empire, but, as we noted in Part One Chapter I, his hopes for an Imperial tariff wall enclosing a vast free-trade area under the British flag were thwarted by the economic nationalism of the Dominions. He then turned to the alternative of a general British tariff which would make possible a reciprocal preference system within the Empire. The advantages of this plan to those with a material interest in reducing the force of foreign competition were obvious, and tariff reformers more and more stressed the need for protecting British jobs and British capital. Chamberlain himself, in his radical youth, had talked the language of Cobden, but, according to John Morley, 'his free-trade convictions, even in those days were ... only skin-deep ... *Au fond*, he looked at the problem from the manufacturer's point of view, which welcomes a tariff as an instrument of monopoly: indeed, in his own business he effected a transaction with American producers in the nature of a commercial treaty, whereby he accepted a subsidy in return for an engagement not to introduce his screws into the United States'.[1]

---

[1] SIR ALMERIC FITZROY, *Memoirs*. Hutchinson (London, 1925), p. 501.

Not all businessmen were seduced by the tariff reformers' propaganda. The Lancashire cotton industry held fast to its faith in free trade, and Chamberlain found few supporters among those directly concerned with the expansion of international commerce — international bankers, dealers in commodities, shipowners and shipbuilders, and the innumerable import and export merchants. Protection was an issue that tended to divide British capitalism although its advocates endeavoured to close the breach by stressing its possibilites as a revenue-raising method less painful than direct taxation. That was a telling argument with the propertied classes as a whole, who felt that the burdens imposed on them were growing unbearable. Seventy per cent of the cost of the South African war, which had proved unexpectedly expensive, had been met by borrowing, but even so, income tax had been increased in 1900 from 8d. to 1s. in the pound, and in 1901 to 1s. 2d. The following year, tariff reformers, who had been urging their panacea as a means of broadening the base of taxation, were cheered by inclusion in the budget of a small duty — 1 shilling per hundredweight — on imported wheat. Embarrassed by their enthusiasm, the Chancellor of the Exchequer, Sir Michael Hicks-Beach, insisted that this tax, which he called 'a registration duty', would have no protectionist effect and would not raise the price of bread to the poor, since it would be borne by the foreign producers. When the bakers unkindly spoiled this argument by making the loaf a halfpenny dearer, he and his supporters fell back on the plea that, in any case, it was desirable for all classes to contribute to the cost of the war. A young Tory backbencher, soon to cross over to the Liberals, joined the debate to point out that what was euphemistically called broadening the base of the revenue really meant taxing the necessities of life. That, said Winston Churchill, would raise 'something much more formidable than a political issue; it would raise an issue directly social'.

The Tories were soon to discover how explosive an issue it could be. In the autumn of 1900, after the capture of the Boer capitals had suggested — falsely as it turned out — that the South African struggle was all but ended, they had seized the opportunity to seek a new mandate. The 'Khaki Election', as it was called, proved a well-timed manœuvre. Badly split on the subject of war, the Liberals were unable to withstand the current of patriotic emotion which responded to such Tory slogans as 'a vote against the Government is a vote for the Boers'. Lord Rosebery is reported to have remarked: 'I never remember dirtier work than at this election. There is a Nemesis attending methods of that kind.' He was a good prophet on this occasion; but the Tories, who had secured a new lease of power on favourable terms, were able for the time being to disregard prophecies.

In 1901, Lord Salisbury retired and was succeeded by his nephew, A. J. Balfour, who had long served as his confidant and deputy. The new Prime Minister was a man, Lord d'Abernon once said, 'hampered by no passionate convictions', but he had to preside over a Cabinet in which the dominant personality was Joseph Chamberlain, whose convictions on the subject of a tariff-bound Empire were becoming more passionate daily. Since a number of other leading ministers were pronounced free traders, the problem of preserving unity was likely to require all Balfour's ingenuity.

On May 15th, 1903, shortly after C. T. Ritchie, who had succeeded Hicks-Beach as Chancellor, had introduced a budget repealing the wheat duty, Chamberlain made a speech at Birmingham setting forth a full tariff reform programme, including food taxes and preferential duties, which he declared imperative for the preservation of the Empire. His colleagues were taken by surprise: indeed, so much so that on the very same day Balfour had told a Tory deputation protesting repeal of the wheat tax that duties on food could not be a permanent feature of the country's fiscal system. Open schism in the party now seemed unavoidable, but the Prime Minister won a respite by promising an inquiry. Four months later, not only Chamberlain, but Ritchie and three other free traders, resigned from the Government. This left the public understandably confused, but, since Chamberlain's son and disciple, Austen, was promoted to the Exchequer, it appeared that on balance the tariff reformers were in the ascendancy.

Free to pursue his agitation, Joseph Chamberlain now began a 'raging and tearing' campaign to convert both his party and the voters to the merits of tariff reform in preparation for the next election. Meanwhile, Balfour refused to commit himself beyond indicating a willingness to use a tariff as a means of retaliation against other nations. He would not even sit on the fence: instead he hovered above it miraculously sustained by a fine-spun web of arguments that maddened his opponents and mystified his followers. 'He was not content,' wrote one of them, 'to make a broad statement of his views without at the same time giving expression to all the qualifications which in his mind it required.'[1] All his Parliamentary skill was exercised in evading any test of the question in the House of Commons. He knew that if he came out squarely for tariffs he was liable to defeat by a combination of Tory free traders and Liberals, while, if he leaned far the other way, the Chamberlainites would be certain to pull him down. Thus on more than one occasion he was forced to the extraordinary step of leading his followers out of the House, leaving the Liberals to debate and carry free-trade resolutions unchallenged.

While the tariff controversy split the Tories, it offered the Liberals a much-needed rallying point. Sharply as they might differ on other matters, on this question the Gladstonian leader of the party, Campbell-Bannerman, Rosebery, Asquith and Haldane, the Liberal imperialists, and Lloyd George, the vociferous young radical, were in full agreement. Moreover, free-trade sentiment remained strong among the organized workers, so that emergence of tariff reform as the predominant political issue served to soften the threatened competition of the new Labour Party. Liberal orators grasped eagerly at their opportunity. They followed Chamberlain up and down the country, challenging his facts and figures, always hammering on the theme that his programme meant dear food — an argument particularly appealing to working-class voters already suffering from rising prices. One of the most effective political posters of all time showed a big 'free-trade loaf' side by side with a little 'tariff loaf', and Chamberlain sought vainly to convince his audiences that an import duty on wheat at the rate he proposed would have scarcely any effect on the price of bread.

Energy and eloquence enabled Chamberlain to make great progress towards one of his objectives; by 1905 he had obtained the support of most of the Tory press, and the party conference that year voted all but unanimously in favour of his programme. But in the arena of public opinion he had no corresponding success.

[1] SIR AUSTEN CHAMBERLAIN, *Down the Years*. Cassell (London, 1935), p. 215.

On the contrary, a series of by-elections showed that the voters were actively aroused against tariff reform and infuriated by the opportunism of the Government. Even Brighton, normally as safe a Tory seat as could be found, was captured by the Liberals in the spring of 1905. Clearly, the longer the Government postponed a general election the worse its plight was likely to become. But Balfour clung to office. He was intent on completing the foundations of the new foreign policy on which, together with his Foreign Secretary, Lord Lansdowne, he had been working ever since he took office. Before he finally handed in his resignation on December 4th, 1905, the Anglo-French Entente had been concluded, the alliance with Japan dating from 1902, reinforced, and the way paved for a *rapprochment* with Russia. The ship of state was set on an international course which a new Liberal helmsman could not alter.

In January 1906, the British public, given at last a chance to pronounce judgment on the Chamberlain programme, repudiated it with resounding emphasis. It is tragic that verdict could not have been rendered earlier, before the development of German naval policy, and of British counter-measures, thereto, had set the stage for 'irrepressible conflict'. For while no single, or simple, explanation of the causes of World War I is possible, it would be unrealistic to ignore the part played by economic rivalry. Fear of German competition lined up an extremely vocal section of British opinion behind Chamberlain's economic imperialism; fear of the effects on their trade if his schemes reached fruition rallied the Germans behind the Kaiser's naval ambitions; fear of German sea power led Britain to accelerate expansion of its own navy and to seek continental allies.

It was in 1897, the year of the Jubilee Imperial Conference at which Chamberlain strove to win Dominion support for an Empire customs union, that Canada, as a small concession to imperial sentiment, granted preferential tariff rates to British goods. The German Government protested, as it had a right to do, that this action violated the Commercial Treaty of 1865, which guaranteed most-favoured-nation treatment for German trade throughout the British Empire, and adopted retaliatory measures against Canadian products. Thereupon the British Government denounced the treaty, offering to negotiate a new one regulating Anglo-German trade but excluding that of the colonies. This relatively minor incident, coupled with imperialist propaganda in Britain, gave William II the powder he needed to blast internal opposition to his long-cherished plans for building a German navy. He telegraphed to Hohenlohe the Imperial Chancellor:

This unqualified step is equivalent to the beginning of a war to the knife against our just developing production . . . If the Socialists had not for years fought against naval construction . . . we would not now be practically defenceless at sea and exposed to attacks on our commerce . . . the denunciation would not have happened. As answer thereto we must now see to a rapid and substantial increase in the building of new ships.[1]

A week or two later the Kaiser was writing to Count Phillipp P. Eulenburg, expatiating on the means by which the navy bill was to be 'put over'. Admiral von Tirpitz had been instructed to set up a large propaganda office to feed material to the press and to maintain contact with 'the professor-class' who were to be encouraged to indoctrinate students on Germany's need for an expanded foreign commerce and sea power to protect it. 'We do not want to put anyone in the shade,' von Bülow, successor to Hohenlohe, told the Reichstag when debate on the bill opened on December 6th, 1897, 'but we demand a place for ourselves in the sun.'

When the bill passed the following March, there does not seem to have been any marked increase in blood pressure at Westminster. Some years previously, nervousness about the naval plans of France and Russia, then regarded as the two most probable enemies, had induced the British Government to enlarge and modernize the fleet. Expenditure on construction in 1898-99 was about three times greater than ten years before, while naval personnel had been increased by some 50 per cent. Britain, in fact, had such a long start that it could safely ignore a moderate German naval programme. However, in 1900, the Reichstag passed a new law the preamble to which declared that Germany must possess 'a battle fleet of such strength that, even for the most powerful adversary, a war would involve such risks as to make that

[1] PRINCE VON BÜLOW, *Memoirs*. Putnam (London, 1931), vol. I, p. 53.

Power's supremacy doubtful'. This policy presented an unmistakable challenge to Britain. If the greatest military power in Europe succeeded in becoming also the second greatest naval power, it would be in a position to reach for the overlordship of the continent. The one fixed principle of British foreign policy was to oppose any nation threatening to attain that position. Moreover, ever greater dependence of Britain's economy on imported foods and raw materials made the nation even more sensitive to threats to its command of the seas than in the past.

The German Government's justification for its course was set forth by von Bülow in a memorandum prepared for the Reichstag committee considering the Naval Bill of 1900:

We could only be sure of maintaining peace with England, as we sincerely wish to do, if an English attack on us seemed less dangerous than it does today . . . England is the only power that could attack us without great risks to itself. There are two reasons why such an attack is possible: first, the fact that the imperialist ideas which have been gaining ground in England for some years, will probably dominate after the South African wars which will undoubtedly end in an English victory. Second, a general antipathy against Germany among the masses of English people will surely find root in England because Germany is now a serious economic competitor in world markets, as a result of our tremendous industrial development, our increasing trade, and our increasing overseas interests.[1]

How far the Kaiser and his ministers really believed in the danger of British aggression and how far they were purposefully creating a bogey in order to frighten the German people into giving wholehearted support to their expansionist ambitions, it is difficult to say. At least a colourable excuse for the fears expressed by von Bülow could be found in writings of British publicists, for example a famous article in the *Saturday Review* of September 11th, 1897, which asserted that:

. . . in Europe there are two great, irreconcilable opposing forces, two great nations who would make the whole world their province, and who would levy from it the tribute of commerce . . . Is there a mine to exploit, a railway to build, a native to convert from bread-fruit to tinned meat, from temperance to trade gin, the German and the Englishman are struggling to be first. A million

[1] VON BÜLOW, op. cit., pp. 411-12.

petty disputes build up the greatest cause of war the world has ever seen. If Germany were extinguished tomorrow, the day after tomorrow there is not an Englishman in the world who would not be richer. Nations have fought for years over a city or a right of succession; must they not fight for two hundred and fifty million pounds of yearly commerce?

There is no reason to suppose that this article, or others in the same vein that appeared in Britain from time to time, were officially inspired, though Germans used to a 'managed' press may have suspected otherwise. The cynical nonsense of its argument was apparent to a majority of Englishmen who still thought in terms of free trade and understood that British and German commerce could prosper simultaneously, as was indeed the case in the years preceding 1914, when exports of both countries expanded with almost equal rapidity. Nor is there the slightest evidence to show that any responsible British statesman at any time contemplated war as a means of destroying German competition. Cecil Rhodes, ardent imperialist as he was, dreamt of an Anglo-German-American union that would assure world peace, and assigned part of his scholarship fund to German students. Chamberlain, the apostle of protection, was markedly friendly to Germany until his overtures were sharply rebuffed.

But while it was absurd to suppose that German economic progress was a threat to the British economy *as a whole*, it was true that the interests of individual British and German capitalists clashed frequently and both were accustomed to identify their personal prosperity with that of their respective countries. To British businessmen seeking outlets for surplus production, tariff reform seemed to offer an opportunity to tie profits and patriotism in a neat knot, and they failed to see why foreign countries, which had protected their home markets, should object. They did not realize that an empire embracing a quarter of the world might seem an intolerable monopoly to other nations if it were surrounded with any kind of ring-fence, whether an imperial tariff or an effective preference system. The British Empire had aroused a minimum of suspicion, jealousy and hostility, just because it had long followed an open-door policy. Germany, now the second largest industrial and trading nation, had grown dependent on Britain's free-trade market and on equal access to those of the

Dominions and colonies. Were entry to those markets impeded, the German economy would suffer. And, if as a result a trade war were precipitated, all the advantages would lie with Britain, whose exports to Germany were of far less consequence than German exports to British countries. As an American student of Anglo-German economic relations has written:

The tariff question thus was one of the stones upon which the knife of Anglo-German antagonism was sharpened. As a standing threat of a tariff war, it was a serious obstacle to any lasting accord with Germany; and moreover, it called out innumerable utterances which planted more firmly than ever in the British mind the fixed idea of German enmity. This had the inevitable effect of stiffening the official policy of linking Britain with the anti-German powers on the continent.[1]

A few years before Queen Victoria died, Britain had begun to reconsider the policy of 'splendid isolation' it had followed throughout her reign. Up to then, the military balance of power in Europe had been fairly well maintained and no nation had seriously attempted to dispute British mastery of the seas and endanger Imperial communications. By the mid-'nineties, however, growing international trade and new colonial interests were stimulating the naval ambitions of several powers. On the continent, Germany, Austria and Italy were bound together in the Triple Alliance and there was a Dual Alliance between Russia and France. But these groups did not necessarily provide the kind of balance that promised security for Britain, which, at the time, had no real friend in Europe and was experiencing constant friction with Russia in Asia and with France in North Africa.

Was there danger of a 'ganging-up' by the continental powers against Britain? That did not seem impossible, particularly at the outbreak of the South African war when 'perfidious Albion' was being execrated as an imperial bully throughout Europe. Salisbury had already taken one precautionary measure by settling all outstanding disputes with the United States and so securing the Atlantic flank. Now Chamberlain in a public speech in November 1899 made a bid for an agreement with Germany. A more unpropitious moment could hardly have been chosen.

[1] Ross J. S. HOFFMAN, *Great Britain and the German Trade Rivalry, 1875-1914.* University of Pennsylvania Press (Philadelphia, 1933), p. 292.

Anti-British feeling in Germany was at its height, and the early disasters of British arms in South Africa had given the German Government and general staff the impression that Britain was degenerate. Although prior to making his gesture, Chamberlain had received encouragement from the Kaiser, he now found himself snubbed by von Bülow in a speech to the Reichstag which hinted ominously at Teutonic ambitions. 'In the coming century', he declared, 'the German nation will be either the hammer or the anvil.'

Nevertheless, Chamberlain still clung to his project. Early in 1901, the Secretary of the German Embassy in London sent home the following report of a private conversation with him:

The day of a policy of 'splendid isolation' was over for England. England must look about for allies for the future. The choice was either Russia and France or the Triple Alliance. Both in the Cabinet and in the public there were those who wished for and eagerly worked for an understanding with Russia; and who were moreover ready to pay a very high price to obtain this object . . . So long as he, Mr. Chamberlain, was convinced that a permanent partnership with Germany was possible, he would resolutely oppose any idea of an arrangement with Russia. But should a permanent partnership with Germany prove unrealizable, he would then support an association with Russia. . . .[1]

This time, negotiations were opened between London and Berlin and a convention was actually drafted. But when the document was submitted to Lord Salisbury in May 1901, he pointed out that in effect it committed Britain to joining the Triple Alliance and to defending the German and Austrian frontiers against Russia, a much greater liability than Germany would incur by undertaking to come to Britain's assistance if it were attacked by France as well as Russia. 'It would be hardly wise,' he added, 'to incur novel and most onerous obligations, in order to guard against a danger in whose existence we have no historical reasons for believing.' For their part, the Germans seem to have been little more enthusiastic. They did not believe that Britain had the alternative at which Chamberlain hinted and they thought that by waiting they could get better terms.

One reason why men like Chamberlain were anxious to reach agreement with Germany was their desire for support in checking

[1] BARON VON ECKARDSTEIN, *Ten Years at the Court of St. James, 1895-1905.* Thornton Butterworth (London, 1921), pp. 185-6.

Russia's advance into China. The Russians had seized Port Arthur in 1898 and two years later occupied the whole of Manchuria; further encroachments, threatening the large British commercial interests centred in the Yangtze Basin seemed probable. Unable to secure effective German co-operation, the Foreign Office responded readily to overtures by Japan, whose particular concern was Russian designs against Korea. The Anglo-Japanese Alliance, signed in January 1902, provided that if either party were attacked by more than one power, the other would come to its assistance. This was a very definite commitment to which Salisbury's objections to the draft Anglo-German convention might well have applied. But the short-term advantages were clear: it gave a measure of protection for British interests in China and, by reducing the necessity for naval strength in the Far East, made possible concentration of a larger part of the fleet in home waters. To the Japanese the treaty afforded an opportunity, soon to be seized, to force a showdown with the Russians, whom they felt confident of beating provided no third party intervened.

On the conclusion of the Anglo-Japanese Alliance, the British Government approached Berlin once more, suggesting German adherence to the new pact and a joint effort to settle the future of Morocco, a state whose internal weakness, strategic position, and potential wealth had aroused the covetous interest of several European powers. Again, no agreement could be reached, and, a few months later, the first, fateful steps towards an Anglo-French understanding had been taken. An accumulation of disputes, ranging from the Newfoundland fisheries to the Siamese frontier, required long and difficult negotiations between London and Paris. But a greater obstacle to agreement was psychological. Public opinion in France, and to a lesser extent in Britain, was strongly influenced by the idea of traditional enmity between the two nations, and there was always a danger that a compromise between governments would be upset by a popular explosion. It was this aspect of the problem that lent importance to Edward VII's visit to Paris in 1903. His reception on arrival was far from friendly but, ignoring signs of hostility, he wooed the French with all his considerable charm and was able to sense a real change in atmosphere before he departed.

The Anglo-French Convention, signed April 12th, 1904, was

nominally no more than an agreement to wipe the slate clean, but there were secret clauses which, in effect, gave Britain a free hand in Egypt in return for a promise of diplomatic support to France in achieving its objectives in Morocco. Was this more than a platonic gesture? The German Government, which had formally expressed approval of Anglo-French reconciliation, sought an early opportunity to obtain an answer to this question. In the summer of 1905, it protested against French activities in Morocco, forced the resignation of Delcassé, chief French architect of the entente with Britain, and insisted on a conference of the powers to reopen the Moroccan question. But when the delegates gathered at Algeciras in January 1906, the Germans found to their chagrin that the new alliance was very solidly based and were forced to swallow a bitter diplomatic defeat.

The outcome of the conference afforded proof also that the advent of a Liberal government in Britain a month earlier had left British foreign policy unchanged. It has been suggested that it was to insure this continuity that Balfour had resigned instead of seeking a dissolution of Parliament in December 1905. Campbell-Bannerman, the Liberal leader, was therefore forced to form his administration before going to the country, and consequently to give very prominent positions to Asquith, Grey and Haldane, the leaders of the imperialist Liberal League, or risk splitting his party before the election. 'Asquith, Grey and I stood together,' Haldane said to the Webbs, 'they were forced to take us on our own terms.'[1] These terms included the appointment of Sir Edward Grey to the Foreign Office, where he had hardly settled in before he was told by the French Ambassador that his government feared an unprovoked attack by Germany and wanted to know whether it could count on British asistance. Grey refused to make any advance commitment, but after consulting Asquith, Haldane, who had become Secretary for War, and the Prime Minister, agreed to intitiate Anglo-French staff conversations. It is strange that the Gladstonian Campbell-Bannerman should have authorized so momentous a step, stranger still that he should have acquiesced in keeping it a secret, not only from Parliament but from the Cabinet. For while the military arrangements which arose from these conversations were always formally treated

[1] BEATRICE WEBB, *Our Partnership*, p. 326.

TARIFFS, TREATIES AND ARMAMENTS

as not binding, they did constitute a heavy moral obligation.

Naturally, it was not long before some inkling of this development reached Berlin, and the disquiet it aroused there was not allayed when, a few months later, Sir Arthur Nicholson, the diplomat who had represented Britain at Algeciras, was sent as Ambassador to St. Petersburg. His mission — to conclude an agreement removing the many frictions that kept Anglo-Russian relations heated — resulted, after much patient negotiation, in an agreement on such questions as Persia, Tibet and Afghanistan, all points where the interests of the two countries overlapped. This treaty, like that with France, was not directed against Germany: its purpose rather was to insure against any alliance of Russia with Germany. But in Berlin this seemed a distinction without a difference. The 'impossible' had happened: Britain had made friends with the two powers, themselves allied, which lay east and west of Germany, and, as a result, German freedom of diplomatic and military action was circumscribed. As Bethman-Hollweg, who succeeded von Bülow as Imperial Chancellor in 1909, was to write:

You may call it 'encirclement', 'balance of power', or what you will, but the object aimed at and eventually attained was no other than the welding of a serried and supreme combination of States for obstructing Germany, by diplomatic means at least, in the free development of its growing powers.[1]

The Anglo-French-Russian combination — the Triple Entente — 'was Europe's automatic reply to the growth of German power'.[2] But while it re-established a balance of forces that temporarily induced Berlin to be more cautious, it in no way modified German ambitions. Rather the sense of frustration created by a series of diplomatic defeats served to increase the inferiority complex which afflicted both the Kaiser and his subjects. In their jealous envy, the Germans saw Britain, a land where democratic decadence was joined with devilish cunning, standing between them and the destiny they deserved by virtue of their soldierly qualities, their industry, and their intelligence.

And now their self-esteem was to suffer a blow in a field where they prided themselves on their superiority. Since 1898

[1] Theobald von Bethmann-Hollweg, *Reflections on the World War.* Thornton Butterworth (London, 1920), p. 12.
[2] Élie Halévy, *History of the British People, Epilogue.* Benn (London, 1929), vol. I, p. 125.

Germany had been forcing the pace in naval construction but in 1905 Britain turned the tables with a surprise coup. Inspired by Sir John Fisher, a supremely aggressive and technically imaginative officer who had been appointed First Sea Lord the previous year, the Admiralty revolutionized naval design with the first dreadnought. The new ship, completed in the sensationally brief period of fifteen months, was ready for sea at the beginning of 1907. It was the largest armoured vessel ever constructed and, with its ten 12-inch guns which compared with four in previous types, and a speed of 21 knots, it made every battleship in the world obsolete. Until it could produce ships as good, Germany was bound to fall behind in the naval race: moreover, since such vessels were too large for the Kiel Canal, the main German fleet would be effectively divided between the North Sea and the Baltic unless this waterway was widened — a work which, in fact, was completed in June 1914.

Fisher's audacious experiment was undoubtedly a tactical success, but it meant, perhaps, as Halévy has suggested, the loss of a certain moral advantage. With Britain moving from the defensive to the offensive, the pleas of its statesmen for limitation of armaments went unheeded, even when they were reinforced, as in 1907 and 1908, by reductions in the naval building programme. Berlin saw in these gestures no more than an attempt to capitalize the advantage the Royal Navy had gained from the dreadnought by freezing the situation and so making German inferiority permanent. Von Bülow announced a veto on discussions of disarmament at the forthcoming International Peace Conference at The Hague, and, in 1908, a new German naval law speeded up the 1900 programme by providing for four battleships to be laid down annually from 1908 to 1911. So the race went on while tension between the participants grew rapidly.

For some account of the later phases of what might be called 'the cold war' between Germany and Britain, the reader must turn to Part Two, Chapter v. Suffice to say here that propagandists in both countries, inspired by successive diplomatic incidents and playing on acute commercial rivalry, created that belief in the inevitability of conflict which makes conflict so difficult to avoid. The lights of Europe, which were to be extinguished in August 1914, had already by 1908 begun to flicker ominously.

CHAPTER III

THE IMPACT OF LABOUR

The Labour Party has profoundly influenced the present House of Commons; more than it realizes itself. It is the sense that there is this power in the background — independent, discontented, hostile — that drives the Government; and that compels it always to keep legislation at the high speed to which it has risen at the present moment . . . As an old member of the House of Commons I am bound to say that the Labour Party has given to Parliament a seriousness, a strenuousness, and an effectiveness which rarely, if ever, existed in that assembly before.

T. P. O'CONNOR, M.P., in *M.A.P.*, August 22nd, 1909

T H E history of the British Labour movement from 1900 to 1914 supports rather neatly Arnold Toynbee's theory of the stimulating effects of adversity. During this period the organized workers, who for thirty years had been content to advance sedately but steadily, were faced, first by an actual decline in their standard of living, second by a powerful counterattack promoted by the propertied classes on what had been regarded as established labour rights. Their response to this challenge was energetic. After temporary retreats to rally their forces, they regained the offensive and went forward into new territory. The House of Lords' decision in the Taff Vale Case, which disarmed the trade unions industrially, swung attention to the political front and turned the Labour Party from an ailing infant to a vigorous youngster, able to secure from Parliament the privileges lost in the Courts. Taken by surprise, the capitalist forces attempted to smash this flanking movement in another legal action, the Osborne Case, and succeeded in blocking further progress by Labour's political wing for several years. But the unions, once again in possession of the strike weapon, returned to the industrial battle with a strength and belligerency of spirit greater than ever before.

For their victories in this period the workers paid a stiff price. These adverse legal decisions, particularly the first, checked any general improvement in wages and working conditions for at least a decade. It may be, as the Webbs have suggested, that 'the capitalist employers, thinking only of their profits for the time being, regarded even a temporary crippling of the trade union movement as well worth all that it might cost them'. But, as they add, 'The historian will not find the balance sheet so easy to construct. The final result of the successive attempts between 1901 and 1913 to cripple Trade Unionism by legal proceedings was to give it the firmest possible basis in statute law.'[1] More than that, these body blows at the trade unions so stirred the working class that they were able to double their membership between 1900 and 1913 and enforce in practically all major industries the principle of collective bargaining. Finally, the Labour Party was established as a permanent institution which, if still a long way from winning power, was able by its competitive position in elections to exert considerable influence over the policies of the older parties.

It was hardly a coincidence that in both these legal assaults the first brunt was borne by the railway workers. No body of employers had so strenuously and bitterly opposed collective bargaining as the railway companies. The Webbs report the general manager of one of the largest as saying in the 'nineties: 'You might as well have a trade union or an amalgamated society in the Army, where discipline has to be kept at a very high standard, as have it on the railroads.'[2] Nearly all the companies refused to have anything to do with the unions, and victimization of workers active in organizing their fellows was commonplace. Hours of duty were very long, often more than twelve a day; wages were exceptionally low. As late as 1907, the official wage census of the Board of Trade showed that 96,000 adult railwaymen were receiving 19 shillings or less per week.

In 1900, a strike broke out on the small Taff Vale line in South Wales. It was at first unofficial, but when the management sought to counter successful picketing by the importation of strike breakers, the Amalgamated Society of Railway Servants agreed to provide strike pay and other assistance. In the course of the dispute some damage was done to railway property, and the company decided to sue for civil damages, not only the men actually

[1] SIDNEY and BEATRICE WEBB, *The History of Trade Unionism*. Longmans, Green (Revised edn., London, 1920), pp. 633-4.
[2] Ibid, p. 525.

responsible but the union. To the general surprise, it won its case on appeal to the House of Lords and the union was ordered to pay £23,000 in damages, while its total costs amounted to £42,000. This was a crushing blow to a relatively small union, and the implications of the verdict staggered the whole trade union movement. Legal justification could be found in the increasing tendency of the courts to permit unincorporated associations to sue or be sued in the name of one or more of their officers in what were called 'representative actions', as well as in the loose wording of the Trade Union Acts of 1871-76 on which the unions had relied for protection against such suits. But the decision was undoubtedly opposed to the intention of those acts and to that of the government which sponsored them.

The Taff Vale Case seemed to cancel most of the gains made by the trade unions in a hundred years of struggle. Theoretically, the right to strike remained, but it could only be exercised at the risk of exposing both union funds and the private property of union officers to employers' suits even, apparently, in cases where there was no question of any criminal action by strikers. One of the most eminent lawyers of the day declared:

These decisions disclose divergencies of views among distinguished men which make it hopeless for anyone to try and say with accuracy what the law is. Speaking for myself, I should be very sorry to be called upon to tell a trade union secretary how he could conduct a strike successfully. The only answer I could give would be that, having regard to the diverging opinions of the Judges, I did not know.[1]

While the sword of strike action was temporarily blunted, the workers had a new weapon to bring into play, thanks to the action of the Trades Union Congress of 1899. (See page 64.) True, the Labour Representation Committee — forerunner of the Labour Party — did not as yet appear very formidable but it was something on which to build. The Committee had been launched in February 1900 at a conference representing half a million trade unionists and some 70,000 socialists. Difficulties involved in laying down principles and policies had been overcome by stating both in the most general terms. The Social Democratic Federa-

---

[1] R. B. HALDANE (VISCOUNT HALDANE OF CLOAN), 'The Labourer and the Law', *Century Review*, March 1903, p. 362.

tion wished to give the new organization a full-blooded socialist and class-war character, but Keir Hardie, who realized how easily scared many of the trade union leaders were, succeeded in shelving this resolution. An attempt to narrow unduly the scope of the committee by a declaration in favour of exclusive representation in Parliament of the working class by the working class was also defeated. But the conference endorsed the one principle for which Hardie had always fought — independence. It was agreed that a 'distinct Labour group' with its own whips was to be established in Parliament, though temporary co-operation with other parties willing to promote legislation in the direct interest of labour was not excluded.

The elected executive of the new committee was made up of seven trade unionists and five socialists. James Ramsay Mac-Donald was appointed Secretary and, despite the sad ending of his career as a Labour leader, this was probably a wise choice. The vagueness of the committee's policies, necessary to gain trade union support, created a great danger of torpidity if direction was not in energetic hands; on the other hand, much tact and patience was required to prevent clashes between the heterogeneous elements combined in the organization. MacDonald possessed these qualities; in addition, he was a fine figure of a man with a commanding presence and, at his best, a magnificent speaker. Some fourteen years earlier, then a penniless boy of twenty, he had come to London from the Highland fishing village where he had grown up. He had worked for a pittance as a clerk, advanced his education in evening courses, become private secretary to a Liberal M.P., and finally made his way as a journalist. The Social Democratic Federation had first attracted MacDonald, but he soon came to dislike its Marxist doctrines and developed a private brand of evolutionary socialism precariously based on biological analogies. After a period of activity in the Fabian Society, where he was snubbed by the Webbs, who never approved of him, he had found a political home in the Independent Labour Party.

The Labour Representation Committe soon proved for practical purposes a partnership between the I.L.P. and the trade unions. The Fabian Society maintained its adherence to the Committee but at this stage, while prepared to offer advice, was unable to give much active leadership. For one thing, the Society was split over the Boer War and educational policy; for another, the Webbs were very actively cultivating Tory and Liberal leaders with, they thought, some degree of success. So little were they interested in the momentous new development that the published portions of Beatrice Webb's voluminous diaries make no reference to the Labour Representation Committee.

Before long, the Social Democratic Federation, fearing to compromise its purity, withdrew, and the I.L.P. was left to carry the burden of propaganda and organizational work for the Committee — a task to which it gave itself with abundant moral fervour. The trade unions supplied a rather inert bulk membership and most of what little money was available. They were still so unwilling to pay for the benefits of political representation that the income of the Committe in its first year was only £243 and but £100 more the next. Nevertheless, at the 'Khaki Election' a few months after its formation, fifteen candidates, nominated and financed by affiliated trade union and socialist organizations, were put forward. They polled a fairly encouraging total of 62,698 votes, or over 35 per cent of those cast in all the divisions contested. Merthyr was won by Keir Hardie, and Derby by Richard Bell, a railway union leader, who was soon to show, however, that his heart belonged to the Liberal Party.

Failing more robust support from the unions, the future of the Labour Representation Committe appeared bleak. 'In February 1901', wrote Philip Snowden, future Labour Chancellor of the Exchequer, in his autobiography, 'I well remember the feeling of despondence which prevailed. It looked as if this new effort was going to share the fate of previous attempts to secure direct representation of Labour.'[1] And a book published that year described the Committee as paralysed by personal feuds and by the reluctance of the trade unions to break with the Liberal Party.[2]

This, then, was the situation when the Taff Vale decision gave a shock to the trade union world that galvanized it into action. The undisguised glee of employers and a large part of the press at the curb on 'labour tyranny' fashioned by the House of Lords gave

---

[1] PHILIP VISCOUNT SNOWDEN, *An Autobiography*. Ivor Nicholson and Watson (London, 1934), vol. I, p. 94.
[2] HENRY W. MACROSTY, *Trusts and the State*. J. Richards (London, 1901), p. 244.

fair warning that redress was not likely in the absence of strong pressure on the Government. Realizing that this 'semi-political decision' had to be countered by the mobilization of political power, a large number of trade unions which had been hanging back now joined the Labour Representation Committee. Its affiliated membership almost doubled, and a series of by-elections gave it an opportunity of spreading its influence and demonstrating its usefulness. At Clitheroe, in 1902, MacDonald's diplomacy secured the nomination of David Shackleton, a leader of the conservative cotton spinners, with the united support of the local unions, co-operative societies, and the I.L.P. Since neither Liberals nor Tories could find a candidate willing to fight this combination, he went to Westminster unopposed. The next year, Will Crooks, a popular figure in London and ex-Mayor of Poplar, won the Tory stronghold of Woolwich with Liberal support, while Arthur Henderson wrested Barnard Castle from the Liberals in a three-cornered fight.

Hoping to quiet the growing agitation in Labour circles, the Balfour Government appointed a Royal Commission on trade-union law. But not even one trade-union leader was invited to join the bevy of lawyers that comprised its membership, and the Trades Union Congress refused to give evidence. The commission, instructed to take its time, made no report until after the General Election of 1906. Meanwhile a bill embodying the principle of non-liability of unions for the 'tortious acts' of their members was introduced into the House of Commons. On its second reading, when the Government permitted a free vote, it was carried by 250 to 130. Thus members from industrial districts had their opportunity to make a voting record. In committee, however, the measure was hacked to pieces with the encouragement of the Solicitor-General, Sir Edward Carson, and eventually withdrawn by its sponsors.

In the field of social reform, the one notable achievement of the Balfour administration was the Education Act of 1902, which made possible a great advance in public secondary and technical education. But since it also reinforced the Church schools, its potential benefits were smothered for a time in the resurrected dust of the old controversy of denominational versus secular education. An Unemployed Workers' Act, passed in 1905, authorized local authorities to form 'Distress Committees' empowered to find work for those 'genuinely' seeking it, and to draw on local taxes to meet part of the expense. A discretionary rather than an obligatory measure, and limited in duration to three years, it was far from an impressive answer to the demands Hardie and others had been putting forward for 'work or maintenance'. Nevertheless, it may be regarded as of historical importance, since it represented the thin end of the wedge of State responsibility for the unemployed. Another small seed planted by the Tory Government that was destined to grow into a large tree was an enabling act authorizing provision of free meals for school children.

At this time, refugees from the Russian pogroms were pouring into London and complaints that they undercut wages were met by an Aliens Act (1905). But any favourable effect this might have had was offset by the almost simultaneous approval by the Government of Chinese contract-labour in the Rand mines. The terms on which the unfortunate coolies were to be recruited outraged the trade unions even though they were not directly affected. It also stirred up the nonconformists, whose consciences were already troubled by the Education Act and the Licensing Act of 1904. The latter measure, which modified the power of magistrates to extinguish public-house licences, hitherto granted annually with no absolute rights of renewal, was widely regarded as an advance payment to the drink interests in return for financial aid in the coming political campaign. Add to such sins of omission and commission the unpopular tariff reform programme and it will be seen that the Tories, who had swept the country in the 'Khaki Election', had good reason to fear their coming encounter with the voters. But even in their most pessimistic moments few of them could have anticipated the tidal wave which overwhelmed them in January 1906.

More will be said about this great victory of the Liberal Party in the next chapter. Here we are concerned with the lesser, though on the long view more significant, triumph of the Labour Representation Committee, which now blossomed out as the Labour Party. Of the fifty candidates it had sponsored, twenty-nine were elected, while a separate, but closely allied, miners' group rose from five to fourteen. This replacement of a scattered handful of independent Labour members by a solid block with the right to call itself a party was a shock to most politicians. There had been, apparently, incomplete realization of the depths of the tides stirring the workers, or of how effective an organization had been built under the guidance of MacDonald and Arthur Henderson, Treasurer of the Committee since 1903. Balfour, who was among the defeated, saw in the election results 'something much more important than the swing of the pendulum or all the squabbles about Free Trade and Fiscal Reform. We are face to face (no doubt in a milder form) with the Socialist difficulties which loom so large on the continent. Unless I am greatly mistaken, the election of 1905 inaugurates a new era'.[1]

The experiences of another ex-minister who lost his seat, as reported by Sir Almeric Fitzroy, Clerk to the Privy Council, provide interesting evidence of the change in the electoral situation:

[Stanley] . . . attributes his defeat and all the disasters in Lancashire to the uprising of Labour. Workingmen who had been his supporters for years . . . suddenly transferred their allegiance to his Labour opponent on the direction of the trade union authorities. The solidarity of Labour throughout the length and breadth of the country had the most striking illustration for wherever a Labour candidate stood no length of service or weight of personal influence counted for anything in the opposite scale. For years Labour has been working to this end but the cross issues that were prominent at the General Election of 1900 assisted to mask what was going on and to prepare the present surprise. Stanley does not believe that the fiscal question as such had much effect . . . it was rather the conviction, for the first time born in the working classes, that their social salvation is in their own hands.[2]

'Upon our party,' Arthur Henderson said at a victory celebration, 'rests the responsibility of keeping this government up to the scratch of their own professions, and a further responsibility of shaping their policy in harmony with public necessity . . . We must therefore guard as a sacred right the principle of independence which has assured the success of our movement.' In relation to these tasks the Labour Party's strategic position in the House of Commons had elements of both advantage and disadvantage. The Liberal majority was so huge that the Government was not com-

[1] BLANCHE E. C. DUGDALE, *Arthur James Balfour, First Earl of Balfour*. Hutchinson (London, 1936), vol. II, p. 20.
[2] SIR ALMERIC FITZROY, *Memoirs*. Hutchinson (London, 1925), pp. 279-80.

pelled to bid for Labour support in the lobbies. On the other hand, its dramatic political advent had given the new party considerable prestige, and as a potential competitor at future elections it was too formidable to be ignored. Moreover, there were in the Liberal ranks many radicals who were pledged to support most of Labour's demands.

The influence Labour could now exert was proved during the 1906 session when the Government brought forward a Trade Disputes Bill restricting the technical operation of the law of agency so that only the immediate organization alleged to have behaved illegally could be sued in tort. 'We had underestimated the extent to which the Labour spirit had operated on the candidates at the election,' Haldane said in his autobiography, explaining why the Government withdrew this bill, which he had helped to draft. The trade unions insisted that they must have the immunity they had enjoyed from 1871 until the Taff Vale decision and, when member after member in all parts of the House rose to announce they were pledged to support legislation of this nature, the Cabinet capitulated.

Tory leaders twitted the Government about their enforced retreat but they themselves did not care to challenge the revised bill on its third reading. More remarkable still, the vast Tory majority of the House of Lords, which was seeking to nullify the verdict of the polls by slaughtering Liberal measures, decided that this was 'unfavourable' ground on which to fight. So, as the first fruit of political organization, the trade unions secured what has since been their main charter — the Trade Disputes Act of 1906 which, in the words of the Webbs:

. . . explicitly declares, without any qualification or exception, that no civil action shall be entertained against a Trade Union in respect of any wrongful act committed by or on behalf of the Union; an extraordinary and unlimited immunity, however great may be the damage caused, and however unwarranted the act, which most lawyers, as well as all employers, regard as nothing less than monstrous.[1]

It was not altogether easy for the Labour Party to live up to its sensational entry on the Westminster stage. Once the Trade Disputes Act was law, the trade union watchdog relaxed and was

[1] SIDNEY and BEATRICE WEBB, op. cit., p. 606.

inclined to resent the efforts of its socialist tail to wag it into a more aggressive attitude towards the capitalist system. The party continued to stress independent action but remained very uncertain about the direction in which that action was to take it. Thus in 1908 the annual conference turned down a resolution which would have made the party definitely socialist, only to accept the very next day a motion declaring it should adopt as an objective 'socialization of the means of production, distribution, and exchange'. Basically at this time the party was a trade-union pressure group rather than a national political organization. Nevertheless, its members resisted right-wing proposals to perpetuate this situation by excluding all but trade-union members. Intuition rather than calculation kept it pursuing a middle way.

No doubt internal contradictions and uncertainty of purpose reduced the effectiveness of the Labour Party in the years following 1906. Still, considered in retrospect, its record was less barren than G. D. H. Cole and his school of labour historians have been inclined to suggest. The very existence of such an independent political force was a considerable factor in the outpouring of social legislation that makes the period 1906 to 1911 in Britain comparable to the New Deal era in the United States. Of course, old age pensions, enactment of an eight-hour day for miners, the institution of trade boards to regulate conditions in sweated industries, the provision of labour exchanges, the launching of national health and unemployment insurance, progress in public housing and town planning seemed rather small beer to impatient socialists demanding social revolution. But each of these measures added a new brick to the rising structure that Beatrice Webb called 'the house-keeping state'. And while all the credit cannot be given to the Labour Party, its advent surely created a climate favourable for such building operations.

There were a number of Liberal ministers who were ardent for social reform. But there is no reason to believe that H. H. Asquith, who succeeded to the premiership in 1908 on the death of Campbell-Bannerman, was among them, and some of his colleagues clung firmly to the economic philosophy of the nineteenth-century Whigs. This led, on occasion, to embarrassment. In 1908, for example, the son of the G.O.M., Herbert Gladstone, who as Home Secretary had charge of the Wage Boards Bill, jibbed at accepting the principle of a legal minimum wage without which this measure to reduce the evils of sweating must have proved abortive. As a result the bill was dropped until the next session, when it was placed in the more radical hands of Winston Churchill, then President of the Board of Trade. There were laments from some exponents of *laissez-faire* economics, but opposition proved unexpectedly feeble.

It had been rather stronger in the case of the Mines (Eight Hours) Bill of 1908, which conceded the principle of legal limitation of hours for adult males, something the Factory Acts had never done. The miners' unions, with the support of organized labour generally, had been pressing for this legislation for years. In 1906 they reiterated their demands, but the Cabinet, not anxious to commit itself, appointed a committee of inquiry which in its report stressed all the difficulties involved without taking a definite stand. When the Government finally decided to introduce the bill, a 'League of Coal Consumers', representing the railways and large industries, organized a lobby to defeat it. But neither Liberals nor Tories were willing to resist the counter-agitation of Labour. The bill passed the House of Commons, and Lord Lansdowne persuaded the Peers, some of whom were tempted to kill it, that they would be ill-advised to use their veto on this occasion.

The unwillingness of the Tories, even in the Upper Chamber, where they held undisputed sway, to oppose resolutely measures popular with the workers, was undoubtedly due to a fear of the consequences in constituencies where they might face Labour opposition. It is true that historically they had never been so hostile in principle to state interference as the Liberals, but they were now the party of business and the peculiar champions of private enterprise. When it came to formulating a programme of their own, their sole specific was the tariff. As J. W. Hills, M.P., one of the few progressive Tories, said to the Webbs in 1910:

They all say they are in favour of social reform, but when you urge them to declare in favour of any single item they shrink back with a cry 'That is Socialism!' In which, of course, they are right.[1]

Lord Salisbury had deplored 'electoral arithmetic' and had felt secure enough to neglect it. His successors could not afford to follow his example, even when the sum total produced by add-

[1] BEATRICE WEBB, *Our Partnership*, p. 465.

ing costly social reforms to restrictions on private enterprise was very disagreeable to the class they mainly represented. It was not surprising, therefore, that a new effort was made to stem the progress of the interloping party whose impact on politics was compelling older rivals to move faster along the road to social change than they would have done if it had not thrust itself forward.

Once again the opponents of Labour resorted to the Courts. In 1908 an action was brought against the Amalgamated Society of Railway Servants by one of its members, W. V. Osborne, who sought to restrain the use of its funds for political purposes. In the lower court the suit was dismissed, but Osborne, who easily found financial assistance to press the case, won in the Court of Appeal and finally in the House of Lords. As in the Taff Vale decision, the judgment conformed with the letter rather than the spirit of the law. The Trade Union Act of 1876, in defining the term 'Trade Union', had referred to collective bargaining and the conduct of strikes but not to other functions long exercised by unions. Now the judges decided that the Act's list of things permissible was not exceptional but exhaustive, which not only meant that the use of union funds for political purposes was illegal but also raised a doubt about the propriety of funeral benefits, educational work, and other common trade-union activities which the Act had not specifically mentioned.

This decision shattered the finances of the Labour Party. Most of its affiliated unions were enjoined from contributing to its funds, meeting election expenses of candidates, or paying salaries to elected members. Naturally there was an immediate demand for remedial legislation, but the Asquith Government, while promising eventual redress, was not sorry to see the Labour Party handicapped and found reasons for delaying action. In 1911 some relief was afforded by provision in the Finance Act for payment (from the Exchequer) of salaries to Members of Parliament — a reform first demanded by the Chartists seventy-five years before. But it was not until 1913 that a Trade Union Act was passed allowing unions to set up special political funds, provided authorization had been given by a ballot of members, and that those unwilling to subscribe to a political levy were allowed to contract out of the obligation.

Meanwhile the Labour Party, by scraping and borrowing, had

survived the two General Elections of 1910 without serious loss of strength. On the other hand, it had been forced to limit the number of its candidates, particularly in the second election, and so had been deprived of an opportunity to expand. Nor was the Parliamentary position favourable for putting pressure on the Government. The Liberals and Tories now had approximately the same number of members in the Commons, so that the Labour Party and the Irish Nationalists held a balance of power. But neither could afford to throw out the Liberals for Labour knew that a Tory government would be most unlikely to do anything to reverse the Osborne Judgment and the Irish were intent on securing their promised Home Rule Act.

The problem of what tactics to pursue under these circumstances caused a good deal of controversy. At one point in 1910 Ramsay MacDonald — not yet the official leader of the Parliamentary Labour Party but an outstanding figure — appears to have considered favourably overtures from Lloyd George for participation in a coalition government. How firm an offer this was it is difficult to say: in any case, nothing came of the project owing to the firm opposition of Arthur Henderson and others. But while the party thus maintained nominal independence, it was constrained to uphold the hands of the Government for several years during which the progress of social reform was effectively halted. This enforced opportunism undoubtedly checked its growth. Playing third fiddle in the Liberal band, it did little to stir the enthusiasm of the workers and could gather few new recruits. Thus the pleasure with which the upper classes had greeted the Osborne Judgment was not unreasonable. On the political front the advance of the enemy had been checked, at least temporarily.

But the damned-up energies of the workers were to find an outlet elsewhere. They were in an aggressive mood. The continued lag of wages behind prices, combined with judicial attacks on their institutions, had made them angry. Now trade and industry were booming; the demand for labour rising. The Trade Disputes Act had restored the strike weapon to the unions and new leaders were coming forward to urge its more vigorous use. The times were ripe for the struggle on the industrial front to which some reference will be made in Part Two, Chapter v.

CHAPTER IV

THE PEERS V. THE PEOPLE

The House of Lords, as it at present exists and acts, is not a national institution, but a Party dodge, an apparatus and instrument at the disposal of one political faction ... When Conservative members go about the country defending a Second Chamber, let them remember that this is the kind of Second Chamber they have to defend, and when they defend the veto let them remember that it is a veto used, not for national purposes, but for the grossest purposes of unscrupulous political partisanship.

WINSTON CHURCHILL in the House of Commons, June 29th, 1907

I N 1906, for the first time in history, the benches of the House of Commons were occupied by something like a cross-section of the population. Until then, members of both traditional parties had been recruited almost exclusively from the upper classes; typically they were sons of peers, well-to-do rentiers, leading lawyers, and top-rank businessmen. Now, among the 377 Liberals elected, a majority of 84 over all other parties combined, there was a considerable small-business element and numerous professional men — teachers, journalists, social workers, promoters of good causes. In addition, in the place of the former sprinkling of working men, there were 53 representatives of labour, 29 of them belonging to a distinct Labour Party, the rest either miners or 'Liberal-Labour' trade union officials. By contrast, the 50 bankers and 53 railway directors who had sat in the previous Parliament were reduced to 16 and 21 respectively.[1]

The rejuvenated Liberal Party was nearly as diverse in its points of view as in its social origins, and the ties binding it together were common antipathies rather than common sympathies. Generally speaking, members of the party were against tariffs, Chinese contract-labour, State support of religious education, and the drink interests. Their positive economic philosophies ran the gamut from Spencerian individualism to Fabian socialism. They formed anything but a tightly knit organization, and the

[1] ÉLIE HALÉVY, *History of the English People, Epilogue*, vol. II, p. 11.

fact that it held together surprisingly well must be ascribed to the glue gratuitously supplied by Tory tacticians.

In constructing his government, Sir Henry Campbell-Bannerman had found places for representatives of all the main groups. He himself was a Liberal of the old school, a believer in Peace, Retrenchment and Reform, but more sympathetic with the new democracy than Gladstone had been. A man of integrity and forthright speech, he had suffered unpopularity within his party and without when he had condemned as 'methods of barbarism' the burning of farms and the use of concentration camps in the later phases of the South African war. The defeated Boers had not forgotten his courage, and the memory assisted his successful negotiation of the Union of South Africa — the outstanding achievement of his brief premiership.

The Cabinet included a number of other Gladstonian veterans, among them John Morley (India Office), Herbert Gladstone (Home Office) and Lord Loreburn (Lord Chancellor). But Campbell-Bannerman had been constrained to give key positions to his former opponents, the leaders of the Liberal Imperialists. H. H. Asquith became Chancellor of the Exchequer and heir apparent; Sir Edward Grey, Foreign Secretary; and R. B. Haldane, Secretary for War. The radicals were represented by David Lloyd George at the Board of Trade and a number of under-secretaries, including several friends and disciples of the Webbs, who were thus encouraged in their hopes of permeation. The most notable junior, however, was Winston Churchill, who, since parting from the Tories on the tariff issue, had been moving steadily to the left. His chief was in the House of Lords, so that as Under-Secretary for the Colonies he spoke for his department in the Commons during the important South African debates — an opportunity of which he made full use. Finally, John Burns was appointed President of the Local Government Board, the first working man to hold Cabinet rank.[1]

[1] It was widely reported that when the Premier offered him the position he said: 'I congratulate you, Sir Henry: it will be the most popular appointment you have made.' It turned out to be one of the worst. Burns, as we have seen, played a notable part in the early Labour movement as political agitator and union organizer. Bernard Shaw had once called him 'a demagogue in the ancient and honourable sense of the word'. But he had allowed the applause of his audiences to go to his head. Jealousy had led him to play the part of a Parliamentary lone wolf and refuse to co-operate with other Labour men. And now vanity delivered him, as it was in later days to

The election of 1906 was a shattering experience for the Tories. In 1900 they had returned 380 strong: now they were an attenuated band of 157. They had been swept out of most of the industrial districts — all nine of the Manchester and Salford seats, including Balfour's own, had been lost — and many of their rural strongholds had fallen. Only in Birmingham and Liverpool, the London suburbs, and the Home Counties, had they held their own. For the representatives of a class who regarded rule as their natural right, who believed sincerely that only members of their class were fit to govern, the situation was almost desperate. Everything they stood for appeared to be jeopardized by the mob returned to Westminster — a mob of dissenters, proletarian agitators, shopkeepers and cranks. Even in the Cabinet were such dangerous characters as the 'red' John Burns and the foxy, pacifist, radical, Welsh solicitor — Lloyd George. This was democracy run riot, the nemesis Conservatives had feared in 1884 and then forgotten during two decades of power. Now the future of their country — which they instinctively identified with the fate of their order — seemed threatened.

Nevertheless, little save fear and a thirst for revenge united the Tories. The tariff had been one of the main causes of their downfall, but ironically the wholehearted followers of Chamberlain had emerged as the strongest section of the party, comprising more than two-thirds of the elected members. Their leader seemed to be in a position to take over the whole party until in July 1906 he suffered a stroke which effectively ended his political life. Thus Balfour, for whom a safe seat was soon found, continued to command an unhappy Tory company in the Commons. In the Upper Chamber the vast Tory host was captained by the Marquis of Lansdowne, former Whig grandee and owner of large Irish properties, who shared Balfour's apathy on the tariff question.

Despite this disunity between leaders and led, a façade of party harmony was erected and tacit agreement reached on a strategy to hamstring the Liberal Government and nullify as far

deliver some of his successors, into the hands of the permanent officials, who flattered him into believing that their conservative decisions were his own. As a result his department, which should have taken the lead at this period, proved a heavy drag on the social reform movement and had to be by-passed. Burns, for instance, so bungled the introduction of old-age pensions in 1907 that next year the bill was assigned to Lloyd George at the Treasury.

as possible the verdict of the electors. The chosen weapon was the veto power of the House of Lords which since 1886, when most of the Whig peers broke with the Liberal Party on Home Rule, had become for all intents and purposes a Tory club. Constitutionally, this change had put the Lords in an exposed position. It was difficult enough in any case to reconcile an unrepresentative, hereditary Upper Chamber with popular democracy: it was impossible to justify one controlled not only by a single class but by its most conservative section. The claim made was that the House of Lords performed a useful function in revising hasty legislation and in checking governments that had exceeded or outlived their mandates. But in fact it operated as a brake only when Liberal hands were on the wheel; when the Tories were in office, it was little more than a rubber stamp.

Writing to Lansdowne on April 13th, 1906, Balfour said:

I do not think the House of Lords will be able to escape the duty of making serious modifications in important government measures but, if this be done with caution and tact, I do not believe they will do themselves any harm. On the contrary, I think it quite possible that your House may come out of the ordeal strengthened rather than weakened by the inevitable difficulties of the next few years.[1]

Seldom has so brilliant a mind made so poor a calculation. True, the Tory campaign was for a time managed with much 'caution and tact' or, as some felt, with unscrupulous Machiavellian cunning. Prompted by their leaders, the peers swallowed — not without some gagging — a number of legislative nostrums that were poison to their class. As we saw in the last chapter, they accepted most of the measures about which working-class voters felt strongly, and although they attempted to amend the Old Age Pensions Bill, which Lansdowne believed 'would weaken the moral fibre and diminish the self-respect of the people', they yielded to the insistence of the Commons.

The Tory aim was to cut down the Government's legislative programme without raising an issue on which the Liberals could appeal to the electorate in the hope of receiving a mandate to 'end or mend' the House of Lords. Among the more notable victims of this policy of selective slaughter were the Education and

[1] LORD NEWTON, *Lord Lansdowne: A Biography*. Macmillan (London, 1929), p. 354.

Plural Voting Bills of 1906 and the Licensing Bill of 1908, all measures offensive to Tory vested interests. The first sought to end denominational teaching in the public elementary schools and to excuse children of dissenters in rural districts, where often only Church schools were available, from attending religious instruction. This attempt to meet nonconformist demands was objectionable not only the Church of England but also to the Roman Catholics, so that the Tories were able to enlist the support of the Irish Nationalists and Catholic trade unionists. It was not, therefore, a measure commanding such overwhelming support that the Government was likely to risk a dissolution. A more dangerous action, perhaps, was the Upper Chamber's unceremonious dispatch, with little more than a pretence of debate, of a bill to abolish plural voting. This system, which permitted electors to vote in each constituency in which they owned property, gave a privileged position to landowners and businessmen from which the Tories benefited much more than their opponents.[1]

Infuriated at the defeat of this long-promised reform, the Commons retorted with a resolution, carried by 432 to 127, calling for limitation of the right of the Lords to amend or reject legislation. Unheeding, the Tory peers went on to kill the Licensing Bill, the main purpose of which was to reduce the total number of public houses. This step, favoured by temperance reformers in all parties, was naturally anathema to the brewing interests; and not even a personal appeal to Lansdowne by the King moved the Tory peers who, meeting in conclave at Lansdowne House, decided by a huge majority to reject the bill. The subsequent discussion and vote in the House of Lords was, therefore, a mere formality.

Lloyd George's charge that the House of Lords 'was not a watch-dog of the Constitution but Mr. Balfour's poodle' seemed to the Liberals more than ever justified. But they still needed an issue to fire the country, some 'measure of social legislation whose effects would be so far-reaching that the House of Lords could neither accept it without humiliation, nor reject it without imperilling its prerogatives and even its existence'.[2] Left to himself, Asquith, who had become Prime Minister in 1908, might not

[1] 'The General Election [December 1910] is in full swing. I have five votes, at Horsham, East Grinstead, Reigate, the New Forest of Hampshire and Westminster.' W. S. BLUNT, *My Diaries*. Secker (London, 1921), Part II, p. 346.
[2] ÉLIE HALÉVY, op. cit., vol. II, p. 118.

have forced a showdown. He was an able advocate, a cool and resourceful Parliamentarian, and an amiable Cabinet chairman. He was not a fighter and most of the reforming zeal of his youth had evaporated. John Morley once said that he had 'not only a constitutional disinclination to anticipate events, but a reasoned conviction that in nine cases out of ten a decision is best deferred till the last moment'.[1] John Dillon, Irish Nationalist M.P., complained to Blunt that Asquith, who had once been unpretentious, had now 'adopted all the feelings of the aristocracy', and asserted 'he had been ruined by his second marriage to one who was a Tory at heart and was always advising him to stand out against Lloyd George and Churchill and the mass of the Radical Party'.[2]

The Prime Minister's lack of drive was more than compensated for by the aggressive energy of Lloyd George and Churchill who together devised a strategy to beat the Lords and took charge of its application. The little Welshman had proved an outstanding success at the Board of Trade and, when the ministry was reshuffled on the retirement of Campbell-Bannerman, had won promotion to the Treasury. Churchill's talents had also brought him rapid advancement. After a brief apprenticeship as Colonial Under-Secretary, he had followed Lloyd George at the Board of Trade and in 1910 was to become Home Secretary. In both these offices he played an important part in shaping and carrying through the social reform programme, winning the approval, not lightly bestowed, of Beatrice Webb. His chief interest, he told Blunt in 1909, was the welfare of the poor. 'I would give my life,' he said, 'to see them placed on a right footing in regard to their lives and means of living. That is what I am paid for.'[3]

Plans for an ambush of the Tory peers, whom success had rendered complacent, seem to have been laid in September 1909 when Churchill visited Lloyd George in North Wales. Early in the new year, the former, in a speech at Birmingham, gave a hint of what was being plotted:

I do not, of course, ignore the fact that the House of Lords has the power, though not I think the constitutional right, to bring the government of the country to a standstill by rejecting the provisions which the Commons make for the financial services of the

[1] Sir ALMERIC FITZROY, *Memoirs*. Hutchinson (London, 1925), p. 557.
[2] W. S. BLUNT, op. cit., p. 313.   [3] Ibid., p. 287.

year . . . And for my part, I should be quite content to see the battle joined as speedily as possible upon the plain, simple issue of aristocratic rule against representative government, between the reversion to protection and the maintenance of free trade, between a tax on bread and a tax on — well, never mind.

Not all Lloyd George's colleagues were as willing as Churchill to aid and abet his scheme for humbling the Tories and, incidentally, 'dishing the Socialists', by a radical challenge to the House of Lords. Most members of the Cabinet belonged, or were closely allied, to the propertied classes, and it was not without misgivings that they approved 'the People's Budget'. However, they had no alternative to Lloyd George's plan for dealing with the Second Chamber's successful sabotage of the Government, and it was clear that commitments for expenditure made a large increase in taxation inevitable in 1909. Old-age pensions had proved more costly than anticipated, and other money-absorbing social reforms were in contemplation. A rapid increase in motor traffic necessitated a large road construction and modernization programme. Last, but far from least, naval building plans were being accelerated with the vociferous approval of most of the press, the armament industry, and the Tory Party. The budget was bound to be a big one: why not make it 'popular' as well?

Altogether the Chancellor of the Exchequer had to find £16 million in new taxation — a larger addition than any of his predecessors in office had ever been required to raise in peacetime. Apart from social theory, or a desire to confound opponents, he was compelled to rely mainly on direct taxation. The trend of financial policy had been in that direction for years, and the Labour Party was pressing for heavier levies on large incomes and reduction of the consumption taxes that burdened the poor. In 1907, Asquith had taken a new step towards income-tax reform by setting a lower rate for earned incomes below £2000 and had increased death duties on estates exceeding £150,000. Lloyd George went considerably further towards a fully graduated system of direct taxation. Incomes over £3000 were to pay 1s. 2d. in the pound instead of 1s. and those over £5000 became liable to a supertax of 6d. in the pound on the amount by which they exceeded £3000 — an idea borrowed from the, then, fiery socialist, Philip Snowden. Steeper graduation of death duties applied the maximum 15 per cent rate at the £1 million level instead of £3 million and, to check evasion, provision was made for the taxation of gifts.

'Soaking the rich' in this manner could not provide enough revenue, and Lloyd George was forced to turn to consumption taxes on drink and tobacco. That too served his reforming purposes, for he believed in 'making as difficult as possible the access of the people to any commodity that injures them'. Moreover, increases in duties on beer and spirits, together with a steep rise in the tax on liquor licenses, struck a blow at the Tory drink interests and afforded revenge for the defeat of the 1908 Licensing Bill.

The forces of property found all these tax increases unfair and burdensome, but what really aroused them to berserk fury was a series of entirely new taxes on land. These were four in number: (1) a 20 per cent levy on increases in site values accruing after April 30th, 1909, payable when land changed hands; (2) a 10 per cent charge on the added value received by a lessor at the end of a lease; (3) an annual tax of one halfpenny in the pound on the value of undeveloped sites; (4) an annual tax of 5 per cent on mineral royalties. Only the last of these imposts was expected to produce any appreciable revenue immediately: from the others the yield, at best, would expand slowly after the laborious task of making a complete land survey and valuation — 'a new Domesday Book' — had been concluded. The concern of landowners, however, was with ultimate consequences. It appeared to them that a precedent was being set and a technique developed which could lead to confiscation; that these 'vindictive and socialistic' taxes were, in the words of Sir Edward Carson, 'the beginning of the end of all rights of property'.

In the perspective of history, their anguished rage appears quite disproportionate to the provocation. Lloyd George, like Joseph Chamberlain in the 'eighties, was seeking to attach the masses to the Liberal Party by posing as their champion against aristocratic privilege. But he was inviting them into that economic blind alley which commemorates Henry George rather than leading them along a broad highway to socialism. The fury of his opponents aided the deception. The more they sought to paint him as 'a swooping robber-gull' (Lansdowne's phrase), the more successfully he dramatized himself as a modern Robin Hood who made the landlord and the capitalist pay for security of property with premiums which could be used to improve the conditions of the poor.

In the House of Commons the Tories could only conduct a fighting retreat: even with the help of the Irish, whose own quarrel with Lloyd George had been excited by the increased tax on whisky, they could not hope to upset the Government majority. There remained, however, their majority in the Lords, a potential weapon against the budget, but one whose use raised grave constitutional questions. Since the seventeenth century, the House of Commons had claimed exclusive rights to determine national revenue and expenditure. This privilege was not formally enshrined in any statute but rested, like most constitutional practice, on a formidable set of precedents. The last occasion on which the Lords had tampered with taxation was in 1860, when they threw out a bill abolishing the paper duties, a move which the Liberal Government of the day claimed was amendment of the budget by indirection. The following session, therefore, it had incorporated in the Finance Bill all tax changes, including cancellation of the disputed duties, and the Lords, unwilling to take responsibility for rejecting the bill and forcing a general election, had capitulated. Salisbury, at the time of Harcourt's 'Death Duties Budget', had spoken of non-interference of the Second Chamber with finance bills as 'accepted practice'; Balfour, as recently as October 6th, 1908, had said in a speech at Dumfries: 'It is the House of Commons, not the House of Lords, which settles uncontrolled our financial system.' Thus, as an astute writer has put it:

The question now was — how silly would their lordships be? By constitutional tradition, they could veto everything but a Budget: yet here was a Budget crying to be vetoed. It was like a kid, which sportsmen tie up to a tree in order to persuade a tiger to its death; and at its loud, rude bleating the House of Lords began to growl.[1]

Some of the Tory elder statesmen saw clearly enough that the peers could not kill the budget without exposing themselves to a crippling blast of Liberal bullets, and urged caution. But whenever the tiger showed signs of retreat, Lloyd George found means

[1] GEORGE DANGERFIELD, *The Strange Death of Liberal England.* Constable (London, 1935), p. 20.

of exciting it anew. In his famous Limehouse speech on July 30th, 1909, he mixed taunts with pathos, contrasting the insolence of wealth with the 'patience and fortitude' of the people. At New-castle on October 9th, a few weeks before the Upper Chamber began to debate the budget, he dared the peers to do their worst. The question was, he said:

Should 500 men, ordinary men, chosen accidentally from among the unemployed, override the judgment — the deliberate judgment — of millions of people who are engaged in the industry which makes the wealth of the country.

From his invalid's couch, Joseph Chamberlain, forgetting he had once proposed a 'ransom from the rich', declared that the issue was between tariff reform and socialism and begged the House of Lords 'to force an election'. His deluded followers thought that an appeal to the country would probably give them both power and the long-sought mandate to introduce protection. Thus tariff reformers and the landed interests, the manufacturers and the aristocracy, were more than ready to accept the lead given by Lord Milner who declared on November 26th, that the duty of the peers was 'to try to prevent a thing they believed to be bad and damn the consequences'.

Four days later, the House of Lords rejected the budget by 350 to 75 and the consequences became manifest. On the motion of the Prime Minister, the House of Commons solemnly agreed that the action of the House of Lords 'is a breach of the Consti-tution and a usurpation of the rights of the Commons', and Parliament was then dissolved. There was no doubt about the major issue on which the election was to be fought. The budget had become of secondary importance, and the Liberal Party was asking the voters to give them authority to reduce the powers of the Upper House so that its Tory majority would no longer be in a position to veto legislation distasteful to it.

The results of the election of January 1910 were disappointing to both major contestants. Almost exactly equal numbers of Liberals and Tories were returned, and the former now had to depend for a majority on support from the forty Labour members and the eighty-two Irish Nationalists. It was the Irish who really held the balance of power and the previous year they had voted against the budget. Now they were prepared to sacrifice their whisky, but only on condition that the Government gave the most binding assurances that the wings of the House of Lords would be clipped so that it would no longer be in a position to veto Home Rule. On these lines an understanding was reached, thus making inevitable a battle over Ireland as soon as the supremacy of the Commons had been secured..

There is no need to retell in detail the oft-told story of the struggle over the Parliament Act, which finally received the Royal Assent in August 1911. The battle was interrupted for some months following the death of Edward VII in May 1910, when, to meet the wishes of his successor, George V, leaders of the two major parties explored the possibilities of compromise. No meeting of minds proved possible. The Tories were willing to reduce the hereditary element in the Upper Chamber, but only if its membership was reformed in such a manner as to ensure a permanent Conservative majority, and if it retained at least sufficient power to force a general election on a constitutional or 'organic' issue, such as Irish Home Rule. To the Liberals, on the other hand, reform of the composition of the House of Lords was a matter of minor interest; their purpose was to make it definitely subordinate to the Commons and responsive to the will of the electorate. It was easier to accomplish this end if the Upper Chamber continued as a palpably undemocratic body with 'no damned nonsense of merit about it'.

When the inter-party conferences failed, the Government proceeded with its plans to enact the Parliament Bill. This measure provided that: (a) the House of Lords should henceforth be without power to reject or amend any bill certified by the Speaker of the House of Commons to be a 'Money Bill'; (b) other bills, when passed by the Commons in three successive sessions and rejected twice by the Lords, should become law, provided that there was an interval of two years between the second reading of the bill for the first time and the final third reading; (c) the maximum duration of Parliament should be reduced from seven to five years. Although drastic, the bill still left the House of Lords considerable scope for influencing legislation. Since the procedure prescribed for overcoming resistance in the Upper Chamber was so time-consuming, governments were likely to avoid resort to it by accepting amendments to legislation unless vital questions of principle were involved. Further, the two-year-interval provision meant that the Lords' veto would become effective after a government had been in office three years — a fact which assumed importance in 1948 when the Labour Government faced the prospect of legislative impotence during the two years that remained to it.

Thanks to the Parliament Act of 1911, Mr. Attlee's administration could seek a remedy by introducing a bill, restricting still further the Lords' suspensive veto, in time for its passage in three successive sessions before an election was due. In 1910, Asquith faced a much more difficult problem: before his bill could become law he was compelled to obtain the consent of the Upper Chamber to the amputation of its own powers. There was only one final sanction available — use of the Royal Prerogative to create peers in sufficient numbers to give the Government a majority. This threat had been successfully used to force through the Reform Act of 1832, but its employment was a matter of considerable delicacy if the Throne were not to become directly involved in party politics. It was not, therefore, until the end of 1910, when it was certain that the House of Lords was going to reject the Parliament Bill and force yet another general election, that the Cabinet asked the King to be ready to exercise his prerogative if the voters again endorsed the Liberal policy and the Lords once more sought to override their decision. The King consented to furnish this club, but Asquith was not disposed to flourish it before the contingency for which it was designed actually arose.

It was, perhaps, unfortunate that the Prime Minister kept his weapon so discreetly concealed. For to many noble lords it seemed incredible that the King would consent to allow their House to be swamped by 500 upstarts — a belief undoubtedly encouraged by some in Court circles who claimed to be 'in the know'. Such wishful thinking led them into reckless courses. 'Let them make their peers,' cried Lord Curzon in May 1911. 'We will die in the last ditch before we give in.' (Three months later he was to crawl out of that ditch, muddied by the abuse of tougher and more obtuse colleagues, to vote for the Parliament Bill and save the 'order' in which he took such pride from ridiculous inflation.) Some of the more romantic Tories actually talked of revolution. In February 1910, George Wyndham, former Chief Secretary for Ireland, said to W. S. Blunt:

The strength of the Tory position is that they and the King together command the whole material force of the country, besides half its voting strength. They have the money, and the Army and the Navy and the Territorials, all down to the Boy Scouts. Why then should they consent to a change in the constitution without fighting?[1]

A year later he was harping on the same theme, urging that the Tory leaders should say to Asquith: 'You threaten us with a revolution: we threaten you with a counter-revolution.'[2] Balfour and Lansdowne, the responsible heads of the party, knew better than to indulge in dreams of a twentieth-century Barons' Revolt. As a last gesture of protest they consented to sponsor a bill limiting the Prerogative of the Crown relating to the creation of peers — a curious proposal to come from a party which had originated as 'the King's Men' and regarded itself as the peculiar buttress of the monarchy. But when, on July 20th, 1911, Asquith sent letters to Balfour and Lansdowne declaring firmly that the King had consented to create sufficient peers to ensure passage of the Parliament Bill, they knew the game was up. By this time, however, they had lost control of their followers. A group of peers, large enough to offset the maximum Liberal strength in the Upper Chamber, rallied to the banner of the octogenarian Lord Halsbury who refused to be intimidated by 'this bogey of the Royal Prerogative'. It was not sufficient, therefore, for the rest of the Tory peers to abstain; some of them had to sacrifice themselves, and Lord Curzon finally persuaded thirty-seven to join the Liberals and most of the Bishops in the Government lobby. The bill was saved by seventeen votes. 'We were beaten,' wrote George Wyndham, 'by the Bishops and the Rats.'

After the lapse of forty years, this whole episode has acquired the comic flavour of old-fashioned melodrama, and it is difficult not to laugh at the passionate rhetoric of the peers as they defended their home and honour against the villainous Liberal mortgage-holders. Nevertheless, the fears that inspired their opposition were not so groundless as some historians have suggested. Undoubtedly, the Parliament Act weakened the political defences of property and so assisted the subsequent advance of socialism. On the other

---

[1] W. S. BLUNT, op. cit., p. 299.   [2] Ibid., p. 353.

hand, a victory for the House of Lords in 1911 might have proved even more dangerous for the interests it represented. It would have given notice to the masses that the Reform Acts had not secured popular sovereignty, that the will of a majority of the people could still be frustrated if it clashed with that of the upper class. It would have blocked the gradualist approach to social democracy and reinforced the Marxian thesis, hitherto neglected in Britain, that only revolution could bring emancipation to the working classes.

Thus in meeting and defeating the challenge of the House of Lords the Liberal Party once again cleared the constitutional channels to progress. And with this service it completed its historic mission. When the last serious political barrier to democracy was down, there was no longer scope for a party which had been both the herald of emancipation and the nurse of capitalism. Now that emancipation had acquired a socialist connotation, these two functions were openly in conflict and, as a consequence, the Liberal Party began to disintegrate, with some of its members pulled to the right and others to the left. Even if the First World War had not produced a fatal schism among the Liberals, it is doubtful whether they could long have remained a major force. The climate of the British Parliamentary system has never been kind to third parties.

CHAPTER V

THE ERA OF ILL-FEELING

> We cannot read the debates [on Home Rule] that continued
> at intervals through April, May and June [1914], without
> wondering that our Parliamentary institutions were strong
> enough to survive the passions by which they were convulsed.
> Was it astonishing that German agents reported and German
> statesmen believed that England was paralysed by faction
> and drifting into civil war, and need not be taken into
> account as a factor in the European situation?
> WINSTON S. CHURCHILL: *The World Crisis*

IN American history books, the presidency of James Monroe,
1817-25, a period of prosperity accompanied by unusual
political harmony, is celebrated as 'the era of good feeling'.
By contrast, the years 1910 to 1914 in Britain deserve to be
known as the era of ill-feeling. Seldom has the public ear been
assailed by so many discords. It was a time when the administration was weak and the opposition irresponsible. Political controversy poisoned social life; normal Parliamentary good manners
went by the board while the parties battled over the House of
Lords and Home Rule; the spirit of compromise fled its Westminster haunts, ousted by the returning ghosts of violence and
bigotry.

The example set by upper-class males was followed by the
politically inferior order of women and the socially inferior order
of workers. An agitation for women's suffrage, which had
gathered force slowly and soberly, turned suddenly into a campaign of hate and destruction that was answered by a police
brutality quite foreign to Britain. A wave of labour unrest, on a
scale never previously known, swept the country. Compared to
the middle-class ladies who organized the militant suffragettes, and
the Tory leaders who incited Ulster to violence and army officers
to disaffection, the workers behaved with decorum and restraint.
In some cases, however, strikes acquired revolutionary overtones
and in general, they aroused a class bitterness to which both sides
contributed. 'May God strike Lord Devonport dead,' prayed the
striking dockers on Tower Hill when that newly ennobled grocer,

who was chairman of the Port of London Authority, refused to recognize their union. 'Of course I'm feudal,' said a society lady to the novelist, Arnold Bennett, during the 1912 coal strike. 'I'd batten them down. I'd make them work. I'd force them down.'

In his extremely entertaining study of this period, *The Strange Death of Liberal England*, George Dangerfield has suggested that the rebellions of Tories, women and workers, were all the fruit of an 'unconscious rejection of an established security'. According to his theory, the turmoil was not an indication of degeneracy but a sign of a new life, a new energy. It expressed a break with the cautious respectability of the Victorians, boredom with old habits of life and thought. The case is best sustained when applied to the suffragette movement, which, undoubtedly, had elements of a revolt against 'a moribund, a respectable, a smothering security'. But it is difficult to accept the view that the workers were likewise turning their backs on the idea of security. They had no soft and cloistered unreality from which they felt the urge to escape; they were constantly faced by the problems of meeting the rent, buying the next meal, and keeping the children clothed and shod. Moreover, as we saw in earlier chapters, Edwardian prosperity had passed them by. Real wages had declined, employment had become more irregular, trade-union activity had been hampered. There is no need to call upon Freud to explain why, when business began to boom in 1910, the workers seized the opportunity to better their lot.

Nor is the suggestion that boredom was an important ingredient in the Tory rebellion very plausible. True, there were among its leaders political adventurers seeking 'glittering prizes', for example, F. E. (Galloper) Smith, M.P., later Earl of Birkenhead. But most of the Tories do not seem to have been trying to elude their Victorian nurse; on the contrary, they were anxious to 'keep a'hold of' her 'for fear of meeting something worse', like the little boy in Belloc's *Cautionary Tales*. They were troubled by the new age that threatened their privileges, their property, and their place in the world. They saw the security they had so long enjoyed undermined by a democratic electorate that insisted on legislation to benefit the masses, by trade unions whose demands cut profits and limited the capitalist's freedom of action, by weak-kneed politicians who capitulated to popular pressures. When they fought the Parliament Bill to the last ditch, they were defending themselves against unpredictable change; when they resisted Home Rule for Ireland, it was because maintenance of 'the Union' symbolized stability; when they built their programme around protection, they proclaimed their fears of foreign competition.

In the autumn of 1910, when the fires of party strife were already burning fiercely, an attempt was made to extinguish them by a cooling coalition. Interestingly, it was Lloyd George, one of the chief fanners of the flames, who sponsored this proposal. At a time when the inter-party conferences on the Parliament Bill were deadlocked, he suggested that the situation might be saved by extending the scope of the conversations to cover all the main issues dividing Liberals and Tories. It was a move highly characteristic of the man. He had, according to a journalist who knew him well, a natural talent for coalition since he was both 'an explosive of party union and a builder of flying bridges between incompatibles'.[1] 'Principles mean nothing to him — never have,' said Balfour reminiscing on this episode years later. 'His mind doesn't work that way. It's both his strength and his weakness. He says to himself at any given moment: "Come on now — we've all been squabbling too long, let's find a reasonable way out of the difficulty." But such solutions are quite impossible for people who don't share his outlook on political principles — the great things.'[2]

In rejecting Lloyd George's overtures, Balfour seems to have been influenced by memories of Sir Robert Peel, whom he regarded as a betrayer of the Tory Party. But if the reported terms of the coalition offer are correct, it was Liberal rather than Tory principles which were to be sacrificed. There is reason to suppose that Lloyd George was ready to leave the powers of the House of Lords undisturbed if provision were made for joint sittings with the House of Commons to iron out differences; to concede Imperial preference on existing customs duties and entrust the tariff question to an impartial commission; to accept a system of 'national training' — an idea close to most Tory hearts, though not

---

[1] HERBERT SIDEBOTHAM, *Pillars of the State*. Nisbet (London, 1921), p. 88.
[2] BLANCHE E. C. DUGDALE, *Arthur James Balfour*. Hutchinson (London, 1936), vol. II, p. 77.

Balfour's; and finally, to dispose of the perennial Irish problem by 'a reasonable federal solution'.[1] Had this plan been accepted as the basis for a united Liberal-Tory government, it is the Liberal Party's left wing and its Nationalist and Labour allies who would really have had cause to complain. Almost certainly the Liberals would have split badly, though a majority might have followed Lloyd George, and when the dust settled the Tories would have found themselves in control of the coalition.

It is a measure of the party bitterness at the time that the Tories should have so blindly thrown away the opportunity Lloyd George's scheme offered them. That bitterness was exhibited in full flower on July 25th, 1911, when Asquith was prevented from addressing the House of Commons on the Parliament Bill by a howling mob of Tories led by that ascetic aristocrat, Lord Hugh Cecil, in strange partnership with the parvenu, F. E. Smith. Never before in Parliamentary history had a Prime Minister been so treated. The scene was premeditated, and George Wyndham, who was privy to the plot, declared it was intended more as a demonstration against the leadership of Balfour, whose cool detachment irked a party that had become mentally unhinged, than as an insult to Asquith.[2] Balfour, he had complained a few months earlier, 'does not want to fight . . . He knows that there was once an ice-age and that there will some day be an ice-age again. This makes him indifferent'.[3]

The B.M.G. (Balfour Must Go) movement was, in fact, rapidly gathering force at this time and soon after the Parliament Act reached the statute books it gained its objective. In early October, the Tory leader received an extremely critical letter from Walter Long, 'my oldest colleague, my *professed* friend and upholder', which amounted to 'a bold and brutal invitation to retire'.[4] A month later he stepped down, leaving to his party a knotty problem of succession. Long himself, a country squire of the old school, was one candidate; Austen Chamberlain another. But neither could command a sure majority of the party, and the mantle fell on Andrew Bonar Law, a Scottish-Canadian iron merchant whose emergence from obscurity symbolized a new era in Tory history. From now on the party was to be dominated by

[1] Ibid., p. 76.
[3] Ibid., p. 353.
[2] W. S. BLUNT, *My Diaries*, Part II, p. 371.
[4] BLANCHE E. C. DUGDALE, op. cit., vol. II, p. 88.

its business wing, in whose hands the leadership remained until it was assumed by Churchill on the resignation of Neville Chamberlain in 1940.

In his memoirs, Austen Chamberlain gave the following account of Bonar Law:

He had no connection with the great Tory families; he was unknown outside political circles; he had never held high office nor even sat in a Cabinet. To the ideas of the landed gentry, so influential and still so numerous in the Tory ranks, he was a stranger. He had singularly little regard for tradition and even less for the forms in which it was enshrined . . . He once said to me, before the war had stirred deeper emotions, that he cared intensely for only two things: Tariff Reform and Ulster.[1]

Since the new Tory leader had little immediate prospect of securing tariff reform, he could devote himself to the task of saving Protestant Ulster from a fate worse than death — subjection to the Papist hordes of Southern Ireland. Indeed, he regarded this cause as so paramount that before long he consented to drop food taxes from the party programme in order to close ranks for the Irish battle.

The new Home Rule Bill was introduced in the Commons on April 12th, 1912. It was a measure based on federalist principles, and there was a suggestion that it might pave the way for local self-government (devolution) in England, Scotland and Wales. The Imperial Parliament at Westminster, with a reduced Irish membership, was to continue as the supreme authority in the British Isles, with power to control defence, foreign affairs, and external trade. Ireland, therefore, was to obtain much less self-government than a Dominion, and the Dublin Parliament promised to be little more than a glorified county council. The very moderation of the bill was turned against it by Balfour. If Irish nationalism were a genuine passion, he argued in his pamphlet *Nationality and Home Rule* (1912), it would never be appeased by a half-way house to independence; if on the other hand the bill satisfied the Nationalists, that would be perfect proof that their agitation had no real depth and didn't deserve appeasement.

The subtle dialectics of this thesis were, however, quite foreign to the turbulent debate that preoccupied British politicians from

[1] Sir Austen Chamberlain, *Down the Years*. Cassell (London, 1935), pp. 223-4.

1912 to 1914. Maintenance of the Union as an issue became swallowed up in the question of Irish unity. Asquith had persuaded the Nationalist leaders to accept a modicum of Home Rule on condition that it applied to the whole island. That meant the inclusion of Ulster against the will of its Protestant majority, large numbers of whom invited Sir Edward Carson, a grim and eminent lawyer hailing from Dublin, to lead them in battle against the bill, swearing great oaths to follow him to the death. It was their right, they claimed, to stay tied to Mother England's apron strings and to keep the other three-fourths of Ireland secured in the same manner. And, if Mother insisted on turning them loose, they were determined to show their love and loyalty by beating her up.

In their stand the Carsonites were fully supported by the official Tory Party. Even before the Home Rule Bill was published, Bonar Law had taken the salute at a huge review of the newly formed Ulster volunteers and so blessed a private army organized to defy Parliament. On July 27th, 1912, addressing a demonstration at Blenheim Palace, he practically abdicated his leadership in favour of Carson, saying: 'I can imagine no length of resistance to which Ulster will go which I shall not be ready to support.' How far that might be Bonar Law indicated five months later when he told the House of Commons that the Northern Irish 'would prefer, I believe, to accept the government of a foreign country rather than submit to be governed by the honourable gentlemen below the gangway [the Nationalists]'.

Asquith deplored this open advocacy of rebellion but took no active steps to deal with it. Tory treason remained unpunished: there was not even an effort to suppress political armies. Worse still, the Government's attitude towards the elementary duty of maintaining law and order was highly discriminatory. Although it was well known that the Ulster Volunteers had some weapons and were seeking others, the old embargo on importation of arms into Ireland, suspended in 1905, was not revived until the Nationalists began to recruit troops. In April 1914, 30,000 rifles and 3,000,000 rounds of ammunition were landed in Ulster in defiance of this ordinance, thanks to what seemed the purposeful inefficiency of the authorites. When a similar gun-running was carried out in July by the Nationalists, troops were summoned and three civilians killed — a blood-letting that greatly added to Irish bitterness.

In 1912, left-wing trade unionists had been jailed for circulating a leaflet urging soldiers not to shoot their striking working-class brothers. The following year, Bonar Law in a speech at Dublin made a plain appeal to the army to disobey the Government. No action was taken against him. Responding to such incitements, officers at The Curragh refused in 1914 to undertake duty in Ulster. They drew no penalty, and Sir Henry Wilson, Director of Military Operations, who as head of an Ulster 'fifth column' inside the War Office aided and abetted them, remained undisturbed at his post. This disaffection in the army shook the Government into a desperate attempt to reach a compromise. But an inter-party conference proved unable to compose a formula which reconciled Liberal pledges to the Nationalists with the unshakable demands of Ulster. In July 1914, as Europe began to mobilize, Britain seemed nearer to civil war than at any time since 1688.

It is hardly surprising that the militant suffragettes should have protested with embarrassing vigour their unrelenting prosecution by a government which gave immunity to the Ulster leaders. They could claim, at least, that they had resorted to violence only when peaceful persuasion had failed; that, denied the rights of citizens, subjected to taxation without representation, they had no alternative means to forward their cause save direct action.

A majority of the M.P.s elected in 1906 had been pledged to support women's suffrage but, when a deputation waited on Campbell-Bannerman soon after the new Parliament assembled, he declared nothing could be done since both the Liberal Party and the Cabinet were divided. 'Go on pestering,' was the Prime Minister's advice and his auditors accepted it with a literalness that was to dismay his successor. Yet it was not until several years later that a section of the suffragettes began to publicize their demands by violence. In July 1910 they had been encouraged by the successful introduction of a bill providing for enfranchisement of about one million women — householders and property owners. But disappointment soon followed, for Asquith was able to secure consideration of this measure by a committee of the whole House, so that it could only go forward if and when the Government allotted time to it. Since the Government was engrossed in its dispute with the Lords, this was the equivalent of putting the question into cold storage.

It was at this point that the Women's Social and Political Union, headed by Mrs. Emmeline Pankhurst and her daughter, Christabel, began a carefully organized campaign of destruction that was soon to reduce the Cabinet, the magistracy and the police to a state of baffled fury. At first they contented themselves with the wholesale breakage of window glass but before long they moved on to arson, picture slashing, snipping telephone wires, and the deposit of acid in letter boxes. Hundreds of women were arrested and sentenced to various terms of imprisonment. They went on hunger strike until released, when they quickly returned to a life of political crime. The authorities then attempted to keep them alive in jail by forcible feeding, but this brutal procedure proved ineffective in giving nourishment and its victims frequently had to be turned loose so that they might not die in prison. Finally, the Government persuaded Parliament to pass what was popularly known as 'the Cat and Mouse Act' which made it possible to release prisoners who had not served their full term and rearrest them when convenient without new charges or a new trial.

Militancy reached its peak early in 1913, following another 'betrayal' by the Prime Minister. More than a year before, he had promised that a forthcoming Franchise and Registration Bill, designed to establish complete manhood suffrage and abolish plural voting, should be so drafted as to admit amendments providing for women's suffrage. And these amendments, he promised, should be left to a free vote of the House. But when on January 23rd, 1913, the bill reached the committee stage and an amendment was moved to delete the word 'male' wherever it appeared, the Speaker ruled that this proposal would entirely alter the character of the bill and was, therefore, out of order. Agitators for women's suffrage, both militants and constitutionalists, were convinced that they had been deliberately cheated: so eminent a Parliamentary lawyer as Asquith, they believed, must have foreseen this denoucment. The Pankhurst followers expressed their angry disappointment with hammer, torch and bomb. They caught the headlines, but it was, perhaps, the persistent, well-organized, and orderly campaigns of the National Union of Women's Suffrage Societies, under the leadership of Dame Millicent Fawcett, which gradually converted a large section of the general public to 'The Cause'.

By the summer of 1914, Asquith suddenly seemed ready to yield. The cause of his change of heart is not entirely clear. It may have been inability to cope with the Pankhurst tactics, or the effective propaganda of the large non-militant suffrage groups, or knowledge that the Labour Party had decided to give adult manhood and womanhood suffrage a foremost place in its election programme. In any case, he promised early action. But now he could not easily satisfy the W.S.P.U. that he really meant it. Moreover, some women had found in militancy a way of life, and the thought of peace filled them with dismay. Insisting there could be no truce until victory was sealed, they continued to smash and burn until war provided a new outlet for their aggressions. From August 4th on, the loud patriotism of Christabel Pankhurst was matched only by that of Carson and 'Galloper' Smith who a few weeks before had been almost ready to seek the protection of the German Kaiser.

In their revolt the workers were far more law-abiding than the Tories or the militant suffragettes. It is true that among their leaders were men who preached the doctrines of revolutionary syndicalism and believed that 'the function of industrial unionism ... is to build up an industrial republic inside the shell of the political state.'[1] But the vast majority of the trade unionists who walked off their jobs between 1910 and 1914 were certainly not consciously aiming at revolution: they were exercising their right to strike for better wages and shorter hours. Not many disputes were fought out to the bitter end, for the conciliation machinery of the Board of Trade proved an effective means of reaching settlements. Strikes seldom led to violence. There was rioting at Tonypandy, South Wales, during a mines dispute in 1910, and the next year both the Liverpool dock strike and a country-wide railroad strike led to disturbances. Each time the Government was quick to send troops and special police and, on the last two occasions, strikers were killed.

[1] JAMES CONNOLLY, *Socialism Made Easy*. C. H. Kerr (Chicago, 1909), p. 58.

Such occurrences are rare in British trade union history and are evidence that the industrial struggle in this period was conducted in an atmosphere of exceptional tension. Yet it would seem that the Webbs, for once, exaggerated when they wrote of

. . . an outburst of exasperated strikes designed, we may almost say, to supersede Collective Bargaining, to repudiate any making of long-term agreements, to spring demand after demand upon employers, to compel every workman to join the union, avowedly with the view to building up the Trade Union as a dominant force.[1]

It is interesting to contrast this passage with the contemporary complaint of G. D. H. Cole, whose guild-socialist theories were closely akin to the ideas of the syndicalists, that trade unionists were insufficiently militant. 'There is a good deal to be said,' he wrote in 1913, 'for the view that we have too much conciliation, and that a big increase in the number of strikes would do us no harm.'[2]

What really irked those who looked to industrial mass action to bring about the transformation of society was not so much a shortage of strikes as the willingness of most trade-union leaders to compromise. From 1901 to 1910 there had been an annual average of 463 industrial stoppages, and 4,258,859 working days lost. In 1912, 821 strikes were recorded and they involved larger numbers and lasted longer, causing a total loss of 40,346,000 working days. Wages were usually the immediate cause, but often the crucial issue was union recognition. For the workers' offensive in these years was being countered by an obstinate rear-guard stand by employers, many of whom had yet to accept collective bargaining as the normal method of settling working conditions. In this sense the unions were engaged in class warfare, but it was for limited objectives which were substantially achieved. By 1914 the workers' organizations had won for themselves a status in the community far greater than they had ever enjoyed before and an authority which both employers and Government were forced to recognize and, frequently, placate.

This outcome of four years of struggle looks more impressive in retrospect than it did at the time. Certainly it fell far short of

[1] SIDNEY and BEATRICE WEBB, *History of Trade Unionism.* (Longmans, Green (London, 1920 Edn.), p. 665.
[2] G. D. H. COLE, *The World of Labour.* G. Bell (London, 1913), p. 316.

the hopes of those who had expected that a mounting series of bigger and better strikes would lead to a revolutionary climax. Clearly a number of unrelated and unco-ordinated strikes were unlikely to overthrow the power of capitalism. Consequently the syndicalists sought to perfect the strategy of the general strike which, by paralysing both industry and government, would produce an atmosphere favourable to their ends. In 1914 they were encouraged by the formation of the 'Triple Alliance' bringing under one general staff the 1,350,000 members of the National Union of Railwaymen, the Transport Workers' Federation, and the Miners' Federation. All three organizations had been left dissatisfied by strikes waged in isolation: now they planned concerted action to enforce their demands.

The date was set tentatively for October 1914. . . .

Amid all their domestic preoccupations, the chief Liberal ministers had never been free, since 1906, from concern about the European situation. There had been alarming incidents at regular intervals. In 1908, at an early stage in the crisis caused by Austrian annexation of Bosnia, Asquith had told Balfour privately that 'incredible as it may seem, the government could form no theory of the German policy which fitted all the known facts, except that they wanted war, and war . . . would certainly involve Russia, Austria, and the Near East — to say nothing of ourselves'.[1] Diplomatic nerves were again jangled in the summer of 1911 by the sudden dispatch of a German cruiser to the obscure Moroccan port of Agadir. The excuse was protection of a German concession, but when Berlin asked for most of the French Congo in return for future 'disinterest' in Morocco, it was plain that a new experiment in international blackmail was being made. On this occasion a strong protest by Grey to the German Foreign Office was backed by an even stronger public speech by Lloyd George, who warned Germany Britain might find the price of peace too high. Coming from the reputed leader of the pacifist section of the Cabinet, this statement caused a sensation. Berlin's immediate reaction was a note which Grey described as 'so stiff that the Fleet might be attacked at any moment'.[2] It provided,

[1] LORD NEWTON, *Lord Lansdowne: A Biography*. Macmillan (London, 1929), pp. 372-3.
[2] WINSTON S. CHURCHILL, *The World Crisis*. Thornton Butterworth (London, 1929); also Odham (London, 1939), vol. I, p. 33.

in fact, cover for a retreat. Once again the Reich had suffered from British support of France; once again it sought to repair its prestige by adding to its Navy.

In the face of these frequent threats of German aggression, the British Government took steps to strengthen the national defences. Under R. B. Haldane the War Office was reorganized between 1906 and 1912. The regular Army was regrouped to form a first-line fighting force of six divisions ready for instant dispatch overseas, and behind it, as a home reserve, were the new volunteer 'Territorial' regiments. Haldane did his work with such efficiency that army costs were not materially increased. Navy appropriations, on the other hand, were inflated year by year as more and larger battleships were added to maintain a wide margin of superiority over the expanding German fleet. This led to controversy inside and outside the Government. In 1909, the request of Reginald McKenna, First Lord of the Admiralty, for six new dreadnoughts met the hot opposition of Lloyd George and Churchill, who, believing the money might better be spent on social reform, urged that no more than four battleships were really needed. They were supported by a majority of the Cabinet, but the 'Big Navy' advocates were assisted by a noisy agitation in the Tory press which popularized the slogan: 'We Want Eight and We Won't Wait'. And after McKenna and his whole Board of Admiralty had threatened to resign, they actually secured two more than they had originally demanded. As consolation, Lloyd George received a Cabinet blessing for 'the People's Budget' which placed the main burden of armaments on the financially strongest shoulders.

At intervals between 1906 and 1914 attempts were made to reach an Anglo-German agreement to end the ruinous and dangerous naval race. But Germany was not prepared to accept permanent naval inferiority except on political conditions insuring the end of the Triple Entente. Grey was ready to offer a 'non-aggression pact' pledging Britain against making or joining 'any unprovoked attack' on Germany — a proposal which alarmed those permanent Foreign Office officials whose major purpose was to conserve and strengthen the agreements with Russia and France. But since nothing short of a guarantee of absolute British neutrality would satisfy Berlin, negotiations proved unfruitful.

Meanwhile, soon after the Agadir incident a significant change in leadership was made at the Admiralty. A strong hand was needed there owing to the reluctance of the professional sailors to fall in with the broad strategic policy of the Government. In the event of war with Germany, plans called for the immediate transport of an expeditionary force to France so that the first task of the Navy would be to secure the safe passage of the Channel. The Navy chiefs disliked this programme: their view was that priority should be given to close blockade of Germany and destruction of its naval power, preparing the way for direct invasion of Germany. McKenna was a good administrator and had fought hard for more ships, but he had not the commanding personality needed to bring the admirals into line. Asquith decided, therefore, to assign the job to Churchill, a choice which may have alarmed the Admiralty in view of his association with the 'pacifist' Lloyd George and his recent opposition to the 'Big Navy' programme.

The gamekeeper turned poacher soon proved, however, that he was just as zealous as his predecessor in raiding the Treasury for the benefit of the Navy. Churchill's motto has always been: 'Whatsoever thy hand findeth to do, do it with thy might.' At the Board of Trade and the Home Office he had found scope for action in social reform and almost persuaded himself this was the mission to which he should devote his life. Now he discovered a new love — the Navy — which quickly succumbed to his energetic and ardent wooing. In October 1912, his old friend, W. S. Blunt, noted:

He [Churchill] has become most truculent about international affairs, being engrossed in preparations for war with Germany . . . He and George [Wyndham] had been talking these two days in absolute accord on Army and Navy affairs and the coming war with Germany. Hearing them talk one might be excused for thinking what is commonly said by the Tories, that Winston will one day return to the Tory fold. His old connection with the Army and now with the Navy has turned his mind back into an ultra Imperialist groove.[1]

This concord between Churchill and Wyndham, then at

[1] W. S. BLUNT, op. cit., p. 417.

opposite poles on domestic questions, exemplified the upper-class united front on foreign affairs. In the inner circles of both parties there was agreement about the necessity for resisting German expansion and understanding that the upshot of this resistance was likely to be war. By contrast, neither the insistent ringing of international alarm bells, nor open preparations for conflict at home and abroad, appear to have penetrated deeply into the public consciousness. This was not because of any lack of discussion. Tory newspapers, particularly those in the Northcliffe group, constantly publicized the German 'menace' both in its military and economic aspects: German spies and imaginary invasions were the stock-in-trade of the thriller-writers. But the man-in-the-street was not seriously aroused either by jingo propaganda or by the warnings of such socialist leaders as Keir Hardie and Ramsay MacDonald, who knew from their international contacts how grave a situation was developing. The Navy — traditional bulwark against foreign foes — found a good deal of public support for expansion: the agitation for conscription, even though it was led by as popular a hero as Field-Marshal Lord Roberts, fell flat.

One reason for this unconcern, perhaps, was the fact that Britain had not been embroiled in a European war for a hundred years, apart from the dim and distant campaign in the Crimea. A world conflict, and its implications, were beyond imagination. Besides, democratic curiosity about foreign affairs was not encouraged. Sir Edward Grey had never considered it his duty to spell out the meaning of the Triple Entente or to explain to the public why an incident in the Balkans might involve Britain in war with Germany. Still less was he prepared to admit, even to himself, the moral obligations incurred by the Anglo-French military conversations which, unknown to all but a few leading politicians and high civil servants, had continued ever since 1906.

In 1912, an even more definite commitment was made to France. Owing to the growth and disposition of the German Navy, the Admiralty was anxious to concentrate its strength in home waters. Consequently, an agreement was made whereby the British fleet assumed responsibility for guarding the northern coasts of France, while the French Navy undertook the protection of British interests and communications in the Mediterranean.

In a memorandum to Asquith and Grey, dated August 23rd, 1912, Churchill said:

The point I am anxious to safeguard is our freedom of choice if the occasion arises, and consequent power to influence French policy beforehand. That freedom will be sensibly diminished if the French can say that they have denuded their Atlantic sea-board, and concentrated in the Mediterranean on the faith of naval arrangements made with us.[1]

How was the implicit contradiction to be overcome? How was 'freedom of choice' to be reconciled with the desired distribution of Anglo-French naval power? The riddle was supposedly answered by an exchange of notes between Grey and the French Ambassador, Cambon, which declared that the Anglo-French military and naval conversations and arrangements did not constitute 'an engagement that commits either Government to action in a contingency that has not yet arisen and may never arise'. Nevertheless if either Government had 'grave reason to expect an unprovoked attack', there were to be consultations between them on possible action to prevent aggression.

The French were happy about this document which, quite logically, they regarded as an assurance of assistance if Germany declared war. Grey and his colleagues apparently believed their hands were still untied. 'It seems almost incredible,' wrote Harold Nicolson, in the life of his father, Lord Carnock (Sir Arthur Nicolson), 'that the British government did not realize how far they were pledged. They had, in fact, committed themselves to a guarantee which would involve England either in a breach of faith or a war with Germany.'[2] Yet only on the assumption that they knew not what they did can the Liberal ministers be absolved of leading their country blindfold towards a catastrophic *fait accompli*. None can deny they had good reason to fear German aggression and to take the strongest possible steps to meet it. But they should have considered, as Lord Salisbury had done when he rejected the draft Anglo-Germany treaty of 1901, 'the impropriety of attempting to determine by secret contract the future conduct of a representative assembly'.

[1] WINSTON S. CHURCHILL, *The World Crisis*. Odham (London, 1939), vol. I, p. 87.
[2] HAROLD NICOLSON, *Sir Arthur Nicolson, Bart., First Lord Carnock*. Constable (London, 1930), p. 374.

Britain then was committed to aid France, but, before the commitment could be made good, it would have to be endorsed by Parliament. The Government, however, was not prepared to ask for this endorsement until the feared 'contingency' had actually arisen. Consequently, Grey had to deal in circumlocutions in warning Germany.[1] He was not able to state the truth bluntly: if Germany went to war with France, Britain would inevitably be drawn in. The dangerous ambiguities of Grey's diplomacy have been clearly stated by Winston Churchill in Volume I of *The World Crisis*:

It is true to say that our Entente with France, and the military and naval conversations that had taken place since 1906, had led us into the position where we had the obligations of an alliance without its advantages. An open alliance, if it could have been peacefully brought about at an earlier date, would have exercised a deterring effect on the German mind, or at the least would have altered their military calculations. Whereas now we were morally bound to come to the aid of France, and it was our interest to do so, and yet the fact that we should come in appeared so uncertain that it did not weigh as it should have done with the Germans.[2]

Had the German Government known without a doubt where Britain would stand, it is possible — though by no means certain — that it would have restrained Austria from using the Sarajevo murders as an excuse to crush Serbia. As it was, the militarist cabals in Berlin and Vienna thought they had found a singularly propitious moment to deal with pan-Slavism in the Balkans and erect an insuperable barrier to Russian advances in that region. The risk of intervention by Britain seemed minimized by the Ulster crisis and by labour unrest. And, if Britain stood aside, would not France, also engaged just then in political feuding, hesitate to fulfil its treaty obligations and so leave Russia isolated? The leaders of the Central Powers decided, therefore, to make their great gamble — a decision encouraged by the weakness of the British Liberal Government and the ambiguities of its foreign

[1] Cf. Grey's minute on his talk with the German Ambassador, Prince Lichnowsky, June 24th, 1914. 'I did not wish to mislead the Ambassador by making him think that the relations that we had with France and Russia were less cordial and intimate than they really were. Though we were not bound by engagements as allies, we did from time to time talk as intimately as allies.' *British Documents on the Origins of the War*, vol. XI, pp. 4-5.
[2] P. 165.

policies, and by the irresponsibility of the Tory Opposition. But they forced their luck too far by invading Belgium, a move which rallied a confused Britain to almost solid support of the war. Had they not taken this step, the Liberal ministers would have been forced, on August 4th, 1914, to ask Parliament to redeem the moral pledges they had secretly given France and would certainly have encountered stormy opposition, if not repudiation. In view of the fact that the Schlieffen Plan for invading France through Belgium was known to the Foreign Office and War Office, is it altogether cynical to wonder whether Asquith and Grey were counting on the Kaiser to cut their Gordian knot?

PART THREE

SOME CONSEQUENCES OF WORLD WAR I

CHAPTER I

THE WAR WOUNDS OF CAPITALISM

Totalitarian war can hardly anywhere stop short of socialism. There is here an inequality of ideological sacrifice which cannot be avoided. Those who want socialism in peace can find war in this respect to their liking. Those who trust to individualism in peace must be ready to surrender it in war. Private enterprise at private risk is a good ship and a ship that has brought us far, but it is a ship for fair weather only. SIR WILLIAM BEVERIDGE: *Some Experiences of Economic Control in War-Time*[1]

IN the last week of July 1914, as the armies began to mobilize, the moneyed world was seized by panic. Hysteria reigned in financial markets everywhere as holders of securities sought frantically to turn them into cash. Commodities moved wildly, some collapsing, others — wheat and sugar, for example — rising sharply. Bankers in London, Paris, and Berlin endeavoured to call in funds from abroad, and there was particularly heavy pressure on the United States, then a debtor country. As early as July 23, the New York Stock Exchange slumped sensationally, owing to liquidation of stocks by European investors. The demand for sterling in America was so heavy that the pound rose from its par of $4.86 to $7.00. On July 31st, the London Stock Exchange — greatest of all international security markets — suspended business, unable to cope any longer with the flood of selling orders, and the bank rate was jumped from 4 to 8 per cent.

Terror in the financial world communicated itself to the rulers of the nations. Was there danger of a complete breakdown of the machinery of credit and trade? Would war bring economic chaos and a revolt of famine-stricken workers? Facing these questions, to which none could give an answer, emperors, chancellors and prime ministers shivered and hesitated to take the fatal plunge. But it was now too late: the forces they had set in motion could not be arrested: they were no longer the masters but the slaves of events.

In Britain, once the die was cast, the business community

[1] Oxford University Press (London, 1940).

recovered its nerve rapidly. The Government proclaimed a moratorium and, in concert with the Bank of England, made various arrangements to relieve financial stringency and provide a breathing spell while the national economy adjusted itself to the exigencies of war. Fears of revolution faded quickly. Years before, the International Socialist Bureau, to which the Labour Party had belonged since 1903, had called on member organizations for co-ordinated action to prevent outbreak of war and, in the event of failure, 'to use the political and economic crisis created by the war . . . to hasten the fall of capitalist domination'. In the spirit of this resolution the British section of the International issued a manifesto on August 1st, denouncing any attempt to involve Britain in war as an ally of Russian reaction. But the invasion of Belgium convinced most members of the Labour movement that German militarism was the immediate enemy. Simultaneously, French Socialists rallied to the flag of *La Patrie* and the powerful German Social Democratic Party persuaded itself that *Das Vaterland* was engaged in a crusade against Czarist tyranny. National sentiment had won an easy victory over international solidarity.

The British workers quickly showed their willingness to aid the Government industrially as well as politically. Pending strikes were called off: disputes in progress, settled. Without waiting for reciprocal action by the employers, national trade-union leaders announced an industrial truce. As Winston Churchill had foreseen, domestic squabbles were cured by 'a higher principle of hatred'. John Redmond, the Irish Nationalist leader, and Sir Edward Carson both turned their energies to recruiting. Suffragette leaders released from jail found employment in hounding young male 'slackers', winding bandages, and organizing war relief.

In this harmonious atmosphere, British capitalists dared to hope that the war, so far from destroying them, might offer new opportunities: in the past, uncertainty and scarcity had often enabled the bold speculator, the astute entrepreneur, to reap a rich harvest. For the moment, trade was badly dislocated. No one was buying anything but daily necessities, and many factories were forced to close. On the other hand, the great army springing into being at the call of 'King and country' would have to be fed, clothed and munitioned. Enormous and remunerative Government orders were in prospect: rising prices of staple commodities promised a widening of profit margins. And, in addition, there was cheerful anticipation of immediate capture of overseas markets where German competition was no longer to be feared. 'This war', said the *Daily Telegraph* of August 19th, 1914, 'provides our businessmen with such an opportunity as has never come their way before . . . There is no reason why we should not permanently seize for this country a large proportion of Germany's export trade.' 'If we rise to the occasion,' echoed the *Pall Mall Gazette* of the same date, 'British trade should see a period of tremendous prosperity . . . and should be supreme not only in the home market but in the whole area of business.' It was long before such illusions were dissipated: longer still before there was full realization of the dismal truth that for British capitalism the war was an unmitigated disaster and 1914 the point at which it turned from slow decline to rapid decay.

There are five major reasons why this was so:

(1) Not only did the war prove costly beyond all anticipation but the effort to shift a large part of the burden led first to inflation, always a prime solvent of social stability, and then to a load of taxation which permanently hindered the effective functioning of private enterprise.

(2) The conflict absorbed so large a proportion of the national resources that the State was forced to develop a war economy on socialist lines and, although the measures adopted were regarded as 'for the duration' only, important administrative and psychological residues remained after the peace.

(3) International trade and credit were permanently deranged with particularly damaging consequences for the British capitalist system, which, more than that of any other major nation, was keyed to foreign commerce.

(4) Serious political and military errors damaged the prestige of the upper classes, on whom responsibility for conduct of the war rested. On the other hand, conditions proved favourable for the growth and consolidation of the Labour movement, particularly after the Liberal Party began to disintegrate.

(5) The adverse effects of all these developments were compounded by the refusal of the representatives of capitalism to

recognize at the end of the war the extent to which the conditions of their continued supremacy had changed. Intent on restoring as nearly as possible their prewar world, they kicked against the pricks for two decades and so completed their ruin.

In the five actual war years Britain's total expenditure was £9,593 million, of which only 28 per cent was met from taxes. Taking account, however, of the two post-Armistice years, during which war assests were being liquidated and taxes maintained at peak levels, total expenditure of £12,454 million was covered to the extent of 44 per cent by revenue. Only by comparison with the achievement of other European belligerents can this record be considered good. If, from the outset, taxation had been increased drastically, the deadweight burden of debt could have been held down and inflation checked. But as late as May 1915, Lloyd George, Chancellor of the Exchequer, was still banking on an early peace, although Lord Kitchener, Secretary for War, had warned his Cabinet colleagues that the conflict was likely to last at least three years. In November 1914, a supplementary budget had doubled income-tax and supertax rates and heavily increased beer and tea duties. These measures added little more than £1 million a week to revenue at a time when expenditure had already reached £1 million a day and was rapidly mounting. Not until almost a year later, when Lloyd George had been succeeded at the Treasury by Reginald McKenna, was there any further attempt to formulate a tax programme commensurate with national needs. Then an excess-profits tax was introduced, but the rate was only 50 per cent and nearly two years elapsed before it was raised to its maximum level of 80 per cent. Most of the indirect taxes on consumption, particularly those on drink and tobacco, were doubled and redoubled in the course of the war years. The standard rate of income tax (prewar 1s. 2d. in the pound) was increased to 3s. in 1915-16, 5s. in 1917-18, and in 1918-19 reached a peak of 6s. where it remained for three years.

The British Government's delay in facing its financial problem was encouraged by (and in turn reinforced) the popular fallacy that the unpleasant task of paying for the war could be conveniently postponed. In vain economists pointed out that, in fact, a nation can only carry on war by means of currently produced goods and services, apart from whatever may be obtained by reducing inventories, liquidating foreign assets, and securing foreign loans. Ideally, a war should be financed 100 per cent from taxes, leaving in private hands only the monetary equivalent of the supply of goods and services available for civilian consumption. Even in a socialist economy, this is an ideal unlikely to be realized in practice, and it is completely out of reach when the State depends on the profit-motive for the procurement of nearly all its needs — except, of course, the services of its fighting men. Nevertheless, in World War I, the Treasury might well have taken a heavier toll of spendable incomes without arriving at the point where lack of incentives diminished production. The consequence of failure to do so was an addition to the National Debt of approximately £7 billion — a sum which Philip Snowden described as 'a monument to the criminal folly or cowardice of our statesmen'. He added:

If the government had had the courage in the early days of the war to levy higher taxation, this debt would never have been contracted. The cowardice of the government . . . left a vast spending power in private hands which was devoted to luxury and other forms of extravagance; and the system of borrowing inflated purchasing power, and led to the increase in the cost-of-living with the disastrous financial and commercial consequences which are now being revealed.[1]

In after years the capitalist classes had reason to regret their general support of this policy of deficit financing. For the cost of servicing the debt was a prime cause of the crippling level of postwar taxation. In the first decade and a half following the Armistice, service of the debt, including modest sinking-fund requirements, called annually for a sum roughly equivalent to one-and-three-quarter times the whole prewar national expenditure. Even after the war-loan conversion scheme of 1932 effected a considerable saving in interest charges, debt services continued to absorb an unduly large share of the budget.

This postwar debt burden was all the more insupportable because it represented money borrowed when prices were seriously inflated. No attempt was made to control prices until a fairly late

[1] PHILIP SNOWDEN, *Labour and the New World.* Cassell (2nd edn. revised; London, 1924), p. 142.

stage in the war, and by the end of 1917 they had risen 125 per cent or at a rate of 27 per cent per annum since August 1914. After that, the rate of increase was checked by price- and wage-fixing measures and higher taxation. Following the Armistice, however, controls were rapidly relaxed and an inflationary boom permitted to develop which carried wholesale prices 225 per cent above the 1914 level before the inevitable collapse came towards the end of 1920. In the next two years prices were cut in half and finally stabilized at around 55 per cent above prewar.[1] Consequently the Treasury paid interest in pounds of much greater purchasing power than most of those it had borrowed.

In spite of lenient tax policies, the Government might have avoided part of the inflation had it made greater efforts to mobilize real savings. War loans, however, were financed largely either by the direct sale of bonds to the banks or by encouraging bankers to lend to would-be subscribers — both methods involving the large-scale creation of credit which was reflected in the doubling of bank deposits between 1914 and 1919. In addition, the Treasury resorted from the beginning to the issuance of uncovered currency — the manufacture of money. In the December quarter of 1914, the average total of currency notes in circulation was £33,719,000. A year later it had risen to £88,598,000 and from that point it mounted steadily to £353,358,000 in the fourth quarter of 1920.[2]

Violent changes in money values both during and after the war had many adverse economic and social consequences. While people living on fixed incomes were not so desperately affected in Britain as in some other countries, their position was seriously prejudiced. So, too, was that of many professional workers who found their incomes lagging far behind the rise in prices. Manual workers, on the whole, were rather more successful in maintaining their real incomes, thanks less to an equivalent rise in wage rates than to overtime, full employment, and an increase in the average number of wage earners per family. When the slump came they struggled to hold such improvements as they had won and to some extent succeeded, but at the cost of greater insecurity of employ-

[1] Arthur L. Bowley, *Some Economic Consequences of the War*. Williams & Norgate (London, 1930), pp. 66-73.
[2] Sir Bernard Mallet and C. Oswald George, *British Budgets: 2nd Series, 1913-14 to 1920-21*. Macmillan (London, 1929), p. 365.

ment. Thus inflation and deflation alike tended to stimulate social unrest. Among all classes it led to an erosion of that confidence in stable progress which hitherto had provided a psychological foundation for the capitalist system. The long-asked question: does capitalism make for social justice? was now ominously supplemented with: does it work?

At the outbreak of the war in 1914, neither Government nor industry felt the necessity for any drastic adaptation of the national economy. Their attitude was expressed in the slogan 'business as usual', attributed to Churchill and popularized by the *Daily Mail*. It was generally supposed that the Army could be fed, clothed and munitioned by placing orders with private firms in the normal way: there was no need to enforce a priority system, and whatever stimulus to production was required would be furnished by rising profits. It was only 'human nature', remarked Walter Runciman, President of the Board of Trade, in 1915, for businessmen 'to get the largest amount they can for what they have to sell'.

There were two early exceptions to this *laissez-faire* policy. The railways, control of which by the Government in time of war was authorized by an act dating back to 1871, were immediately taken over on a rental basis and operated as one system. This made possible elimination of competitive practices which might have interfered with the movement of essential traffic. Passenger services were drastically reduced and freight hauls shortened by such measures as requiring consumers to obtain coal supplies from the nearest mining district. Another advantage was that the Government could deal directly with the railway unions, whose relations with the companies had long been bad.

It was labour difficulties that led to the next important example of state interference with freedom of contract. By the autumn of 1914 the war industries had already begun to experience a manpower shortage which they sought to overcome by recruiting men from other trades and employing women. This 'dilution of labour' brought protests from the unions, who objected to under-cutting of long-established standards by low-paid women workers. The Engineering Employers Federation retorted with a demand for the abolition of all trade-union rules which hindered production. Negotiations between the two sides proved abortive until the Government equipped itself for effective intervention by assuming power, under the Defence of the Realm Act of March 1915, to commandeer any factory required for war work and to issue orders to labour employed therein. The same month a conference representing all the trade unions agreed to abandon the strike weapon during the war, to accept government arbitration in all disputes, and to 'relax' rules which interfered with production. In return the Government undertook to obtain from all war contractors guarantees that 'dilution' would not be used to depress wages, that suspended rules would be restored when peace returned, and that in the postwar period preference in rehiring would be given to prewar employees. The Amalgamated Society of Engineers, most important of all unions in the munitions field, remained dissatisfied. It was not prepared to sign such an agreement until the Government pledged itself to limit profits and so ensure 'that the benefit resulting from the relaxation of trade restrictions and practices shall accrue to the state'. On these lines a bargain was struck.

The unions thus relinquished most of their freedom of action but they were encouraged by a Government proposal to institute Local Armament Committees, representing labour, the employers and the State, which would supervise 'dilution', conversion of factories to war purposes, and so forth. Hostility on the part of employers to any union share in management problems wrecked this plan, which might have prevented many later troubles. Consequently, the Government turned to more direct methods of control. In June 1915, the Ministry of Munitions was set up under a special act which also gave legal force to the March agreements and provided for limitation of profits in 'controlled establishments'. At the same time, further restrictions were imposed on labour, including a system of 'leaving certificates' which workers in munition plants had to obtain from their employers before moving to another job. This order was perhaps necessary to prevent disorganization of production through the poaching of manpower. But it meant that workers, particularly those with special skills, were effectively barred from selling their services to the highest bidder and, in view of the half-hearted manner in which the pledge to restrict profits was honoured, it caused great resentment.

The first strike proclaimed as unlawful under the Munitions Act broke out in July 1915 in the South Wales coalfield, following the breakdown of negotiations for a new wage agreement. Theoretically, all the strikers were liable to imprisonment, but it was no more possible to jail 200,000 men than to force them to hew coal under armed guard. Hence, Lloyd George found it expedient to assist the negotiation of a settlement which conceded most of the miners' demands. Moreover, the strike called attention to the unsatisfactory state of the coal industry, in which output had been curtailed and prices sharply increased. The Government, therefore, took steps to fix domestic prices, though it deferred complete control of the industry until the following year.

At the beginning of the war a number of merchant vessels had been requisitioned, but the shipping industry as a whole had been left to its own devices, apart from some assistance in insuring against war risks. Dislocation of world trade at first reduced demand for tonnage, but in 1915, after the submarines had begun to take their toll and supplies had started to pour in from America, freight rates doubled and tripled. Although huge fortunes were made by speculative deals in ships, the Government was disinclined to interfere until scandalized public opinion forced it to take over refrigerator ships in April 1915 and eventually to extend control to all ocean-going vessels.

Thus, reluctantly the Government found itself controlling one industry after another. Every extension of its powers was attacked as bureaucratic interference but it was also held responsible for shortages and high prices and was under constant pressure from the workers, who felt, with reason, that their rights were being restricted far more than those of their 'bosses'. Moreover, with the adoption of conscription, for the first time in national history, the ideological case for non-interference was shattered. If men could be drafted to save the country, property could hardly be accorded a more favourable position, particularly when 'business as usual' had obviously failed to mobilize as large a proportion of the national resources as a war that had become 'total' demanded.

It was indicative of the hesitant approach to economic planning that the Government, anxious though it was to keep wages from soaring, deferred any rounded attempt to deal with the main stimulus to wage demands — rising food prices — for more than two years. Early in the war an *ad hoc* commission had been appointed to control sugar supplies and prices, and similar bodies were later created to deal with imported meat and cereals. But only in December 1916, after food hoarding and profiteering had aroused much grumbling, was a Ministry of Food set up. At the time there was a theory that only a big-business man with practical knowledge of the industry concerned could successfully administer economic controls. Sir Joseph Maclay, a prominent shipowner, had been made Shipping Controller: Lord Devonport, chief of a vast grocery chain, was given the job of policing the food trades. He hoped to accomplish this task by exhortation rather than by sanctions, but the situation was rapidly becoming far too precarious to be saved by voluntary appeals to 'eat less bread'. Not until June 1917, when Devonport was replaced by Lord Rhondda, coal magnate and Liberal politician, with J. R. Clynes, a Labour M.P., as his deputy, did the Ministry of Food begin to develop as an effective instrument. By that time, food prices had risen 104 per cent above their prewar level. For the next two years they were held reasonably close to this point, only to mount skyward again in 1919 when controls were removed or relaxed.

Sir William (now Lord) Beveridge, one of the top officials of the Ministry of Food, and its historian, has explained how at first attempts were made to fix prices of selected articles at particular stages of their production or distribution. It was soon found that such partial measures led to worse shortages and price distortions.

The wide extension of control came as the result of experience and conveys an economic lesson. To control the price of food in one form while leaving free some other form in which the material may be used is futile. If milk prices are fixed, those of butter and cheese must be fixed also: otherwise if there is any shortage of milk at all . . . the shortage will be turned into famine, as much milk as possible being diverted for sale in the uncontrolled forms. Again, fixing of prices for some foods only was accompanied or followed by a peculiarly rapid rise in the prices of other foods; the power of the purse, neutralized in one direction . . . was concentrated on the uncontrolled foods and drove up prices so as to reserve them for the rich.[1]

[1] SIR WILLIAM H. BEVERIDGE, *British Food Control*. Oxford University Press (London 1928), pp. 166-7.

Another lesson learned by trial and error was that 'it is fatal
to remove the ordinary machinery — price adjustment — by which
supply and demand are regulated, without putting some definite
control in its place'.[1] That meant rationing, the classical method
of stretching supplies in a beleaguered fortress, which Britain,
blockaded by submarines, had in fact become. The Government,
however, was very reluctant to accept the Food Controller's advice
on this point: it feared an adverse popular reaction. Actually,
'when the test came, Lord Rhondda found that the public were
prepared to endure any and every restriction . . . so long as they
felt that to be a necessary condition of fair play for all'.[2] The war,
indeed, had made possible, even among people normally individualistic in their thinking, a certain acceptance of the old socialist
slogan: 'From each according to his ability; to each according to
his need.' A conservative magazine pointed out that enlarged
family incomes due to full employment, together with the rationing, meant that 'for the first time in the history of England, the
necessaries of life are distributed with some reference to social
justice . . . Far fewer families in the British Isles failed to get
not only a full but even an extravagant Christmas dinner in 1917
than in 1913'.[3]

Such experiences encouraged the idea that State interference
might prove beneficial in other circumstances. Many begin to ask:
'Is it only in wartime that we can have social justice? Should we
not look to the Government to provide in peace against unemployment and hunger?' Businessmen and the newspapers that reflected
their opinions might rail at bureaucratic muddlings and insist
that every vestige of State interference must be removed as early
as possible. The man-in-the-street often drew a different conclusion. As an American observer wrote shortly after the war
ended:

It may be accepted without question . . . that in the popular mind
government operation and control of industry in the past four
years has not merely driven the last nail into the coffin containing
the defunct *laissez-faire* theory of government; it has dumped that

---

[1] Ibid., p. 289.
[2] SIR WILLIAM H. BEVERIDGE, *Some Experiences of Economic Control in War-Time.*
Oxford University Press (London, 1940), p. 27.
[3] *The Round Table*, March 1918.

coffin without benefit of the clergy into the grave already dug to receive it.[1]

Those pleasant dreams of vast trade captured from the Germans, of the re-establishment of British commercial supremacy, soon fled, though hope remained that defeat of the German war machine would be followed by the crippling of German competition. For the present it was clear that British industry could not fight a military war with one hand and a trade war with the other. Concentration of the engineering industries on munition-making precluded maintenance of their exports, to say nothing of their expansion. Other industries hampered by lack of manpower found it increasingly difficult to fill foreign orders. Then the growing shipping shortage introduced a new impediment both to exports and the import of raw materials from which they were so largely made.

Exports of United Kingdom produce in 1914 were valued at £526 million — over £100 million less than in 1913 — and the following year there was a further fall to £483 million. 1916 saw an apparent recovery to £603 million, and the totals for both 1917 and 1918 were higher than in 1914. But this improvement was due to rising prices which masked a rapid decline in the actual volume of goods shipped. All through the war British manufacturers were, in fact, losing markets, and the legatees of the moribund German trade were the United States in Canada and Latin America, and Japan in the Far East. These new competitors were to prove hard to dislodge. Moreover, shortages and high prices in such countries as India, Brazil, and Argentina encouraged the launching of local consumer-goods industries and the raising of tariff walls to protect them. Economic nationalism, one of the causes of the catastrophe of 1914, found the atmosphere of the war — and its aftermath — conducive to luxuriant growth.

As British exports declined, imports mounted, rising from £696 million in 1914 to £1316 million in 1918. Here too, of course, inflated prices exaggerated the increase, but, on the other hand, up to July 1917 the figures were reduced by the exclusion from import returns of goods which were British or Allied govern-

[1] CHARLES WHITING BAKER, *Government Control and Operation of Industry in Great Britain and the United States during the World War*. Oxford University Press (New York, 1921), p. 5.

ment property. In any case the problem of financing the adverse visible trade balance grew steadily more acute. Before the war, surplus imports had been easily covered by overseas investment income and other 'invisible' items. Now it became necessary to draw on capital to meet current obligations, particularly as British credit was used to sustain Allied purchases in the United States and other neutral countries. British investors' holdings of saleable foreign securities, such as American stocks and bonds, were requisitioned by the Government and sold to swell foreign exchange reserves — an unprecedented form of interference with private property rights. Altogether some £1 billion of foreign investments — a quarter of the British total — were liquidated, but even so, by the time the United States entered the war in the spring of 1917, the shortage of dollars had become desperate. For months that year, food purchases in America were seriously curtailed for this reason and, on July 29th, Balfour, then Foreign Secretary, cabled to Colonel House, President Wilson's adviser:

We seem on the verge of a financial disaster that would be worse than defeat in the field. If we cannot keep up exchange, neither we nor our Allies can pay our dollar debts. We should be driven off the gold basis, purchases from U.S.A. would immediately cease, and the Allies' credit would be shattered. . . . You know I am not an alarmist, but this is really serious.[1]

The crisis was eventually overcome by large American government loans to the Allies, aggregating by 1919 £1890 million, of which the British share was £850 million (calculated at $4.86 to the pound). However, in the course of the war, Britain had lent the Allied and associated countries £1740 million and even, after writing off as irrecoverable £568 million owing by Russia, it was on balance a creditor. France, by contrast, although it had also made some loans, owed far more than it was due to receive.

International war debts, together with reparations, were to prove the most potent cause of economic maladjustment and political tension during the stormy years of peace. Before 1914, the creditor position of Europe *vis à vis* the rest of the world had not created undue strains because, generally speaking, foreign investments represented productive assets and interest and dividends

[1] BLANCHE E. C. DUGDALE, op. cit., vol. II, p. 211.

were in effect received in the form of goods. But the great load of war debt had no real assets behind it, and the residual creditor, the United States, would not accept payment in anything but gold. Thus there arose an insoluble 'transfer problem' to bedevil the delicate machinery of international exchange, on whose smooth operation British prosperity and the stability of British capitalism so greatly depended.

The problem could only have been overcome, within the terms of a free-market economy, by driving down British working-class standards of living to levels at which consumption and imports would have been drastically reduced and British goods so cheapened that lost markets could be recaptured. Some postwar British governments, as we shall see, moved as far as they dared in this direction, but their freedom of action was restricted by democratic pressures they could not withstand. Unable to squeeze labour sufficiently to produce an external surplus from which the American debt could be paid, the representatives of British capitalism in the end resorted to *de facto* repudiation with all its moral implications for a system based on sanctity of contracts.

CHAPTER II

THE DISINTEGRATION OF THE
LIBERAL PARTY

The war gave the new party [Labour] just the opportunity it
needed to get established ... But for the war it is possible
that Liberal and Labour would have been welded into a
Progressive party which would have carried on for another
generation. But organized Liberalism was divided and
shattered by Coalition politics, and the war had kindled a
certain fanaticism which favoured the clean cut between
classes.

J. A. SPENDER: *The Public Life*[1]

DISSOLVED in the acid bath of war, British political life
recrystallized in unfamiliar patterns. One of the historic
parties was broken in pieces, ostensibly by the violent colli-
sion of personalities, actually on the rocks of history. The Liberal
Party, like the competitive capitalism it had once fostered, was by
nature internationalist; when it turned to nationalism it was
inevitably displaced by those who had stronger convictions on the
subject. Moreover, the Tories, in view of their protectionist lean-
ings, were more acceptable champions of a private enterprise
avid for the fruits of monopoly. Thus the moneyed men in the
Liberal Party tended to swing to the right while working-class
supporters and radical intellectuals joined the ranks of Labour,
which had laid claim to the libertarian tradition. Meanwhile,
the Irish Nationalists, long-time allies of the Liberals, were
smothered by the republican Sinn Fein and vanished from
Westminster for ever.

The strangest consequence of the conflict was the emergence of
Lloyd George, erstwhile pacifist and radical, the scourge of dukes
and terror of millionaires, as the 'man who won the war' and
undisputed leader of a predominantly Tory coalition. For four
years after the Armistice he was to continue as captain — and
captive — of a reactionary host. In his rise Lloyd George hastened
the disintegration of the Liberals: after his fall, cast out by his

[1] Cassell (London, 1925), vol. I, p. 154.

new friends, he sought in vain to gather together his old ones, but not all the Welsh wizardry at his command could infuse life into a dead party. The sole result of his efforts was the haunting of Westminster for a spell by two Liberal ghosts, each claiming to be the only genuine apparition.

The final direction of the split in the Liberal Party was all the more curious because on the eve of the war it had shown signs of cracking in quite a different way. In those last days of July 1914, Lloyd George had been the leader of the Cabinet majority — according to Churchill it comprised 75 per cent of the total membership — which opposed British participation in the conflict unless the country were actually attacked. Then it was Asquith and Grey who found Tory backing for their view that Britain was bound to go to the aid of France. Learning from Churchill on Sunday, August 2nd, that at least half the Liberal ministers were likely to resign if war was declared, Balfour said he was certain his colleagues would be ready to join a coalition. The same evening he and other Tory leaders assembled at Lansdowne House and authorized Bonar Law to write Asquith that 'any hesitation in supporting France and Russia would be fatal to the honour and future security of the United Kingdom' and to offer him every assistance.

The next day the German ultimatum to Belgium settled the issue and reunited the Government. Lord Morley, John Burns, and a junior minister, Charles Trevelyan, alone continued their opposition to the point of resignation, and only a handful of Liberal back benchers endorsed their action. John Redmond swung the Irish Nationalists behind the Government, and the great majority of the Labour Party, although sharply critical of Grey's diplomacy, followed suit. There were, however, some notable opponents of this policy. Ramsay MacDonald, who was offered a place in the Cabinet by Asquith, refused to accept and resigned as leader of the Parliamentary Labour Party. His view that the country should have remained neutral was shared by Keir Hardie, Philip Snowden, W. C. Anderson, the able chairman of the party's national executive, and by most members of the Independent Labour Party. Nevertheless, the hostility of this group to the war was not very actively expressed in the early months.

August 1914 saw, in fact, a complete political truce. The parties agreed not to fight each other at by-elections, and war credits and emergency legislation were speeded through Parliament without opposition. The Home Rule and Welsh Disestablishment Acts, great bones of contention between Liberals and Tories, became law, but their enforcement was suspended. Balfour and other Tory leaders were brought into consultation by the Government and given access to secret information.

This political moratorium lasted for several months, but by the new year the Tories were growing restive. They thought of themselves as *the* national party and felt instinctively that war, a form of activity for which they had a hereditary talent, could not properly be conducted by anyone else. In January 1915 their growing sense of frustration was expressed by the patrician Lord Curzon in an explosive memorandum to Lord Lansdowne. The situation, he declared, was becoming intolerable: the Government 'have all the advantages, while we have all the drawbacks of a coalition'.[1] Tory irritation began to vent itself in sharper questioning of ministers, with the Home Secretary, Reginald McKenna, a favourite target because of his alleged 'softness' in dealing with enemy aliens.

As the spring advanced, disappointment at the deadlock on the Western Front and the failure to force the Dardanelles added to the tension. To the Tories, with whom they had close family and social ties, high officers in the fighting services brought grievances against their civilian chiefs. Lord Fisher, First Sea Lord, was at odds with Churchill over the Dardanelles campaign, which he had always regarded without enthusiasm: Sir John French, commander of the forces in France, had bitter and justified complaints against the War Office, headed by Lord Kitchener, which had failed to organize a supply of munitions on a scale commensurate with that of the war. Despite censorship, the disquieting knowledge that lack of shells was impeding operations and adding to casualties was becoming widely spread.

Although closely connected with the shells scandal, the political crisis of May 1915, which ended in the formation of the first Coalition Government, was actually precipitated by the proffered resignation of Lord Fisher, who immediately informed Bonar Law, leader of the Opposition, of his action. Law went to Lloyd

[1] Lord Newton, *Lord Lansdowne: A Biography*. Macmillan (London, 1929), p. 444.

George — they had long been intimate — to say he could not restrain his followers from raising this matter in Parliament. It was a particularly bad moment for open disunity, since Italy was hesitating on the brink of joining the Allies, and Asquith agreed, therefore, to reconstruct the Government on an all-party basis. The Irish Nationalists declined an invitation to participate, but Arthur Henderson came in to represent Labour, and a large group of Tories joined the Cabinet. Their terms were stiff: Haldane, victim of yellow-press slanders, was forced out of the Government altogether and Churchill was demoted from the Admiralty to a minor office. However, McKenna, for whom many Tory knives had been sharpened, was agile enough not only to save himself but to win the chancellorship of the Exchequer. Lloyd George, the previous holder of this office, took over the newly created Ministry of Munitions and responsibility for military supplies. It was, perhaps, the boldest move of his astonishing career, for failure would have ruined him irretrievably. But he had the energy, resourcefulness and imagination that the task required and his success in performing it made him the outstanding figure in the administration.

Coalition averted crisis but established only a façade of unity. Inside the unwieldy Cabinet controversy continued, cutting to some extent across party lines. On the one side were the Asquithian Liberals and some of the older Tories who were unable to adjust themselves mentally to the conception of total war: on the other were the men of action, impatient of procrastination, eager for short cuts, and not over-solicitous for democratic procedures. The key issue was conscription. Over three million men had already volunteered, but the hungry fronts were demanding ever greater reinforcements. Moreover, the voluntary system had made for haphazard use of manpower. Skilled men desperately needed for munition-making were in the trenches while some non-essential industries had a surplus of able-bodied labour. There was, however, a deep-rooted national antipathy to conscription. The trades unions hated the idea, fearing it would mean further inroads on their rights (as indeed it did), and there was strong sentiment against it in religious circles.

For a long time the proponents of the voluntary system were supported by Lord Kitchener, who regarded any departure from it as a reflection on his extraordinary achievements in recruiting a vast army by traditional methods. But the inexorable logic of war strengthened the case of the majority of Tory ministers who, with Lloyd George and Churchill, favoured conscription. In the autumn of 1915 a last recruiting campaign, backed by the threat of compulsion for single men, was organized by Lord Derby. It was only moderately successful and, in January 1916, the first Military Service Act was passed. One Liberal minister, Sir John Simon, resigned in protest and, on the third reading of the bill, 31 Liberals and 6 Labour members voted against it while 84 Liberals and a majority of the Labour Party abstained. The act applied to bachelors only and was generally regarded as unsatisfactory. But once the principle of conscription was conceded, it was not hard to make it applicable to all of military age, as was done by the second Military Service Act of May 1916.

The end of this controversy failed to restore harmony inside the Cabinet. Asquith's surrender did nothing to lessen the animosity with which he was regarded by many Tories and, as the months passed with no victories to fortify his prestige, he was subjected to increasingly sharp attacks in the press, some of them inspired by his own colleagues. Towards the end of 1916, Lloyd George, who had been made Secretary for War on the death of Kitchener, began to organize a cabal against his chief, aided by the newspaper magnates, Lord Northcliffe and Sir Max Aitken (later Lord Beaverbrook), and Sir Edward Carson. Details of this intrigue, of which there are exhaustive and conflicting accounts in the memoirs of all concerned, are too complicated even for summary. Lloyd George's immediate objective was to concentrate full authority for the conduct of the war in the hands of a small committee over which he would preside and from which the Prime Minister would be excluded. Not unnaturally, Asquith balked; but he appeared ready to consider a compromise until a series of articles in papers controlled by Lloyd George's friends gave the impression, in his words, 'that I am being relegated to the position of an irresponsible spectator of the war'.

At this point, Lloyd George withdrew from the Government. It was a gambler's throw, for by now he had lost the confidence of many Liberals without gaining the full trust of the Tories. But he had calculated the risks correctly. Asquith, told by Bonar Law that he and his friends would also leave the Government, tendered the resignation of the Cabinet. The King sent for Law, but he declined the task of forming a new administration since the Tories were in a minority in the House of Commons and he could not count on the support of either the Liberals or Labour. This left a clear road for Lloyd George. True, barely half the Liberals were ready to follow his lead, and, as he says in his *War Memoirs*, the majority of Tory ministers in the first Coalition 'accepted the prospect of serving under my leadership with bitter reluctance'.[1] They had no alternative, however, and, shepherded by Law and Carson, hastened to enter the fold. The Labour Party proved rather more difficult but succumbed to Lloyd George's persuasive eloquence and comprehensive, though vague, promises and offered its full support. Arthur Henderson joined the small new War Cabinet, John Hodge and G. N. Barnes accepted invitations to head two new ministries, Labour and Pensions, and a number of others received minor posts.

Asquith retired feeling injured, as well he might, for the loyalty with which he had always supported Lloyd George had been repaid in other coin. But he appealed to all Liberals to back the new Government and on only one occasion did he challenge the policies of his former lieutenant. The issue in this instance was the accuracy of a speech in which Lloyd George blamed General Gough, commander of the Fifth Army, for the German breach of the British lines on March 21st, 1918, and denied charges that the defeat was due to failure of the Government to send adequate reinforcements to meet an enemy offensive known to have been in preparation. When General Sir Frederick Maurice, just replaced as Director of Military Operations, publicly questioned his statements, he was able to show serious errors in the General's own statistics. But the figures the Prime Minister offered in rebuttal were far from clear, and Asquith, disclaiming any intention of censuring the Government, asked for a Select Committee of inquiry. When this was denied — Lloyd George spoke angrily of 'a conspiracy to overthrow the Government' — Asquith pressed a division and was heavily defeated. The historic importance of this incident is that it caused a wound in the Liberal Party which

[1] DAVID LLOYD GEORGE, *War Memoirs*. Ivor Nicholson & Watson (London, 1933-37), vol. III, p. 1041.

was never to be healed. At the general election seven months later, the Maurice division was the guide used to separate Coalition sheep from Liberal goats, and all the 98 Liberals who voted against the Government were opposed by candidates in receipt of 'coupons' (testimonials of trustworthiness), signed by Lloyd George and Bonar Law.

There can be little doubt that, as a war leader, Lloyd George was vastly superior to his predecessor. He had a driving energy and no regard for obstructive traditions. The mistakes he made were seldom due to hesitation, for he had both boundless self-confidence and unshakable resolution. In total war, when the end sought is total victory, these are invaluable qualities. As Churchill wrote, looking back on the 1916 crisis:

There is no place for compromise in War . . . Clear leadership, violent action, rigid decisions one way or the other, form the only path not only of victory, but of safety and even of mercy. The State cannot afford division or hesitation at the executive centre. To humour a distinguished man, to avoid a fierce dispute, nay, even to preserve the governing instrument itself, cannot, except as an alternative to sheer anarchy, be held to justify half-measures.[1]

Asquith's virtues — tolerance, patience, equanimity — were certainly not ones that facilitated 'violent action'. Had he remained at the head of affairs, he might well have shrunk from the ruthless determination which carried Britain through the last and bloodiest years of the war. In November 1914 he had promised 'never to sheath the sword . . . until the military domination of Prussia is wholly and finally destroyed' but he was not so thoroughly committed as Lloyd George was to the policy of 'the knockout blow'. It has, in fact, been suggested that prior to his resignation he was decidedly receptive to the idea of a negotiated peace.[2] In November 1916 a memorandum written for the Cabinet by Lord Lansdowne had argued that, although the Allies would undoubtedly win the war, the human and economic costs might prove disproportionate to the benefits of complete victory. Was it not, therefore, wise to explore the possibilities of negotiation with the Central Powers, who at the time were putting out peace

[1] WINSTON S. CHURCHILL, *The World Crisis*. Odham (London, 1939), vol. III, p. 1101.
[2] F. W. HIRST, *The Consequences of the War to Great Britain*. Oxford University Press (London, 1934), p. 15.

feelers? This view had the 'complete concurrence' of Asquith, according to his friend and colleague, Lord Crewe, who has also suggested that the Lansdowne memorandum may have been the real cause of the political crisis that ended the first Coalition. 'It has been rumoured,' he wrote in a note contributed to Asquith's memoirs, 'that Mr. Lloyd George regarded this document as a danger-signal . . . a supposed invitation to the "elder statesmen", or soberer spirits of the Government, to anticipate an enforced conclusion to the War'.[1]

Whether any statesman could have succeeded in making peace at that stage is, of course, extremely doubtful. War-weariness was already apparent in Austria and beginning to affect Germany, but it was not so pronounced as to induce these countries, which had not yet suffered military defeat, to accept terms corresponding in any way to the aims of the Allies. Nevertheless, it can hardly be denied that a negotiated peace in 1916, or even a year later when Lansdowne publicly renewed this proposal, would have served the world better than war to the bitter end. Certainly from the point of view of the propertied classes, whose stout champion he always was, Lansdowne's unheeded warnings were farsighted. Had the war been abbreviated by even one year, British capitalism would have been far better able than it was to resist the ravages of decay.

The success of the Labour Party in surmounting its wartime divisions and achieving a fundamentally stronger position must be ascribed largely to the patient common sense of Arthur Henderson, who was elected Parliamentary leader on MacDonald's resignation in August 1914. Stirred by patriotic emotion, many of the party's pro-war majority were anxious to purge from their ranks the pacifists, who seemed to them little better than traitors. Henderson, while fully supporting the war, used his great influence with both the industrial and political wings of the party to preserve unity. Thanks to his efforts, MacDonald remained Treasurer of the party and *ex officio* a member of the national executive, and other anti-war leaders — Snowden, Anderson and Robert Smillie of the Miners' Federation — also kept their places in the inner

[1] EARL OF OXFORD AND ASQUITH, *Memories and Reflections 1852-1927*. Little Brown (Boston, 1928), vol. II, p. 152.

circle. Thus the minority was always able to air its views in party councils and, if this caused some bitter internal quarrels, an open schism was avoided.

As time went on, MacDonald and his friends found more and more workers ready to listen when they attacked the secret diplomacy that preceded the war, and demanded peace by negotiation. In some parts of the country they encountered great hostility, even mob violence, but in Scotland, Wales and the industrial north of England, they attracted large and enthusiastic audiences. Their opposition to conscription was shared by many trade unionists who saw class discrimination in the readiness of the Government to draft men at a time when business and property were still treated with much tenderness. The trade unions were also disgruntled by their ever-increasing subjection to regimentation and coercion. In 1917 there were a number of unofficial strikes, organized by committees of shop stewards, many of whom were members of the Independent Labour Party and other socialist groups. Some of these outbreaks expressed general war-weariness; others were due to specific grievances — the lag of wages behind prices, housing shortages, resort by the authorities to conscription as a punitive measure against 'troublemakers'.

Another cause of unrest in 1917 was the Russian Revolution. British workers had always been unhappy about their country's alliance with Czarist despotism and they were deeply stirred by its downfall. The left-wing element, which included pacifist socialists, revolutionary socialists, and not a few who attempted to combine pacifism with advocacy of full-blooded class war, called mass meetings to celebrate the event. In June a large conference at Leeds declared in response to a telegram from Kerensky that:

... the largest and greatest convention of Labour, Socialist, and Democratic bodies held in Great Britain during this generation has today endorsed Russia's declaration of foreign policy and war aims, and has pledged itself to work through its newly constituted Workmen's and Soldiers' Councils for an immediate and democratic peace.[1]

A few weeks earlier, the Petrograd Council of Soldiers and

[1] Among the supporters of this declaration were those two desperate Jacobins – in contemporary Tory eyes – MacDonald and Snowden. Its suggestions of British 'Soviets' created a real scare until it became clear that nothing was going to be done to organize them.

SOME CONSEQUENCES OF WORLD WAR I

Workers had issued invitations to an International Socialist Congress, representing all countries, to be convened in Stockholm for an exchange of views on war aims. This project was blessed by the Provisional Government of Russia, which asked officially for facilities to enable British Labour delegates to participate, and thus presented the British War Cabinet with an awkward dilemma. Should British Labour men — including perhaps such dangerous characters as MacDonald — be permitted to fraternize at Stockholm with enemy socialists? To the Tories the whole notion was preposterous, but Lloyd George was inclined to move cautiously. He wished neither to offend the new Russian Government, if it were really set on this scheme, nor to alienate the Labour Party, whose support he needed to save him from over-dependence on the Tories. He proposed, therefore, that Henderson, himself a member of the War Cabinet, should go to Russia and explore the situation.

Henderson returned after a six weeks' visit with the decided opinion that the Stockholm conference should be encouraged. His fellow ministers, however, had grown more obdurate in their opposition and they objected vigorously when he proposed to go ahead with plans for a special Labour Party conference to decide definitely whether or not representatives should be sent to Stockholm. On July 26th he was asked to attend a meeting of the War Cabinet to consider the question, but on arrival at Downing Street was kept waiting 'on the door mat' while his colleagues discussed his attitude. Now it was his turn to be angry, especially as, on his return from Russia, he had offered his resignation and been begged to stay. In any case, he had made up his mind about the course to follow and he was a hard man to swerve. Two weeks later, on August 10th, he put the arguments for and against Stockholm before the party conference and ended by urging participation. 'In a war in which losses of such terrible magnitude are being imposed on all the nations,' he said, 'it appears to me not only wise but imperative that every country should use its political weapons to supplement its military organization . . . That is why I continue in favour of a consultative Conference with proper safeguards and conditions.'[1]

[1] MARY AGNES HAMILTON, *Arthur Henderson, A Biography.* Heinemann (London, 1938), p. 151.

Despite strong opposition, this lead was followed and Stockholm approved by 1,846,000 votes to 550,000. Then the storm broke. A large part of the press was outraged and attacked Henderson with extreme violence.[1] The Prime Minister in a talk with him the same evening seems to have told him he must give up the secretaryship of the Labour Party or leave the Government.

Henderson chose to resign, freeing himself for the pursuit of two objectives — formulation of a policy on war aims and the reorganization of the party. The first task was the more urgent because a growing section of the public felt it had been too long neglected by the Government. That feeling was to be reinforced by the Lansdowne letter already mentioned, published in the *Daily Telegraph* of November 29th, 1917, and, two weeks later, by publication of the secret treaties between the Allies which the now victorious Bolsheviks had found in the archives of the Russian Foreign Office. These documents, breathing a spirit of imperialism quite at variance with the Allies' public statement of motives, helped to explain the embarrassed silence on war aims in high places. They also gave point to the question asked with increasing frequency by many who were not pacifists: what are we fighting for?

A Memorandum on War Aims, drafted by Henderson, MacDonald and Sidney Webb, was adopted by a special Labour conference at the end of December 1917. It stressed the necessity for complete restoration of Belgium and other invaded countries and the return of Alsace-Lorraine to France. But it placed the strongest emphasis on protection of the right of self-determination and the prevention of new wars by 'a Super-National Authority', a 'League of Nations, which not only all the present belligerents but every other independent State should be pressed to join'. The same principle was given even greater prominence in a statement adopted in February 1918 by an Inter-Allied Socialist Conference held in London.

Labour's ventilation of this question was not wholly without effect on the Government. In a letter read to the December conference, Lloyd George had disparaged discussion by insisting that

[1] It was a calculated violence, aimed at a reversal of the decision when the conference reconvened on August 21st, and it nearly succeeded, as reaffirmation was carried by a bare margin of 3000 votes. No delegation, however, went to Stockholm, as the Foreign Office refused to issue passports.

'a statement with regard to the war aims of the Allies can, of course, only be made in agreement with the other nations who are fighting together in the war'. Nevertheless, on January 8th, he made a detailed speech on the subject to a trade-union audience which demanded information about the purposes of the war before agreeing to further 'dilution of labour'. True, this statement was vague about a future international organization and notably evasive regarding the secret treaties. But it gave a decidedly broader picture than had hitherto been available to the public and satisfied his listeners, who made the required concessions.

Another subject very much in the public mind at this time was 'Reconstruction'. The word had first been used in 1916, when Asquith set up a Reconstruction Committee to prepare for the restoration of peacetime conditions whenever the war ended. But there was widespread feeling that mere restoration of pre-war social conditions was not good enough: instead there should be real improvements in health, housing, education and labour relations.

In his appeal for Labour support when he formed the second Coalition Government, Lloyd George had indicated that such matters would receive increasing attention and he had even hinted at nationalization of the railways and coal mines. Early in 1917 he enlarged the scope of the Reconstruction Committee and, not long afterward, turned it into a fully fledged ministry which was to pour forth a stream of reports suggesting all manner of social reforms. 'We seem definitely to have entered upon a period of revolutionary change,' a well-known quarterly commented. 'Legislative projects which, according to pre-war standards of political action, it would have taken years or even decades to prepare are now being carried through Parliament almost as a matter of course, in the space of a few months.'[1]

This was an overstatement: most of the blueprints of reconstruction were for schemes to be enacted, if at all, after the war. Nevertheless, two reforms of the first magnitude were approved by Parliament in the course of 1917 and 1918. One was the Representation of the People Act, which Lloyd George described as 'by far the biggest advance since the Reform Bill of 1832, and in some respects . . . even more revolutionary'.[2] It enfranchised

[1] *Round Table*, June 1917.   [2] DAVID LLOYD GEORGE, op. cit., vol. IV, p. 1981.

all adult males and introduced women's suffrage, but only for those over thirty. This was a typical British compromise with no good logical basis, since women normally mature earlier than men. It served, however, to calm the nerves of timid males who, noting the preponderance of females in the population, feared a political division on sex lines leading to Amazonian rule.

The act as a whole constituted a draught of democracy which many Tories found hard to swallow and, except for the domestic political truce, it would not have passed without prolonged party conflict. As it was, it gave rise to heated debates inside the War Cabinet with Curzon and Carson representing the die-hards in opposition to Lloyd George, Henderson and Lord Robert Cecil.

Curzon was against any extension of the franchise; above all he was against any admission of females. On this Henderson thumped the table: did he want the workers to get their rights by compromise or by revolution? As for the women it would be an abominable breach of faith if they were not brought in, and he, for one, would not stand for it.[1]

The second great reform was the Education Act of 1918, which was the work of H. A. L. Fisher, one of the best of Lloyd George's 'finds'. It abolished the half-time system for children under fourteen, gave encouragement to nursery schools, made possible important extensions in secondary and university education, and provided for compulsory part-time education for young people between fourteen and eighteen. (This last section, however, never became operative owing to opposition from both employers and their young employees and many technical difficulties.) The act was supplemented by grants making possible large increases in the salaries and pensions of teachers, previously miserably underpaid, which gave their profession an entirely new status. To Fisher, Britain is indebted for much of the solid, if unspectacular, progress which public education made in the inter-war period.

Legislation of this sort was welcomed by the Labour Party, but its own ideas about reconstruction went far beyond social reform. The party had long paid occasional lip service to the need for a socialist transformation of society but had never defined just

---

[1] MARY AGNES HAMILTON, op. cit., p. 117.

what it meant by that phrase. Now the time was ripe for attempting this task. The war had created a demand for fundamental changes both in the methods by which wealth was produced and the ways in which it was distributed; and it had induced a re-examination of economic dogmas.

There was, as a consequence, a large and attentive audience, stretching beyond the ranks of organized labour, for the party's official statement on postwar reconstruction — the famous report, *Labour and the New Social Order*. This pamphlet, drafted largely by Sidney Webb, did not supply complete working drawings of the proposed new order. It was rather a skilfully sketched 'elevation' of a social and economic structure, resting on foundations of 'democratic control of society in all its functions', and built around four key 'pillars'. These were: A national minimum for all; the democratic control of industry; a revolution in national finance; the use of surplus wealth for the common good.

'Every member of the community, in good times and bad alike' was to be assured 'of all the requisites of a healthy life and worthy citizenship'. Democratic control of industry was to be brought about by 'genuinely scientific reorganization . . . on the basis of the common ownership of the means of production'. This did not necessarily mean wholesale nationalization; but early acquisition by the State of coal mines, railways, power resources, the liquor industry, and life insurance was suggested. The most radical item in the plan for financial revolution, though one approved by some non-socialist economists, was a graduated levy on capital for the purpose of paying off the National Debt. In addition, there was to be sharply progressive taxation of incomes and inherited wealth, not just to meet current expenses but as a means of diverting 'the economic surplus' from 'senseless luxury', to provision for the aged, sick and disabled, and to forms of communal consumption — education, recreation, research and the advancement of culture.

The whole programme, even though it fell short of the demands of the extreme left, seemed to many Tories and Liberals little better than Bolshevism. They consoled themselves with the reflection that, although the ultimate aims of the Labour Party might be revolutionary, it was firmly committed to democratic methods. With but forty members in a House of Commons of nearly 700, it was obviously a long way from attaining power. There was always hope, provided the Labour movement was not captured by its 'wild men' who talked 'direct action', that, if and when a Labour government was formed, it would be sobered by responsibility and jettison most of its programme. To some extent the history of the next twenty-five years justified this estimate. The Labour Party remained in the hands of the moderates and, until 1945, was never in a position to translate into legislation the Webbian vision of 1918. What was not anticipated was that in the interval a substantial portion of the new social order would be erected, mainly by non-socialist builders.

A precondition of that paradoxical development was the rebirth of the Labour Party, for without the stimulus of its competition it is reasonable to suppose that successive Tory governments would have accomplished much less than they did. At the beginning of 1918 it was still a federation composed of many trade unions, with a total membership of two and a half million or more, and a few socialist societies which together mustered less than one hundred thousand. This lack of balance was, in practice, partially compensated by the fact that most of the socialists were politically active and most of the trade unionists passive. Nevertheless, the party was dominated by the rather narrow, professional purposes of the unions, and Henderson, as its chief organizer, felt that its base had to be broadened before it could play a truly national role. The next general election would be fought on new registers compiled following the passing of the Representation of the People Act. Millions of men and women, many not members of trade unions, would be voting for the first time and it would be necessary to appeal to them as individuals. Moreover, if the party wished to grow in numbers and influence, it had to attract a following among the professional and white-collar workers.

In 1912, Henderson, after organizing an individual-members' section in his own constituency, had proposed an amendment to the party's constitution to enable this idea to be applied generally. He received very little support: the trade unions feared their control might be weakened, and the Independent Labour Party, largest and most active of the socialist societies, suspected encroachment on their membership. Similar objections were again heard in 1918 but, with the aid of Sidney Webb, Henderson overcame them and, after two special conferences in January and February, a revised constitution was formally adopted. The changes it introduced may be summed up under two heads:

(a) *Broadening the base*: All workers by hand or brain, whether trade unionists or not, were to be admitted to direct membership. A new section of the party was to be composed of local Labour parties, consisting of individuals who collectively were to be represented by five members of the Executive. Special provision was also made for representation of women.

(b) *Extension of principles*: The party now definitely declared that its objects included a socialist system of society. The relevant clause read: 'To secure for the producers, by hand or brain, the full fruits of their industry, and the most equitable distribution thereof that may be possible, upon the basis of the common owner-ship of the means of production and the best obtainable system of popular administration and control of each industry or service.'

Immediate policy was the occasion in June 1918 of yet another party conference, which fashioned an election programme out of *Labour and the New Social Order*. The delegates were also called upon to consider an important question of tactics: what should be Labour's relation to the Coalition? At the January conference a resolution requiring Labour members of the Government to resign had been heavily defeated. Now the Executive asked for a declaration that 'the political truce should no longer be recog-nized'. This, Henderson explained, meant not withdrawal from the Government but freedom for the party to contest by-elections and carry on propaganda for the general election which was cer-tain to be held immediately the war ended. Although right- and left-wingers alike complained of its contradictions, this resolution was carried by a substantial majority. It might be thoroughly illogical but it expressed an instinctive feeling that, although the national front had to be maintained while the fighting lasted, it was imperative for the party to reassert its independence.

Victory was now near and a new era dawning. Old allegiances were broken; political and economic ideas were in flux. Never was there such an opportunity for a party that looked forward. But to seize it, Labour had to keep its hands free, resisting Lloyd George's seductive offer of a Parliamentray bed wide enough to accommodate every political faith. To accept that offer meant sacrificing all hopes of growth for a fractional share of the fruits of office, and even less real influence. Some were tempted, including most of the office-holders: the majority, remembering the principle on which Keir Hardie had founded the Labour Party, declared, albeit hesitantly, for fighting alone. And so, as the last great battle in France neared its climax, the postwar pattern of British politics began to take shape.

PART FOUR

THE DECADENCE
OF
BRITISH CAPITALISM

CHAPTER I

PROCRUSTES' BED OF GOLD

The truth is we stand mid-way between two theories of economic society. The one theory maintains that wages should be fixed by reference to what is 'fair' and 'reasonable' as between classes. The other theory —·the theory of the economic Juggernaut — is that wages should be settled by economic pressures, otherwise called 'hard facts', and that our vast machine should crash along, with regard only to its equilibrium as a whole, and without attention to the chance consequences of the journey to individual groups.

The gold standard, with its dependence on pure chance, its faith in 'automatic adjustments', and its general regardlessness of social detail, is an essential emblem and idol of those who sit in the top tier of the machine. I think they are immensely rash in their regardlessness, in their vague optimism and comfortable belief that nothing really serious ever happens. JOHN MAYNARD KEYNES: *The Economic Consequences of Mr. Churchill*[1]

B RITISH statesmen in 1919 had few precedents to guide them in directing the transition from a war to a peace economy. The conflicts in which Britain had engaged in the nineteenth century had been relatively minor: they had been fought by small armies of professional soldiers and had neither seriously dislocated industry nor caused abnormal financial strains. For war on anything like a comparable scale it was necessary to look back to the long struggle with Napoleon. That, in relation to contemporary population and national income, had been perhaps as costly as the war of 1914-18 and had left a similar legacy of burdensome debt. And, like World War I, it had forced Britain off the gold standard and led to serious inflation, though changes in money values were not so extreme as those experienced between 1914 and 1920.

The final defeat of Napolean had been followed by an economic crisis which, apart from a brief recovery in 1818, continued until 1822. These were years of real distress for industrial workers and farmers, but the government of the day, following the newly

[1] Hogarth Press (London, 1925).

DECADENCE OF BRITISH CAPITALISM

triumphant philosophy of *laissez-faire*, made no attempt to intervene. On the contrary, it pursued an orthodox financial policy of encouraging deflation by reducing its debt to the Bank of England, which, as a result, was able to resume gold payments in 1821. Meanwhile wages were forced down to a point at which manufacturers were in a position both to cut prices low enough to attract foreign customers and to earn satisfactory profits. 'Savings' squeezed out of the workers eventually provided the means to overcome depression and launch a new era of industrial and trade expansion. The victims protested, but they were weak and their employers, backed by the full power of the State, were strong. Agitation for better labour conditions was repressed with a heavy hand and, to protect the free market in manpower and other commodities, the Government did not hesitate to restrict the free market in ideas. These years of depression and recovery after 1815 saw the massacre of Peterloo, the imprisonment of Cobbett and numerous other popular champions, and severe discouragement of all efforts to organize the workers.

Clearly, in 1919 a Lloyd George, with twenty million electors to consider, could not imitate the methods of a Wellington who represented a minute oligarchy. The coalition of Tories and Liberals, which triumphed in the 'snap' election of December 1918, had promised 'a land fit for heroes', and to the masses this meant a higher standard of living, more leisure, better housing, more security. On the other hand, the Government was immediately dependent on what a conservative historian has described as 'the wealthiest, the least intelligent, and the least representative House of Commons since Waterloo'.[1] Thus Lloyd George and his colleagues were subject to pressures which forced them into contradictory courses. A large, if still somewhat amorphous, body of public sentiment looked for accentuation of the prewar collectivist trend: well-organized and articulate business opinion wanted a world safe for capitalism and expected the Government to restore and protect the essentials of a free-market economy.

Among these essentials, in the eyes of most leaders of financial opinion, was restoration of the gold standard. That was 'the only effective remedy for an adverse balance of trade', a small Treasury

[1] D. C. SOMERVELL, *The Reign of King George the Fifth*. Faber (London, 1935), p. 206.

Committee headed by Lord Cunliffe, then Governor of the Bank of England, reported in August 1918, the only means of reinstating the Bank of England's time-tested methods of credit control. Nor were these financial experts satisfied merely to re-establish a fixed gold value for the pound: they insisted it must have the same gold content as before 1914, or, in other words, that the sterling-dollar exchange must be restored to, and maintained at, the prewar rate of $4.86. This policy implied deflation of wages and prices and a fluid labour market which responded automatically to monetary pressures. It was not one that could easily be reconciled with programmes of social security that tended to diminish the mobility of labour and to strengthen resistance to wage reductions.

Yet, at the time, only a few eccentric economists challenged the Cunliffe Report which, broadly speaking, was accepted as gospel by every Government, including the two Labour ones, holding office between 1919 and 1931. The magic of gold was still powerful — and what Briton did not desire that the pound sterling should once more 'look the dollar in the face'? It was believed that restoration of the gold standard would enable London to regain its old commercial and financial dominance, for there was little appreciation of the extent to which world economic currents had been deflected by the war. Nor was there understanding of the way in which successful deflation would enhance the burden of the National Debt and enlarge the claims of bondholders — the passive receivers of income — to the detriment of entrepreneurs and workers — the active producers of wealth. Finally, there was no realization that the probable price of stable exchange rates would be instability of employment. These were lessons to be learnt by painful experience through a decade of depression.

To do the authors of the Cunliffe Report justice, they themselves underestimated the human costs of their programme. The hardships of deflation in Britain would, they expected, be softened by the effects of continued inflation in other countries. In particular, they believed that wartime inflation in the United States, which had been less intense than in Britain, would be extended as a steady flow of bullion to its shores enlarged the basis of credit. Thus the painful process of cutting down sterling prices to fit Procrustes' bed of gold would be eased by a simultaneous stretching of dollar prices. Something of this sort might have happened if the Government had stopped deficit financing immediately the war ended, as the Cunliffe Committee recommended. In that event Britain would have started to deflate while America was experiencing its postwar boom and the awkward gap between the price levels of the two countries might have been closed.

The suggestion of a balanced budget in 1919 was, however, a counsel of perfection. National expenditure was still so enormous that an immense increase of taxation would have been required to cover it fully. Probably nothing short of a capital levy, advocated by the Labour Party as a means of trimming the National Debt, would have sufficed, and that was too heroic a measure for a government representing the propertied classes. The serried ranks of businessmen in Parliament were, in fact, clamouring for lower taxes, while industry, anxious to catch up with arrears of investment and to rebuild its stocks of raw materials, favoured an easy-money policy. Moreover, the temper of the public was opposed to austerity. During the general election, citizens had been led to expect that the unpleasant task of paying for the war would be transferred to German shoulders and they thought the budget might as well stay unbalanced until the peace treaty was signed and the promised reparation billions began to flow into the Exchequer.

Again, the mood of labour had to be considered. The transition from war to peace involved finding normal employment for millions of munition workers and soldiers, and some temporary unemployment was inevitable. Deflation of credit would immensely complicate the problem of re-absorption and probably leave large numbers idle for a long period. That could create a dangerous situation, for labour, already restive, might become more willing to listen to the small but vocal group of leaders whose revolutionary ardour had been aroused by events in Russia. As it was, the atmosphere was decidedly tense at the beginning of 1919, and labour disputes, some marked by unusual violence, broke out in various parts of the country. Even the police threatened to strike, and unrest was also evident among soldiers impatiently awaiting their release from service. Demonstrations by men in uniform, which in a few places developed into riot and mutiny, were no doubt local and spontaneous, but they appeared ominous to those who had always looked upon the Army as a potential ally against the workers. In the light of such occurrences, the Government deemed it better to appease the revolutionary spirit than to suppress it. Demobilization was hastened, and to ease the transition period a scheme of 'unemployment donations' for both ex-servicemen and former munition workers was instituted. Moreover, in order to head off attempts to cut wages in industries affected by the cessation of Government orders, an act was passed making going rates of pay the legal minima for six months.

Altogether, it seemed advisable in the spring of 1919 to postpone for a season the programme of the Cunliffe Committee and give inflation its head. That was exactly the effect of the budget presented by Sir Austen Chamberlain to the House of Commons on April 20th, a feature of which was the reduction of excess-profits duty from 80 to 40 per cent. True, the Chancellor increased some other taxes with the intention of providing enough revenue to meet estimated future 'normal' expenditure. The most important and permanent change was a drastic upward revision of the death-duties scale, unaltered since 1914, on estates of over £15,000. The gradation was made much steeper, with estates exceeding £2 million charged 40 per cent, double the previous rate — a sharp reminder to the wealthy that even an anti-socialist government might find itself forced to impose 'confiscatory' taxation.[1] Despite this and other revenue-raising measures, the estimated deficit for the financial year 1919-20 was put at £234 million. And since conditions were unfavourable for long-term borrowing, the probability was that most of this sum would have to be found by adding to the floating debt. That meant enlarging the credit base of the banking system and giving a new fillip to inflation.

Nevertheless, the Treasury had not lost sight of the long-term objective — deflation to the extent necessary to stabilize sterling exchange at its prewar dollar parity and restore the gold standard — and, in conjunction with the Bank of England, it began preparations for its attainment. One essential preliminary was to test the actual depreciation of sterling against gold. To this end,

[1] One die-hard Tory was so shocked by this proposal that he denounced it as 'a kind of Bolshevism'. Lenin and Trotsky, he said, were thieving scoundrels who stole 100 per cent of a man's property but the Chancellor was treading on their heels when he pocketed 30 to 40 per cent of an estate.

exchange controls, which had helped to peg the pound at just under the prewar rate of $4.86, were partially lifted in March 1919 and, a few months later, a free gold market was permitted to reopen in London. At the same time the financial authorities pressed for rapid decontrol of British domestic prices so that the internal purchasing power of the pound, as well as its external value, could be set by the free play of economic forces.

Although these moves were designed to pave the way for deflation, their immediate effect was to stimulate inflation. Relaxation of exchange controls assisted a spurt in foreign trade calling for liberal extensions of bank credit. Heavy spending by consumers encouraged a great expansion of imports while war-starved foreign markets poured in orders for British goods. The demand for textiles was particularly strong, and Lancashire began to enjoy one of the most prosperous spells it had ever known. Immense profit-margins inspired reckless speculation in mill properties and recapitalization of dozens of cotton companies on an absurdly extravagant basis, to the great future grief of unwary investors. Nor was this the only industry in which smart promoters made fortunes overnight.

Once controls were lifted, prices soared and, with a labour shortage soon developing, there was little resistance to wage increases. As always, rising prices encouraged manufacturers and merchants to invest in new facilities and to build inventories. They had no difficulty in financing such activities, either by obtaining advances directly from the banks or by seeking funds through the Stock Exchange where a credit-fed boom was in progress. For, so long as the Government depended on deficit financing, it could not effectively curb the growth of credit.

Inflation was rampant in the United States also, but the gap between American and British price levels was fully maintained. Consequently sterling fell fairly steadily throughout 1919 to reach a low point of $3.30 in February 1920. This proved to be about the peak of the boom, for shortly afterward the authorities suddenly shifted their pressure from the throttle to the brakes. On April 15th, the Bank of England raised its rediscount rate from 6 per cent to the near-crisis level of 7 per cent, where it was to remain for a full year. This was high enough to discourage speculators and a warning to businessmen to liquidate inventories and reduce bank debits. Four days later Chamberlain produced a staggering budget containing a host of tax increases which, with some decline in expenditure, were estimated to provide a surplus of £234 million compared with a realized deficit of £326 million in the year ending March 31st. Thus the Treasury would be in a position, not only to stop borrowing, but to start reducing the floating debt — a prime factor in credit inflation. The necessary price was the highest tax bill on record. Consumers of wine, beer and spirits were called upon for a heavy contribution; super-tax exemption was cut to £2000 and the graduated scale revised upward to reach 6 shillings in the pound on the largest incomes; excess-profits duty was advanced to 60 per cent and a brand-new corporation-profits tax of 5 per cent added; postage, telephone and telegraph charges were raised to put the Post Office on a paying basis

Such a multiplication of imposts dampened inflationary enthusiasm, which, in any case, was waning as consumers at home and abroad found goods too dear for shrinking purses. Wholesale prices reached their peak in May 1920, retail prices six months later, and money wages in January 1921. By that time the depression was well under way. Its extent can be illustrated by the collapse of coal export prices, which fell from a height of 115 shillings per ton in the autumn of 1920 to 24 shillings (15 shillings below average costs of production) in the spring of 1921. At the same time the Government hastily abandoned control of the industry, which included a guarantee of profits, and the coal-owners demanded wage cuts. The result was a prolonged strike, the first of a disastrous series in the industry.

Throughout 1921 unemployment mounted. During the coal stoppage over 2,500,000 were out of work not counting the miners, and at the end of the year the total was still nearly 2,000,000. Other industries, particularly the 'unsheltered' ones dependent on exports, followed the coal owners in cutting wages. However, towards the end of 1920, just as the boom expired, the Government had extended unemployment insurance, which had formerly covered only about 4,000,000 workers, to an additional 8,000,000. The benefits paid were far from generous and could be drawn for a maximum of 15 weeks in one year, but they served to some extent to soften the effects of unemployment as a depressant of wages.

While factories closed and the lines of workless men grew longer, the campaign to put the pound back on gold was being carried forward relentlessly. Budget Day in April 1921 saw provision for another large surplus which would make possible further reductions in the floating debt. Boom-level taxation in the face of mounting depression was, however, arousing the Government's supporters to demand stringent economy, and to pacify them the Chancellor appointed a committee of businessmen to suggest methods of reducing expenditure. Its Chairman, Sir Eric Geddes, promised to tackle the job 'with an axe' and his assault on education, one of his major victims, indeed proved murderous. By such methods the budget was reduced in the course of the next two years to its postwar norm — about four times the highest prewar figure. Any further shrinkage was inhibited by the fact that upwards of 50 per cent of the total was accounted for by untouchable commitments, the largest of which by far was war-debt interest. It was difficult to reconcile so inflated a charge on national income, a charge which increased relatively as prices fell, with the deflation of all other incomes. Was it social justice, some asked, to create unemployment and squeeze wages so that bondholders could enjoy more purchasing power? Since the Government had lost the opportunity to diminish the National Debt by a capital levy when prices were high, it could only answer this question with soothing assurances that the depression was temporary and prosperity would return with the gold standard.

In 1922 the backers of the gold-standard policy had some reason for confidence. Business in the United States was recovering rapidly and American prices were advancing while British prices continued to fall. This was exactly the concurrence of events that the Bank of England had expected as a result of the heavy flow of gold to America since the beginning of 1920. By the end of 1922, the gap between wholesale price levels in the two countries had been closed and, in terms of purchasing power, the pound was definitely undervalued at the current market rate of $4.57.

Unfortunately for the plans of Montagu Norman, now Governor of the Bank of England and chief strategist of the campaign to rehabilitate sterling, the directors of the Federal Reserve Bank were not prepared to allow gold inflation to run an uninhibited course. With business activity threatening to reach the point of speculative excess, they took steps to reduce the expansive pressure of bullion imports on currency and credit. Partly as a result, the American price curve turned downward again early in 1923. For a time the British curve paralleled it and sterling continued to rise, reaching $4.70 in March. The improvement was a tribute to an ill-fated gesture of British financial strength made by Stanley Baldwin, then Chancellor of the Exchequer, when he agreed to a funding scheme for the British war debt to the United States involving annual payments of $160,700,000 for sixty-two years. Although that placed a load on Britain's balance of international payments which eventually helped to break sterling, the immediate response of the market was encouraging. Reaction followed swiftly, however, owing to mounting tension created by French occupation of the Ruhr.

Another halt on the long road back to the gold standard occurred at the beginning of 1924, when the first Labour Government took office. As it had not an independent majority, and enjoyed its tenure subject to a Liberal Party veto, there was no reason to expect any revolutionary changes in British policy. Moreover, Ramsay MacDonald, the Labour Prime Minister, was clearly more intent on establishing a record for respectability than one for daring. Nevertheless, some timid men of wealth staged a mild flight from the pound, which was not arrested until both MacDonald and his Chancellor of the Exchequer, Philip Snowden, publicly declared their devotion to 'sound money'. Then sterling again began to rise and British prices to fall. American confidence in Europe revived when MacDonald's success in reconciling France and Germany paved the way for evacuation of the Ruhr, the Dawes Plan for restoring the German economy, and the Locarno Treaty. Investment funds once more began to flow from Wall Street to European countries, Germany in particular, and part of this new supply of dollars in time reached Britain, either in the form of reparation payments or through the channels of multilateral trade. Moreover, high interest rates in London attracted considerable amounts of short-term American money.

These varied influences were reflected in a final upward movement in the sterling-dollar exchange rate which started in the middle of 1924. Defeat of the Labour Government and its replacement by a Tory administration in October provided a new impetus. The climax was reached on April 28th, 1925, when Winston Churchill, now Chancellor of the Exchequer, announced the immediate introduction of a bill re-establishing the gold standard.[1] Surprisingly little opposition was encountered. Labour deplored the move as premature, and Sir Alfred Mond, the great industrialist, suggested it was likely to hinder exports. But the generally accepted view was that of Walter Runciman, a shipping magnate, who declared that the Government's action was 'calculated to re-establish London as the financial centre of the world without throwing undue burdens on the poorer classes or the trading community'.

The British monetary system was once more anchored to gold, but not too securely, and constant vigilance was required to keep it from drifting. Since the country's international balance of payments was precarious, it was thought necessary to discountenance any expansion of domestic trade For that would tend to increase the demand for imported raw materials and consumers' goods and might even bring about a rise in prices and wages which would in turn check exports. Consequently, home investment had to be discouraged and, with this end in view, bank rate was advanced from 4 to 5 per cent in March 1925 and kept at that level until August, when it was cut by ½ per cent. In October it was again reduced to 4 per cent, but this proved the low point for five years and throughout 1926 it was held at 5 per cent.

One great difficulty facing the monetary managers arose from the fact that the final 10 per cent rise in the gold (and dollar) value of sterling had been achieved without a corresponding fall in British prices. As J. M. Keynes pointed out at the time, the improvement in the exchanges was due to speculative anticipation of restoration of the gold standard, not to any increase in the real

[1] Churchill had lost his seat in Parliament in 1922 and picked the wrong constituency for a 'comeback' in 1923. Thus he was temporarily exiled from Westminster and, as a result, he has written, was able 'to make an independent and unbiased judgment of the situation when the Liberals most unwisely and wrongly put the Socialist minority Government for the first time into power . . . But for my erroneous judgment in the General Election of 1923, I should never have regained contact with the great party into which I was born and from which I had been severed by so many years of bitter quarrel'. *Thoughts and Adventures.* Thornton Butterworth (London, 1932), p. 18. It must be said that the Tories greeted the prodigal generously: he could hardly have hoped for a fatter calf than the Exchequer.

purchasing power of the pound. Consequently, for foreign customers British goods were now 10 per cent more expensive than in 1924. In order to compete in world markets, export industries would have to reduce wages and other costs, an adjustment not easily made unless industries catering to the home market followed suit and brought about a fall in the cost of living. 'Thus Mr. Churchill's policy of improving the exchange by 10 per cent was, sooner or later, a policy of reducing everyone's wages by two shillings in the pound. He who wills the end wills the means. What now faces the Government is the ticklish task of carrying out their own dangerous and unnecessary decision.'[1]

But the Government hesitated to will the means, for to do so required a public avowal of the implications of its policy. The mechanism relied upon to adjust wages and prices, so as to bring them into line with the revalued pound, was the free market. Curtailment of credit was to curb business activity and create enough unemployment to drive the workers to accept wage cuts. That mechanism had worked, though at great human cost, in the nineteenth century; but now trade-union resistance to wage cuts created so much friction that its efficiency was greatly reduced. Moreover, social security measures had deprived the whip of unemployment of some of its sting. If the Government had been consistent, it would have abolished unemployment benefits so that competition of the jobless, faced with starvation or the workhouse, would break down the resistance to lower wages of those at work. But both the humanitarianism of the age and political considerations forbade so ruthless a logic. The Government was not a dictatorship: sooner or later it had to face the electors, who would certainly punish a party that used the weapon of hunger to force down living standards.

Perhaps, as Keynes suggested, the Government might have found a way of solving the problem by putting the facts frankly before the trade unions and asking for their co-operation in securing an all-round cut in money wages in return for a guarantee that prices would then be reduced proportionately so that the workers' real incomes would not be affected. But how could such a guarantee be implemented? Labour costs were not the only 'sticky' ele-

---

[1] JOHN MAYNARD KEYNES, *The Economic Consequences of Mr. Churchill*. Hogarth Press (London, 1925), p. 6.

DECADENCE OF BRITISH CAPITALISM

ment in the price structure, the adjustment of which might prove
a slow process. Moreover, the trade unions would want to know
if rents, profits and interest were also to be reduced. So far as
rents and profits were concerned, they should, theoretically,
adjust themselves in time to a lower price level, but receivers of
interest would be the ultimate beneficiaries of an agreed deflation unless they were subjected to a special tax. Altogether, this
Keynes plan pointed towards more interference with the private-
enterprise system than a Tory government could yet contemplate.

Since such a frontal attack on labour costs presented too many
difficulties, the only alternative seemed to be piecemeal revisions
of wages, initiated by those private industries which were most
severely handicapped by high export prices. Among these coal
mining was outstanding. It had reaped an unexpected harvest of
profit when French occupation of the Ruhr knocked out German
competition for many months. But by 1925 the German mines
were rapidly recapturing the continental market: they were
newer, they were being mechanized with the aid of dollar loans,
and their labour was cheaper. At the same time the static condition of British industry generally prevented any expansion of the
domestic market. All through the winter of 1924-25, the situation
in the British coalfields was growing progressively worse. By
April, two-thirds of the collieries were losing money and unemployment was becoming acute.

The return to the gold standard, raising the cost of British coal
to foreign consumers, was the final blow. The miners, wrote
Keynes, 'represent in the flesh the "fundamental adjustments"
engineered by the Treasury and the Bank of England to satisfy the
impatience of the City Fathers to bridge the "moderate gap"
between $4.40 and $4.86. *They* (and others to follow, are the
"moderate sacrifice" still necessary to ensure the stability of the
gold standard'.[1] The extent of the sacrifice became known on July
1st, 1925, when the mine owners put forward proposals for lower
wages and longer hours. No agreement seemed possible and, in an
effort to avert a crisis, the Government appointed a commission
of inquiry which speedily reported that the difficulties of the
industry were 'to a large extent the creation of neither party to the
dispute'. True as this statement was, it left the position unchanged

[1] JOHN MAYNARD KEYNES, op. cit., p. 23.

and on August 1st, the miners, having secured a promise of an embargo on coal shipments from the railway and transport unions, were set to walk out. There was an ominous suggestion that the final outcome might be a general strike, but at the last minute Prime Minister Baldwin stepped in with an offer of a nine-month subsidy to the coal industry, affording time for a Royal Commision to investigate the whole problem.

It also gave the Government time to prepare for the crisis which inevitably arose in April 1926 when the breathing spell ended. The Commission, headed by Sir Herbert Samuel, had made many useful recommendations for the long-term rehabilitation of the industry; but it opposed any continuance of the subsidy, and its main suggestion for meeting the immediate problem of costs was a cut in wages. This the Miners' Federation, backed by the whole trade-union movement, refused to accept, and on May 3rd, the dreaded General Strike began.

Ten days later it collapsed, for reasons which will be discussed in Part Four, Chapter III, and although the miners held out alone for months they finally accepted defeat. It was a victory for the Government and the employers, which might have been exploited to secure a general reduction in wages. The previous July, Baldwin had told a trade-union delegation: 'All the workers of this country have got to take reductions in wages to help put industry on its feet.'[1] But now that divisions in the dispirited labour movement provided an opportunity to put this policy into effect, he counselled moderation. An astute politician, as well as a humane man, he realized the danger of pushing the workers too far. Although their industrial arm might be temporarily paralysed, they still had votes.

For the next three years, while the great American boom rushed onward, Britain remained in the doldrums. The price level sank slowly and real wages, for those at work, increased. Some of the newer 'light industries' which had developed in the Midlands and the south of England were flourishing and the economic picture, judged by conditions in London, was moderately bright. But in the old industrial districts the depression had become chronic and, for the country as a whole, a 10 per

---

[1] R. PAGE ARNOT, *The General Strike, 1926.* Labour Research Department (London, 1926), p. 35.

cent unemployment rate had become normal: that was the price of equilibrium.

The sterling exchange rate held, exports expanded somewhat and the balance of international payments included a surplus available for overseas investment. Stability, however, was keyed to American prosperity, which produced a large demand for such British-controlled raw materials as rubber and tin, and to the apparently insatiable appetite of American investors for foreign securities. Consequently, the flow of dollars through international trade channels was sustained until the collapse of Wall Street in 1929 heralded a reversal in American fortunes that was to shake the world.

Ironically, it fell to the lot of a British Labour Government to try to save sterling in the great crisis by obstinate adherence to economic orthodoxy. It had taken office — again as a minority government — following the election of May 1929, with a programme which emphasized reduction of unemployment. But by the middle of 1930 it found itself faced by a rapid deterioration of trade. That year an average of 16.1 per cent of the insured workers were jobless, and in 1931 the rate jumped to 21.3. The unemployment insurance fund was speedily bankrupted and had to be supplemented from the general revenue on a scale that wrecked the budget.

The story of how Ramsay MacDonald and Philip Snowden split the Labour Party when they sought to save the gold standard at the expense of the unemployed belongs to another chapter. Here we need only note that their efforts were doomed to futility. The paper balancing of the British budget could not restore the confidence in Britain of a capitalist world that had lost confidence in itself. How otherwise can we explain the panic-stricken rush of the moneyed men in all countries to hoard, not real wealth in the form of goods — *they* were glutting markets everywhere — but the symbols of wealth? No dike could have been built to resist the universal wave of liquidation that swept sterling from its gold anchorage in September 1931.

The crisis was more than the breakdown of the international monetary system; what was really involved was atrophy of the international free market. Montagu Norman, Governor of the Bank of England and arch-exponent of financial orthodoxy, seems to have recognized that fact even while he urged the Labour Government to make the conventional sacrifices to the golden calf. For in the very weeks when foreigners with short-term claims on London took £200 million worth of gold from the Bank of England's vaults, no attempt was made to utilize the traditional defence of a high interest rate. There had been a time when it was said in Threadneedle Street that a 10 per cent bank rate would pull gold out of the earth. But then exchange stability had been insured by the constant responsive movements of international prices of goods, money *and men*. Now workers, in most countries, refused to have their labour treated as a commodity or to allow their living standards to be subjected to 'automatic adjustments'. In America this refusal took the form of support for high tariffs and immigration restrictions; in Britain the workers looked for protection to social security. The effect in both cases was a loss of elasticity in the pricing of labour which gradually undermined the functioning of the whole free market. The year 1931 signalled the urgent need for an alternative economic system. The problem was to find one that combined both humanity and efficiency.

CHAPTER II

POSTWAR FERMENT: 1919-1922

> The fundamental causes of Labour unrest are to be found
> rather in the growing determination of Labour to challenge
> the whole existing structure of capitalist industry than in
> any of the more special or smaller grievances which come
> to the surface from time to time.
> Memorandum signed by Arthur Henderson and G. D. H.
> Cole, 1919.

THE four years following the end of World War I were a
period of almost universal political commotion and social
upheaval. A conflict breaking all previous records of
slaughter and destruction had shattered the relatively stable
world of the nineteenth century. Three great European empires
had collapsed and the problem of filling the vast void they left
behind was being settled by wars and revolutions while the statesmen at Versailles quarrelled in their attempts to agree on a new
map. Accompanying all this turmoil was a tremendous churning
of ideas, many of them violently contradictory. International
liberalism, looking towards the outlawry of war, supported efforts
to build a League of Nations, but also upheld the conception of
self-determination which was expressing itself in the narrowest
kind of nationalism. International communism warred against
both these rival ideologies.

Everywhere the comfortable assumption that economic progress and the profit system were mutually dependent was being
challenged. In Russia a full-blooded revolutionary socialist state
was established and effectively resisting its enemies within and
without. In central Europe capitalism seemed to be succumbing
under attacks by socialist and communist movements. Even in the
victorious western countries, where there had been no actual
breakdown of the economic system, organized labour was enjoying
a mushroom growth and loudly demanding social and economic
changes.

This ferment bubbled in Britain as on the continent. The
trade unions had increased their membership 50 per cent during

the war and, since the Armistice, had stepped up the pace of their recruiting campaign. The Labour Party, despite indifferent success in the General Election of 1918, had become the official opposition and a national political force with unlimited potentialities. It, too, was attracting a host of new supporters, among the middle classes as well as the workers, partly because of the appeal of its international policies, partly because it stood for social justice. Thousands of young people joined it with but hazy notions of the principles of socialism but with the firm conviction that any change from the existing system, controlled as it was by tired and cynical old men, would be for the better.

Thanks to the success of Lloyd George's election coup immediately after the Armistice, very little of the intellectual and emotional excitement of the times was reflected in Parliament. The Coalition Government had sought a new mandate from the voters while they were still gasping with relief at the return of peace and before they had had any opportunity to consider soberly the manifold problems facing Parliament. Moreover, the new register, compiled following passage of the Representation of the People Act (see Part Three, Chapter III), was far from complete, and arrangements for recording the votes of servicemen were totally inadequate. Only 59 per cent of the eligible electors went to the polls, and of the 2,400,000 absentee ballots issued — mostly to soldiers — less than 1,000,000 were returned.

It is probable that if Lloyd George and his colleagues had said to their countrymen: 'We have carried the war to a successful conclusion; give us the authority to finish the job,' they would still have won. Their majority might have been smaller, but it would have been of better quality and they would not have been burdened with so many rash pledges. Lloyd George's first thoughts were, in fact, better than his last. On November 12th, 1918, he spoke to his Liberal followers of a peace based on 'fundamental principles of righteousness' and denounced 'base, sordid, squalid ideas of vengeance and avarice'. His original election manifesto was moderate in tone: no mention of 'hanging the Kaiser' or of extracting from Germany 'the uttermost farthing'. However, the Tory newspapers — in particular those controlled by Lord Northcliffe, whose once warm friendship for Lloyd George had cooled — were dissatisfied with this reticence. They hinted darkly at a plot to let Germany off lightly and demanded pledges that all war criminals would be tried and executed, and reparations of astronomical amounts collected. Scared by this propaganda, the Coalition managers insisted on a more belligerent programme, and the Prime Minister and his colleagues yielded to the pressure. They were, Churchill was to explain apologetically, 'to some extent overborne by the passions they encountered in their constituencies . . . Hatred of the beaten foe, thirst for his just punishment, rushed up from the hearts of deeply injured millions . . . In this uprush and turmoil state policy and national dignity were speedily engulfed.'[1]

On domestic issues, Lloyd George expanded his Celtic soul freely, and, whether from fear of revolution or from a belief that election promises were not debts of honour, his Tory friends made no effort to restrain him. There were pledges 'to make Britain a fit country for heroes to live in', to abolish slums, to restore the countryside and settle large numbers of ex-servicemen on the land. 'Let us make victory,' said Lloyd George in the peroration to the first of his 'reconstruction' speeches, 'the motive power to link the old land up in such measure that it will be nearer the sunshine than ever before, and that at any rate it will lift up those who have been living in the dark places to a plateau where they will get the rays of the sun.'

The Coalition stew of jingoism and social evangelism was spiced with virulent attacks on Liberal and Labour opponents, who were denounced as 'friends of the Hun' and 'deserters of the national cause'. A sharp division between those Liberals who followed Lloyd George and those who regarded Asquith as their leader was necessary to meet the Tories' demand for greater representation. They were the strongest section of the Coalition but a minority of the House of Commons, and to improve their position needed a chance to attack constituencies held by Liberals. The joint blessing of Lloyd George and Bonar Law ('the coupon') was, therefore, bestowed on Tory assailants of the Asquithians, only twenty-eight of whom escaped defeat. Asquith himself and most of his chief lieutenants were among the victims. A bitter and successful onslaught was also made against the Labour Party

[1] WINSTON S. CHURCHILL, *The World Crisis; The Aftermath.* Thornton Butterworth (London, 1929), pp. 41-2.

pacifists, who were blackguarded as pro-German Bolsheviks. In some places they were opposed by a bogus Labour outfit, 'The National Democratic Party', created for the occasion, financed by Coalition funds, and fully supported by local Tory machines. Henderson, MacDonald, Snowden and Anderson all lost their seats and, as a result, the Parliamentary Labour Party, while increased in numbers from 42 to 62, was woefully lacking in experienced leadership. It was composed largely of solid but unenterprising trade-union leaders, men who had been in almost perfect agreement with Lloyd George during the war and now found it hard to oppose him. Their chosen leader was William Adamson, a sincere but slow-thinking Scots miner. Later he was succeeded by J. R. Clynes, a man of fine qualities with a good record as wartime Minister of Food, but hardly a forceful personality.

On the Government benches no less than 530 M.P.s jostled each other. There were 136 National Liberals, a handful of Coalition Labour men, and 384 Tories, or a clear majority of the House, even if the 73 Sinn Fein members who refused to take their seats were included. This Tory mass included the most remarkable collection of second-raters the Halls of Westminster had ever known. Many of them were businessmen of the narrowest type, with little political experience and less social conscience. As a group they were completely out of sympathy with the notions of a new world that were stirring the country at large: the old world had been kind to them and they saw no need to improve it. One of Lloyd George's biographers has written:

An assembly so composed was a most unlikely instrument of 'social reform'. But, while scornful of the 'country fit for heroes' schemes, except perhaps as a temporary ruse to sidetrack Bolshevism, the Coalition majority was, according to its lights, eminently patriotic. It was quite in earnest as to 'making Germany pay', and almost as ignorant as the economic experts themselves concerning the possibilities of that policy. Mr. George had indeed created a monster that was to haunt and afflict him.[1]

[1] E. T. RAYMOND, *Mr. Lloyd George*. Odham (London, 1922), p. 272. SIR AUSTEN CHAMBERLAIN in *Down the Years*, Cassell (London, 1935), p. 243, reports Lloyd George's own opinion of 'the monster'. Replying to an inquiry about the nature of the new House, he smiled and said: 'I'll tell you. I made a speech to them. I addressed myself at first to the opposition benches in front of me. They were cold and hostile; I couldn't get a cheer. This, I said to myself, is not the House of Commons; it's the Trade Union Congress. So I turned ... to the benches behind me, but neither was that the House of Commons; it was the Associated Chambers of Commerce.'

DECADENCE OF BRITISH CAPITALISM

Even at the moment of its election this House of Commons was barely representative of opinion in the country and it rapidly became less so as people recovered from their post-Armistice emotional debauch.[1] The result was a general revulsion against politics, and the workers, in particular, turned their eyes away from Parliament and sought to attain their ends by other means. During the war, the industrial truce had both assisted accumulation of trade-union funds and bottled up many resentments. Thus in 1919 and 1920 the workers were in a belligerent mood and their organizations were in a strong position to take advantage of the shortage of labour and the anxiety of employers, who were making abnormal profits, to keep production going. There were numerous strikes — 35 million man-days in 1919, 27 million in 1920, were lost in labour disputes — and many were highly successful.

Under the circumstances, industrial action to secure better conditions was only to be expected, but there were some strikes, or threats of strikes, tinged with political purpose. The syndicalism of prewar years still had advocates in the trade unions, and they were reinforced by men under the influence of Russian communism. While the theoretical ends of the two groups were different, they agreed on immediate strategy — a succession of strikes culminating in a general strike as a means of overthrowing the capitalist system. However, the appeal of 'direct action' at this time was not confined to outright revolutionaries. In the debates on the subject that enlivened Labour gatherings throughout 1919 and 1920, many who rejected the full class-war theory of Moscow toyed with the idea of using industrial pressure to force concessions from a reactionary Parliament. Thus in 1919, Herbert Morrison made his first speech at a Labour Party conference a strong plea for industrial action to halt the undeclared war against the Soviet Union.

British troops were then operating in northern Russia, various 'White' generals were being armed and subsidized by the British Government, Poland and other border states encouraged to grab pieces of the defunct Czarist Empire. This attack on what was considered, with all its faults, to be the first 'workers' state' was

---

[1] Excluding Ireland, Coalition candidates, together with Tories who ran without 'the coupon' but generally supported the Government, polled 57 per cent of the votes cast, but returned 84 per cent of the members.

bitterly resented even by right-wing Labour leaders, and the slogan 'Hands Off Russia' united the whole movement.

In May 1920, London dockers refused to coal the *Jolly George*, a freighter loaded with munitions for the Polish army which was then invading the Ukraine. Their union, the Transport Workers, backed this action and, under the leadership of Ernest Bevin, banned the handling of war material for use against the Soviet Union. Later in the summer, when the Red Army gained the upper hand and began to advance towards Warsaw, the British Government sent a note to Moscow threatening intervention. Immediately there was an outburst of protests from all sections of the Labour movement. On August 9th, the Trades Union Congress Parliamentary Committee, the Labour Party Executive Committee, and the Parliamentary Labour Party, meeting in joint emergency session, declared that 'war is being engineered between the Allied Powers and Soviet Russia', and warned the Government that the whole industrial power of the workers would be used to prevent so 'intolerable a crime against humanity'.

A 'Council of Action' set up to organize resistance to intervention then summoned a special Labour conference which instructed it to press for absolute guarantees against the use of British armed forces to aid Poland and for the withdrawal of naval units directly or indirectly assisting the blockade of Russia. For a few days both war and a general strike seemed near, but while no promises were secured from Lloyd George, the Government modified its stand and gradually wound up its intervention policy. How far this outcome was due to Labour pressure, it is not easy to say. The inroads of the undeclared war against Russia on its budget may also have influenced the Government; moreover, the Poles, rallying before Warsaw, succeeded in driving the Red Army back. All the same, the Labour movement felt that the threat of 'direct action' had justified itself by results.

It was on the strike weapon that the Miners' Federation relied in their campaign to secure nationalization of the coal industry. This demand was first put forward, together with claims for increased wages and shorter hours, at the beginning of 1919. From the Government's point of view a strike would have been disastrous. Coal stocks were very low and a stoppage would have speedily curtailed industrial production. To postpone a decision, the Government, therefore, appointed a Royal Commission on the Coal Industry and undertook in advance to accept its findings. Half the members were nominated or approved by the Miners' Federation, and Sir John Sankey, a judge known to be sympathetic to Labour, was appointed chairman. Within three weeks this body published an interim report recommending wage increases and a seven-hour day and condemning 'the present system of ownership'. The miners were encouraged but still felt some doubt about the value of the Government's pledges. However, when Bonar Law, Tory Leader of the House of Commons, stated in writing that the Commission's report would be accepted 'in the spirit and in the letter', the union withdrew its strike notices, previously held in suspense.

Hope of success grew during the public hearings of the Commission, which attracted immense attention. Noble receivers of coal royalties and the great magnates of the industry were subjected to stringent cross-examination by Robert Smillie, veteran leader of the Scottish miners, and other commissioners. For the first time the profit system was on trial and its beneficiaries called upon to justify their role in the national economy. The outcome also provided a sensation. A majority of the Commission — the chairman and the six members on the labour side — urged nationalization. Five of the six business members, including three coal owners, defended the existing system; the other, Sir Arthur Duckham, outlined a plan for unification of the industry by private enterprise, subject to government regulation.

Lloyd George's chickens had now come home to roost. Naturally, the miners demanded that effect be given to the Sankey plan, but it was all too plain that the House of Commons would overthrow the Government sooner than agree. The Prime Minister, therefore, sought escape from his pledges by emphasizing the marked division of opinion in the Commission — unanimity would have been a miracle — and offered as a compromise a scheme, based on the Duckham Report, which clearly satisfied no one.

Embittered as they were by this 'betrayal', the miners now hesitated to strike alone. Instead they sought aid from the Trades

Union Congress, which, after uttering some vague threats, also postponed the issue by undertaking a campaign to popularize 'the Mines for the Nation'. Although public response was not notable, the miners continued to press for a general strike to compel government action. But this was a step from which most trade-union leaders shrank; it had, they felt, not without reason, revolutionary implications and threatened to carry them too far from their proper sphere of securing better labour conditions.

In that more familiar field some impressive victories had been won. A ten-day national railway strike in the autumn of 1919 had been denounced by Lloyd George as an 'anarchist conspiracy' and met with an elaborate display of force supplemented by a volunteer road-transport system. Very few goods moved, however, and the strike ended in a resumption of negotiations which brought the men most of their demands. Not long afterward, the dockers, a section of the Transport Workers Federation, secured a national minimum of sixteen shillings a day through a special Court of Inquiry. It was on this occasion that Ernest Bevin first won national fame: his exposition of the dockers' case was so effective that the press nicknamed him 'the Dockers' K.C.'

The last major strike, before the collapse of the postwar boom ended the trade-union offensive, broke out in the coal fields in October 1920. Owners were still earning exceptional profits in export markets, and the miners considered they were entitled to a larger share. A two-week stoppage won a wage increase on a temporary basis; negotiations for a permanent agreement were deferred until the following March. By that time, as we saw in the last chapter, deflation, intensified by monetary policy, was rapidly adding to the army of unemployed. The coal-export bonanza had petered out and mine owners were not only resistant to increases in wages but set on securing reductions. No settlement could be reached, and on March 31st, 1921, the men were locked out. The Miners' Federation called on its associates in the Triple Alliance (see page 148) for sympathetic action, and their response indicated the imminent possibility of a halt in all forms of transport. A 'State of Emergency' was proclaimed by the Government, reservists mobilized, volunteer strike-breakers enrolled. But the leaders of the railway and transport workers' unions were most reluctant to enter a battle in which their members had no direct

DECADENCE OF BRITISH CAPITALISM

interest and, at the last moment, found a pretext to rescind their
strike orders. Left to fight alone, the miners stayed out until the
end of June, when they were forced to accept very disadvantageous
terms.

'Black Friday' — the day the Triple Alliance proved a broken
reed — bitterly discouraged those who had hoped to open the door
to a new society with the key of industrial action. The Government and the employers, correspondingly elated, pressed forward
their counter-offensive. Lloyd George's promised social reforms —
most of them still in the blueprint stage — were forgotten as the
economy axe fell on education, housing and unemployment benefits. Wages were cut in one industry after another, and by the end
of 1922 reductions added up to £10 million a week. Even though
real wages suffered much less and, in some industries, actually
increased, the trade-union movement was baffled and dispirited.
Membership declined; funds were depleted; militancy subsided.
And, once again, the Labour movement began to flex its political
muscles and look towards Westminster.

Entwined with trade-union controversy over direct action
was a political debate on the rival merits of Parliamentarianism
and Dictatorship of the Proletariat. This question pre-empted
much time at British socialist gatherings between 1919 and 1921,
when the prestige of the Russian Revolution was high and that of
Parliament low. As we have noted, the dramatic transformation
of the despotic Empire of the Czars into a socialist republic stirred
even the mildest members of the Labour movement. Moreover,
sympathy with Russia was deepened by the Government's intervention policy and by the wordy warfare carried on against the
Bolsheviks by British conservatives. The Slogan, 'Workers of the
World, Unite', made all the more appeal when bitterly anti-
Labour papers like the *Daily Mail* assailed Lenin and Trotsky in
one column and damned MacDonald and Henderson in the next.
At the same time the patent absurdity of some of the Russian
'atrocity' stories in which British Tories delighted, blinded many
to the less sensational, but sufficiently horrifying, methods of
terror employed to fortify Soviet rule.

Sympathy for the Soviet Government as a victim of capitalist
aggression did not necessarily mean ideological agreement.

Indeed, there was little comradely love lost between the Russian Communist Party and most of the leading lights of British Labour. The pretensions of Moscow as a red Rome, holder of the only key to socialist salvation, and infallible interpreter of the sacred writings of Karl Marx, were keenly resented by British and other western socialists. There were those, however, who, stressing working-class unity above all other principles, strove to build a bridge between the Second International and the newly formed Third International (the Comintern). At the first postwar meeting of the former, at Berne, February 1919, the question whether a socialist society should be sought through democratic methods or by dictatorship of the proletariat was hotly debated. Democracy carried the day, but the controversy left its mark on the European socialist parties, most of which suffered from splits and desertions to the Communist camp.

In Britain the Labour Party, as a whole, held firmly to the line laid down at Berne. It was an independent group, the British Socialist Party, that formed the nucleus for the Communist Party of Great Britain in 1920.[1] A very vocal section of the Independent Labour Party also favoured adoption of communist policies and tactics, and affiliation to the Third International. They succeeded in stirring up an acute controversy which animated branch meetings and party conferences for many months. Their argument that the Second International had proved a hopelessly feeble instrument of working-class solidarity in 1914 was not easily answered; their assertions that British democracy was a sham carried a certain conviction in the days of the Coalition. But the whole tradition of the I.L.P. was out of tune with Communist dogmas. Moreover, in the dark days just past, the party had been united by a belief in the futility of force, and most members found it difficult to reconcile their opposition to war with advocacy of bloody revolution. Gradually, the anti-Communists gained the upper hand and, at the I.L.P. annual conference in 1921 a resolution to affiliate with the Third International was finally and decisively defeated.

[1] The British Socialist Party had been created in 1911 by a merger of the old Social Democratic Federation with some dissident I.L.P. branches and Clarion Clubs. It turned sharply to the left early in the war after expelling a minority group, headed by the veteran, H. M. Hyndman, which took a violently anti-German position and favoured full support of the Government.

Some members of the minority broke away and joined the Communist Party, then busily seeking to 'capture the masses' in preparation for the revolution which, the Comintern had persuaded itself, was imminent throughout western Europe. The quarry proved elusive, however, and the Moscow Road a *cul-de-sac* where the British Communist Party was bottled up, unable to maintain effective contact with the main body of the workers. To break out, it sought affiliation to the Labour Party, but the Labour Party was unco-operative. Unity of the workers, Henderson pointed out at the 1921 annual conference, was all very well but it must be based on unity of purpose and principle. Was that to be achieved by the admission of a group which, at the direction of Moscow, pursued polices completely inconsistent with those of the Labour Party?

The supporters of Communist affiliation were voted down by a large majority and, in after years, again and again experienced the same fate. The Labour Party had adopted the common-sense view that it was absurd to appeal to the workers to use revolutionary means for ends which could be secured by votes. Admittedly, the democratic process might be hampered by difficulties in gaining a hearing when the Labour Party had but one small daily newspaper with which to make itself heard above the din of the capitalist press. But this handicap had not hindered growth in the past and there was no reason to suppose it would do so in the future. In 1918, without even that one voice, the party had polled 2,244,802 votes compared with 370,802 in the previous General Election of December 1910. Allowing for a much larger electorate, such results indicated how greatly the Labour Party had widened its appeal with its new organization and programme. In local elections, too, sensational gains had been achieved since the close of the war and numerous city and borough councils were now ruled by Labour majorities. With the Liberals a divided and diminishing force, hopes of a future Labour government no longer seemed a fantastic dream.

There was little doubt that when the day came the Prime Minister would be Ramsay MacDonald. He had his severe critics both on the right and the left but since 1918, in spite of his absence from Parliament, he had established a much greater ascendancy in the Labour Party than he enjoyed prior to the war.

In the debates on aims and tactics, into which he had thrown himself with ardour, his position was well to the right of centre. Nevertheless, his record as an opponent of the war kept him in good odour with a majority of the I.L.P., which, as the most active of the Labour Party's affiliates, exercised an influence out of proportion to its numbers. His pacifism also added to his prestige in the Labour movement as a whole, once wartime passions had subsided. To large numbers of workers he was the man who had told the truth when truth-telling was unpopular. They were proud of him, too, as a boy of humble origin who had educated himself so that he could meet and defeat upper-class politicians on their own ground. And he was equally congenial to the ex-Liberals and middle-class intellectuals drawn to the Labour Party primarily by their opposition to secret diplomacy and militarism.

In these postwar years MacDonald was in great demand as a speaker, and he responded energetically, travelling constantly about the country to address large meetings and confer with small groups of the most active comrades. His oratorical powers were then at their peak. On analysis his speeches might be found lacking in substance, but he had a happy knack of appearing to appeal to the intelligence of his listeners while actually plunging them into an emotional warm bath of exactly the right temperature. One of his greatest assets was his unmistakable but easily understood Scotch burr — a classless accent which for the workers had no overtones of superiority and for the middle classes no suggestion of inferior education. To an attractive voice was added a manner both reserved and commanding and an almost heroically handsome figure. No wonder he secured, and for long held, a devoted following, or that from many of the newly enfranchised women he received something like adoration.[1]

By 1922, when the Labour Party again had a chance to test its strength in the country, MacDonald was its acknowledged, if still unofficial, leader. The General Election in November of that year followed the break-up of the Coalition. There had long been

[1] The author well remembers the scene at Labour headquarters in Woolwich when the results of the by-election of 1921 were announced. Men and women who had flocked from all parts of London to aid MacDonald's return to Parliament, were waiting in the committee room for the end of the count. A great victory had seemed assured, and when the figures came in showing defeat by a narrow margin there was an incredulous silence, broken after a minute by loud, uncontrollable sobbing.

friction between the Cabinet and the Tory back-benchers over Ireland, India and Lloyd George's special political fund, which rumour associated with his lavish distribution of titles. Unemployment and deterioration of the European situation following French invasion of the Ruhr had accelerated a steady slump in the Government's stock. The Prime Minister and most of his Tory colleagues wished to continue the Coalition as a united front against socialism and, indeed, to extend it by bringing in the independent Liberals. But the Tory Party, having lost some of its fears of Labour, had decided that Welsh wizardry was now more of a liability than an asset.

On October 19th, Austen Chamberlain, Tory leader since ill-health had retired Bonar Law, summoned a party meeting at the Carlton Club. His purpose, according to some accounts, was to explain plans for an early general election; another story is that he intended to suppress murmurings engendered by the Chanak crisis which almost plunged Britain into war with Turkey. At any rate, he seems to have been taken by surprise when Stanley Baldwin, President of the Board of Trade and still an unknown quantity politically, moved a resolution declaring that, when the election came, the Tory Party should fight 'as an independent party with its own leader and own programme'. It was carried by 187 to 87 — a clear vote of no confidence in the Coalition — and Lloyd George resigned. Bonar Law, who had almost certainly helped organize the Carlton Club coup — Baldwin was his henchman — consented to form a new government and immediately appealed to the country.

Labour entered this contest with high hopes, not of winning a majority but of substantially enlarging its numbers. Since 1918 its political machine had been overhauled and more professional organizers and elections agents engaged. But the party's strength, as always, lay in its ability to attract the enthusiastic services of volunteers to man committee rooms, address envelopes, canvass voters, and speak at street corners. It was this army of workers that more than compensated for chronic lack of funds and enabled Labour to win elections with a fraction of the expenditure incurred by its opponents.

The results on this occasion were encouraging, if not spectacular. Bonar Law won a comfortable Tory majority of 70, but the Liberal Party suffered further depletion and its 117 M.P.s were almost exactly divided between the Asquithians and the Georgites. The Labour Party nominated 414 candidates, polled a total of 4¼ million votes — 2 million more than in 1918 — and returned 142 members, thus confirming its claim to be the official Opposition. More important than this improvement in numbers was an improvement in calibre. Supporting the solid core of trade-union leaders were men drawn from all classes — teachers, writers, social workers, doctors, lawyers, merchants, manufacturers and even landowners. For the first time the Parliamentary Labour Party represented a cross-section of the nation and was able to draw on a wide variety of experience and knowledge. A feature of the election was the return of the pacifists, MacDonald and Snowden, and the ex-liberals, Arthur Ponsonby, Charles Trevelyan, E. D. Morel, and many others. From Glasgow, where but one seat had been secured in 1918, came ten lively Independent Labour Party members.

It was this last group that led an immediate fight for a change in the party rule that officers were to be elected at the close of each session. This meant that J. R. Clynes should have continued as leader, but the new members felt he was too unaggressive and insisted that they should be allowed a voice in the matter. As a result MacDonald was elected by a narrow margin — a fateful choice which nearly all those who helped to make it were bitterly to regret. For although he was undoubtedly the party's outstanding Parliamentary tactician, as a general he was to prove like that noble Duke of York who marched his army up the hill and marched them down again.

CHAPTER III

SEARCH FOR TRANQUILLITY:
1923-1929

The nation is not interested in politics, it is interested in economics. It has in the main got the political system it wants; what it now asks for is more money, better times, regular employment, expanding comfort, and material prosperity. It feels that it is not having its share in the development of the modern world, and that it is losing its relative position. It feels that science and machinery ought to procure a more rapid progress. It complains that the phenomena of production, consumption, and employment, are at this time in our country exceptionally ill-related. It turns to Parliament asking guidance, and Parliament, though voluble in so many matters, is on this one paramount topic dumb.
WINSTON S. CHURCHILL: *Romanes Lecture*, Oxford, June 19th,
1930

BONAR LAW's slogan for the General Election of 1922 — 'Tranquillity and Stability' — expressed in more elegant language the same thought as President Harding's promise of 'normalcy'. Undoubtedly, it was a sentiment with considerable popular appeal. Four years of war, followed by four years of political and social turmoil, domestic and foreign, had given the country its bellyful of excitement. Making peace had proved a drawn-out and disillusioning process. Conferences and crises had recurred with wearisome monotony and still no permanent settlement was in sight. At home the economy had lurched from boom to bust to the accompaniment of loud social discord. Swift changes in the value of money and sharp fluctuations in incomes had forced difficult adjustments of living standards. No wonder, then, that many people, longing to relax and cultivate their gardens, gladly accepted Bonar Law's colourless leadership in exchange for the chameleon-hued politics of Lloyd George.

'Tranquillity', however, was an aspiration, not a policy. Translated into practical terms, what did it mean? In foreign affairs it obviously implied an effort to bring about the long-delayed pacification of Europe, to make possible a return to normal political and economic relations, above all to settle the question of reparations. At the moment Bonar Law took office the outlook was far from auspicious and, a few weeks later, in January 1923, French occupation of the Ruhr made it a great deal worse. The intention of the French Government was to enforce its reparations mortgage but it could not overcome the passive resistance it encountered. German production fell catastrophically, the mark finally collapsed, and the collection of reparations seemed more remote than ever.

Lord Curzon, Tory Foreign Secretary, was hardly the best man to deal with this problem. The pompous lectures he addressed to Paris did nothing to improve relations between France and Germany, but much to embitter those between Britain and France. He also started a quite unnecessary new quarrel with the Soviets by attempting to assume the role of protector of the Russian Church. On the other hand, he played a constructive part in the negotiation of the Treaty of Lausanne which ended the war between Turkey and Greece and gave peace to the Near East for the first time since 1911.

Within the Empire, tensions created by nationalist agitations at the end of World War I had eased. The Cromwellian policy of the Coalition, which had sought to suppress the lawlessness of the Irish Republican Army by allowing the 'Black and Tan' auxiliary police to conduct a reign of terror, had failed dismally. Lloyd George and his colleagues had been forced to negotiate and, by the end of 1922, the Irish Free State was settling down to *de facto* independence. India, too, was temporarily quiet, though it was a sullen quietness that foreshadowed future difficulties. Restricted self-government, provided by the Montagu-Chelmsford reforms, had been accepted as an installment; and the country now enjoyed a fiscal autonomy that made it possible to protect local industry against competing British goods. As a result, while the Flag still waved over India, trade was receding and one of the most useful Imperial props of British capitalism was beginning to sag.

At home the problem of defining 'tranquillity' in a way that would give general satisfaction offered formidable difficulties. The postwar depression had passed its acute stage but was threatening to become chronic in the absence of some new economic stimulus. In the course of the election campaign, Bonar Law had remarked: 'I do have at the back of my mind this feeling that in a condition so critical as ours the real cure must come from better trade and better industry.' Presumably this statement of the obvious meant that if private enterprise were left alone, the situation would improve. Certainly, the vast majority of his supporters felt that the necessity of the hour was to return, as far as possible, to prewar social and economic conditions. Given strict economy, lower taxes, and an end of the 'pampering' of labour, capitalism could again become dynamic. To the workers such ideas spelt reaction, for the prewar era had little glamour in their eyes. They were not prepared to rely on unrestricted private enterprise to determine their conditions of life. In such matters as social security, employment and housing, the State, they insisted, had assumed responsibility and must assume more. No doubt only gradual progress could be expected — hope of a revolutionary rate of change had faded — but progress towards better social conditions and higher standards of living there must be.

Very early in Bonar Law's premiership an issue arose which illustrated the difference between these two attitudes. The Government announced a measure to remove rent restrictions by progressive stages: this was the way, it believed, to induce new investment in housing, which was discouraged by low yields on existing property. It was, of course, the orthodox free-market remedy for shortage, but to the workers, whose wages had been sharply reduced in the past two years, it appeared as another attack on their standard of living. Their anger was made manifest at by-elections in three supposedly safe Tory constituencies where vacancies had been created for the benefit of ministers who had lost their seats at the general election. All three, including the Minister of Health, whose department was responsible for housing, were defeated. Clearly, higher rents were not part of the average voter's conception of 'tranquillity' and Bonar Law found it advisable to reverse himself. Decontrol of rents was postponed and Neville Chamberlain appointed Minister of Health with a commission to attack the housing shortage by government action.[1]

[1] Neville Chamberlain, son of Joseph and half-brother of Austen, had entered national politics late in life. He had, however, gained administrative experience as an efficient and progressive Mayor of Birmingham.

Chamberlain's Housing Act of 1923, which thus owed its birth to rude pressure from the electorate, was later hailed by the Tories as a masterpiece of sound social reform. One party pamphleteer calls it 'the first really practical measure to overcome the housing shortage', and claims that 'as a result of this Act when the Conservative Party returned to power (1924-29) all previous housing records were broken'.[1] The first statement is true — the Coalition's housing programme had been a dismal failure — the second needs some amplification. For the broken records of 1924-29 were just as much due to the Wheatley Act of 1924, a Labour measure, as to the Chamberlain Act. Each made possible the erection of about half a million houses, but only the former produced dwellings which the average worker could afford to rent. The latter, by means of modest subsidies to private builders, encouraged the speculative production of houses for sale at prices too high for all but the best-paid manual workers. Nevertheless, the Chamberlain Act was a measure of real significance. It was an admission by the champions of private enterprise of the social and political necessity for large-scale State intervention to ensure that the supply of shelter at reasonable prices would be equal to the demand.

The housing shortage, however, was still regarded as a special case. Government action to deal with it did not, according to Tory views, set a precedent for, say, State investment to provide work for the unemployed. At this time there was only one form of interference with the free market which supporters of the Government could greet with enthusiasm — Protection. This, indeed was their favourite recipe for reviving trade and increasing jobs. Unfortunately, Bonar Law, in the interests of 'tranquillity', had promised at the general election not to raise the tariff issue, and Stanley Baldwin, who succeeded him as Premier in May 1923, treated this pledge as binding. Thus his Cabinet, for all its substantial majority, found itself cornered. Faced by demands to tackle the unemployment problem, it could not attempt the only solution in which it believed.

In October 1923, Baldwin decided to end this stalemate by dissolving Parliament and seeking a mandate for a tariff on manu-

[1] CHARLES E. BELLAIRS, *Conservative Social and Industrial Reform 1800-1945*, Conservative Political Centre (London, 1947), p. 28.

factured goods, but not foods, coupled with imperial preference. The ensuing election showed that free-trade sentiment was still strong in the land, strong enough even to reunite the warring Liberals and revive their drooping spirits. With tariffs the issue, the free-trade vote in the many constituencies contested by all three major parties was concentrated on the strongest of the opposition candidates, whether Labour or Liberal. As a result, although the Tories received almost the same proportion of the aggregate votes cast as the previous year, their strength in the House of Commons fell from 344 to 257. The Labour and Liberal Parties increased their numbers to 192 and 157 respectively, making a free-trade majority of over 90.

The disastrous consequences, from a Tory point of view, of Baldwin's experiment precluded any further attempt to revolutionize the fiscal system of the country until after the 1931 crisis. When the Tories returned to power in the autumn of 1924, following the defeat of the first Labour Government, they had again forsworn a general tariff. They did not, however, regard the introduction of separate tariffs as inconsistent with this pledge, and during the next five years a number of protective duties were imposed either on the ground they they were needed for 'revenue' or required to 'safeguard' key industries. Consequently several of the newer industries — motor cars, tyres and rayon were the most important — were given a privileged position which was denied to the worst sufferers from depression, the old staples such as iron and steel. In fact, it may be argued that this piecemeal protection directly added to the difficulties of the export trades, where unemployment was concentrated, by raising their costs, penalizing their potential overseas customers, and diverting investment capital to the favoured branches of manufacture.

The verdict of the electors in 1923 was negative: 60 per cent were *against* tariffs, but only 31 per cent voted *for* the Labour Party's alternative programme of moderate socialism. Nearly as many had cast their ballots for the Liberal Party and so given it the balance of power. Under these circumstances Baldwin chose to stay in office until Parliament reassembled late in January 1924, leaving the onus of the next move on the Liberals. The question was: would they throw their support to the Labour Party and permit it a lease on office terminable at their pleasure; or would they combine with the Tories 'to keep the socialists out'? In many quarters the prospect of MacDonald as Prime Minister was regarded with the utmost dismay, and strong pressure was brought to bear on Asquith, the Liberal leader, to adopt the second course. 'You would be amused,' he wrote a correspondent, 'if you saw the contents of my daily post-bag: appeals, threats, prayers from all parts, and from all sorts and conditions of men, women and lunatics, to step in and save the country from the horrors of Socialism and Confiscation . . . The City is suffering from an acute attack of nerves . . . One of the leading bankers came to see me this morning with a message from the City Conservatives, that if only I would set up an Asquith-Grey Government, all the *solid* people in the country would support it through thick and thin.'[1] Asquith, however, saw no reason for maintaining a discredited Tory administration in office and he had no desire to renew the painful experience of Coalition. 'If a Labour Government is ever to be tried in this country,' he said in a speech to his followers on December 18th, 1923, 'as it will sooner or later, it could hardly be tried under safer conditions.'

There were those in the Labour Party who felt that to take office subject to a Liberal check-rein would be a great mistake: it meant acceptance of responsibility without power. However, MacDonald, together with most of the senior members of the party, took the view that refusal of the opportunity, restricted as it might be, would fatally damage Labour's prestige. A party that shied at responsibility could not expect to be entrusted with power. Nor would MacDonald consider for a moment left-wing suggestions that the party should accept office but court immediate defeat by making the King's Speech a full-blooded socialist manifesto. He knew that such a gesture would invite, and receive, a heavy rebuke from an electorate that was hoping to find 'tranquillity' and wanted neither old-fashioned capitalism nor pure socialism. There were two things, he argued, that a minority Labour Government could do: make a contribution to the pacification of Europe; and provide an affirmative answer to the much-debated question: 'Is Labour fit to govern?'

These limited ambitions were, in fact, realized. MacDonald's

[1] EARL OF OXFORD AND ASQUITH, op. cit., vol. II, p. 248.

team, a judicious mixture of elderly trade-union leaders and ex-Liberals, if not brilliant, was, on the whole, capable. Haldane, the Liberal elder statesman who was brought in as Lord Chancellor, had expressed the fear, while the Cabinet was in the making, that 'inexperience in administration' might discredit it within a few weeks. In retrospect, however, he paid his colleagues a handsome tribute:

Ramsay MacDonald managed his Cabinets very well . . . All the members of the Cabinet worked hard and came prepared . . . They made their points briefly and forcibly, trained to do so by Trade Union discipline . . . We always got through our business . . . The Cabinet . . . contained some men of first-rate administrative ability. Ministers like Snowden, Thomas, Wheatley, and Sidney Webb were as capable in the conduct of affairs as one could wish to see and were also excellent in council.[1]

But while the first Labour Government demonstrated its ability to carry on day-to-day business with some efficiency, its domestic policies failed to strike public imagination. It was much too inclined to treat the constant threat of a Liberal veto as an excuse for inaction rather than as a stimulus to ingenuity. The one first-class measure carried to completion was the Housing Act, mentioned on an earlier page, which was pertinaciously pushed through by John Wheatley, the dour Catholic publisher from the Clydeside who was the sole left-winger in the Cabinet. Lesser reforms accomplished included an increase in old-age pension rates, restoration of the farm workers' legal minimum wage, and an act extending unemployment insurance benefits. But the Government proved no more able than its predecessor to reduce the total number of unemployed. Any feasible programme for that purpose was blocked, not merely by the Liberals, but by Philip Snowden, who, as Chancellor of the Exchequer, was proving himself to be the best Gladstonian of them all. His budget was notable for reductions in food taxes and abolition of the

[1] RICHARD BURDON HALDANE, *An Autobiography*. Hodder & Stoughton (London, 1929), pp. 327-30. The author's account (p. 216) of the Liberal Cabinet of 1906-10, in which he was also a leading member, makes an interesting contrast. 'It was a congested body of about twenty, in which the powerful orator secured too much attention. The Prime Minister knew too little of the details of what had to be got through to be able to apportion the time required for discussion. Consequently, instead of ruling the Cabinet and regulating the length of the conversations, he left things much to themselves.'

so-called 'McKenna Duties', imposed during the war ostensibly to discourage luxury imports and since retained for frankly protective purposes. He made no effort to revise or offset the deflationary policies of the Bank of England (see Part Four, Chapter 1), for instance, by making provision for public works. Little wonder, then, that poor Tom Shaw, the elderly textile leader who as Minister of Labour was expected to create new jobs, was driven to telling back-bench critics that 'remedies for unemployment cannot be produced like rabbits out of a hat'.

Against the background of a domestic record little better than mediocre, Labour's success in handling the Franco-German problem positively glowed. MacDonald, who had chosen to be his own Foreign Secretary, immediately discarded the Curzonian manner which had so throughly annoyed the French. Instead, in a series of letters written to M. Poincaré, the French Prime Minister, but addressed in fact to the people of France, he set forth in plain but sympathetic terms British views about the reparations problem and the need for a co-operative effort to liquidate the war spirit. Some critics complained the tone was too friendly and would only bolster the prestige of Poincaré and the right-wing parties that supported him. But at the French General Election of May 1924 the Radicals and Socialists won handsomely and the French press unhesitatingly gave much of the credit to MacDonald's open diplomacy.

The sequel was a meeting between Herriot, the new French Premier, and MacDonald, followed by an Allied conference to which, in due course, the German Government was invited to send a delegation. On August 16th, 1924, an agreement was reached providing for evacuation of the Ruhr and acceptance of the Dawes Plan for funding reparations and restoring the German currency system by means of an international loan. But beyond this the conference really relaxed the tensions that had so long gripped Europe and opened the door for the brief but bright period of European co-operation that was ended by the great depression. 'Mr. Ramsay MacDonald', said the London *Daily News*, 'has induced France and Germany to shake hands ... He has achieved in six months what British statesmen have been trying in vain to accomplish for six years.'[1]

[1] August 18th, 1924.

In these negotiations MacDonald showed a sureness of touch which afterwards deserted him. They were the high point of his career and, possibly, success went to his head. Certainly from this time on his friends began to observe increasing evidence of those delusions of grandeur which statesmen so often develop. In any event, it was a case of pride coming before a fall, for in the following six weeks he fumbled badly on two issues. The first was the draft commercial treaty with Russia, in regard to which he allowed himself to be goaded into making inconsistent statements by pressures from the extreme right and extreme left; the second was the prosecution of a communist editor for sedition which was ordered by the Attorney-General and then dropped. This action was sharply criticized by both Tories and Liberals in the House of Commons and, when MacDonald made the question one of confidence, quite unnecessarily in the opinion of Snowden and other ministers, the Government was defeated. Thus the general election that followed was fought, not on ground of Labour's own choosing, but on issues which enabled the opposition parties to suggest that sinister 'red' influences were operating in Downing Street.

In the course of the campaign an already confused situation was confounded by the publication of a letter, purportedly signed by Zinoviev, then head of the Comintern, directing the British Communist Party to form cells in the Army and Navy in preparation for civil war. A copy of this missive — no original was ever produced — was received by the Foreign Office early in October. MacDonald in the intervals of electioneering drafted a note of protest to the Soviet Government but gave instructions to delay action pending proof of the letter's authenticity. However, learning that the *Daily Mail* had a copy and was about to publish it, the Permanent Secretary of the Foreign Office released both letter and draft note on October 24th. From the Tories' point of view it was the exact psychological moment, and in the six days remaining before the polls they talked of little else. They accused the Government of trying to suppress the letter until after the election; they hinted darkly that Labour was caught in the 'Red Web'; and MacDonald, by delayed and characteristically vague explanations, did little to elucidate the situation.

The effect of this scare was to stir the politically apathetic into going to the polls in unusually large numbers to the great benefit of the Tory Party, which gained 161 seats and came back with an over-all Parliamentary majority exceeding 200. Labour, however, had no reason to feel unduly downhearted for, while it lost 42 seats, it increased its popular vote by more than a million and raised to 33 per cent its proportion of the aggregate vote. The real victim was the Liberal Party, which fell heavily between the two stools of socialism and conservatism and permanently broke its back. The Liberal share of the total vote fell from 30 per cent in 1923 to 18 per cent, and only 40 Liberals returned to Westminster.

The irrelevancies of the 'Red Letter' election had again produced a negative result. During the campaign there was little serious discussion of fundamental economic issues, for the Tories were still a party without a policy. They had undertaken to stay away from the tariff bottle but they could not turn to the pure water of *laissez-faire*, the only drink, as we saw in Part Four, Chapter I, proper to the deflationary diet prescribed by the Bank of England: to do so would require them to deny the workers those social-security anodynes that softened the pains, and checked the effective functioning, of the free labour market. Theoretically, the Tories as upholders of the private-enterprise system should have favoured that step; technically, with their undisputed control of Parliament, they were in a position to take it; practically, as they well understood, it offered a short way to political suicide. The luck of the ballot in three-cornered fights had enabled them to win two-thirds of the seats with only 48 per cent of the total vote. That was not a popular mandate to put back the clock of social reform.

It was the good fortune of the Tory Party in this period to have a leader who almost instinctively clung to the middle of the road. Stanley Baldwin was a traditionalist and a humanist: he believed in the capitalist system but not in the unrestricted sovereignty of the market. In earlier years he had headed a family business, conducted on paternalistic lines, and he sought now to soften the antagonisms of capital and labour by reproducing on a national scale the spirit of mutual confidence he had fostered in the Baldwin ironworks. It was with this end in view that, in March 1925, he asked for the defeat of a bill, introduced by members of his own party, which required trade unions to collect political levies only from those of their members who signed an authorization. The transparent hope of its sponsors was that substitution of 'contracting-in' for 'contracting-out' would reduce the trade-union funds that were the Labour's Party's mainstay. Baldwin, in an earnest speech, pointed out that, even though the bill was just in principle, its passage would foment the spirit of class war. He begged his followers, therefore, not 'to push our political advantage home at a moment like this,' and ended by expressing the belief that 'there are many in all parties and all ranks who will re-echo my prayer: "Give peace in our time, O Lord" '.

Unfortunately the brutal facts of the economic situation could not be altered by such appeals. A few months later, the efforts of the coal owners to save their hopelessly inefficient industry by slashing wages brought the country to the verge of a general strike. As we have already noted (see page 203), the Government postponed the crisis for nine months by granting a subsidy and used this interval to build up an elaborate strike-breaking organization. When the showdown came on May 3rd, 1926, the Government was ready while the trade unions were not. Most of the top men in the General Council of the Trades Union Congress had long been more than dubious about the strategy of the general strike and, to the last, they sought some concession which would enable them to retreat without loss of dignity. If they could have dealt with Baldwin alone, they might have succeeded, but there were tougher men in the Cabinet, notably Churchill, eager to provoke a battle that would once and for all dispose of the menace of a general strike.

When the call finally came, the three million union members instructed to cease work showed remarkable solidarity and discipline; despite provocations, there were relatively few serious incidents. Yet successful as the strike was in bringing industrial life to a standstill — Government volunteers could maintain little more than a token transport service — it was doomed to failure unless it could be turned into a revolution. That was a logic from which all save a militant Labour minority shrank. In threatening a general strike, the trade-union leaders had unconsciously attempted a bluff; when their bluff was called they sought to persuade themselves that they were merely engaging in normal industrial action on an unusually large scale. However, as the contest developed, they were forced to recognize that the Government had taken a stand from which it could not budge without complete loss of authority. Even if the general strike was strictly legal, in a larger sense it was unavoidably unconstitutional.

Unwilling to conduct a revolution, the trade unions surrendered after nine days. They had suffered the worst defeat in their history and were almost at the mercy of their opponents. Many employers, including the railroad companies, wished to improve the occasion by ending collective bargaining. Baldwin, however, urged prudence. 'I am not out to smash trade unions,' he told the House of Commons, 'and I will not allow the Strike to be made a pretext for the imposition of worse conditions.' But he could not, or would not, deprive his party of the satisfaction of a revenge which took the form of a major revision of labour law. The Trade Disputes and Trade Unions Act of 1927 pronounced general strikes, and indeed most sympathetic strikes, illegal. It also prohibited organizations of State employees from affiliation to the Trades Union Congress and the Labour Party, restricted rights of picketing, and confined trade-union political assessments to members giving their consent in writing. Drastic as this legislation was, it might easily have been still more severe had not a series of by-election defeats reminded the Tories of the dangers of pushing political advantage too far.

The narrow limits within which the Baldwin Government, strong as it was on paper, could move between 1924 and 1929 are illustrated by its budgets. Its upper-class supporters, the providers of political funds, pressed for reduced expenditures and lower taxes; the masses, whose votes were required to obtain power, insisted on expensive reforms. The problem of satisfying these opposing demands fell primarily on Winston Churchill, Chancellor of the Exchequer from November 1924 to June 1929, whose financial policies, perhaps inevitably, proved full of contradictions. He began by reducing income tax to 4s. in the pound — the lowest rate in the inter-war period — and by promising a searching scrutiny of departmental estimates: a progressive reduction in expenses of £10 million a year was, he suggested, possible. However, at the same time he restored the gold standard — a move which necessitated dear money and so blocked much hope of saving on debt charges, by far the largest budget item. He also announced a Widows, Orphans and Old Age Pension scheme, eventually to become self-supporting but immediately requiring contributions from the Exchequer.

The promised economies never did materialize. Cuts in some places were more than balanced by increases in others and, despite a gradual decline in prices which should have proved of assistance, Churchill's last budget was several millions greater than his first. In a somewhat frivolous apology to the Commons in 1927, he protested that he had not promised to effect a reduction of £10 million but only to 'aim at' that figure: 'One may aim at a reduction,' he said, 'as one may aim at a target, but one does not promise to hit it.' After 1928, Churchill suggested, there might be some hope of lower expenses, but, he remarked significantly, a general election would then be approaching and nothing was more costly, since 'every new administration, not excluding ourselves, arrives in power with bright and benevolent ideas of using public money to do good'.

Apart from the Pensions Act, the most expensive of the Government's measures was the reform of local government sponsored by Neville Chamberlain, Minister of Health. An Act passed early in 1929 in effect adopted the functional approach to the relief of destitution which the Webbs had advocated twenty years before in the Minority Report of the Royal Commission on the Poor Law. It abolished the Boards of Guardians, transferring most of their duties to the county and county borough councils, whose public health and education committees, in co-operation with new public-assistance committees, became responsible for destitute children and the destitute sick. This act all but demolished the 'Principles of 1834' which had prescribed treatment of paupers as semi-criminals, to be isolated from the community and subjected to 'deterrents' of a penal character. Five years later the work was completed by creation of the Unemployment Assistance Board to assume responsibility for able-bodied unemployed whose insurance benefits had become exhausted.

The Act of 1929 also dealt with other local government problems and, in connection with it, Churchill introduced legislation freeing agricultural land from liability for local taxes and relieving productive industrial property of 75 per cent of this burden. To compensate local authorities for their loss of revenue, Treasury grants were correspondingly increased and their distribution governed by a new formula which took some account of the greater needs of poor areas. This was a very commendable reform but one hardly compatible with promises of economy since the estimated annual cost to the Exchequer was upwards of £30 millions. It was only by resort to a 'raid' on the National Debt sinking fund that Churchill was able to finance the scheme without increasing direct taxes.

Dependence on what he once called 'adventitious aids or windfalls' was, indeed, a regular feature of Churchill's administration of the Exchequer. He claimed in his last budget speech that such Micawber-like expedients were fully justified as a means of tiding the country over a difficult period. Certainly they helped to solve temporarily the problem of appeasing the politically powerful many without imposing tax increases that would have aroused the economically powerful few.

Thus, in the three years following the General Strike, Baldwin's Government provided the country with tranquillity of a sort. At least there were no new crises, and trade, foreign and domestic, showed some signs of expansion. An economic equilibrium had been achieved, but it was one in which the moderate prosperity of some sectors was balanced by deep depression in others. Despite all the sacrifices made on their behalf, most of the industries dependent on foreign trade had enjoyed no real recovery. From 1924 to 1929, the volume of Britain's exports had increased only 8 per cent and its share of world markets had fallen from 12.94 per cent to 10.76 per cent. Commenting on this situation, an authoritative writer has stated:

A considerable decline in manufacture for export is not necessarily a disastrous symptom. It may merely represent a partial abandonment of the practice of capital exporting, or it may reflect an improvement in terms of trade with raw-material producing countries, such as we have indeed witnessed since the war. What proved disastrous, however, was the effect of this decline in exports on the volume of employment. The expansion of manufacture for the home market and the development of other occupations failed to provide the employment required for workers displaced

DECADENCE OF BRITISH CAPITALISM

from the older trades as well as for new recruits to industry. Between July 1924 and July 1929, it is true, the numbers insured actually in employment increased from 10,600,000 to 10,900,000. But throughout the last ten years unemployment has never fallen below 8.8 per cent of the insured workers and the average has been far greater than in the prewar period.[1]

This record was all the more dismal when contrasted with the simultaneous unprecedented prosperity of the United States. It suggested that the 'stability' of which the Tories boasted was a euphemism for stagnation, that the economic system of the country had experienced not a temporary breakdown but a permanent loss of efficiency. No one could assert that the people were surfeited with goods or that their capacity to consume was exhausted. Yet no outlet could be found for the potential production of a million or more workers, an army of the idle who advertised what R. H. Tawney had called 'the sickness of an acquisitive society'.

Inevitably, the General Election of May 1929 was fought on the issue of unemployment. The Tories had no new proposals to make: they could only offer the hope of better times ahead provided the electors put 'Safety First' and voted against dangerous economic experiments. The slogan proved uninspiring to a public bent on change. Despite another big increase in the electorate, due to the enfranchisement of women under thirty, the Tory Party's total vote was much the same as in 1924 and its Parliamentary membership fell from 396 to 260.

Labour, on the other hand, gathered in some three million new supporters and, with 290 M.Ps, became for the first time the largest party in the House of Commons. It still lacked an absolute majority, but dependence on the Liberal Party, numbering sixty members, seemed likely to prove less of a hindrance to a Labour Government than in 1924. More or less reunited under Lloyd George, the Liberals had decided that a return to radicalism offered the best chance of political survival. They had put forward a detailed programme for the conquest of unemployment by an attack 'in the same spirit as we attacked the emergencies of the war', and could not logically oppose any bold measures to promote

[1] G. C. ALLEN, *British Industries and their Organization*. Longmans, Green (London, 1939), pp. 275-6.

recovery. Consequently, Labour accepted the responsibilities of office for the second time with the highest hopes, blissfully unaware that a great storm brewing across the Atlantic was to blow the last rags of socialism from their chosen leader and drive him to seek shelter under Tory blankets.

CHAPTER IV

THE ECLIPSE OF LABOUR

THERE is reason to believe that Ramsay MacDonald was well content with the Parliamentary position when he became Prime Minister for the second time, on June 6th, 1929. Had Labour won another thirty seats and so secured a majority, he would have faced the problem of translating a socialist programme into legislation — an uncongenial occupation for one who had come to disagree sharply with the I.L.P. slogan — 'Socialism in our Time'. Dependence on the Liberals was far less irksome than dependence on the impatient Labour left-wingers: it provided him with a strong argument for moderation. His first 'King's Speech', apart from some vague allusions to possible nationalization of coal mines, was so cautiously phrased that Churchill sarcastically offered 'cordial co-operation in the Government's self-imposed task of carrying out the Conservatives' policy and making the world easier, if not safer, for capitalism'.

MacDonald's Cabinet was heavily weighted with representatives of the right and centre of the Party. The only left-winger included was George Lansbury, who as first Commissioner of Works was to win a deserved popularity by making the Royal Parks more accessible to the people. Arthur Henderson proved a sound choice for the Foreign Office, where he laboured against increasingly heavy odds to shore up the foundations of peace and launch a practical disarmament programme. The task of finding work for the unemployed was placed in the hands of J. H. Thomas, once a vigorous leader of the railway workers, who was now going rapidly to seed. Neither his delight in public dinners, which led the cartoonist David Low to lampoon him as 'Right Honourable Dress-Suit', nor his habits of association with speculative financiers, seemed to qualify him for this job. But he was closer to MacDonald than any of the other leading trade unionists.

Under more favourable circumstances, the second Labour Government might have made a dull but not unworthy record. Conditions in the summer of 1929 appeared to favour Mac-

Donald's desire to promote tranquillity with a reformist flavour. Britain was as near prosperity as it had been for many years. Unemployment was slowly declining; most indices of trade pointed upward; hopes for recovery that would permit gradual improvement of the condition of the workers seemed to most people solidly based. Few paid attention to small clouds in an otherwise clear sky. There was, for example, the disturbing fact that American investors, engrossed in their frenzied bull market, were losing interest in foreign securities at the very time when high money rates in New York were pulling in funds from all over the world. One consequence had been an increase in the Bank of England's rediscount rate on February 7th, 1929, from 4½ per cent to 5½ per cent — a move to protect the gold reserve that had discouraging implications for domestic industry. Reduction in the flow of dollars through international channels was also beginning to have an adverse effect on world trade. However, so long as Wall Street continued to boom, its glittering façade concealed the deterioration of economic conditions. For a few months, the Labour Government could plan its course with some sense of confidence.

One of the first measures put in had provided for an extension of 'transitional benefit' for those of the unemployed who had exhausted their insurance rights. It also abolished the restriction of benefits to those 'genuinely seeking work' — a mockery in the chronically depressed areas — and slightly increased allowances for dependants. But while these changes did something to alleviate conditions for the workless, they did not still complaints of harsh administration which often deprived the genuinely needy of assistance.

Perhaps the most portentous piece of legislation completed by the Labour Government was the Coal Mines Act of 1930, which partially redeemed a pledge to the miners to reduce their legal working day. Maximum hours were cut from 8 to 7½ — the union had asked for 7 — and, to conciliate the owners, the coalfields were divided into statutory areas, each with a marketing scheme and an output quota. The bill also made provision for badly needed reorganization of the industry, but this section was weakened by the House of Lords. Thus the coal owners secured the monopolistic benefits of a government-blessed cartel with no corresponding obligation to increase efficiency. In the 'thirties, the Tories were to make considerable use of this precedent.

Among other Acts carried to completion was a useful housing and slum-clearance measure for which Arthur Greenwood, Minister of Health, was responsible. But a large part of the Government's programme fell by the wayside. Liberals combined with Tories to pass a killing amendment to a Trade Union Bill designed to reverse the Trade Disputes Act of 1927. The House of Lords rejected on grounds of expense an Education Bill which provided for raising the school-leaving age to fifteen — a long-promised reform which was thus postponed until 1946. The one piece of attempted nationalization was Herbert Morrison's scheme for a London Passenger Transport Board to take over both municipal tramways and privately owned bus companies and underground railways in the Metropolitan area. Swept aside in the 1931 crisis, this plan was subsequently enacted in a somewhat changed form by the National Government and provided a prototype for the public corporations which after 1945 were created to manage various nationalized industries.[1]

Before the Government had been in office many months, its legislative programme was pushed to the background by the overriding problems of world economic crisis. The great Wall Street bubble burst in the autumn of 1929, inaugurating an international deflation of unprecedented severity. Owners of stocks and commodities rushed to liquidate, and prices plunged downward. Trade shrank rapidly, businessmen curtailed commitments, postponed investments, reduced production. Week by week the army of unemployed in Britain received thousands of new recruits, with the total rising from 1,100,000 when the Government took office to 1,700,000 the following May. During those eleven months, Thomas produced nothing but optimistic statements and mysterious hints at plans 'up his sleeve'. However, Sir Oswald Mosley, who had been given a minor post in the Government and assigned to assist Thomas, submitted proposals of his own to the Cabinet. Their main feature was a big public-works scheme to be

[1] This was the second occasion on which a Tory Government carried to completion a collectivist project launched by Labour. The Electricity Act of 1926, which set up the Central Electricity Board to operate the 'Grid' and exercise extensive authority over private power companies, followed a plan drafted by the first Labour Government.

financed by public borrowing, a plan for which the Government might reasonably have expected to obtain Liberal support in view of the Lloyd-Georgian election programme. Nevertheless, it was pigeoned-holed by the Cabinet and Mosley resigned. There was at first a good deal of sympathy with him among rank-and-file members of the party, who were deeply disturbed by ministerial apathy in regard to the unemployed, but in attempting to organize a revolt against the Government he overplayed his hand and aroused suspicion of his motives.[1]

The truth was that the Labour Government had already reached an impasse. It could not hope to influence the volume of unemployment favourably unless it was prepared to unbalance the budget, pledge public credit on a large scale, and so risk a loss of foreign confidence in sterling which might endanger the gold standard. On the other hand, if the increase in unemployment were not checked, the cost of supporting the workless would put an unbearable strain on the Exchequer unless rates of benefit were reduced. It was a choice, therefore, between bold socialist planning and economy at the expense of the unemployed, who already received little more than enough for bare subsistence. The first alternative involved the risk of defeat in Parliament and the gamble of an appeal to the electorate; the second meant an almost certain split in the Labour Party.

Actually, Snowden, again Chancellor of the Exchequer, had committed the Government to deflation by his 1930 Budget. He had convinced himself that deficit financing was the unforgivable sin and that departure from the gold standard would lead the country straight to an economic hell. Revenue was declining owing to the depression, and expenditure rising chiefly because the Unemployment Insurance Fund required heavy subventions from the Treasury in order to remain solvent. Snowden, determined to maintain the sinking funds regardless of the deflationary effects of debt repayment, plugged the gap with heavy increases in taxation and sternly resisted all appeals for money to finance new social reforms.

The tradition that held war to be the only emergency justi-

[1] Within a year he formed the New Party, which, despite lavish expenditure of funds and much publicity, failed to win any seats in the 1931 General Election. Then, inspired by Hitler's success, he launched the British Fascists with a complete set of Nazi trappings, including anti-semitism and black-shirted thuggery.

fying deliberate unbalancing of the budget was a weighty one and Snowden's policies were not strongly challenged. No doubt most Labour members would have responded eagerly if their leaders had repudiated orthodoxy and challenged the Opposition parties to defeat a socialist solution to the unemployment problem. But, when leadership pointed in the opposite direction and adopted measures bound to increase deflationary pressure, they acquiesced although they did not accept the logical consequence — a purge of the economic system to force down costs, including wages, to the point where prices fell so low that hoarders of money would once again be tempted to exchange it for goods.

Had MacDonald and Snowden put the position bluntly before their followers in the summer of 1930, there is no doubt that they would have been faced by irrepressible revolt. The Cabinet itself would not have sustained them and the Government would have been compelled to resign. That would have meant the end of MacDonald's political career for, in such circumstances, he could hardly expect to be retained as the party's leader; and, having had one long sojourn in the wilderness, he had no desire for another.

Consequently, the Government drifted through 1930 while the number of unemployed passed the two-million mark and continued to rise. MacDonald, whose own understanding of economics was meagre, made no effort, we are told by a writer who knew him well, to consult either Labour economists or sympathetic non-party professionals like Keynes. 'This abstention from contact with the thinkers and experts on his own side, or what might have been presumed to be his side, in effect handed him over, tied and bound, to the business magnates and other important persons and the orthodox among the civil servants by whose professional negativism and scepticism he allowed himself to be overwhelmed.'[1]

MacDonald had indeed lost touch with most of the members of his own party. His contempt for all but a few was hardly more concealed than his pleasure in the company of the rich and titled. By November 1930, when a new session opened, discontent among Labour M.P.s was spreading rapidly. 'The Prime Minister made a

[1] MARY AGNES HAMILTON, 'James Ramsay MacDonald', *Atlantic Monthly*, April 1938, pp. 459-60. Mrs. Hamilton was a Labour M.P. from 1929 to 1931.

speech which sent the spirits of his followers down to zero. Talk
in the lobbies, over dinner, in tea-room and map-room was
gloomy . . . Would it not be better, members began asking each
other, if MacDonald, who so heartily disliked his own Party . . .
were replaced by Henderson?'[1] Such talk was sternly discouraged
by Henderson himself, but inevitably it reached MacDonald's
ears and must have strengthened his belief that only an all-party
government, which he naturally would lead, could adequately
cope with the crisis. Not long afterwards, if Lloyd George's testi-
mony can be accepted, top leaders of the three parties started a
series of private meetings. Henderson was not invited.[2]

Early in 1931, an economy campaign began to take shape.
A Treasury memorandum presented to the Royal Commission on
Unemployment Insurance stated that continued borrowing by the
Unemployment Insurance Fund without adequate provision for
repayment threatened British financial stability. The largest
employers' organization asked for a one-third reduction in
unemployment benefits, which, it declared, were hindering
'unemployment from acting as a corrective factor in the adjustment of wage levels'. In February, resisting a Tory motion
censuring Government extravagance, Snowden agreed with
opposition speakers that expenditure possible in prosperous times
was intolerable in a depression, and approved in principle of
'temporary sacrifices' of social gains. Shortly afterwards, in
response to Liberal pressure, he appointed a committee to recommend economy measures, choosing as its chairman Sir George
May, head of the gigantic Prudential Insurance Company.

Snowden's 1931 Budget had to provide for another large
prospective deficit as revenue continued to fall away and expenditure to rise, mainly on account of unemployment. Apart from a
50 per cent increase in petrol duty, he did not, however, add to
taxes, but solved the problem, on paper, by raiding the 'Exchange
Account' and speeding up income-tax payments. Amid general
relief at the relative mildness of these proposals, too little attention
was paid to his warning that, unless the world depression lifted,
there would have to be substantial cuts in expenditure or higher
taxes or both.

[1] MARY AGNES HAMILTON, *Arthur Henderson.* Heinemann (London, 1938), pp. 352-3.
[2] Ibid., p. 384.

Throughout the summer of 1931, while the May Committee sharpened its axe, the economic situation in central Europe went from bad to worse. In May, the dominant Austrian bank, the *Kreditanstalt*, to which the Bank of England had made substantial loans, announced its insolvency. That meant in effect the bankruptcy of the Austrian State, and fears that Germany would be the next to suffer financial collapse prompted a flight from the mark. On June 12th, President Hoover proposed a one-year moratorium on all inter-governmental debts, but a delay in securing the agreement of France dissipated much of the psychological effects of this plan. Next month the *Darmstädter und Nationalbank* — one of Germany's largest — failed. It was the very day that the Macmillan Committee on Finance and Industry reported that Britain had been financing long-term foreign investments with the aid of short-term foreign funds and that its current foreign liabilities were greater than its quick foreign assets. Since British banks were known to have large sums tied up in Germany, this combination of events encouraged foreigners to withdraw balances from London. As a result, sterling fell in terms of both francs and dollars, forcing the Bank of England to part with large sums of gold. A hurriedly called international conference in London attempted in vain to find a solution for the German situation: all adequate remedies were blocked by French insistence on political conditions which no German government could accept.

On July 31st, while all the financial nerve centres of the world were tingling, the Treasury released the May Committee's report indicating a British budgetary deficit of £120 million unless there were immediate and heavy cuts in the social services. Parliament had just recessed, so ministers could not be questioned; there was no covering statement from the Treasury or declaration of Government policy. Little wonder, then, that there was another panicky flight from sterling, checked only temporarily by a £50 million joint American and French credit.

Nevertheless, MacDonald seemed willing to allow the crisis to ripen before taking action. He appointed a Cabinet subcommittee — himself, Snowden, Henderson, Thomas and William Graham, President of the Board of Trade — to examine the May Report, but scheduled its first meeting for August 25th. Following consultations between MacDonald, Snowden and leading bankers, the date was advanced to August 12th, when the members were told that the actual deficit for 1932-33 would be nearer £180 million than £120 million. It was agreed that the budget must be balanced by drastic economies as well as new taxes, but difficulty arose in regard to a proposed 10 per cent cut in unemployment pay. Snowden refused to consider alternatives — a tariff to correct the adverse balance of trade, reduction in the sinking fund, review of the gold-standard position. Meanwhile, he and MacDonald talked to the Tory and Liberal leaders, who, like the bankers, insisted that there must be bigger cuts than the Cabinet so far had been willing to make. Reluctantly they also consented to meet the National Executive of the Labour Party and the Trades Union General Council. Snowden said on this occasion: 'We believe firmly that if sterling collapses . . . you will have chaos and ruin in this country. You will have unemployment rising not merely to five million but to ten million.' The Labour Cabinet held its last meeting on Sunday, August 23rd, when it learned that the American and French bankers were adamant in demanding a 10 per cent cut in unemployment pay as a condition of the credits without which sterling would immediately topple from its gold throne.[1] A vote showed the members almost evenly split on accepting these terms, and MacDonald asked them all to resign before he left to see the King. His colleagues naturally expected he would resign himself and that Baldwin, as Leader of the Opposition, would be asked to form a government. But next morning they were astounded to hear from MacDonald that he had accepted a commission to head a National Government to cope with the emergency. 'There was no suggestion in MacDonald's tone or manner of regret at the break-up of the Labour Government . . . He did not appeal for support from his old associates in this new venture. On the contrary, he gave them the sense that he was glad to be rid of them.'[2] Stunned, the ex-ministers filed out: only Snowden, Thomas, and the Lord Chancellor, Lord Sankey, were asked to remain.

---

[1] Snowden later vehemently denied that such conditions had been made by the bankers. However, in the final stages of the Economy Bill (see *infra*) MacDonald, when asked to make some concessions to the unemployed, stated: 'The handling of the unemployment cuts was necessitated by special conditions of borrowing and they must remain.'

[2] MARY AGNES HAMILTON, op. cit., p. 385.

There were but ten men in the new Cabinet — four Labour, four Tory, and two Liberal. It was not, MacDonald insisted, a coalition: it was a salvage squad formed solely to balance the budget and restore sterling 'to its old reputation for reliability'. Thanks to the National Government, he said on the hurried reassembly of Parliament, 'this House meets . . . with the pound worth twenty shillings'.

Snowden's emergency supplementary Budget was introduced on September 10th, and four days later a bill providing for economies totalling £70 million in a full year received its second reading. In addition to the 10 per cent cut in unemployment benefits and their limitation to 26 weeks in any one year, there were to be reductions of 10 to 20 per cent in the salaries of all public servants. Additional taxes included higher duties on beer, tobacco and entertainments and an increase in income tax to 5s. in the pound coupled with reductions in allowances that doubled the charge on small incomes. By accepting these 'drastic and disagreeable' proposals, said Snowden, 'the country will show the world an example of the indomitable British spirit in the face of difficulty'.

The world, however impressed it may have been, remained dubious about the value of sterling, especially when it learned, despite Admiralty censorship, that British naval ratings at Invergordon had 'struck' against the proposed cuts in their pay. The frantic scramble for liquidity continued and, on September 15th, the Berlin Stock Exchange collapsed, while a slump on the Amsterdam Bourse featured the heavy selling of British Funds. Realization of foreign balances in London continued on so huge a scale that the large American and French credits were rapidly exhausted. By September 18th, the Treasury was forced to ask for further assistance from the same sources but met a refusal. Three days later, suspension of gold exports was announced and sterling fell fairly rapidly to about 70 per cent of the dollar parity at which it had been so painfully held since April 1925.

All the experts who had been explaining that devaluation of the pound would be The End now turned around and assured the public that it was really A Very Good Thing, in fact just the tonic needed to revitalize industry. Ordinary citizens, legitimately bewildered, braced themselves for a shock that never came. They had been led to expect that a departure from gold would mean frantic inflation, but internal prices remained steady: the pound was still worth twenty shillings.

Unblushing at this spectacular failure to perform the task which provided its *raison d'être*, the National Government now turned to the problem of safeguarding its own existence. At its formation, MacDonald had declared that it was a temporary combination that would dissolve into its component parts once its job was done. But the Labour Party had no further use for him — he was soon to be formally expelled — and his personal following was but a corporal's guard: he had no future except as head of a National Government. The Tories were willing to retain him in that position for a time, provided they were given a free hand to bring in tariffs as part of a National programme. Snowden, who had just jettisoned his socialist principles to follow a *laissez-faire* policy, objected to this bargain. About half the Liberals also jibbed, but the remainder, led by Sir John Simon, decided to accept the Tory terms with the result that the already splintered party suffered further fragmentation.

After some weeks of wrangling, MacDonald issued a manifesto asking for a 'Doctor's Mandate', which included authority to consider 'every proposal likely to help, such as tariffs ...' and on this basis the appeal to the electorate was made. But the general election campaign turned not on tariffs but on the misdeeds of the defunct Labour Government, with its two most prominent members leading the hue and cry. Every effort was made to terrify the voters. MacDonald at his meetings waved bunches of worthless German marks to show what might have happened to the pound; Snowden described the policy of Labour as 'Bolshevism run mad'; a last-minute statement from National headquarters declared that, if Labour won, Post Office savings deposits would be endangered.

These tactics were remarkably successful. As in 1924, the winds of fear piled the 'floating vote' on to the Tory shore, and the National Government was able to win no less that 554 seats out of a total of 615.[1] Labour suffered a crushing defeat; its Parliamentary strength was reduced to 56 — a smaller number than in 1918 — and almost all its leaders were among the casualties.

---

[1] They were divided as follows: 471 Tories; 35 National Liberals (Simonites); 33 Liberals (Samuelites); 13 National Labour; 2 plain National.

George Lansbury, the only ex-Cabinet member to survive, was elected Leader of the Parliamentary Party; Clement R. Attlee, who had been a junior minister in the Labour Government, became his deputy.

Defeat, however, did not mean destruction. Labour's popular vote declined only some 2,000,000 to 6,363,561 — almost one-third of the total cast — and as an organization it remained completely intact. A mere handful of individuals followed MacDonald while, on the left, the Independent Labour Party, whose members had chafed against official discipline for years, decided to secede. This move was followed by a split in the I.L.P.s own ranks, and a considerable minority of its members broke away to help form the Socialist League, a 'ginger group' which, under such able leaders as Sir Stafford Cripps and Aneurin Bevan, was to prove a thorn in the flesh of the Labour Party executive throughout the 'thirties.

Previous political setbacks suffered by Labour had usually led to greater activity by the movement's industrial wing. In 1931, however, and for some years to come, the trade unions were in no mood for militant action. They had been losing members for years — bottom was not touched until 1933 — and massive unemployment discouraged campaigns for improvement of conditions. Their best hope was to defend existing wage rates, a task which they carried out with some degree of success, so that, thanks to the continued fall in prices, workers fortunate enough to hold regular jobs improved their living standards between 1930 and 1933.

The Labour Party's loss of prestige, the apparent failure of constitutional methods, and the passivity of the trade unions, might have been expected to favour the growth of revolutionary groups. Certainly the Communist Party did its best, diligently advertising the contrast between the flourishing state of the Soviet Union, just completing the first five-year plan, and the prolonged depression of the capitalist world. But although the communists were vocal, as always, and exceedingly energetic in their efforts to organize the unemployed, every electoral test exposed them as a stage army. Their impact on the workers remained limited, despite their capture of some key trade-union positions, and it was chiefly among the intellectuals that they were able to find new recruits.

Labour Party recovery during the 'thirties was accompanied by a series of internal debates on ways and means. The first issue'to be disposed of was: How to profit by the lessons of 1929-31? Some of the old guard were still inclined to avoid specific commitments, but a majority of members felt that the relation of principles to tactics must be more clearly defined. They wished to make sure that no future leader would be able to tread the path of 'Mac-Donaldism' and to this end the 1932 Party Conference passed a resolution declaring that 'the next time Labour takes office, with or without power, it should stand or fall on definite socialist legislation'.

'Next time', however, was probably a long way off and a more immediate question was the policy which Labour, as His Majesty's Opposition, should follow on foreign affairs and armaments. Ever since the end of World War I, pacifist sentiment had dominated the Labour movement. There was a strongly held conviction that in 1914 the workers had been tricked into fighting imperialist battles on the pretence that they must 'save the world for democracy'. Now, it was felt, Labour must be on guard against any attempt by a reactionary government to maintain itself in power by the classic method of promoting foreign adventure.

The advent of Hitler, with his undisguised ambition to destroy the Treaty of Versailles and to expand his Third Reich at all costs, for a long time hardly changed this attitude. British Labour was, of course, outraged by Nazi ideas and methods, but it did not at once recognize the new Germany as the uncompromising enemy of every democracy, an enemy incapable of negotiating in good faith. Thus in 1933 the Annual Party Conference unanimously approved a Socialist League resolution which called on the workers 'to take no part in war, and to resist it with the whole force of the Labour movement'. Although by this time the Hitler regime had been established for some months and the Brown Terror had made clear its nature, the debate was strangely academic; although for nearly two years Japan had been carrying on an invasion of China in defiance of the League of Nations, the problem of how to deal with nations that waged aggressive war was not squarely faced. True, the Labour Party had upbraided the Government for not urging stronger League action to protect

China and had even advocated economic sanctions against Japan. But it glided over the difficulty of reconciling use of this weapon, which was unlikely to prove effective unless the nations' wielding it were prepared as a last resort to back it by military action, with total opposition to war.

The dilemma of the Labour Party became crystal-clear in October 1935 when Italy invaded Ethiopia and Mussolini threatened to resist forcibly any really inconvenient sanctions such as a denial of oil supplies. At the Party Conference, actually in session when the blow was struck, Sir Stafford Cripps, speaking for the Socialist League, insisted that 'no League system is a reality within imperialism'. A capitalist government, he said, could not be entrusted with sanctions; they must, therefore, be opposed until Britain had a socialist government. Lansbury supported him in a speech advocating total non-resistance, but his eloquent plea was swept aside by Ernest Bevin, who complained that he was 'tired of having George Lansbury's conscience carted about from conference to conference'. The brutality of this attack on one of the most revered veterans of the Labour movement was resented by many delegates but when a vote was taken a large majority supported sanctions. Lansbury thereupon resigned as Parliamentary leader and Attlee, who, much as he hated war, believed that non-resistance was an irresponsible policy, was elected in his place.[1]

Labour had taken a step forward but not a very long one. While demanding British leadership in enforcing League sanctions against an aggressor, even at the risk of war, the party continued to oppose any increase in armaments and thus laid itself open to the jibe that it wished Britain to police the world without any truncheon. The country, at that time, was woefully ill-prepared for war though strong enough, perhaps, to have exposed the hollow character of Mussolini's boasted power had it taken really resolute measures to stop the Ethiopian war. But by this time a much more dangerous enemy was rapidly regaining its armed strength. In March 1935, the Nazi Government openly announced the existence of the air force it had been building in merely nominal

[1] This choice was confirmed after the General Election of November 1935, which resulted in the return of another Tory-dominated 'National Government' but enabled the Labour Party to raise its numbers to the more respectable total of 154.

secrecy and the immediate introduction of conscription. Both these steps were gross violations of the Treaty of Versailles.

Yet even in the autumn of 1936, when Ethiopia had been conquered, Germany had remilitarized the Rhineland, and Franco's revolt against the Spanish Republic was thriving on aid from Hitler and Mussolini, the Labour Party's position remained ambiguous in some respects. Speaking at the Annual Conference at Edinburgh, in October 1936, Attlee said:

We must fix our level of British armaments with regard to our position in a system of collective security, not with regard to a competition with other armed powers . . . We are not prepared to support a Government that has betrayed the League . . . and that has not related its arms policy to any intelligible foreign policy . . . We recognize the dangers of our position owing to Fascist dictatorships but I will never be a party to taking a fatalistic line and suggesting that it is inevitable there must be a line-up for a war.

The extraordinary behaviour at this time of the Government, which was combining half-hearted rearmament with whole-hearted appeasement, helps to explain the Labour Party's attitude. It had no confidence that the Government would employ increased armed strength solely to hinder aggression: it feared, on the contrary, some kind of deal with Hitler; or even, under cover of foreign dangers, the transformation of the Government, which still called itself 'National', into a semi-Fascist regime. But such fears could not excuse the Labour Party's timorous approach to the problem of Spain. At Edinburgh, David Grenfell, speaking for the national executive, said: 'Do not ask for intervention [in Spain] meaning not to fight . . . If you are for intervention in these circumstances you must be for war and you must take the responsibility.' Labour was not prepared to take the responsibility: it was content to send bandages, chocolate and sympathy to the hard-pressed Spanish Republicans and to urge the British Government to check violations of the arms embargo by the Fascist powers. It refused, along with Chamberlain, and even Churchill, to face the fact that the Spanish battle was the opening skirmish in the world war which appeasement was rapidly making inevitable.

A year later, the heat of events forced the party to shed more of its long-cherished pacifist garments. In the summer of 1937 it denounced the farce of non-intervention as 'a policy foredoomed to failure'. The same year the annual conferences of both the Labour Party and the Trades Union Congress passed resolutions supporting rearmament and demanding 'a stand against aggression, whatever the risks', and the Parliamentary Labour Party ceased its opposition to appropriations for the Armed Forces. Nevertheless, as late as April 1939, when the Government decided, very reluctantly, to introduce conscription, the Labour Party challenged the bill at all stages. Abandonment of the principle of voluntary service, argued Arthur Greenwood, 'at the cost of creating new divisions within this country, is not merely fantastic, it is criminal'. 'We have lost, and Hitler has won,' declared Aneurin Bevan. 'He has deprived us of a very important English institution — voluntary service . . . What argument have they [the Government] to persuade the young men to fight except in another squalid attempt to defend themselves against a redistribution of international swag?'

Sloganeering of this kind, on the eve of World War II, is evidence of a curious time lag in thought. To some extent the Labour movement had become the victim of its own propaganda. For years, socialists had maintained that war was a purely capitalist institution, a struggle for economic power, the most profitable means of disposing of surplus production. This interpretation, although always oversimplified, had historic justification in the era of limited wars, but 1914 to 1918 had proved that total war was a deadly menace to the capitalist system. And the efforts of a British Government, thoroughly representative of capitalist interests, to buy off Hitler indicated a desperate anxiety to maintain peace. When Labour attacked Chamberlain as an appeaser, it was on strong ground: when simultaneously it strove to picture him as a war-monger, it promptly blew up its own case. Thus by the pursuit of contradictory policies, as well as by refusal to face squarely the implications of fascism, the Labour Party helped to confuse the public and incurred not a little responsibility for the tragic failure of the democracies to call a halt to Nazi aggression before it was too late.

CHAPTER V

UNDER THE UMBRELLA

THE victory of the National Government in 1931 opened up brighter vistas for British capitalism than it had known since 1914. At last its political representatives had united for a counter-offensive and, having subverted the enemy generals, had succeeded in recapturing the machinery of the State. Labour, if not completely crushed, seemed unlikely to recover rapidly from its wounds, so that the capitalist forces could count on a clear run of five years, probably ten, before they would again be seriously challenged. Thus they could concentrate on rebuilding the fortress of free enterprise without continually breaking off to repel Labour sorties.

Although an ex-Labour leader nominally headed the National Government and some important positions were held by Liberals, there was no doubt about which party controlled it. Eighty-five per cent of its vast array of supporters belonged to the Tory Party, which by itself composed three-quarters of the House of Commons. The Tories, therefore, had no need of allies but were prepared to tolerate them so long as they permitted the marketing of Tory products under a National label. This most of them were willing to do, though in the course of 1932 Snowden and the Samuel Liberals withdrew from the Government in protest against its tariff policies.

MacDonald, an increasingly unhappy and lonely man, whose once robust health was breaking down, stayed at 10 Downing Street until May 1935. He retained the trappings of power, but his influence on policy steadily diminished. His speeches, long noted for cloudy generalization, now became positively foggy — reflecting, perhaps, a difficulty in reconciling his past with his present — and finally reached a stage of semi-mystical incoherence which was visibly embarrassing to his colleagues. Great was the relief when he retired in favour of Stanley Baldwin, who had served since 1931 as deputy Prime Minister and had been the real head of the Government.

Next to Baldwin, the outstanding figure in the Cabinet was

DECADENCE OF BRITISH CAPITALISM

Neville Chamberlain, Chancellor of the Exchequer and *de facto* director of domestic policy. That policy included harsh treatment of the unemployed in the interests of economy but it was not as downright reactionary as some critics charged. Although the period 1932 to 1939 saw no new major social reforms, the building-up of the welfare state continued. A considerable number of Acts were passed consolidating and extending existing legislation in such fields as the regulation of working hours and factory conditions, workmen's compensation, health insurance, pensions and public health. Several measures providing financial assistance for slum-clearance enabled definite progress to be made before work was interrupted by the war.

Much of the drive for such reforms was supplied by Chamberlain, who, as a former municipal administrator, was particularly concerned about housing. His conservatism was not of the static variety: indeed, he liked to think of himself as a bit of a radical. 'How false is the suggestion,' he exclaimed to a Cambridge audience, 'that this is a safety-first government destitute of new ideas; and how in fact it is continually introducing changes of a really revolutionary character.'[1] Considering the profound structural alterations in economic institutions effected by State action during the 'thirties, we may agree. Yet the Chamberlain economic revolution was, to some extent at least, an involuntary one and its results — the rapid growth of State capitalism, sometimes referrred to as 'socialism of the right' — went well beyond the original intention of strengthening private enterprise by increasing its profitability. The aim of Chamberlain's economic policy, like that of his foreign policy after he became Prime Minister in 1937, was expressed by that unexciting symbol — the umbrella. It was to provide shelter for industry through fiscal protection, which has been well defined as 'the effort to maintain the *status quo* even at the sacrifice of the greater wealth which might be secured by readjustment'.[2] But since in the circumstances of the 'thirties readjustment could not be altogether avoided, Tory ministers found that planning by tariff involved more State intervention in the economy than they had bargained for.

[1] KEITH FEILING, *The Life of Neville Chamberlain.* Macmillan (London, 1946), p. 229.
[2] G. C. ALLEN, *British Industries and Their Organization.* Longmans, Green (London, 1939), p. 13.

In his 1936 Budget speech, Chamberlain reviewed with much satisfaction the improvement in national finance and trade during the four and a half years he had held office. 'The two main pillars of the policy,' he said, 'have been the introduction of the tariff and the establishment of cheap money.' It was, perhaps, a little brazen for a leading member of the National Government to claim credit for the second pillar, for it was depression that had made money cheap in the first place and devaluation of sterling that had kept interest rates low. Had the National Government achieved its expressed aim of keeping the pound tied to gold, it is inconceivable that in the first six months of 1932 the bank rate could have been reduced by successive stages to 2 per cent, a low point since 1897, nor could it have been held there through the period of recovery right up to the eve of World War II. Only when defence of a fixed exchange parity had been abandoned, was it possible for monetary management to relate the supply of credit to the needs of trade and industry.

The fortunate failure to 'save' sterling was thus the foundation of one of Chamberlain's greatest successes — conversion in 1932 of £2 billion 5 per cent War Loan to a $3\frac{1}{2}$ per cent basis. Together with some minor refunding operations, this coup made possible an annual saving in National Debt interest of some £40 million. Another major contribution of cheap money to the economy was a housing boom financed largely through the Building Societies, whose outstanding mortgage loans rose from £268 million in 1929 to £587 million in 1936. With the average rate of interest on such loans reduced from 6 to $4\frac{1}{2}$ per cent, home purchases became a possibility for large numbers of white-collar workers and even some wage earners. Altogether in the 9 years, 1931-39, 2,400,000 houses were built, three-quarters of them by private enterprise and the remainder by public authorities whose operations were also facilitated by low interest rates.

However, cheap money had less influence in promoting other forms of investment than might have been expected. The commercial banks had difficulty in finding outlets for their plentiful funds, and not until 1937 did the total of advances return to the 1929 level. Long-term private investment also lagged. According to the estimates of Colin Clark, net capital investment in 1907 was equal to 12.2 per cent of the national income, in 1929 to 7.2 per cent, and in 1935 to 6.9 per cent.[1] This trend did not reflect any lack of saving; in fact, other of Mr. Clark's calculations support Keynes's thesis that the propensity to save was steadily tending to outrun willingness to invest.[2] In 1934 Keynes had proposed that the Government should attempt to compensate for the inadequacy of private investment, which he regarded as a prime cause of unemployment, by a large development loan for housing, roads, and other useful public works. His advice was virtuously rejected by Chamberlain, who, strictly orthodox in his budgetary policies, frowned on all New Dealish pump-priming experiments. Consequently, the opportunity to arrange a fruitful marriage between cheap money and idle resources, represented in 1934 by over 2,000,000 unemployed, was missed. As Keynes wrote in 1937, when urging the Government to prepare for a new slump:

The capital requirements of home industry and manufacture cannot possibly absorb more than a fraction of what this country, with its present social structure and distribution of wealth, chooses to save in years of general prosperity; while the amount of our net foreign investment is limited by our exports and our trade balance. Building and transport and public utilities, which can use large amounts of capital, lie half-way between private and public control. They need, therefore, the combined stimulus of public policy and a low rate of interest . . . If we know what rate of interest is required to make profitable a flow of new projects at the proper pace, we have the power to make that rate prevail in the market. A low rate of interest can only be harmful and liable to cause an inflation if it is so low as to stimulate a flow of new projects more than enough to absorb our available resources.[3]

The setback in business, which Keynes had forecast, duly arrived in 1938. If it proved short-lived, that was because mounting international tension persuaded the Government to borrow heavily to pay for armaments. That, of course, is the one form of public investment which, offering no competition to the existing stock of capital and hence no threat to profits, is regarded as 'sound' by Treasury officials, bankers and businessmen in general.

None could deny Chamberlain full credit for the first of his

[1] COLIN CLARK, *National Income and Outlay*. Macmillan (London, 1938), p. 185.
[2] Ibid., pp. 187-91.
[3] *The Times*, 'How to Avoid a Slump', January 14th, 1937.

pillars of policy. The tariff programme was his by inheritance and, when he introduced the Import Duties Bill on February 4th, 1932, he exulted in fulfilment of the hopes of his father, Joseph Chamberlain. His bill provided for: (1) a general tariff of 10 per cent, *ad valorem*, subject to a small free list which included the staple foods and such raw materials as cotton and wool; (2) a statutory Import Duties Advisory Committee to make recommendations to the Treasury of higher or lower rates of duty on individual items. This measure, which was indeed revolutionary in that it shattered a fiscal tradition of some eighty years standing, was rushed through Parliament within a month.

No Chamberlain could consider the tariff a purely domestic question. Joseph's original dream had been one of an economically unified Empire, separated from the un-British world by a continuous tariff wall but as innocent of internal barriers as the United States. He had suffered rude awakening when the Dominions, asserting their fiscal independence, had obstinately insisted on protecting their infant industries from British as well as foreign competition. Nevertheless, the dream had stayed with him and he had bequeathed it to his sons. Thus filial devotion prompted Neville Chamberlain to arrange for an Imperial Economic Conference at Ottawa in the summer of 1932 and, pending its deliberations, he postponed application of the new tariff to the produce of Empire countries.

The Ottawa Agreement, initialled on August 20th, 1932, was hailed by Chamberlain as 'the crowning achievement of a year wonderful in endeavour'. His biographer, more soberly, declares: 'The conference was not a failure, yet neither was it a success,' and writes of it as a 'disillusioning' experience for him.[1] The Dominions proved no more willing than thirty years before to reduce substantially, for the benefit of British industry, the margin of protection afforded to their own manufacturers. At the same time their claims for a preferred share of British food and raw-materials markets were embarrassing to Chamberlain and his Tory colleagues. Even the most docile 'National' Liberals, not to mention the great consuming public, were likely to rebel at high taxes on food. Besides, the interests of British farmers had to be taken into account: from their point of view imports of cheap

[1] KEITH FEILING, op. cit., pp. 211-12.

wheat and meat were just as obnoxious when they originated in Canada or New Zealand as when they came from the United States or the Argentine.

Reconciliation of all the conflicting interests whose spokesmen thronged the Ottawa lobbies proved impossible; but concessions by both sides prevented a deadlock although the agreement fell considerably short of Chamberlain's hopes. Several Dominions removed special tariff surcharges imposed during the depression and increased the preferential position of British goods, usually by raising the duties payable by foreigners. Britain, for its part, conceded continued free entry to over 80 per cent of all Empire imports, and undertook to place new or increased duties on foreign wheat, butter, eggs, fruits, linseed and unwrought copper in order to improve the competitive status of Empire producers of these commodities. Further, for the benefit of both British and Dominion farmers, foreign imports of meat were to be restricted by quotas.

Changes in the direction of trade during the next six years suggest that the Dominions and colonies gained more from the Ottawa Agreement than the Mother Country. Comparing 1930 (the last fairly normal year before Britain abandoned free trade) with 1938, we find that the Empire increased exports to Great Britain by 22 per cent in value and its share of the British import market rose from 29 to 40 per cent. By contrast, while the percentage of British exports taken by Empire countries increased from 43.5 to 50 per cent, their absolute total fell by 5 per cent. For Britain's long-ailing export industries, the fruits of Ottawa were disappointingly scanty.

In recommending the Import Duties Bill to the House of Commons, Chamberlain claimed that 'moderate protection' offered the country three major advantages:

(1) It would help correct an adverse balance of payments and so provide insurance against depreciation of sterling to an extent that would cause a large increase in the cost of imported essentials.

(2) It would fortify the revenue by a method fair to all sections of the community.

(3) It would assist agriculture and industry by transferring to them work 'now done elsewhere' and 'thereby decrease

256

unemployment in the only satisfactory way in which it could be diminished'.

Naturally the tariff produced some revenue — enough to permit a small reduction in income tax in 1934 and to restore the 1931 cuts in unemployment benefit and government salaries. But the question of how far protection served to strengthen sterling and to increase employment is more debatable. The fact that there was no collapse of the pound and that, after 1933 unemployment gradually diminished is far from proof positive of Chamberlain's case, since other economic developments must be taken into account.

During the first two tariff years, when unemployment was still at its worst and consuming power was low, imports certainly declined more steeply than exports. But they also increased fairly rapidly when the tide turned, while export trade remained stagnant. As a result, Britain's merchandize deficit rose from £287 million in 1932 to £501 million in 1937, the most prosperous year of the 'thirties. For a time the gap was filled by recovery in foreign investment income, shipping receipts, and other 'invisible' items, but in the last years before World War II, Britain was forced to liquidate foreign capital assets to sustain its balance of payments. Whether this point would have been reached earlier, except for the discouragement of imports by the tariff, it is hard to say.

In any case, little more than twelve months after the passing of the Import Duties Act, the United States lowered the gold value of the dollar and Chamberlain grew anxious lest too swift a rise in sterling should start a new deflation. British policy, he told the World Economic Conference in 1933, was to raise prices from their unduly depressed state. Unfortunately, tariffs were not helpful for this purpose. The new fence around what had been the world's freest and largest market caused a further shrinkage in international commerce and spurred other nations to heighten their trade barriers. More and more countries in the 'thirties adopted more and more tortuous devices to repel foreign goods from their shores while simultaneously pressing their own products on the world market. The inevitable result was the accumulation of unmanageable surpluses of primary commodities which exerted a terrific downward thrust on prices.

Since prices of British imports fell much more steeply than

R   B.C.   257

those of its exports, a given volume of British manufactures exchanged for a larger quantity of food and raw materials. But this improvement in 'the terms of trade' was not wholly advantageous. It meant the impoverishment of Britain's traditional trade partners, the producers of primary products, forcing them to restrict their consumption of British goods. Thus while cheap food tended to raise the living standards of those with jobs, it contributed to chronic unemployment among men who normally worked for the export market. If the new tariff transferred to Britain some work formerly 'done elsewhere', it also, in combination with the tariffs of all the other nations, served to reduce the total amount of productive labour everywhere. An entry in Chamberlain's diary, dated February 17th, 1934, shows he had some inkling of this difficulty:

The largest problem I see in front of us is what is to be the future of international trade. It has shrunk to $\frac{1}{3}$ of what it was in 1929. Is it going to recover, or is the spirit and practice of economic nationalism going to prevail, and each country try to live by taking in its own washing?[1]

In Britain unemployment reached an all-time peak in January 1933, and thereafter declined steadily until 1937, when the number actually at work was slightly higher than in 1929. This increase in jobs, however, was smaller than the increase in working population, so that the total on the unemployment registers still exceeded that of early 1929. Moreover, this seemingly irreducible residue, amounting to some 10 per cent of the whole labour force, was concentrated in those districts that had been almost continually depressed since 1921 — Wales, Scotland, Tyneside, Lancashire, Cumberland — the homes of the major export industries.

Tariff-making is a form of economic planning, a means by which resources of labour and capital are diverted from one kind of production to another, which the State wishes to encourage. In Britain, in 1932, the objective of the Government was to increase the profitability of certain key industries, allegedly injured by foreign competition and, in general, to make the country rather more self-sufficient. It soon discovered that tariffs by themselves were an inadequate tool: it was, moreover, faced by demands to 'do something' for sections of the economy which were hurt

[1] KEITH FEILING, op. cit., p. 229.

rather than helped by a protectionist system. As a result the next eight years saw a rapid, if rather haphazard, development of State intervention, regulation and control, which sensibly modified the economic structure of the country.

Two vital branches of industry unfavourably affected by tariffs were shipping and shipbuilding, which found themselves with fewer imports to carry, and exposed in a world of shrinking trade to increasingly bitter competition. There was talk of reviving the Navigation Acts and reserving certain Empire routes for vessels flying the British flag. But the British mercantile marine, as a common international carrier, was too exposed to retaliation for that course to be adopted. As an alternative, the Government provided subsidies to tramp steamers and set up a 'scrap and build' scheme to give shipowners willing to scrap two old vessels financial assistance in buying a new one. Loans and insurance guarantees were also made available to the Cunard Line to help build the 'Queens'.

Coal mining, with its large export surplus, was another unprotectable industry. However, the Government attempted to aid it through use of the bargaining power which the tariff afforded. Thus a trade agreement signed in 1933 allotted Denmark a guaranteed proportion of British bacon imports and a minimum butter quota in return for a pledge that at least least 80 per cent of Danish coal imports would be obtained from Britain. Similar arrangements were made with a number of other countries but, since the result was intensified German and Polish competition elsewhere, the benefit to the British mines was dubious. Moreover, bilateral bartering of this kind set a dangerous precedent.

The coal owners were compensated to some extent for loss of foreign markets by restricted competition at home. Through the 'thirties, district marketing boards, authorized by the Coal Mines Act of 1930 (see page 237), continued to fix prices and limit production. Unfortunately, by sustaining submarginal producers and diminishing incentives to efficiency, this scheme hindered the task of the Coal Mines Reorganization Commission, established by the same Act. In 1936, therefore, the Government introduced a bill to enlarge the Commission's powers, but the ruggedly individualistic coal owners inspired a back bench Tory revolt which killed it. Two years later, however, an Act was passed nationalizing coal-royalties, an essential preliminary to any large-scale programme for concentrating production in the most efficient pits. Then the war prevented any further test of the possibility of State-supervised voluntary re-organization.

The Government was equally unsuccessful in realizing its declared hope of using tariff leverage as a method of rationalizing and modernizing the iron and steel industry. In April 1932, the Import Duties Advisory Committee recommended duties of 20 per cent on finished steel goods and $33\frac{1}{3}$ per cent on primary and semi-finished products. This assistance was supposed to be temporary and conditional on early adoption by the industry of a programme for technical re-organization which would lower costs to the level of up-to-date continental producers. But there are few things more adhesive than a tariff and, after several short-period renewals, the Government agreed in 1934 to make the rates permanent.

By that time trade associations representing various branches of the industry had been brought together in the British Iron and Steel Federation. The zeal of this new body in promoting technical progress was hardly as conspicuous as the energy it devoted to 'stabilizing the market', a process which, when undertaken by private enterprise, always seems to mean higher prices. In pursuit of this end, the Federation in 1935 signed a treaty with the continental steel cartel, whose members reluctantly agreed to restrict imports to Britain when the Treasury, to 'facilitate negotiations', suddenly announced a further increase in the tariff. With foreign competition thus curbed and demand rising, the industry was able to raise average prices by 39 per cent in the next three years.

Admittedly, the resultant expansion of earnings stimulated new investment in the industry which led to some improvement in average efficiency. But protection plus cartelization also encouraged continued operation of obsolete facilities while hindering capacity use of low-cost plants. In addition, high steel prices handicapped other industries, particularly in export markets, and probably inhibited the realization of some capital projects requiring large quantities of steel. All in all, the steel tariff provided a prime example of the way protection tends to freeze the *status quo* and foster monopolies which, sooner or later, the community is compelled to regulate or destroy. There appears, in fact, to be a direct link between Chamberlain's Import Duties Act of 1932 and G. R. Strauss's Steel Nationalization Bill of 1948.

Some of the most elaborate planning of the 'thirties was designed to give a larger share of the national income to agriculture. This was indeed a depressed occupation. For years, both the population employed on the land and the cultivated acreage had been shrinking, for only the most efficient farmers working on the best soils could hope to compete with imported wheat and meat. However, to restore agriculture to the point at which it could supply even 50 per cent of home food requirements called for higher duties than urban consumers would tolerate: nor would such duties be really protective unless they applied to Empire as well as foreign products.

Consequently the Government soon abandoned the tariff as the main instrument of agricultural revival and relied instead on a combination of controls and restrictions which made farming the most regulated of all occupations. It would take a whole chapter even to outline the different schemes, many of them exceedingly complicated, adopted for each of the principal foods by authority of the Agricultural Marketing Act of 1933 and subsequent ancillary measures. It is enough to say that numerous boards and commissions were created to guide both production and distribution. In some cases tariffs were supplemented by import quotas, in others by subsidies. Farmers whose woes sprang not from foreign competition but from 'overproduction', the dairymen and the potato growers, for instance, had to be prevented from competing among themselves. Thus a Milk Marketing Board fixed minimum prices and decided how much milk could be sold in 'liquid' form: a Potato Marketing Board allotted 'acreage quotas' to established growers and penalized newcomers tempted by high prices.

Eight years of Tory economic planning strengthened British capitalism in only one important respect: it helped the recipients of rent, interest and profit to secure temporarily a larger share of the cake.[1] But this gain was achieved by State intervention on a

[1] Colin Clark estimates rent, interest and profit at 31.6 per cent of home-produced income in 1929, 29.2 per cent in 1932, and 34.5 per cent in 1935. (*National Income and Outlay*, p. 94.) The official series of the Central Statistical Office, which is not strictly comparable, shows that in 1938, the first year for which its figures are available, these items comprised 37 per cent of private income after taxes. (*Annual Abstract of Statistics*, No. 84, 1935-46.)

scale difficult to reconcile with the theory of private enterprise, which asserts that the real test of economic efficiency is ability to make a profit in a free market. How could that test apply when the market was rigged by means of tariffs, doles to industry, legal restriction of competition, and deliberate instigation of monopoly?

The fact was that the Tory Party, seeking an alternative to socialism, had resuscitated the mercantilist system — collectivism for the well to do — sweetening it for the masses with an admixture of social reform. Conceived as a remedy for ailing capitalism, this treatment proved fatal to the patient. Under the artificial sun lamps of a protective State, private enterprise became less and less enterprising and ever riper for socialization.

Economically decadent as it was, British capitalism might have withstood for a time the challenge of the 'internal proletariat' if it had been able to avoid a clash with the 'external proletariat', represented by the 'have-not nations' in general and Germany in particular. The necessity of doing so was well understood by the upper classes, who, if not strictly speaking pacifist, were as unbelligerent in the 'thirties as at any time in British history. The commercial jingoism conspicuous prior to 1914 was no longer prevalent, for businessmen had learnt that total war could not be a paying proposition. A new conflict, whether or not it encompassed the physical destruction of the country, as many feared it might, would surely mean the rise of taxation to ruinous heights, tightening of the State's grip on private enterprise, and further drastic modifications of the social and economic structure.

The Labour movement, as we noted in the last chapter, was equally wedded to peace, both on general principles and for fear that war might lead to a reactionary dictatorship. In fact, the nation at large was so loath to take up arms again that for a long time it refused to understand the significance of the Nazi revolution. Thus, ironically, the very ardour of the desire for peace in Britain and in the other democracies made war inevitable. Hitler's first aggressive moves could almost certainly have been exposed as bluffs had they been boldly called. But Britain, the greatest power in the League of Nations, failed to give a lead, unwilling to incur even the slightest risk of having to back collective security with force.

Neville Chamberlain is now regarded as the arch-appeaser, but it is only fair to note that his policy was inherited from his predecessors, MacDonald and Baldwin. Indeed, when he became Prime Minister in May 1937, the odds against a bloodless halt to Fascist aggression were already long. Prior to that time, determined and united action by Britain and France on any one of several occasions when broken pieces of the Versailles Treaty were rudely hurled at them might have ended the Hitler myth. One chance was lost in March 1935 when Germany returned to conscription and the *Luftwaffe's* creation was announced. That merely produced a solemn conference of British, French and Italian statesmen who agreed in a wordy resolution to uphold 'collective maintenance of peace' and oppose 'unilateral repudiation of treaties'.

Twelve months later Hitler denounced the Locarno Agreement and ordered the *Reichswehr* to reoccupy the Rhineland — another flagrant breach of the Treaty of Versailles. This was a direct threat to French security, and the first impulse of the current French Government was to mobilize and march. Unfortunately, it hesitated and decided to consult London before making a move. In great alarm the British Cabinet refused to commit itself to any definite support of France and invited Flandin, French Foreign Minister, to come and talk matters over. When he arrived, he urged strongly the importance of stopping Germany now: it might well be the last chance. But he found few who accepted this view. 'Talked to Flandin,' Chamberlain notes in his diary (March 12th, 1936), 'emphasizing that public opinion here would not support us in sanctions of any kind. His view is that if a firm front is maintained by France and England, Germany will yield without war. We cannot accept this as a reliable estimate of a mad dictator's reactions.'[1] Baldwin, still Prime Minister, told his French visitor: 'If there is even one chance in a hundred that war would follow from your police operation, I have not the right to commit England.'[2] We now know that

---

[1] KEITH FEILING, op. cit., p. 279.
[2] WINSTON S. CHURCHILL, *The Second World War, The Gathering Storm*. Cassell (London, 1938), p. 154.

Flandin was right: Hitler had promised his generals to withdraw from the Rhineland at the first sign of real opposition.

In support of their claim that the British public would not stand for sanctions against an aggressor, if that involved any risk of war, Baldwin and his colleagues were apt to refer to the 'Peace Ballot' sponsored by the League of Nations Union in the summer of 1935. This attempt to gauge public opinion on fundamental foreign policies had attracted enormous interest. Well over 11 million persons voted on one or more of the questions posed on the ballot and a vast majority indicated support for the League of Nations, for all-round reduction of armaments by international agreement, for abolition of military aircraft, for prohibition of private manufacture of arms, and for use of 'economic and non-military sanctions' against 'a nation [which] insists on attacking another'. On the matter of military sanctions 'if necessary', opinion was more divided, but even so there were 6,833,803 'yeas' to 2,366,184 'nays'. As Churchill has said, the ballot affirmed 'a positive and courageous policy which could, at this time, have been followed with an overwhelming measure of national support'.[1]

The fact that the British public, although opposed to war as an instrument of national policy, was ready to take risks to check an aggressor was demonstrated when Italy invaded Ethiopia in October 1936. Great enthusiasm was aroused by the strong line on collective security which was at first taken by the British delegation to the League of Nations Assembly. Nor was the public dismayed when simultaneous naval concentrations in the Mediterranean suggested that this time words were to be backed by deeds. Rather there was disappointment because the economic sanctions actually proclaimed seemed carefully calculated to cause Italy no more than inconvenience.

Later it became obvious that the British Government's spasm of energetic leadership was little more than electoral window dressing. Baldwin had decided to call a general election in November 1935 and, in view of the Peace Ballot, to stress in his programme support of the League and collective security. If this policy was to have an air of conviction, some demonstration at Geneva was necessary. But once the Government had secured a

[1] WINSTON S. CHURCHILL, op. cit., pp. 132-3.

new mandate, with a reduced though still handsome majority, it relaxed. Only a few weeks later, Sir Samuel Hoare, British Foreign Secretary, who had addressed such brave words to the League about resistance to unprovoked aggression, was conniving with the French Foreign Minister, Pierre Laval, in a plan to reward the Italian aggressor by conceding to him control of a large part of Ethiopia. Details of this scheme leaked out prematurely, causing such a storm in press and Parliament that the Baldwin Government was forced to jettison both Hoare and his plan. Nevertheless, Baldwin clung to his determination to oppose all sanctions that might possibly involve Britain in war; and Mussolini's legions advanced on Addis Ababa according to schedule.

So a great opportunity to establish the authority of the League of Nations was lost. There can be little doubt that really determined enforcement of sanctions, including a denial of oil supplies, would have stopped Mussolini. If he had been rash enough to act on his threats to resist forcibly, the combined British and French fleets would have been more than a match for his navy: his armies in East Africa could have been cut off and Italy itself blockaded. Had this been done, it is probable that the Fascist regime would have collapsed, giving an eloquent warning to Hitler. As it was, the fiasco of sanctions against Italy reinforced Nazi contempt for the League and the democracies which nominally supported it. It led to creation of the Berlin-Rome Axis while increasing mutual distrust between Britain and France. And the Hoare-Laval plan, temporarily abortive as it was, provided a model for the Munich Pact, which later delivered Czechoslovakia into Hitler's grasping hands.

In May 1937, when Chamberlain replaced Baldwin as Prime Minister, he wrote in a private letter: 'I believe the double policy of rearmament and better relations with Germany and Italy will carry us safely through the danger period.'[1] This assumption that time could be bought by appeasement proved fallacious. Better relations with Germany, at least, could be secured only by acquiescence in the successive coups from which Hitler gained both prestige and tangible assests. Annexation of Austria gave him a new source of manpower, important raw materials, and, above all, strategic facilities for his campaign against the Czechs:

[1] KEITH FEILING, op. cit., p. 319.

Munich produced another three million *Volksdeutsche* and subtracted forty first-class divisions from the military potential of the democracies: the final seizure of all Czechoslovakia placed in his hands a large and efficient munitions industry. Thus, even though the pace of British rearmament was gradually accelerated after 1936, Germany continued to extend its lead. Time worked for Hitler, not Chamberlain.

In any event, the British Prime Minster could not match Germany's economic mobilization for rearmament. At the end of 1936 he had written: 'If we were now to follow Winston's advice and sacrifice our commerce to the manufacture of arms, we should inflict a certain injury on our trade from which it would take generations to recover, we should destroy the confidence which now happily exists, and we should cripple the revenue.'[1] Besides, the double policy posed an insoluble problem in public relations. In order to win support for appeasement, Chamberlain had to play down the Nazi danger and profess faith in Hitler's palpably false assurances of peaceful intentions: to gain backing for even a moderate arms programme, he had to convince the people that threats to peace made this an urgent necessity. It was impossible to resolve this contradiction, to grasp with equal firmness the umbrella and the big stick.

The story of the last phase of appeasement is a familiar one and there is no need to follow it step by step to its bitter ending. What concerns us are the mental and emotional processes which led the upper classes as a whole to support so fatal a course. How came they to reject the traditional foreign policy of their ancestors — the policy of unshakable opposition to any power that sought to dominate Europe? How could they deceive themselves into thinking that Hitler's ambitions were limited and that, unlike other successful blackmailers, he would be satisfied by one or two modest payments? It has already been suggested that one upper-class motive was the perfectly reasonable belief that another war would destroy the existing social and economic system. But, as Churchill and a few others recognized, the only way to avoid war was to halt the Third Reich before it had gathered strength.

The question arises, therefore: Was it merely because of inertia and lack of foresight that Churchill's warnings were ignored, or

KEITH FEILING, op. cit., p. 314.

was judgment distorted by a conflict between patriotism and ideology? Certainly there was one upper-class group whose support of appeasement was joined with acceptance of all or part of the Nazi creed. Among the members of such organizations as 'The Link' and 'The Anglo-German Fellowship' were men who defended Hitler, Mussolini and Franco on all occasions, cultivated the friendship of Nazi leaders, applauded suppression of the German labour movement, and advocated an Anglo-German alliance. Although relatively small, this pro-Nazi element was influential, including, as it did, a considerable number of Members of Parliament and Peers and some of the most powerful bankers and industrialists in the country.[1]

Most of Chamberlain's followers — the real umbrella brigade — were not in any sense pro-Nazi. In fact, they considered Hitler a vulgar upstart and regarded Nazism as thoroughly 'un-British'. But they were also isolationists who wanted to believe that Britain could steer clear of continental squabbles. Moreover, they hated and dreaded Communism more than Nazism and were fearful lest the overthrow of Hitler might create a vacuum in Central Europe for Soviet Russia to fill. That, perhaps, was a major cause of the blindness and paralysis of judgment that afflicted the ruling classes during the appeasement era.

The temper of the general public began to stiffen very soon after Munich. When he returned to London bringing what he claimed was 'peace in our time', Chamberlain was greeted with genuine enthusiasm, but the vast relief of the people at their narrow escape from war was succeeded by scepticism and disillusion. Hitler's refusal to honour even the slight safeguards provided for the Czechs by the Munich Agreement, and his continued contemptuous attacks on the democracies, gave warning that conflict had been postponed, not averted. And before the end of the year there was another eye-opening event — a new and terrible pogrom against the German Jews.

However, the umbrella brigade held its ranks until March 14th, 1939, when Czechoslovakia was occupied by the *Reichswehr* and proclaimed a German protectorate. Chamberlain's first

[1] It is fair to add that there is no evidence of 'Fifth Column' activity by this group during the war, though one or two of the more extreme members of 'The Link' were locked up as a precautionary measure.

reaction was mild indeed: on March 16th, he was not even prepared to assure the House of Commons that he would protest to Berlin. His indecision troubled his followers, and a cynically appeasing speech by Sir John Simon, Chancellor of the Exchequer, the same evening, positively angered them. In Parliament, as throughout the country, there were signs of revolt, while inside the Cabinet a bloc led by Lord Halifax, Foreign Secretary, insisted on a change of policy. Chamberlain bowed to the storm. In a speech at Birmingham on March 17th, he dropped his umbrella at last and indicated both his awareness of an 'attempt to dominate the world by force' and his determination to resist it.

Chamberlain still refused to admit, even to himself, that war was inevitable, but in fact it was far, far too late to stop Hitler by any other means. Nothing now could prevent a conflict which, whatever the outcome, British capitalism could hardly expect to survive.

PART FIVE

THE LAST DAYS OF
BRITISH CAPITALISM

ONE WAR TOO MANY

FOR Britain the Second World War was 'total' in a much fuller sense than the First. Once the struggle had passed its 'phoney' stage, there was never any question of business as usual, trade unionism as usual, or anything else as usual. For a time the nation stood alone, supported only by the Commonwealth, against a foe who appeared as strong as he was ruthless. The island was both front-line and base, under heavy bombardment, partially blockaded, threatened with imminent invasion. Nothing less than complete mobilization of resources, human and material, could match the dangers of this hour or satisfy a people determined never to surrender.

It was a far more popular war than the struggle against the Kaiser's Germany, though accompanied by far less flag waving. There was no question this time of the masses blindly following upper-class leaders into action. From the beginning the workers grasped the fact that survival of the whole democratic way of life was at stake and they did not need to be aroused by parades and propaganda. It was, indeed, a Labour leader, Arthur Greenwood, who 'spoke for England' in the Commons, amid cheers from all sides, when on September 3rd, 1939, thirty-six hours after the invasion of Poland, the Government appeared to be hesitating to honour the pledges which it had made to that unlucky country.

Such opposition as there was to the war was to be found only at the polar fringes of public life. On the right, Mosley and his handful of British Fascists parroted the Nazi line by blaming the war on the Jews and supported the 'peace offensive' launched by Goebbels once Poland was crushed. On the left, the Communist Party first decided to join the struggle against Fascism, but rapidly changed fronts on re-establishing communications with Moscow and learning that the Nazi-Soviet pact had changed the war's nature. Naturally, it switched sides again when Hitler attacked Russia. The I.L.P., clinging to old slogans, steadily opposed a 'capitalist-imperialist war'; but it was now merely the sliver of a splinter, with nothing like the influence among the workers it had possessed in 1914-18.

From the outset, the political and industrial sections of the Labour movement gave the Government full co-operation except in one particular: the Labour Party was not willing to accept Chamberlain's offer of places in the Cabinet. This refusal was due to lack of confidence in the Prime Minister, who was suspected, perhaps unjustly, of a certain lukewarmness in carrying on the war, and even of readiness to negotiate with the enemy if an opportunity presented itself. Moreover, the Labour Party wished to be free to apply a critical spur to the lumbering progress of economic mobilization.

On paper a large part of the apparatus for the organization of production, the allocation of resources, and the control of manpower which existed at the close of World War I was rapidly reinstated. In practice, however, the Government did not utilize these powers fully in the first six months, with the result that the opportunity to expand output offered by the sinister pause between the conquest of Poland and the invasion of Norway was partially wasted. At this time there was manpower to spare, but the authorities seemed unable to direct it to productive work. As late as March 19th, 1940, Clement Attlee was complaining in the House of Commons that there were still 1,400,000 men unemployed and that precious steel was being used to build cinemas. In the course of the same debate a Tory member furnished an example of the lackadaisical manner in which financial questions were handled. Any foreigner, other than an enemy, he pointed out, could sell securities in London and transfer the proceeds abroad. Since the Chancellor of the Exchequer, as Churchill mentions in *The Gathering Storm*, was already groaning about dwindling dollar resources, this failure to establish complete control of the foreign exchanges was certainly an amazing omission.

No doubt the atmosphere during these months when, except at sea, the war appeared suspended was inimical to intense effort. Britain had been keyed up in September 1939 to resist immediate fierce attack: immense air-raids had been expected, an early clash along the French frontier. When the Germans remained inactive, the Allies followed suit. They were hardly ready to force the pace and, in any case, both Chamberlain and the French Premier Daladier, wished to stay on the defensive. The initiative, therefore, remained in Hitler's hands and, when he prolonged the *Sitzkreig*, Britain tended to pass from puzzlement to relaxation. It was an imaginative strategy and, had *Der Führer* persevered with it, he might almost have bored Britain into talking peace.

The Nazi hammer blows that began to fall in April 1940 with the invasion of Denmark and Norway provided a terrible but stimulating shock. From all sides came demands for a change in men and methods, which culminated on May 8th, with what was in effect a Labour motion of censure on the Government. It was defeated by a relatively small margin. Over fifty Tories voted with the Opposition and many others abstained. There could be no doubt that Chamberlain had ceased to command the confidence of both Parliament and public and two days later he resigned.

Only one man could possibly succeed him. Technically, Churchill, as First Lord of the Admiralty, was as much to blame for the Norwegian disaster as any minister, and in the censure debate, loyally defending Chamberlain, he accepted full responsibility. Yet it was felt intuitively that he alone had the proper qualifications for leadership at this hour — the drive, the offensive spirit, the ability to unite the country for a supreme effort. When he asked Attlee and Greenwood to join his War Cabinet, they agreed at once and the Labour Party Annual Conference, then in session, endorsed their decision by a tremendous majority. Rather more than one-third of the places in the Government were filled by Labour men, with three of them, Bevin, Morrison and Hugh Dalton, assuming responsibility for key economic tasks as Ministers of Labour, Supply and Economic Warfare respectively.

At the very moment that this new and truly National Government was taking over, the Germans struck at the Low Countries and France. In the next few weeks one catastrophe followed another until, by the end of June, Britain, deprived of allies, faced the prospect of imminent invasion of its thinly defended coasts. The Navy was intact; the Air Force, despite heavy losses in the Battle of France, had maintained at Churchill's insistence its essential home reserve. But the Army had been stripped of a large part of its heavy weapons in the evacuation of Dunkirk, and there was not even a stock of small arms for the spontaneously organized Home Guard.

American aid was to make good a part of these deficiencies, but, in the main, the crying need for production and more production could only be satisfied by the toil and sweat of the British workers. The problem was to bring men and tools together and make sure that nothing interfered with the most efficient use of both. 'The Government demands,' Attlee told the House of Commons on May 22nd, 1940, 'complete control over persons and property; not just some persons and some particular sections of the community, but of all persons, rich and poor, employers and workers, men and women, and all property.'

From this point on, Britain's war economy was organized, by general consent, on broadly socialist lines. Private interest gave way before communal necessity. The kinds and amounts of goods produced were determined not by the market but in accordance with the plans of the State. More than half the real national income was devoted directly or indirectly to the war effort: the reduced balance available for civilian consumption was distributed so as to insure priority for basic requirements for health and efficiency of the whole population. Something approaching an equalitarian regime was established. The power of large incomes to command goods and services was greatly diminished by taxation and rationing, while living standards of low income groups were raised above prewar levels.

What did complete control of persons and property, as it developed in the course of war, actually imply? To a skilled mechanic it was likely to mean working wherever the Ministry of Labour decided he could be most usefully employed. He might be told to stay at his job or he might be shifted to a different one in a different plant, perhaps in another part of the country. He could not change his employment of his own volition and he was liable to prosecution if he stayed away from work without a valid excuse. If he and his fellow-workers were dissatisfied with wages and other conditions, they could not down tools: failing a negotiated agreement with their employer, they had to abide by the decision of an arbitration board. On the other hand, he was guaranteed 'the rate for the job' and the Government made itself responsible for his welfare in many respects.

A worker in a non-essential industry, whose operations were restricted by Government order, might find his job at an end. He would have to look for a new one through his local Employment Exchange and might be required to take a training course if his existing skills were not those urgently needed. All adults, men and women, of working age were obligated to register for national service and might be directed, under penalty, to accept a particular job. Married women were not, however, forced to go to work far from their homes and those with young children were exempt. Women without family responsibilities, on the other hand, could be ordered to employment in distant parts of the country.

Employers were just as much under orders as their employees. The owner of an engineering plant could not decide what would be the most profitable lines to manufacture but had to adapt his production schedules to Government plans. If he failed to do so, he could be denied raw materials and manpower; his machine tools could be seized and removed to some other plant; his very buildings could be commandeered. When he signed a contract with the Government, he became subject to directions from the Factory Inspectorate of the Ministry of Labour in regard to working conditions. He might be ordered to provide certain health and first-aid services or, if he employed upwards of 250 persons, to install a canteen.

As long as he was co-operative, the owner of a plant suited to the production of war material in its manifold forms was probably sure of orders. But the manufacturer of civilian goods, or the businessman supplying civilian services, was likely to find his trade subjected to compulsory slimming. The owner of a clothing factory, for example, was first given a production quota — some fraction of his prewar output. Then, in 1941, he was called upon to assist in the concentration of industry — a policy adopted to reduce the waste of manpower and factory space caused by many plants operating on a part-time basis. If he received a 'nucleus certificate' he was required to produce the quotas of firms that were closed, providing them either with actual goods or a share of the profits. Later, when the quota system was abandoned, he had to comform to specific instructions of the Board of Trade in regard to the quantity and quality of his output and devote a large share

275

of his facilities either to the production of 'utility' articles or to filling export and Government orders.

Regimentation of labour and industry in this manner naturally led to some losses through friction. On the whole, however, it worked surprisingly well. One reason was that its purpose was well understood and almost unanimously approved. Then, too, the method of the responsible Government departments was normally to reach a desired end by voluntary agreement, either with individuals or representative groups. Had they depended mainly on their coercive powers, they would never have achieved the results they did. It was private zeal under public direction that made it possible for Britain to attain greater efficiency in the pursuit of total war than did the totalitarian states themselves.

The effective conscription of both labour and capital was, of course, on a temporary basis; it was 'for the duration' only. Trade-union privileges were suspended on the understanding that they would be restored in full after the war: owners of productive property were assured that control and direction would not affect their title deeds. When Churchill formed his National Government there seems to have been a 'gentlemen's agreement' among the parties with Tory endorsement of profit-limitations and a policy of 'fair shares', offset by Labour's willingness not to press nationalization of industry as a war measure. In any event, there was no attempt to make the war an excuse for the introduction of fundamental changes in economic institutions.

No one, however, could guarantee a complete return to the *status quo ante*. For one thing, the economic effects of the war were such as to force extensive alterations in the future pattern of production and distribution no matter what the political complexion of postwar governments might prove to be. Six years of intense struggle were to drain the country of its foreign resources and seriously to deplete its domestic capital. That, as we shall see, raised problems which could not, in an advanced democratic State, be solved by capitalist methods.

Nor could the revolution in distribution of income, developed in a semi-siege economy, be swept away with the return of peace, if only because it had exercised so powerful an influence on popular thinking. The cost of the war from 1940 to 1945 absorbed about half the current production of goods and services in Britain —

almost all that could be taken while leaving the civilian population a standard of living that was tolerable, if austere. That
required specifically a reduction in aggregate personal consumption
of 16 per cent in 1944 as compared with 1938, although money
incomes, after direct taxes, were some 50 per cent higher. If the
distribution of the limited supply of goods available had been
determined by bidding in the open market, the pressure on prices
would have been terrific. Obviously, the Government had to take
steps to prevent inflation, and it could not achieve this end by
enforcing an equal percentage cut in everybody's consumption.
That would have meant depriving the well-to-do merely of some
of the superfluities while reducing many of the poor to a level
below bare subsistence. Moreover, quite apart from considerations of social justice, a crudely mathematical interpretation of
'equality of sacrifice' was incompatible with efficiency. Full production required the labour of every able-bodied man not in the
fighting services and that of as many women as possible. And this
working force had to be supplied at least with the essentials of
physical health if the war effort were not to suffer.

Before 1939, most of the unemployed and many of those with
jobs had not steadily enjoyed that minimum. Sir John Orr in 1936
had estimated that about half the population could not afford an
adequate diet and that nearly one-third suffered from definite
malnutrition. Seebohm Rowntree and other social investigators
of the inter-war period had published surveys indicating that
from 20 to 30 per cent of the working class were below 'the poverty
line'.[1]

Planned wartime distribution of real income posed, therefore,
the problem of dividing a diminished national cake in such a
way that some sections of the population received considerably
larger, and others considerably smaller, slices than in peacetime.
The solution required use of such tools as rationing, price control,
subsidies and taxation, in addition to an extension of communal
services. Price control covered most articles of common consumption. All important foods were included and most of them, with
the exception of bread and potatoes, were rationed either quanti-
tatively or on the point system. A basic minimum diet for all

[1] For a summary of these investigations see G. D. H. COLE and RAYMOND POSTGATE
The Common People, 1746-1946. Methuen (London, 1946), pp. 640-7.

was made a first charge on supplies. Higher costs of both imported and home-produced food, had they been reflected in prices, would, however, have put the full ration out of reach of the lowest income groups and stimulated demands for more wages. Hence resort to subsidies which held down the rise in retail food prices between 1939 and 1945 to 23 per cent although wholesale prices increased 62.6 per cent.

Efficiency and social utility dictated the issue of special rations to certain categories of the population. For example, expectant mothers and young children were entitled to extra quantities of milk and eggs and also benefited by a free distribution of cod-liver oil and fruit juice.[1] Children and young people from five to eighteen received a larger milk ration than adults, further supplemented for many by a daily distribution in the schools. Agricultural labourers, miners and certain other manual workers were permitted extra cheese for lunch sandwiches. Those employed in the larger factories could be certain of a square meal daily at low cost in the canteens, which were allotted rationed foods on a higher scale than ordinary catering establishments. Differentiation in another field was restriction of purchases of utility furniture (the only kind made after December 31st, 1942) to the newly married and the 'bombed-out', who could also procure 'priority-dockets' for such scarce articles as blankets and floor coverings.

The one important price not ultimately subjected to direct control was the price of labour — an omission for which the Government was severely criticized. Indirectly, however, the ban on strikes and the existence of price ceilings set fairly strict limits to wage increases negotiated between employers and their employees. Several million workers were covered by agreements which linked advances in pay to the cost-of-living index, and in all trades this factor had a marked influence on wage scales. However, some categories of workers, whose peacetime remuneration had been exceptionally low, for example miners and farm labourers, had to be granted especially large increases. This was one reason why the index of weekly wage rates rose from 100 to

[1] It is worth noting that in the last three years of the war infantile mortality in the United Kingdom was reduced to the lowest point ever recorded – 49 deaths of infants under one year per 1000 births, compared to 53 in 1939. This trend became still more marked after the war, and in 1948 the loss per 1000 was only 34.

152 between September 1939 and December 1945 although the cost of living advanced only 31 per cent. The index of average weekly earnings (October 1938=100) moved still higher to a peak of 180 in June 1945, thanks to overtime, incentive bonuses, and so forth.

As a whole, the working classes not only increased their money incomes during the war but secured a larger share of the national product than in the previous decade.[1] This was only to be expected. In the 'thirties, no productive use could be found for 10 to 20 per cent of the workers and the marginal utility of labour was low. On the other hand, the exigencies of war placed manpower at a premium and, if the workers had not patriotically refrained from exploiting their scarcity value, they could probably have secured a larger share of the cake than they did.

How far actual living conditions of different groups were changed is a matter that deserves the attention of social statisticians. Broadly speaking, it may be said that one-third or more of the workers, who prior to the war had been unemployed, underemployed, or in unusually low-paid occupations, were able to increase their command of goods and services: that is to say that the full ration of food and clothing, which they could now afford to buy, exceeded their prewar consumption. Wage earners in the middle range continued, perhaps, to enjoy about the same standards as before, although not necessarily the same kind of goods. The best paid, those accustomed to incomes yielding a surplus for conveniences and comforts, suffered like the middle classes a fall in standards, due to sheer inability to procure such goods in normal quantities. This group, too, found its money income trimmed through downward extension of direct taxation. Prior to the war, less than one million manual workers had been liable to income tax, and their payments had averaged little more than £3 per head. By 1943-44 this number had increased to 7 million, averaging over £28 apiece. Indirect taxation also sharply restricted popular consumption. In addition to large increases in those old stand-bys of the Exchequer — the tobacco, beer and liquor duties — there was the new purchase tax, applic-

[1] After taxes, wages were 39 per cent of all private income in 1938, salaries 24 per cent, and rent, interest and profits, 37 per cent: corresponding percentages for 1945 were 44, 22 and 34. *Annual Abstract of Statistics*, No. 84, 1935-46, p. 223.

able to most goods other than food, which ranged from 16⅔ to 100 per cent.

In the First World War, financial policy had been more or less 'pure'; its aim was to raise as much revenue as taxpayers could supposedly bear (a low estimate) and at least enough to cover the rapidly increasing burden of debt interest. There was little attempt to relate taxation to the general economic planning of the war and, in particular, to use it as a weapon against inflation. By contrast, in World War II, 'the financial policies of the Government were always "impure" in the sense that they were interwoven with the manifold intricate threads of the nation's economic and social life'.[1]

At the end of 1939, J. M. Keynes warned the Government that it must move to close 'the inflationary gap' and, even before he joined the Treasury as economic adviser in the autumn of 1940, financial policy showed the impress of his thinking. As far as was compatible with the maintenance of incentives, direct taxation was used to reduce the pressure of expanding money incomes on the restricted supply of goods. Standard rate of income tax was raised to 7s. 6d. in the pound at the outset of hostilities, and the following spring to 10s. (in World War I the peak rate of 6s. was imposed only in the fourth year): with surtax the maximum rate applicable to the largest incomes rose to 19s. 6d. The top rung of the Death-Duties scale was lifted from 50 to 65 per cent. Excess Profits Tax started at 60 per cent in 1939 and was advanced in 1940 to 100 per cent, subject to a postwar refund of 20 per cent. Of equal importance from the point of view of inflation control were the various indirect taxes already mentioned, since by adding to prices they discouraged spending on non-essentials and promoted personal savings.

Drastic tax policies enabled the Government to meet out of revenue an increasing proportion of an increasing expenditure: in 1940, 39 per cent; in 1944, 55 per cent — a notable improvement over the record of 1914-18. This still left large sums to be borrowed, but the Treasury, using the techniques it had developed since the gold standard was abandoned, kept a firm hand on the

---

[1] W. K. HANCOCK and M. M. GOWING, *British War Economy*, History of the Second World War, United Kingdom Civil Series, H. M. Stationery Office (London, 1949), 511.

money market and succeeded in financing the war on a 3 per cent, instead of a 5 per cent, basis.

Whether war is financed mainly by taxation or mainly by borrowing, its real costs, as we remarked in Part Three, Chapter 1, must be largely a charge against current national output. That was certainly true in 1939-45: nevertheless, in addition, Britain drew heavily on the accumulated capital of the past and mortgaged part of its future production. In the five years, 1940-45, Government expenditure and personal consumption combined averaged 113 per cent of the national income. Only by 'disinvestment' at home and abroad could the nation live above its income in this fashion. Sales of foreign capital assets during the war totalled £1,118,000,000, and there was a net reduction of £152,000,000 in gold and dollar reserves. In addition, debts to the Commonwealth and foreign countries increased by £2,879,000,000 making with £49,000,000 'unallocated', a total for external disinvestment of £4,198,000,000. [1]

Failure to make good depreciation of property and machinery was the chief cause of capital wastage at home. Only maintenance and repairs essential to the war effort could be effected: with this exception, worn-out machines were not replaced, the use of transport equipment was extended beyond its normal 'life', buildings went unrepaired and unpainted. To these items must be added losses from enemy action — a net reduction of 30 per cent in the prewar merchant fleet, the destruction of 202,000 houses and the major damage sustained by 255,000 others. Over 4 million additional houses were hit in bombing raids, although not rendered uninhabitable, while thousands of factories, schools, hospitals, business buildings and churches suffered anything from total demolition to minor injury. Altogether, according to a rough estimate produced during the American loan negotiations in 1945, internal disinvestment plus physical destruction represented a loss of 10 per cent of the national wealth: including external disinvestment, 25 per cent of Britain's total capital was sacrificed. [2]

Undoubtedly these losses would have been much greater — assuming the war could have been won at all — but for the timely

[1] Ibid., p. 548.   [2] Ibid., p. 551.

arrival of American aid. Lend-Lease, however, did not directly improve Britain's external economic position, for instance, by facilitating the release of resources to swell exports. On the contrary, the agreement with the United States provided that material aid received should be balanced by allocation of more manpower to the fighting services, and to the production of munitions.[1] Relieved for the duration of concern about the balance of payments, Britain in fact deliberately cut exports to the bone until by 1944 they were no more than 31 per cent of their 1938 volume.

The grave future risks which this policy involved had to be disregarded in view of the present risk of defeat. Nevertheless, as the end of the war in Europe approached, the Government was forced to plan for restoration of external trade. Lacking ability to pay for a sufficiency of imports, Britain could barely find the means of subsistence, let alone maintain a tolerable standard of living. A major part of its food, a large proportion of its raw materials, had to be obtained from overseas. Shipping losses and the liquidation of foreign investments had wiped out most of the 'invisible income' which had financed the habitual excess of imports over exports.[2] In addition, huge external liabilities had been incurred which eventually would have to be paid off in goods. The conclusion was that to ensure an import programme no greater than in 1938, when consumption had been restricted by serious unemployment, the volume of British exports must be increased by upwards of 50 per cent over the prewar level.

What were the implications of this need for so large an expansion in production for the foreign market? In the first place, a smaller proportion of the nation's manpower would be available in future to supply the home market, hungry as people were for the clothes, pots and pans, furniture, motorcars, and all the other consumers' goods of which they had been deprived during the war. Again, the need to sell to foreign customers was not the equivalent of ability to sell: once immediate postwar demands were satisfied, export trade was likely to become highly competi-

[1] To allay American fears that Lend-Lease might underwrite competitive exports, the British Government made a unilateral declaration in September 1941, pledging itself not to allow the use of Lend-Lease material for export production.

[2] Even before the war, Britain had a balance-of-payments problem and had begun to draw regularly on external assets.

tive. In the inter-war period, investment in British industry had been held at a low level and much of its equipment was obsolete in comparison with that of other countries, especially the United States. Six years of enforced neglect of repair and maintenance had intensified this deficiency. It would be imperative, therefore, to devote a much larger fraction of the national income to investment than in the 'thirties.

In pondering this situation, the Cabinet also had to take into account the vehement and widespread demand for social reconstruction. 'There existed, so to speak, an implied contract between Government and people; the people refused none of the sacrifices that the Government demanded from them for the winning of the war; in return they expected that the Government should show imagination and seriousness in preparing for the restoration and improvement of the nation's well-being when the war had been won. The plans for reconstruction were, therefore, a real part of the war effort'.[1]

Foremost among popular expectations was maintenance of full employment, not just for the duration of the postwar boom, as after World War I, but permanently. The workers, whether they were engaged in military action or toiling in factories and mines, were haunted by memories of enforced idleness during the inter-war decades. They were grimly determined that, come what may, there should be no repetition of that experience. 'I am convinced,' Bevin told the Commons opening a debate on employment policy on June 21st, 1944, 'that any party which faced the people of this country at a General Election and refused to accept the principle of full employment would not be returned to this House.'

The National Government's official White Paper on Employment Policy had, in fact, asserted that 'the maintenance of a high and stable level of employment' must in future be one of the 'primary aims and responsibilities' of the State. That was a declaration of historic significance and it was backed by a programme which, albeit cautiously, committed the Government to checking swings in the trade cycle by planned public investment and other compensatory measures.

Second only to insistence on full employment was the demand

[1] W. K. HANCOCK and M. M. GOWING, op. cit., p. 541.

for a comprehensive social security system. That was made manifest when the Beveridge Report was published at the end of 1942. In form, a series of recommendations for which the author was solely responsible, this document aroused enthusiastic interest. Some members of the Government considered that its proposals went much too far, but public pressure was irresistible and, after long hesitation, the Cabinet accepted most of them in principle. It also agreed to Beveridge's 'Assumption B' that the logical corollary of complete national health insurance was a broad national health service which would make free medical care available to all.

Social security plans aimed at the overthrow of what Sir William Beveridge called the 'giant evils' of want and disease. Their brothers, squalor and ignorance, were also marked down for attack. The latter was challenged by an Act passed in 1944 on which agreement between the several parties proved possible. Its chief innovation was abolition of the 'free place' system, which barred the secondary schools to all but a minority of working-class children, and substitution of free education up to university entrance standards. The minimum school-leaving age was to be raised to fifteen by 1947 and, as soon afterwards as possible, to sixteen. There was also provision for compulsory part-time education in county colleges for those between sixteen and eighteen, and for additional grants for university students. Implementation of this Act called for tens of thousands of additional teachers and a very extensive school-building programme.

It was harder to secure agreement between the Tory and Labour sections of the Government on the proper strategy to employ in the battle against squalor. The need for a very large, public-assisted housing programme, both to take care of wartime wastage and destruction and to eliminate slums and overcrowding, was common ground. So, too, was the necessity for providing public authorites with extensive planning powers in connection with redevelopment of bombed towns and congested areas. The difficulty was the relation of private property rights to these requirements. In 1942, a committee of experts, over which Lord Justice Uthwatt presided, rejected proposals for land nationalization but recommended a tax on increments of value in built-up districts and public acquisition both of land scheduled for development and of all future development rights. This plan was too strong meat for the property-conscious Tory Party and was shelved. The Town and Country Planning Act of 1944 represented a compromise which neither side found very satisfactory. Its main purpose was to extend the powers of local authorities to acquire private property needed either for reconstruction of bombed areas or for slum-clearance.

Despite many disagreements, some on questions of principle, others on practical matters of timing and administration, all parties in Parliament were deeply committed before the war ended to a vast elaboration of the Welfare State. Said Anthony Eden, on behalf of the Tory Party, in the House of Commons on December 2nd, 1944:

We have set our hands to a great social reform programme . . . and even though there be an interruption it is the intention of each one of us who are members of the Government to carry that programme through. I have no doubt that . . . if a Labour Government were returned, that Government would put through what was outstanding in this programme. And I can say, on behalf of the Prime Minister, that we, as members of the Conservative Party, would give them support in putting through that programme to which the members of each party in the Government have put down their names . . . The undertaking I want to give the House is that there is no question of that programme being allowed to be lost or to fade away.

We see then that three categorical imperatives faced whatever government took office in Britain after peace returned. First, it would have to take steps to divert an increased share of the country's current output of goods to the export market so that the balance of payments could be restored; second, it would have to find means of directing into investment a larger proportion of the national income in order to satisfy the necessity for greater and more efficient production; third, it would have to provide for a tremendous new outlay on the social services and, consequently, maintain taxation at a high level.

The first and second of these tasks implied restriction of consumption, the third would tend to increase it. Under any circumstances, therefore, their concurrent performance would pose exceptionally difficult problems. The question was: Could a solution of these problems even be attempted without a greater change in the economic system of the country than one of the major claimants to postwar office — the Tory Party — was willing to undertake? Since any answer to that question given in 1950 is bound to be coloured by the events of the past five years, perhaps the author may be allowed to quote from a book he wrote in the summer of 1945:

It appears that Britain can have more consumption in the early years after the war only at the cost of foregoing additions to capital without which a rising standard of living is likely to prove impossible. But how is the choice between alternative uses of scarce means to be made? 'The classical method of a free economy,' according to the *Economist*, 'would be to issue unlimited credit to those who want to undertake capital expenditure and let it exert an inflationary effect on prices.' [February 24th, 1945] The result would be a fall in the purchasing power of wages and fixed incomes but an increase in profits which, it is assumed, would be reinvested in new plant.

Still more orthodox, and perhaps still more painful, would be the deflationary solution to the problem. This would entail drastic reduction in government expenditure with a view to repayment of debt. Taxes on profits would be reduced but excise and other levies which restrain consumption maintained. Prices would fall sharply and, for a time, production would slacken and unemployment rise. This would make possible a downward revision of wages, particularly if government economy measures included a decrease in the rates of unemployment pay. A shrinking home market and low prices would discourage imports but stimulate exports, thus providing British industry with profits and the means of capital accumulation.[1]

Both these methods involve imposing austerity on the many, indirectly perhaps for the common good, directly certainly for the benefit of the owners of the means of production: neither method was feasible in the political and economic climate of 1945.

The first would let loose on a bare market a pent-up hunger for goods, backed by a vast accumulation of purchasing power. Long before prices reached a height at which spending was drastically

[1] KEITH HUTCHISON, *Rival Partners: America and Britain in the Postwar World*. Macmillan (New York, 1946), p. 82.

curtailed, the demand for imported commodities would be certain to strip Britain of its last dollar and send the pound the way of the mark in 1924. Deflation would be economically sounder under the circumstances but, barring a dictatorship, it was out of the question. Any possible government would be composed of men who had but recently endorsed full employment and had promised extended social security. How then could it pursue a policy of creating unemployment and reducing social security?

Indeed, in the months before V-E day it was generally conceded that there could be no return to any kind of a free market in the early days of peace. Rationing and most controls over prices, manpower and materials would have to continue, at least until industry was fully reconverted and definite progress had been made towards restoration of the balance of payments. Thus far Tories and Labour agreed. But the latter aimed frankly at a permanent adaptation of wartime socialism to peacetime purposes. The Labour Party believed that a government which had taken responsibility for maintaining employment would have to continue to budget manpower and resources; that if top priority was to be given to exports and domestic investment, then distribution of the balance available for consumption must follow the principle of 'fair shares'. Further, Labour insisted, to attain the greater productive efficiency that was so urgently needed, key industries would have to be nationalized as a first step to reorganization and modernization.

The Tories' long-term programme was far more elusive. They did not deny that State planning might prove a necessary tool — after all they had experimented with it in the 'thirties — but they continued to express their attachment to private enterprise and their belief in its dynamic virtues. Just how the freedom and incentives, which private enterprise requires in order to function, were to be combined with their expensive programme of social betterment, the Tories did not explain. In the election of June 1945 they preferred to expatiate on the supposed danger of a 'Labour Gestapo' while pinning their hopes of success on the tremendous and well-deserved popularity of their leader.

But on this occasion the voters knew what they wanted. They sensed the difficulties of the Tory Party in trying to ride two horses apt to move in opposite directions and had few doubts about which one it would cling to in a crisis. Memories of the early 'twenties, when so many bright hopes had been buried in the grave of 'economic necessity', lingered; those of the great depression were still fresher. Capitalism, the voters felt, had had its chances, many of them, and its performance in terms of human welfare was not good enough. They decided, therefore, to turn to the party which not only promised a new and better social system but gave evidence of believing in it.

CHAPTER II

LABOUR IN POWER

The Labour Government will not dissipate its strength when returned to power by dealing only with minor matters. It will proceed at once with major measures while its mandate is fresh.

CLEMENT R. ATTLEE: *The Labour Party in Perspective.*[1]

THE extent of the swing towards the Labour Party in 1945 was exemplified not only by a huge increase in its popular vote, but by its capture of a great many constituencies where it had never before come within sight of success. For the first time it won victories in areas where the suffrages of the middle class were of decisive importance. In the inner and outer London suburbs Labour candidates, sometimes much to their own astonishment, found themselves returned by substantial majorities. A considerable number of districts in which agriculture was the main occupation also turned away from Toryism: the war, the unionization of farm labourers, and the raising of rural living standards, had at last, it seemed, begun to dissipate the feudal atmosphere of county politics.

Surprising as the 1945 election results were at the time, we can in retrospect distinguish a number of the forces which helped to swell the Labour tide. Ever since the foundation of the Party, there had been evidence of a secular trend in its favour. In 1900 the majority of the workers were strongly attached to the Liberal Party, or, less frequently, to the Tories, and their loyalties were not easily shaken. But these passed on, and the new party recruited ever greater numbers of their sons and daughters. From 1906 onward the curve of Labour's popular vote shows a steady ascent broken only once by the relatively small dip in the 1931 election, following the fiasco of MacDonald's second Government.

This rise in Labour support paralleled the spread and improvement of education. The average voter of 1945 was better informed and better able to understand difficult political and economic issues than his father and grandfather. Since 1918 a large minority

[1] Gollancz, (London, 1937).

of the workers had received the benefits of secondary education, and a very considerable number of them had attended W.E.A. or university extension courses.[1] One consequence was a much wider audience for political literature of a fairly sophisticated type, an audience which eagerly bought the publications of the Left Book Club, founded in 1935, and the topical volumes of the Penguin series. Thus the electorate of 1945 was decidedly more mature than that of twenty, or even ten, years earlier. It was not readily swayed by oratorical effects, but demanded facts and arguments. And so Churchill's fustian 'Gestapo' speech fell flat, while Attlee scored with his quiet appeals to reason.

However, it was not from books that voters had learned the chief lesson that they applied when marking their ballots in 1945. The most powerful force impelling them to vote Labour was memory — memory of disillusion in the 'twenties and despair in the 'thirties. As Lord Lindsay of Birker has written:

More than anything else, what helped to put the Labour Government into power was the country's experience of long-term and large-scale unemployment in the early 'thirties ... Modern industry as it developed after the first World War suffered great fluctuations which had terrible results.[2]

The apparent complacency with which the Baldwin and Chamberlain governments accepted one-and-a-half to two million unemployed as normal, and their niggardly treatment of the depressed areas, had made the deepest possible impression on the working classes. True, nobody actually starved, but hundreds of thousands of chronically unemployed men and their families suffered from malnutrition and, what was worse, from a sense of moral degradation. They were the outcasts, the great unwanted, rotting on the refuse heaps of a capitalist society.

Even men and women with steady jobs were afflicted with a sense of insecurity as they saw so many of their fellows deprived of the opportunity to earn a living. Would their industry, they wondered, be the next to fall into decay? Would they be thrust

[1] Over 100 of the Labour M.P.s elected in 1945 had been either students or tutors, or both, in the adult education movement. See MARGARET COLE, *Growing Up into Revolution*. Longmans, Green (London, 1949), p. 119.
[2] 'The Philosophy of the British Labour Government', in *Ideological Differences and World Order*, ed. by F. S. C. Northrup. Yale University Press (New Haven, 1949), p. 256.

out to join the hopeless queues at the Employment Exchanges? Nor were the middle classes altogether immune to the malaise of the economy; many experienced under-employment if not unemployment, although the secular trend towards a greater proportion of white-collar jobs in business and elsewhere softened for them the depressing effects of industrial stagnation. But for those with a modicum of imagination personal financial security often served to heighten a sense of guilt. As two exponents of the middle-class point of view have written:

The middle classes accepted cuts, increased taxes, and earlier tax payments in the early 'thirties, but the working class endured unemployment, poverty, and even near-starvation, thus burdening the middle-class conscience with another sin . . . The achievements of the first World War were forgotten, its sacrifices proved vain, its dead betrayed. Whose fault was it? Whose could it be — but a generation's which had mistaken comfort for civilization? In the new world the traditional middle-class philosophies seemed useless guides.[1]

The war brought jobs for all and appeared to show that with proper organization it was possible to provide the necessities of life for all, even when a large proportion of national production was being hurled against the enemy. As a result the prestige of capitalist economics sank lower than ever before while that of socialist planning soared. The soil was now fully prepared for the ideas that Labour had been propagating for nearly fifty years and the political temperature was perfect for their rapid growth.

In *Let us Face the Future*, its 1945 election manifesto, the Labour Party declared that it was 'a socialist party and proud of it', whose 'ultimate purpose at home is the establishment of the socialist commonwealth of Great Britain — free, democratic, efficient, progressive, public-spirited, its resources organized in the service of the British people'. Admittedly this goal could not be reached 'overnight', but the Labour Party promised that both long and short term policies would be inspired by a democratic socialist philosophy. The programme it offered to the electors set forth its plans in some detail. 'Suitable economic and price controls' would be employed to ensure that 'necessities for all'

[1] Roy Lewis and Angus Maude, *The English Middle Classes*. Phoenix House (London, 1949), p. 84.

took precedence over 'luxuries for the few'. Provision of new homes was to be given particular consideration although it was recognized that 'there must be a balance between the housing programme, the building of schools, and the urgent requirements of factory modernization and construction'. Wide extension of social insurance on the lines of the Beveridge Report was pledged together with a new national health service and measures to implement the educational reforms provided by the Act of 1944.

Translating the Party's long-held belief in public ownership of the means of production, distribution and exchange, into practical terms, the programme listed a few large key industries — coal, electricity, gas, inland transport, iron and steel — as 'ripe for nationalization': others would be left in private hands, but would be required to meet 'the test of public service'. However, new investment, whether in public or private industry, would be subject to government planning so that scarce capital resources could be allocated in accordance with the nation's most pressing needs. And in this connection the Labour Party proposed to nationalize the Bank of England, thus securing State control of credit policies.

In itself this programme was radical rather than revolutionary. The ground had been prepared for it by more than half a century of collectivist 'gradualism' topped off by wartime experience of a planned economy. Precedents could be quoted for almost every separate item, a point of great importance to the average Briton, who combines a readiness to experiment with an instinct for continuity. Nevertheless, approval of the programme by the electorate marked one of the turning points in British history. It presaged a change from a society which was still essentially capitalistic, although tempered by many socialist innovations, to one basically socialist despite numerous capitalist survivals. For while most economic enterprises were still to be privately owned, the decisions of their managers on such major matters as the scale and nature of their operations, the distribution of their products, the disposal of profits, and the investment of new capital, were henceforth to be strongly influenced, and indeed often determined, by government plans rather than by market pressures.

The first British Government with power to put a socialist programme into effect took office at the end of July 1945. At the polls three weeks earlier — the count was delayed by the collection of servicemen's ballots from all over the world — the Labour Party had secured nearly 50 per cent of the votes cast and nearly 3,000,000 more than the Tory Party, its only serious rival. Under the British electoral system the luck of the ballot has usually tended to give the largest party over-representation in the House of Commons, a result which made for strong and stable government, however deplorable it might be from the point of view of advocates of proportional representation. In the 'thirties the Tories had been the gainers from this tendency; in 1945 the swing of opinion towards the Labour Party gave it 61 per cent of the Parliamentary seats and an overall majority of 146, quite sufficient to insure it a full term of office.

If the opportunities of the new Government headed by Clement Attlee were great, its responsibilities were still greater. No previous British administration had been faced with more baffling and complex tasks. The war against Germany had been won and that against Japan was about to reach its sudden and shattering conclusion. But although external physical perils were, for a time, overcome, the country remained exposed to grave dangers. It was in a sense bankrupt. Quick assets were entirely inadequate to meet enormous foreign liabilities piled up during the war; immediate sources of international income were far from sufficient to pay for the minimum of imports without which Britain was unable to exist. Even with the most intense effort and sacrifice, the nation could not hope to balance its external trade account for several years.

The gravity of the situation was emphasized on August 22nd, 1945, immediately after V-J Day, when the United States Government abruptly cut off Lend-Lease. Britain had not anticipated that the American law which limited this form of aid to the duration of 'hostilities' would be interpreted quite so literally. The end of the fighting had not lessened greatly the expense of maintaining millions of fighting men scattered around the globe. Months must elapse before they could be brought home, demobilized, and put to work in factories reconverted from munition-making to production of export goods. But imports of American food and raw materials could not be suspended until exports were revived or a dollar loan negotiated. They could be, they had to be, reduced, and the first fruits of victory for the war-weary British people were shorter rations.

In *Let us Face the Future* the Labour Party had discouraged expectations of easy times. 'The problems and pressures of the postwar world', it pointed out, 'threaten our security and progress as surely as — though less dramatically than — the Germans threatened them in 1940. We need the spirit of Dunkirk and the Blitz sustained over a period of years.' Production and more production was once again the key to salvation. Only by the greater output of its factories could Britain earn the means to pay for vital imports, to restore the ravages of war, to provide capital for a larger and more efficient industrial plant, and eventually to make possible a higher standard of living.

Some self-appointed advisers told the Government to scrap most of its programme and concentrate on the expansion of production and exports. But it was Labour's belief that this objective could be attained only by broadly socialist methods, and it pointed to the record of the inter-war period as proof of the inability of a capitalist system to prevent chronic under-production and persistent shrinkage of exports. Now sheer existence depended on the full mobilization of national resources and energies. The Labour Government proposed, therefore, to adapt for peacetime use many of the planning tools that had been fashioned during the war to relate means and needs. In accordance with the principle of 'fair shares', which was the keystone of its programme, it continued rationing and the subsidization of basic necessities to ensure that they would remain within the reach of low-income groups. Power to allocate raw materials was also retained so that priority could be given to production for export.

Among the Government's major objectives was improvement and enlargement of the nation's industrial and social plant. Its plans called for investment of a much larger proportion of national income than in pre-war years, but even so demands for capital were greater than the means of satisfying them. It was necessary to weigh the urgency of new factory construction against the desperate shortage of housing, of power stations against harbour works, of shipbuilding against railway equipment, of farm machinery against motor-vehicles, and to apportion the available resources accordingly. Building licences, control of the capital market and, again, power to allocate materials, were the chief instruments used to enforce Government decisions. Moreover, as the nationalization programme developed, the Government acquired direct control of those industries where the heaviest new investment needed to be made.

A common charge against Mr. Attlee and his colleagues was that in persisting with party plans for nationalization they ignored practical considerations and adhered blindly to abstract theories. Their answer was that although as confirmed socialists they believed in the principle of public ownership, they were applying the principle only to those industries which were monopolies or which under private ownership had proved manifestly incapable of meeting public needs. Some, like the coal-mines, were hopelessly inefficient; others — electricity and gas supply for example — were composed of a large number of relatively small units and required co-ordination in order to gain the technical benefits of large-scale operation; all needed infusions of new capital in amounts too large to be satisfied by private investment. In the view of the Labour Government, therefore, nationalization was an integral and essential element in the drive for production.

Whatever the verdict of history on the first Attlee Government may be, none can say it followed the common practice of ignoring election pledges; in fact it made delivery on them to an extent without precedent. When it went to the country in February 1950, just four and a half years after it took office, it could claim that its five-year plan was virtually completed. All but one of the industries scheduled for nationalization were operating under public management. Only the iron and steel industry, acquisition of which by the State had been resisted with fierce determination by the Tory majority of the House of Lords, had won a temporary reprieve. On paper its fate was settled, for an Act vesting the principal iron and steel concerns in a publicly owned holding company had received the Royal Consent. But the Government had agreed to an amendment postponing the date on which this measure took effect until after the General Election of 1950, and thus left the final decision to the voters, since a Tory victory would mean speedy repeal of the Act.

Five major acts sponsored by the Labour Government had rounded out provisions for social security 'from the cradle to the grave'. The promised national health service had been inaugu-rated in the middle of 1948; after eighteen months it was a firmly established and popular institution although the personnel and clinical facilities for its full development were still lacking. A Town and Country Planning Act extended powers of public authorities to acquire land and secured for the State those 'betterment' values arising from growth of population and public improvements which hitherto had endowed landlords with unearned increment. The Distribution of Industry Act (1945) turned the 'Depressed Areas' of the 'thirties into 'Development Areas', in which hundreds of new factories, mostly producing consumer goods, provided thousands of new jobs and helped to create a more balanced economy in districts hitherto over-dependent on heavy industry. To many acquainted with the physical and moral decay that characterized, for example, Merthyr Tydfil or Jarrow in 1938, the fruits of this legislation represented a triumphant justification for government planning.

The housing programme, placed in the vigorous hands of Aneurin Bevan, Minister of Health, had gathered speed despite building material bottlenecks and other difficulties. During its term of office the Labour Government could boast of the provision of vastly more new homes, mostly for rent, than were built under the Lloyd George-Bonar Law Coalition which ruled Britain in the corresponding years after World War I, 1919-22.[1] The Trade Disputes and Trades Union Act of 1927 had been repealed. A new Parliament Act had stiffened the strait-jacket imposed on the House of Lords in 1911 by limiting its suspensory veto of legislation passed by the Commons to one session, instead of two. Burma had been separated from the Empire in accordance with its desires, and India, Pakistan and Ceylon granted independence under conditions which made them willing members of the Commonwealth. Large schemes for the social, economic and political advancement of the African and other colonies had been put in hand. All in all, the claim of the 1945 election posters — 'Labour Gets Things Done!' — had been made good.

[1] Up to December 31st, 1949, 623,347 new permanent and 157,146 temporary houses were completed. In addition, 323,826 dwellings were made available by the recon-struction of unoccupied, war-damaged buildings and the conversion of large houses. Thus altogether accommodation was provided for 1,104,319 families. From January 1st, 1919, to December 31st, 1922, 210,257 houses were built.

No attempt will be made here to offer a detailed appraisal of the Labour Government's legislative and administrative record: more time must elapse before there is either material or perspective for sober judgment. Partisans may declare that the nationalization programme has proved a great success or a spectacular failure; the outside observer, writing in 1950, can only report that results so far hardly justify either assertion. The national boards and corporations, set up to operate the various publicly-owned industries, have still to complete the 'shakedown period' during which they may legitimately ask, not for freedom from criticism, but for suspension of any final verdict. An intricate piece of new social machinery as it comes from the designer's hand is no more likely to be perfect than mechanical equipment embodying new principles. Only actual working experience will show, as American engineers say, what 'the bugs' in it are, and how they can be eliminated. Moreover, with the exception of the Bank of England and, perhaps, Cable and Wireless, none of the nationalized industries and services were operating smoothly when they were taken over. Some required complete re-organization; all were in need of extensive replacement and enlargement of plant. Thus their new managers, while carrying on day-to-day operations, had to plan and implement long-term programmes of investment, the fruits of which could not be garnered for several years.

In the case of the coal-mines, the first industry to be nationalized, the results of nearly three years working undoubtedly fell short of the Labour Party's hopes. There had been no dramatic improvement in production and efficiency, and the morale of the miners still left something to be desired. Although the steady drift of workers away from the industry had been checked, total manpower remained well below the level required if Britain was to resume exports on the prewar scale as well as satisfy all domestic demands for fuel. The lost generation of miners — boys who grew up in the coalfields during the 'thirties and were driven to other employment by the dismal prospects of the industry, boys now men in their prime — had not yet been replaced.

Output increased about 10 per cent in the first two full years after the National Coal Board took over on January 1st, 1947, and further gains were registered in 1949. Production per man-shift, which in 1945 and 1946 had fallen well below the 1938 average of 1.14 tons, rose to 1.20 tons in December 1949, but was still disappointing in view of the advance in mechanization. Absenteeism continued to present a serious problem, and while time lost through strikes since 1945 had been incomparably less than in the years after World War I, many unofficial local stoppages interfered with production.

For 1947 the National Coal Board reported a deficit of £23¼ million, after meeting capital charges, but the following year earned a surplus of £1.3 million. The improvement was partly due to better productivity, but more to an increase in coal prices which occasioned much criticism. However, the increase was unavoidable in view of the necessity for paying higher wages to attract workers to the industry, and because in order to meet demand many uneconomic pits had to be maintained in operation. An outstanding fact about the British coal industry was the wide difference in costs between different areas: some earned large profits, other equally large losses. Under public ownership prices were fixed with a view to securing an overall profit; had private ownership continued they would almost certainly have been still higher so that marginal units could cover their costs.

Provisionally it could be said at the beginning of 1950 that the coal industry was in a healthier state that before 1947; if it was a long way from full recovery, it was at least on the mend. But before nationalization could be a proved success, performance had to be a great deal better than before, not merely a little better — that would be no great achievement. Hopes for the future depended largely on the long-term plans of the Board, which included reconstruction of many existing mines and the sinking of a number of new ones large enough to benefit from the most modern equipment and techniques. As production was enlarged by such measures, it would be possible to dispense with the least efficient collieries (quite a few, in fact, had already been closed) and so gradually reduce average costs. But it would be a good many years before completion of the development programme made it possible to ascertain the worth of Britain's investment in coal. What could be said was that if the risks of the venture were considerable, those of allowing the industry to continue its slide to ruin were even greater. For no permanent economic recovery could be expected in Britain unless the country's one important native source of energy became both cheaper and more plentiful than had been the case in recent years.

Despite the fact that the coal industry was not pulling its full weight, British production and exports both expanded in a remarkable fashion between 1945 and 1949. In 1946, the year of demobilization and reconversion, industrial output as measured by the 'interim index' of the Central Statistical Office, just equalled the average for the years 1935-38. The 1947 winter coal crisis gave that year a bad start, but for the full twelve months an average gain of 8 per cent was recorded. During 1948 production was 21 per cent above 1946, and in the second half of 1949, 29 per cent. The volume index of exports (1938=100) showed an even more rapid advance. From 45.8 in 1945, it rose to 99.3 in 1946, 108.7 in 1947, 136.3 in 1948, and 150 in 1949.

These figures spelt solid progress, but it was a progress punctuated by crises and the burdened British pilgrim still had far to go before he reached his goal — the Delectable Mountains of economic independence. Whether the delays he encountered in his journey up to 1950 were due mainly to natural obstacles or whether they were to be ascribed chiefly to poor guidance was the subject of acute controversy. Supporters of the Labour Government naturally placed particular stress on the first factor; their opponents emphasized the second. The historian must take some account of both.

Foremost among the troubles inherited by the Labour Government was the trade deficit. This had long been an outstanding British problem, but the war had vastly aggravated the difficulties of its solution. Ever since 1918 Britain had found it hard to earn enough foreign exchange to pay for its immense import requirements, and, as we have seen, the gold standard broke down under the strain. Yet the situation never became really desperate, thanks to the existence of three cushions. They were: favourable terms of trade created by relatively low world prices for foodstuffs and raw materials; a large and fairly steady net income from foreign investments; and unemployment on a scale that limited demand for imports, since unemployed men do not use raw materials, and their families eat less than those of the employed.

The war punctured all three cushions. Reduced output of primary products was unequal to the demands of a growing world population, and the terms of trade shifted against manufacturing countries. Liquidation of Britain's most dependable overseas investments had sharply reduced income from this source. Unemployment as a means of checking imports had become both impossible politically and irreconcilable with the clear need for greater national production.

It was essential, therefore, not merely to restore exports to their prewar volume but to overcome the secular decline in international demand for British products. Without the near-monopoly that leadership in invention and industrial organization had given it in the nineteenth century, without the advantages of cheap coal and financial supremacy it had once possessed, Britain had to find means to sell manufactures to an increasingly industrialized world as successfully as it had once sold them to a world of farmers and miners. The difficulties of this task were greatly enhanced by the dominant position in world trade of the United States, a nearly self-sufficient economy. North America was the main supplier of many goods which Britain had to buy, but a poor market for those it wished to sell. Before the war it had usually been possible for countries with a North American trade deficit to earn dollars in other markets. But multilateral exchanges were possible only so long as the United States maintained a balance of trade with the world at large; now it could no longer do so except by throwing on the scales a heavy mass of capital exports in the form of either gifts or loans.

The unexpectedly high cost of postwar foreign policy provided an addition to Britain's balance-of-payments problems widely accepted as unavoidable. Critics on the extreme left maintained, however, that the fault lay with Ernest Bevin, Labour Foreign Secretary, who, under the influence of his permanent officials and his own antipathy to communism, continued 'to base British foreign policy on Conservative imperial and social assumptions'.[1] Thus, according to this view, the opportunity for establishing harmonious relations with Russia was rejected and Britain commited to the heavy military costs of 'the cold war'.

Applied to particular situations, the charge that Mr. Bevin

[1] KONNI ZILLIACUS, *I Choose Peace*. Penguin (London, 1949), p. 122.

erred in pursuing Tory objectives may have had some validity. Was it really wise for him to continue Winston Churchill's passionate support of reactionary monarchical elements in Greece? Would not Britain's interests in the Mediterranean have been better served by reconstruction of Greece on democratic lines? There can be little doubt that the danger of Greek adherence to the Soviet bloc was greatly exaggerated. The Macedonian question and the claims made on Greek territory by other Balkan states made that development improbable; so too did the dependence of Greece on international trade and its many economic and political ties with the West.

Again, continuity of the Palestine White Paper policy, promulgated before the war by the Chamberlain government, proved an expensive failure. After holding large forces in Palestine to combat Israeli demands for independence and incurring heavy moral and financial costs, the Labour Government was compelled to withdraw. It then discovered that the league of Arab states which it had fostered was a very poor team indeed, and that Bevin's policies had seriously weakened the economic, political and strategic position of Britain in the Near East, to which it properly attached great importance.

However, errors of this kind did not alter the fact that in the largest sense continuity of foreign policy was inevitable. Given a world of sovereign nations, the external relations of any state will be determined by a mixture of national interests and international pressures. The notion, briefly held by many members of the Labour Party, including Mr. Bevin, that socialism would prove a common bond between Britain and Russia, was always a sentimental illusion. Ideologically British social democracy and totalitarian communism were poles apart, and in any case geography and economics count more in the formation of foreign policy than ideology. That was surely proved by Soviet Russia's close pursuit of imperial ambitions held by a long line of Czars.

The Kremlin's expansionist postwar aims were bound to be opposed in Whitehall, for the interests of the two countries overlapped at many points. Moreover, the dominant position of Russia in Europe and its penetration of Asia would have compelled Britain to strengthen its links with the United States even if economic necessities had not driven it in the same direction. Now that there were no more blank spaces on the map, balance-of-power politics were unavoidable unless all nations were willing to stay within their own borders. But they were expensive politics, and for Britain, with global interests to defend despite partial liquidation of the Empire, the burden was almost unbearable. That explains why a French writer commented in 1949: 'For the first time in her history, England now finds herself in the part of a subsidized power — the part which in former times she has had played for her, now by Prussia and now by Austria'.[1]

Even with American aid, British defence costs, which constituted a larger proportion of national income than in the United States, represented a charge on production which seriously hampered the recovery effort.

Another drag on Britain's economic resources was the weighty burden of sterling debts accumulated during the war by payment for goods and services received from India, Egypt, Australia, Eire, Irak and some other countries. Up to the beginning of 1950 the Treasury had not succeeded in negotiating agreements for the funding and gradual liquidation of these debts, which at the end of the war aggregated £3.3 billion. Since this sum represented irrecoverable expenditures incurred in winning the war, an enterprise of mutal benefit to debtor and creditors, many in Britain felt that repayment in full would be unjust. However, as Professor Lionel Robbins pointed out, 'it is gratuitous on our part to assume that these feelings are necessarily shared by our creditors . . . Moreover, we must not let the difficulties of the moment obscure the fact that, in many cases, we, the debtors, are comparatively rich while they, the creditors, are absolutely poor'.[2]

Pending final settlement these debts remained in the form of frozen balances in various London banks, but fairly large releases were authorized from time to time by the British Treasury, giving rise to so-called 'unrequited exports'. That is to say a considerable fraction of Britain's exports to India and other creditor countries represented repayment of debt and gave rise to no import equivalent. It was a profitable form of business for British manufacturers since the purchasers, unable to use their pounds for

[1] BERTRAND DE JOUVENEL, *Problems of Socialist England*. The Batchworth Press (London, 1949), p. 34.
[2] 'The Sterling Problem', *Lloyd's Bank Review*, October 1949, p. 26.

other purposes, were willing to pay high prices; but for the country as a whole it meant a dissipation of earning power which it could ill afford. It was, in effect, an export of capital at a time when Britain was dependent on imports of capital from the United States. In addition, convertibility of sterling was impossible until the sterling debts were segregated by some plan which provided for repayment in modest instalments. The crisis of 1947, when the pound was made convertible in accordance with the American loan agreement, had illustrated the difficulties of any less stable arrangement. Prior negotiations designed to prevent holders of London balances from demanding too many dollars ended in an agreement by which £140 million was made available to seven creditor countries. This sum was fully convertible, but Mr. Hugh Dalton, then Chancellor of the Exchequer, anticipated that the resultant demand for hard currencies would be spread over many months. He was speedily disillusioned: the recipients, avid for dollars, turned in their pounds immediately. Within a few weeks Britain was forced to pay out a large part of the dollars it had borrowed from the United States and Canada, and then, to protect its remaining reserves, to suspend convertibility of the pound again.

One reason why the Government hesitated to grasp this nettle was fear of adding to the inflationary difficulties of the creditor countries, difficulties which could be traced to wartime expansion of their currencies in response to British needs. India in particular was in a precarious economic position. The grant of independence to that country had been, perhaps, the most effective British counterstroke to the spread of communist influence in Asia, but its beneficial effects might be lost if the efforts of the Nehru regime to raise the abysmally low Hindu standard of living were impeded. Britain's debt was India's major investment reserve, on which all its development plans were based. Unless the United States was prepared to undertake the financing of India, the British Government had to consider very carefully the possible consequences of more strict limitations on the use of Indian balances. Nor could it resign its banking duties to America with equanimity, for that would mean industrialization of India with American equipment, and the loss of a market which would be needed in 1959 even if it constituted a drain on British resources in 1949.

Opponents of the Labour Government, while often critical of details of its imperial and foreign policies, reserved the weight of their oratorical fire for attacks on the home front. As Mr. Attlee and his colleagues forged steadily ahead with their programme and the shape of socialist things to come grew plainer, the Tory barrage became heavier and louder. Its effectiveness, however, appeared rather questionable. Judging by the usual test — by-elections — the Government retained its popularity to a remarkable degree. During its four and a half years of office, thirty-five Labour M.P.s died or retired. In every one of the subsequent contests a new Labour candidate was returned. It was a record without parallel in British parliamentary history, albeit one achieved partly by luck, as the results of the General Election of 1950 were to reveal.

Nevertheless, the Labour Government had some reason to believe that there was more public support for its policies than scrutiny of the press suggested. It had had its full share of misfortunes, of the kind for which governments are apt to be blamed, and made at least the normal number of mistakes. Its plans were sometimes both ill-conceived and poorly co-ordinated. This was particularly true in the first two years when the Treasury, under Hugh Dalton, was both too lenient with tax-payers and too liberal with grants of credit. As a result inflationary pressures developed, causing a diversion of resources from exports to domestic consumption and an increase in imports that contributed to early exhaustion of the American and Canadian loans.

Throughout its career the Labour Government was frequently accused by the Tories of pursuing austerity for its own sake, and this charge sometimes intimidated the Cabinet. Certainly that seems to have been the case in the autumn of 1946, when Emanuel Shinwell, then Minister of Fuel and Power, decided not to ration coal, electricity and gas, although fuel reserves were abnormally low. Gambling on a mild winter, he had the bad luck to experience the worst in many years. A breakdown in transport caused by heavy snows, together with inadequate power-station and factory stock-piles, forced the partial or complete closing of many industries. For several weeks some 2 million workers were idle and curtailed production led to a loss of exports estimated at £200 million.

Britain had barely recovered from the 1947 winter coal crisis when it was hit again by the summer convertibility crisis, to which reference has already been made. Again the Government was unlucky, but it could also be justly blamed for improvidence and poor calculation. Moreover, the crisis could have been avoided if, in accordance with a clause in the American Loan Agreement, the United States had been asked to agree to postponement of convertibility.

Stripped of dollar resources intended to cover the trade deficit until 1949 or 1950, the Government was compelled to recast its plans, to curb imports further, and to impose drastic increases in taxation so that surplus purchasing power could be mopped up and inflationary tendencies checked. Sir Stafford Cripps, one of the most brilliant minds in the Cabinet, was placed in charge of a new Ministry of Economic Planning, and a few weeks later, on the resignation of Hugh Dalton, took over the Exchequer as well. This combination of offices was to make for much better co-ordination of fiscal and economic policies.

With a firm new hand on the wheel, the economy was put back on its course, and for eighteen months Britain enjoyed relatively smooth sailing. Marshall Aid removed immediate anxieties about the dollar gap; production and exports made regular gains; inflation was held so firmly in check that people who had formerly complained that there was nothing on which to spend their money grumbled because they had not enough cash to buy the goods on offer. In the second half of 1948 Britain achieved a small overall surplus in current international transactions and, even though this concealed a large trading deficit with the western hemisphere, it was possible to hope that the balance-of-payments problem was being reduced to manageable proportions.

Sir Stafford Cripps, however, continued to decry complacency and to urge still greater productive effort. He was unwilling to relax any disinflationary measures, and his 1949 Budget, presented in April, made no concessions to demands for lower taxes, to the dismay of some members of the Labour Party, who joined the Opposition in condemning unrelenting austerity. But the controversy rapidly died away as the country realized it was headed for a new dollar crisis.

The mild recession which overtook the United States in early 1949 caused a slump in sales of British manufactures to that country, and, what was more serious, reduced both the volume and the prices of American imports of such raw materials as rubber, tin and cocoa, which were among the most important dollar earners of the sterling area.[1] Since there was no corresponding decline in imports from hard currency countries, the result was a widening of the dollar gap and a heavy drain on Britain's gold and dollar reserves. A quarterly statement published at the beginning of June showed that these reserves had dropped almost $400 million below the figure regarded as a safe minimum — $2000 million.

This revelation reinforced the opinion long held in international financial circles that Britain would eventually be compelled to devalue sterling in order to protect its reserves and strengthen its competitive position in world markets. During the summer of 1949 there was a scramble by traders and speculators to get rid of pounds by hook or crook, intensifying the pressure on the exchanges. Sir Stafford Cripps, however, continued to deny that he contemplated devaluation; he could, of course, do nothing else, for to admit the possibility of alteration in a controlled exchange rate is to destroy the effectiveness of the control. But in any case he was very dubious of the worth of such a move. Would the stimulus to exports provided by a cheaper pound compensate for the greater cost of imports and all the internal strains that would involve? It seemed very much of a gamble, and the British Government attempted to meet the situation by planning a 25 per cent cut in imports from hard currency countries, and persuading Commonwealth members of the sterling area to take similar action. But the pressure proved irresistible, and on September 22nd, 1949, the value of sterling was officially reduced from $4.02 to $2.80.

Devaluation meant an increase of the buying-power of dollars in Britain and a decrease in that of pounds in the United States. More concretely, Britain now offered larger quantities of its own wares in return for the same amount of American goods. Before

[1] The sterling area comprised all Commonwealth countries, except Canada, together with Eire, Irak, Burma and Iceland. Britain acted as central banker for the area, and its gold and dollar reserve represented the pooled resources, and served the needs, of the whole group.

devaluation it had, perhaps, bid one yard of cloth for a bushel of wheat; now it could propose a bargain rate of $1\frac{1}{3}$ yards. But trading on such terms was possible only so long as there was no important rise in British production costs. Hence, as Sir Stafford Cripps explained, there could be no increases in incomes to compensate for any rise in the cost of living that occurred as the result of devaluation. For the time being it was necessary to ask the weaver to accept some decline in real wages, to be willing to exchange an hour of his labour for fewer loaves of bread. It was not easy for a Labour Government to demand such a sacrifice from the workers who supported it. But the facts of the situation left no choice, as the Trades Union Congress recognized when, after prolonged discussions, it agreed to support the continued freezing of wage rates so long as the retail price index, which stood at 112 at the time of devaluation, did not rise above 118.

Something more than this was needed, however, if British prices and costs were to be held down so that advantage could be taken of the new opportunity to expand exports. Since only a gradual improvement in production could be anticipated, additional overseas sales would require diversion of goods from the home market, giving rise to inflationary pressure unless domestic purchasing power was reduced proportionally. The Labour Government, therefore, adopted an economy programme which included some cuts in the social services and in food subsidies as well as reductions in defence, general administrative expenses, and investment outlays. The total saving effected was estimated at £280 million in a full year, or about $8\frac{1}{2}$ per cent of the current budget. Observers abroad hailed as an act of political courage this readiness of a government with an already balanced budget — a comparatively rare phenomenon at the time — to risk its popularity by retrenchment on this scale. But the opposition at home denounced the economy programme as 'too little and too late' or, as *The Economist* scornfully put it: 'Salvation by fleabite.'

The devaluation crisis, coming as it did when the days of the 1945 Parliament were numbered and election fever was mounting, inevitably prompted a concerted attack on the Labour Government with the Tory press joined by such influential independent organs of opinion as *The Manchester Guardian* and *The*

Economist. In some opposition quarters the hope was entertained that the Prime Minister, alarmed by the storms besetting him, would follow the example of Ramsay MacDonald, who, in a similar crisis, had jettisoned his crew and socialist cargo and accepted Tory sailing directions. But Mr. Attlee, a man whose mildness of manner concealed great steadfastness of purpose, proved singularly unresponsive to suggestions that only an all-party government could handle the situation. He shortened sail, and trimmed the ship, but held to his course.

Meanwhile heated criticism of Labour plans and policies continued. The Government had, it was claimed, reduced the nation's economy to a state of *rigor mortis*. Lack of incentives, the result of 'over-full employment', crushing taxes, and an inflexible wage structure, had immobilized manpower. There were no longer 'carrots' to inspire ambition nor 'sticks' to counteract sloth and, as a result, plans which called for shifts of labour from one industry to another were constantly thwarted. Nor were there spurs to prick business enterprise into adapting itself to national need. Inflationary pressure made profit-making too easy, especially when controlled prices were fixed at levels which covered the costs of the least efficient firms. A sterling market, insulated by exchange controls, offered 'a soft option' to exporters; until devaluation, at least, they had little inducement to venture into the risky North American market.

Enterprise, the indictment continued, was also inhibited by high taxation. Profits might be abundant but the proportion demanded by the Treasury, together with a semi-voluntary restriction of dividends, left a meagre return for investors. 'High profits today, like high wages,' *The Economist* declared on October 22nd, 1949, 'are neither a proof of, nor a spur to, efficiency; until they are there will be less efficiency in the British economy than there might be.' Moreover, the same authority insisted, excessive taxation was not merely a disincentive affecting both management and workers, but an active inflationary force. It discouraged saving and induced members of the wealthier classes to maintain their accustomed standard of living by liquidating capital assets; it stimulated evasion. Thus inflationary pressure grew despite a massive budget surplus which, theoretically, should have provided a safety valve. With high domestic prices limiting exports and attracting imports, recurrent balance-of-payments crises were unavoidable.

What was the remedy for this alleged paralysis of planning? How were the 'rigidities' in the economy to be overcome? The answer of *The Economist*, the most articulate voice of the business classes, was that economic efficiency required more 'freedom to move' and more motives impelling movement in the right direction. It was necessary, therefore, to summon self-interest to serve national ends by liberating prices, wages and incomes, from the dead hand of government control. But before that move could be safely made, there must be a 'determined disinflation, sufficient to make a job worth holding and a profit difficult to come by'. In other words, total demand for both goods and labour must be held slightly below total supply. This could be achieved, *The Economist* said, by coupling credit restriction with government economies large enough to permit a substantial cut in taxes deterrent to enterprise without reduction of the budget surplus. Abolition of food subsidies would yield more than half the minimum amount required: the remainder could be secured by imposing small charges on clients of the public health service, by ending free secondary education, and by some reductions in defence and general administrative costs.[1]

Many Labour supporters were prepared to admit that there were elements of truth in this picture of an economy tied in knots. They agreed that full employment had created some rigidities and had helped to maintain inflationary pressure. But they were not at all convinced that an increase in the unemployment rate from under 2 per cent, as it was in late 1949, to, say, 4 per cent, would make a great deal of difference to the fluidity of manpower. The natural resistance of the worker to uprooting — a resistance strengthened by the housing shortage — could not be overcome so easily. To create a really free labour market far more drastic action would be required. It would be necessary, in fact, to restrict or abolish unemployment insurance and to curb trade-union activity. But even the stoutest right-wingers refrained from proposing such excursions to laissez-fairyland; indeed, they were always careful to disclaim any desire to use unemployment as a club.

[1] *The Economist*, 'A Policy for Efficiency', October 29th, 1949.

A modest rise in unemployment might have certain advantages, but there would be offsetting disadvantages which could not be ignored. The Labour Government, for instance, had made a great effort to convince workers that they need no longer be afraid of 'working themselves out of jobs'. It was part of a campaign to end deliberate limitation of output and opposition to labour-saving machinery, which was beginning to show results. By the beginning of 1950, systems of incentive payment, formerly anathema to most workers, had been started in the majority of manufacturing industries, as well as in the building trades, and the T.U.C. General Council was recommending their extension. But further progress might very easily have been blocked by any significant growth of unemployment, for memories of the old insecurity were still strong.

Again, the Government could not go back on its promise to maintain full employment without antagonizing the organized workers, who, by and large, had voluntarily shouldered the new responsibilities thrust upon them by a planned economy. Close co-operation between the Government, the Trade Union Movement, and management was a vital factor in the drive for production, and, to an extent that amazed many observers in other countries, that co-operation had been achieved. Since 1945 Britain had enjoyed a degree of industrial peace such as it had not known, except in wartime, for generations. True, there had been a good many unofficial strikes, but few had lasted long or involved large numbers of men. Thus from 1946 to 1948 only $8\frac{3}{4}$ million working days were lost through industrial disputes; the comparable figure for the period 1919-21 was 167 million.

This record showed that the unions had not pressed the advantage given them by full employment. Nor was it possible to sustain the charge that job security had led to general slackness. The long-term economic programme adopted by the British Government in 1947 had set as a target an expansion of industrial output of 25 per cent in the years 1948 to 1952 inclusive. Actually in the first two of these years production increased by 20 per cent over the 1947 base, although the labour force was enlarged by little more than 3 per cent in the same period. Despite the alleged lack of incentives, not only production but productivity — output per man-hour — had risen at a rate seldom recorded previously in Britain or any other country. There remained, of course, room for improvement, but the Labour Government could claim that planning implemented by voluntary co-operation had achieved some impressive results. Would partial restoration of the free market, greater reliance on self-interest as a motive force, less security of employment, and a change in the distribution of national income to provide for larger rewards to a minority — in short the programme of *The Economist* — have yielded still bigger returns? Perhaps, but possible gains from greater elasticity had to be weighed against probable losses through friction.

One of the cardinal features of Labour policy, which preachers of 'economic liberation' wished to modify, was the principle of 'fair shares'. Continued rationing of scarce commodities was but one application of this principle. More fundamental was the acceleration since 1945 of the process of levelling real incomes up, and down, that had been going on for forty years. As a result Britain had moved nearer to the ideal of economic equality than any other major nation, not excluding Soviet Russia. This achievement had been made possible, partly by measures securing a minimum income to every citizen under all circumstances; partly by the growth of communal services, such as the national health service; partly by the use of subsidies to keep the cost of basic necessities within reach of all; partly by means of direct taxation of so drastic a nature that in 1948 only 70 persons had incomes exceeding £6000 after payment of income tax and surtax. Ultimately, it had been authoritatively stated, Labour's aim was a range of *net* income extending from a lower limit of £250 to an upper of £3000.[1] Thus it was hoped to effect a permanent reduction of the once yawning gap between rich and poor while leaving room for differentials to provide incentives.

Labour's practical implementation of equalitarian ideals posed a difficult problem for its opponents. The Tory Party was in fact,

[1] FRANCIS WILLIAMS, *The Triple Challenge.* Heinemann (London, 1948), p. 125. Changes in the distribution of total personal incomes, after taxes, are shown by the following table:

	1938	1949
		percentages
Wages	37	45
Salaries	24	24
Pay of Armed Forces	2	3
Interest, profits and rents	37	28

if not in theory, a class party whose top echelons were drawn almost exclusively from the higher income groups. Inevitably, therefore, the solid core of the party — its officers, local and national, its major financial contributors — had a vested interest in inequality which it expected a government of its own men to perpetuate as far as possible. Yet Tories who sought election in working-class areas could hardly defend a wide degree of inequality as a matter of principle; at best they could uphold it as an expedient, a necessary incentive in this wicked world, or seek to prove that all the socialists were offering was 'the equal sharing of miseries'.[1]

Such arguments might carry conviction with those who had been levelled down, but they were less likely to impress the larger number levelled up. To a very considerable section of the community a fair share of postwar austerity seemed more satisfying than an unfair share of prewar plenty. The benefits of Labour's social programme were very tangible. In any working-class district they shone out of the faces of the children, who looked better fed, better clothed, and better shod than ever before. They were reflected in the vital statistics which showed record low death and infant mortality rates. They were manifest in the diminished psychological tensions of a people enjoying a new-found security.[2] Facts such as these enabled Sir Stafford Cripps to claim, at the annual conference of the Labour Party in June 1949, that:

Anyone today looking objectively at the over-all standard of living of our people must agree that for the vast majority of the lower income groups it is better than ever before. That is not to say that we are satisfied — far from it — but it does mean that the Labour Party in its first term of effective power has benefited the people in a way that no other party has, or ever could.

[1] Winston Churchill, House of Commons, October 22nd, 1945.
[2] It must be admitted, however, that there were indications of increased tension among upper and middle-class people, many of whom suffered a deep sense of deprivation and found adjustment to the new society an exceedingly trying process.

CHAPTER III

THE ROAD AHEAD

Fifty years ago, England was a bourgeois democracy in the sense that the bourgeoisie could run the country, its industry, politics, religion and everything else without much caring what the workers thought . . . Today, on the other hand, nothing can be done without the positive consent of the workers, whether it be achieving mobility, or maintaining investment, or using more productive equipment or what you will . . . That the working-class democracy has arrived is not generally realized, and this adds greatly to our difficulties. It is not realized by the workers themselves, whose mentality is still appropriate to the under-dog days. Power has come, but understanding, restraint, and responsibility will still take time to learn . . . Neither is its arrival fully understood by the bourgeoisie. There is too much atmosphere of 'Wait till we get you after the next election'. It won't in this sense matter who wins the next election. A conservative government will no more be able to act without the consent of the workers in the 1950's than will a Labour Government.
PROFESSOR W. ARTHUR LEWIS: 'The Prospect Before Us', *The Manchester School*, May 1948

THIS chapter, written in the summer of 1950, will not attempt to discuss the policies of the second Attlee administration or to describe its first few months of precarious life. Nor will it deal with the intensification of the cold war following the invasion of South Korea — a development which threatened socialist progress by curtailing the resources available for welfare and by distorting industrial reconstruction but, at the same time, brought no comfort to thoughtful proponents of capitalism who had come to realize that a military economy was the worst enemy of private enterprise. These events are too recent for comment in a book of this nature. However, to round out the story told in these pages, it is necessary to analyse in some detail the general election campaign of 1950 and its results with a view to ascertaining whether it denoted a change in the long-term politico-economic trend.

On February 23rd, 1950, when the people of Britain swarmed

to the polling stations in unprecedented numbers, they divided
their favours so evenly that the outcome was a political stalemate.
Although the Labour Party's total vote rose by over 1,100,000 to
almost 13¼ million — the largest total it, or any other British
party, had ever received — its percentage of the poll declined to
46.1, or 2.4 per cent less than in 1945, and it lost 86 seats, which
reduced its former huge majority to a corporal's guard. The
Tories garnered 2½ million additional votes, increased their proportion of the poll by 3.5 per cent to 43.4 per cent, and came back
to Westminster with 84 new members. A very modest rise in the
Liberal Party's vote was entirely due to the fact that it had contested about 175 more constituencies than in 1945: its average
score per candidate was some 25 per cent lower.

The election results seemed to show not only that the country
was evenly divided, but that the division was rather strictly along
class lines. Labour had made a nearly clean sweep of the
industrial districts; the Tories had been equally successful in
residential and rural constituencies. To some observers this
suggested that there were two irreconcilable nations of almost
balanced strength confronting each other. Were we, they asked,
facing the prospect of a permanent stalemate which would
paralyse Parliamentary government?

However, a study of the poll area by area, which took into
account votes received rather than seats won, tended to modify
such fears. The strongholds of neither of the two leading parties
were, on closer inspection, quite so solid as the distribution of
winning members appeared to indicate. Leaving aside Northern
Ireland, a special case, the heaviest concentration of Tory Party
strength was to be found in the southern Home Counties, where its
candidates secured 55.1 per cent of the total vote as compared
with Labour's 34.3 per cent. Contrariwise, even in Glamorgan
and Monmouth, where Labour's predominance was proclaimed
by a 66.5 per cent share of the poll, the Tories could still tally
26.4 per cent. In between these two extremes there were a number
of geographical areas where the electorate divided much more
evenly.[1] The very large votes received by unsuccessful Labour
candidates in many dormitory areas afforded proof that middle-

[1] The election statistics used above are derived from the very complete summary in
The Economist of March 4th, 1950, pp. 466-7.

class electors had not shifted *en masse* to the right; and if Labour support in the agricultural counties fell short of expectations, it was by no means negligible. On the other hand comparison of the total Labour poll with the total number of adults in wage-earning families showed that several millions of workers must either have voted Tory or Liberal, or abstained.

Taking such facts into consideration, it was possible to regard the election results as expressing the collective opinion of the whole nation rather than as an automatic mustering of hostile class armies. But since this opinion appeared to be negative rather than positive, its interpretation offered difficulties. The emphatic discouragement given to the ambitious attempt of the Liberal Party to stage a come-back, the sweeping aside of numerous independent and splinter-group candidates, certainly suggested a general preference for a clear-cut two-party system. Moreover, whatever degree of dissatisfaction with the Labour Government's record the poll reflected, it was clearly not of a nature to swing electors towards the left. There was nothing indecisive about the total disaster suffered by the Communists and those regarded as their fellow-travellers. Yet it could hardly be claimed that the country was sounding an urgent call for a retreat from socialism; at most it seemed to be asking for a pause to take stock. Finally, the election results could not be interpreted as undermining in any way the foundations of the Welfare State, full support for which had been pledged in unison by candidates of all colours.

Indeed, beneath the verbiage which decorated the party platforms not a few similarities could be discovered. In their manifestoes all used variations of what may be called 'the highway theme' to put over the point that they alone knew the best route for the nation to follow. *Let us Win Through Together*, the Labour Party urged, calling on 'electors of all classes . . . to continue along the road of ordered progress which the people deliberately chose in 1945'. Its allies of the Co-operative Party echoed this sentiment in a document headed, *Forward with the People*.

The popular version of the Tory statement of policy, entitled *The Right Road for Britain*, had a photographic cover loaded with symbolic values. It showed a healthy young family — father, mother, son and daughter — striding vigorously up the middle of a broad, sunlit, concrete highway (fortunately devoid of traffic) — the Conservative road that led 'forward ánd upward', the only alternative to the dangerous path curving 'downward to the Socialist State and inevitably on to Communism'.

The Liberals' approach to the same theme was more hesitant. *No Easy Way*, their manifesto was labelled; but it compensated for this note of uncertainty by using as its motto Hannibal's bold boast as he prepared to cross the Alps: 'I will find a way, or make one.'

Although these several roads were advertised as leading to different destinations, they appeared to intersect at a number of wayside-stations. Workers travelling by any of them were assured that there would be no by-passing of social security or full employment: farmers were promised that their journeys would be assisted by guaranteed prices and other benefits. There was less unanimity about methods of locomotion. Labour favoured greater use of nationalizèd buses and controlled speeds for all vehicles. Tories and Liberals thought that, as far as possible, travellers should supply their own transport, and, while agreeing that some restrictions on drivers might be necessary part of the way, promised that these would be lifted as soon as open country was reached.

Tory and Liberal programmes were, in fact, so similar in content that there seemed no ideological barrier to an electoral pact. Such an arrangement was strongly urged by Mr. Winston Churchill, who, in his anxiety to prevent a split in the anti-socialist vote, wooed the Liberal leaders with cave-man vehemence. But those experienced maidens rejected his advances with scorn; they knew all too well their probable fate should they consent to a marriage of convenience with Bluebeard. So long as they remained free and unencumbered they had, they told themselves, a nuisance value at least, and could continue to cherish the hope that the voters would recognize their virtues. Hence their reckless strategy of contesting enough seats — often with candidates selected at the last minute, backed by merely skeleton organizations — to make good their claim that the Liberal Party was a national party capable of returning enough members to Parliament to form a government.

In the upshot, they failed to convince the electors that 'a vote for a Liberal was not wasted'. True, their aggregate poll of over $2\frac{1}{2}$ millions was not unimpressive evidence of a survival of the Liberal tradition. But their support was spread so thinly over the country as a whole that they could win but nine seats, and they suffered both in purse and prestige by the forfeiture of no less than 314 deposits. After the election Liberal leaders continued to talk bravely about carrying on the fight, but observers found it difficult to believe that their party could survive except, possibly, as a very minor independent group. That was the conclusion of a sympathetic article in *The Economist* of March 11th, 1950, which after examining, and finding futile, every possible political strategy, tentatively suggested that attempts to represent the Liberal vote directly at Westminster should be abandoned, and the party transformed 'into an extra-Parliamentary body capable of influencing the course of policy by other means'.

Checked at the very threshold of Downing Street, the Tories in February 1950 charged the Liberals with responsibility for maintaining the Attlee Government in office. Their disappointed rage was understandable, but analysis of the election returns suggested that, even if the Liberals had stood aside altogether, the outcome might not have been very different. It is true that in seventy-one constituencies won by Labour on a minority vote the addition of a major fraction of the Liberal poll to the Tory total would have changed the result. However, it cannot be arbitrarily assumed that, in the absence of candidates of their own, Liberals would have moved *en masse* to the Tory camp. A Gallup Poll taken at the end of 1949 indicated that under such circumstances $42\frac{1}{2}$ per cent would have voted Tory and $22\frac{1}{2}$ Labour: the balance said they did not know or would abstain. Yet even if the Tory candidates in the 71 vulnerable constituencies had secured a *net* gain amounting to 30 per cent of the Liberal vote, they would have won only 17 more seats, and would still have fallen short of a working majority.[1]

It was clear, therefore, that the abdication of the Liberal Party would not automatically provide the Tories with a victory at another election. How then were they to win the 30 to 40 additional seats that they required to give them a strong working majority? In February 1950 they had fought under favourable

[1] See *The Economist*, March 4th, 1950, p. 467.

circumstances. Since 1945 under the guidance of Lord Woolton, Chairman of the Conservative organization, they had built up a well-financed and extremely efficient machine. For the first time they could rely upon an army of enthusiastic volunteers to match that which the Labour Party had always been able to put into the field. As the Opposition the Tory Party was able to exploit all the grievances which accumulate during any government's term of office, especially that of one grappling with circumstances as difficult as those Britain had faced since the war. It enjoyed the effective leadership of Winston Churchill, who succeeded in keeping his opponents on the defensive and avoided the mistakes in tactics which he had committed in 1945. It could, and did, promise all things to all men – and women: full employment and fewer controls; more social security and lower taxes; more food, more petrol, more houses; reduced prices for consumers and bigger returns for farmers. But the bright moon of the Tories' programme failed to attract anything like a tidal wave of support and, although, as an American broadcaster reported, their faithful followers turned out 'with blood in their eyes', and they polled their strength to the last invalid, they failed to reach their goal. It seemed likely to remain beyond their grasp unless they could find a way to loosen Labour's firm grip on the major industrial areas.

The Labour Party entered the election aware that it was bound to lose a considerable number of seats. For one thing the redistribution of constituencies effected by the Representation of the People Act of 1948 had corrected anomalies from which it had benefited in 1945. This change alone would, it was estimated, cost it thirty members. In addition, no government which has held office for any length of time can expect to dodge the swing of the pendulum: there are always some citizens who make a habit of voting against the 'ins'.

Nevertheless, when Mr. Attlee sought a dissolution in January 1950, he appeared to have reasonable prospects of returning with a majority of 50 or 60. The country had weathered the shock of devaluation and in the last quarter of 1949 about half the dollar and gold reserves lost earlier in the year had been replaced. Production and exports were continuing to expand; retail prices had advanced only slightly following the change in the sterling-dollar exchange rate; unemployment remained at a minimal figure; food was a little more plentiful and better supplies of other consumers' goods had helped to make Christmas of 1949 the least austere in a decade. But the government was aware that there was rough water ahead. The increase in wholesale prices of many imported foods and raw materials made some rise in the cost of living inevitable before long; and although the T.U.C. was standing by its endorsement of wage stabilization, many important unions were growing restive and beginning to press for improved pay. It was clear, therefore, that the Government's policy of maintaining employment while keeping inflationary pressure within bounds was due for a test to meet which a fresh mandate was desirable.

The chief objection to a February election was the weather; there was a fear — unjustified as it turned out — that a wet polling day would hold down the vote to Labour's disadvantage. However, owing to the financial time-table and the incidence of local elections, the alternative was postponement of the appeal to the country until June. That would have meant a period of several months when little more than routine business could have been transacted, particularly as the Government had exhausted its 1945 programme. At the same time election fever would have infected all members of the Commons and the country would, in effect, have been subjected to the kind of protracted campaign that is one of the curses of American politics. All in all there seemed to Mr. Attlee and his colleagues nothing to be gained and much to be lost by hanging on until the penultimate minute of their legal life.

In its election strategy the Labour Party tended to rest on its laurels. Its appeals dwelt on the achievements of the Government, emphasizing in particular maintenance of full employment and its pursuit of the ideal of 'fair shares'. As the party in office it could not escape blame for whatever had gone wrong since 1945, and naturally enough it sought to establish as strong a defensive position as possible, taking full credit for every bit of brightness in the national picture. Moreover, the party managers felt sure that they could count on the solid support of the industrial workers. Their chief anxiety was a loss of the middle-class elements who had been attracted to Labour in 1945; their chief hope lay in winning over the agricultural workers and small farmers whose lot had been markedly improved by government policies. Neither of these groups could be expected to respond to a belligerently socialist, class-conscious campaign. And, tactics aside, Mr. Attlee and some of his chief lieutenants undoubtedly believed that, before there was another broad advance towards socialism, it was desirable to have a period of consolidation during which defects in new institutions revealed by actual operation could be remedied.

Reflecting such considerations, the Labour election programme proved to be a rather mild document which stressed the most popular party policies, skipped a little lightly over difficulties in their application, and was inclined to play down developing problems whose solution might call for unpleasantly drastic action. The subject of nationalization was not entirely neglected, but neither was it featured. A brief half-page reported soberly on those industries and services already acquired by the State. Proposals for public ownership of the sugar-refining and cement industries were included, somewhat ambiguously, under the heading of 'Encouragement of Industry', and were justified by references to monopoly of too brief and undramatic a nature to carry much conviction.[1]

The strategy of the soft-pedal, as applied by Herbert Morrison and other Labour generals, was not without its critics. There were those who believed that it was dangerous, even from a purely electioneering angle, in that it might cause a loss of enthusiasm among the workers which would more than offset any possible gains in middle-class votes. Such critics did not ask for sweeping new nationalization plans: the extension of public ownership, they agreed, was not a burning issue nor would it automatically advance the cause of socialism. What was much more urgent, they suggested, was the permeation of all economic institutions with the spirit of social democracy, a spirit they considered to be sadly lacking in some of the nationalized industries.

The failure of the official party programme to develop definite

[1] It is surprising that the Labour Party did not make more of the opportunity to turn Tate and Lyle's anti-nationalization campaign against its authors, when the extent of that concern's monopoly of sugar-refining was so perfectly illustrated by 'Mr. Cube's' insistence on forcing himself into every housewife's shopping bag.

tax proposals disturbed some left-of-centre back benchers. Admitting that the Government had done much to bring about a fairer distribution of incomes, they pointed out that glaring inequalities in economic power and privilege remained, which should be relentlessly attacked by means of heavier imposts on capital. Finally, advocates of a more positive, more aggressive socialist policy contended that physical controls of production and investment should be treated not as 'temporary expedients to meet postwar shortages, but [as] essential and permanent bulwarks of full-employment and fair-shares policy'.[1]

It is doubtful whether the outcome of the election would have been changed by a more radical Labour Programme. The results provided little or no evidence of a decline in working-class support for the Labour Party. On the other hand, Mr. Morrison's seductive gestures failed to prevent the loss of enough marginal seats, where the middle-class vote was decisive, to reduce Labour's majority almost to a vanishing point. There could be no doubt that significant numbers of salaried and professional men and women and of suburban housewives, who had voted Labour in 1945, had since become sufficiently disillusioned to turn back to Toryism.

To some extent disillusion was inevitable. Examining his party's setback in 1950, a young Labour M.P. wrote:

To millions of Labour voters in 1945, Socialism was not a corpus of doctrine. It was a state of mind, an outlook that preferred planning to a free-for-all, social justice to trampling down the weakest. The slogan 'Let Us Face the Future' inspired a generation that wanted hope in contrast to the prolonged dejection of the 'thirties. Labour was swept to power in 1945 on a wave of optimism.[2]

It was not easy for many of the middle class to sustain that optimism amid post-war realities. They had voted for a programme that envisaged an improvement in workers' standards in the expectation that a fuller use of resources would make some levelling up possible without a corresponding levelling down, except, perhaps, of the very rich. Thus they were taken aback

[1] *Keeping Left*, by a Group of Members of Parliament (London: *New Statesman and Nation*), January 1950.
[2] MAURICE EDELMAN, M.P., in *The New Statesman and Nation*, March 11th, 1950.

to find themselves, four years after the end of the war, heavily taxed, forced to pay much higher prices for their special amenities when they could get them at all, restricted in the pursuit of their favourite hobby — motoring — compelled to waste time in queues, and deprived of that prop and badge of middle-class comfort — cheap domestic service. It seemed unfair that while their standard of living remained depressed that of many workers had visibly risen. Some believed that the hardships they felt they were suffering were quite unnecessary, and accused the Government of inflicting them maliciously. Others clutched at the notion, popularized by bank chairmen, the editors of *The Economist*, and a few back-bench Tories with very safe seats, that both the troubles of the nation and their personal difficulties could be removed by a moderate dose of unemployment. That would restore labour discipline, and, by reducing working-class purchasing power, and consumption, ease the inflationary pressures that bore so hardly on middle-class incomes.

The possible penalties, as well as the alleged advantages, of deflationary measures to induce a certain amount of unemploymen have already been discussed in Part Five, Chapter II. But in any case such measures were not practical politics in February 1950. Had not the Tories dismissed as 'rather shabby' the Labour charge that they would seek to promote unemployment, and declared in their manifesto that 'the maintenance of full employment would be the first aim of a Conservative Government'? Possibly some Tory supporters did not take such pledges too seriously or believed that they allowed for a re-definition of 'full employment' which would re-create the 'pool or reserve of labour' that some businessmen claimed was necessary to the proper functioning of industry.[1] On the other hand, the makers of Tory policy could not have failed to observe, expecially after assessing the results of the February 1950 election, that if Labour needed some middle-class support to obtain a secure majority, their own chances of victory depended no less on winning over a larger proportion of the workers to whom full employment had come to mean not only physical security but a badge of freedom. Nor was it so certain that a deflationary policy would prove a boon to large numbers

[1] See Statement by Sir Graham Cunningham of the Federation of British Industries, July 30th, 1946.

of middle-class people. Full employment might have worsened the 'terms of trade' of the salariat in relation to the proletariat; but it had also meant more openings, more security and speedier promotion for a host of technical, administrative and clerical workers. A reversal of the situation would, therefore, have repercussions in Woodford as well as West Ham.

Just as the Tories had inscribed 'full employment' on their banners, so too had they underwritten the whole gamut of social services. 'The Welfare State', Mr. R. A. Butler declared on behalf of his party, 'is as much our creation as it is that of the Socialists.'[1] And Mr. Churchill had been willing to give his opponents hardly as much credit as that. 'In the last four years', he said in a speech at Wolverhampton on July 23rd, 1949, 'they [the Labour Government] have carried out plans prepared by the National Coalition Government with its large Conservative majority, of which I was the head.' The implications of these statements had been spelled out in the Tory election manifesto which promised to conserve and extend the social services. 'We are determined', it announced, 'to give a solid base of social security below which none shall fall and above which each must be encouraged to rise to the utmost extent of his abilities.' In addition, it promised 'to maintain and improve the Health Service', to ease the means tests applied to recipients of various kinds of pensions, to reduce the size of classes in primary schools, and to extend facilities for higher education.

It appeared, then, that in trimming their windows for the 1950 election the Tories borrowed not a few ideas from their competitors across the street. There was a marked similarity between the two displays, especially since the Labour store was not featuring nationalized industry quite as prominently as it had once done. Under the circumstances it seemed that the patronage each attracted would depend on the customers' assessment of the quality of the goods offered by the rival merchants and their respective reputations for prompt delivery. Doubts about the Tory shop might be engendered by unsatisfactory past performance and by the fact that it was trying to cater to both the popular and the carriage trade. Besides there was a rather obvious lack of enthusiasm among many of the older salesmen for the wares

[1] Statement to press, July 23rd, 1949.

they were supposed to push. And the manager himself, at the very moment when the merchandizing plan was endorsed by the shareholders, had urged the importance of giving the customers as little detailed information as possible and appealing for their business on the basis of trust in the old firm.[1]

How to reconcile the promises it felt compelled to make in order to win power from a largely working-class electorate, whose chief stake was in jobs, with the sectional interests of its own membership, whose chief stake was in property — that was the dilemma that faced the Tory Party. Labour scoffers asserted that, if the Tories succeeded in regaining office, they would have little difficulty in resolving the conflict: either the promises made would be speedily forgotten, or their fulfilment would be indefinitely postponed on the grounds that the country must first be rescued from the ruin into which the previous government had plunged it. History hardly justified such scepticism for while the Tories had usually fought major reforms to the bitter end, they had seldom attempted to repeal them on returning to power. Sir Robert Peel accepted the Great Reform Act to the disgust of his die-hard followers; Tory governments of the interwar period not merely accepted but extended many measures that their party had previously denounced as 'socialistic' and made no more than the feeblest effort to amend the Parliament Act of 1911.

Moreover, account had to be taken of the fact that a Tory Prime Minister in the 1950's was going to find himself in a very different position from any of his predecessors. They had been able to dribble out concessions to the workers without impinging too seriously on the rights of property or endangering the *status quo*. But nearly five years of Labour Government had established a new *status quo* with the result that the interests of Tory supporters could no longer be protected by merely resisting further advance; a halt would fail to satisfy them; they required a retreat. That was likely to prove a difficult, if not impossible, operation in a democratic country. In the past the British workers had been persuaded to acquiesce in a very uneven distribution of wealth. But once

[1] 'A programme of words can be pulled to pieces one item at a time without there being any compensating advantages to show in the general welfare of the State. That is why I have advised you consistently, during these last four years, not to commit yourselves to detailed, rigid programmes.' Winston Churchill at the Conservative Party Annual Conference, London, October 12th-14th, 1949.

redistribution had been brought about it was not to be expected that they would agree to return to anything like the old pattern. Yet a Tory cabinet which wished to change the incidence of taxation so as to improve the position of those in the higher-income ranges, would be compelled to make drastic reductions in the scope and costs of the social services. In other words, they would have to diminish the welfare of the majority in order to increase that of the minority — a very different thing from resisting demands by the many for a larger slice of the cake.

Again, the Tory pledge to maintain full employment was not one that could be thrust aside save at the cost of great political risks. Experience since 1939 had convinced British workers that by taking thought a government could ensure a plenitude of jobs. They would never again believe that the trade cycle was a force of nature which man was powerless to control. If a depression threatened, particularly during a Tory regime, they would suspect a deliberate move to undermine their standards and their indignation would create irresistible pressure for counter-measures. Consequently, however much Tories might talk about giving free enterprise its head they would, on returning to power, drop the reins at their peril. However much they might protest their opposition to socialism, they had in *The Right Road for Britain* made commitments which would compel them to adopt socialist policies.

The undertaking to foster the Welfare State precluded any drastic revision of the equalitarian system of taxation which had been developed during World War II and consolidated by the Labour Government. Yet the charge that such a system was incompatible with the efficient operation of a free-enterprise economy was fully justified. It was not to be expected that private savings would provide for national investment needs when confiscatory taxation of large incomes and fortunes both inhibited risk-taking and cut the supply of funds available for that purpose. But a government which had assumed responsibility for full employment could not afford to be indifferent to the problem of investment. If private channels were blocked, it would have to create public ones and ensure that capital flowed through them in sufficient amounts and reached its planned destinations. That was what the Labour Government had attempted to do with some degree of success and it was difficult to believe that any successor could do other than follow its example. Yet once the function of deciding the extent and main direction of capital investment had been taken over by the State, was not the back of the capitalist system broken?

Before the 1950 election some of the younger Tories, at any rate, had realized that their party could not safely continue to pursue inconsistent objectives. 'We are committed', wrote one of them, 'to a great experiment — the creation and maintenance of a Social Democratic State', and he urged the necessity of accepting whole-heartedly the implications of this fact.[1] The alternative was put with crude logic by the writer of a letter printed by the *Evening Standard* shortly before the election. 'The Tories', he declared, 'if returned to power should disenfranchise the masses of the proletariat, both male and female.'[2] Needless to say Tory head-quarters ignored this wildly impracticable suggestion. No party could put such a proposition before the electors without incurring overwhelming defeat: no government lacking a popular mandate for returning to a property franchise could attempt legislation for that purpose without inviting revolution.

Whatever a few Colonel Blimps might say, the leaders of the Tory Party understood very well that 'politics is the art of the possible' and that, in the words of Professor Arthur Lewis quoted at the beginning of this chapter, 'a Conservative Government will no more be able to act without the consent of the workers in the 1950's than will a Labour Government'. The workers might agree to pause in the march which had taken them through social reform towards socialism; they might appreciate the desirability of a period of consolidation. But it was inconceivable that they would permit any government to take away from them the substance of their hardly won gains.

Nevertheless, some observers, particularly in America, hailed the setback suffered by the Labour Party in the February 1950 election as proof that the socialist tide had turned. That appeared to be a wishful snap judgment which could not easily be sustained when the implications of the Tory position were studied. What the election did indicate was that the British people — pragmatic

[1] Quintin Hogg, M.P. Letter to *The Times*, March 16th, 1949.
[2] Quoted in the *New Statesman and Nation*, January 14th, 1950.

as ever — were not concerned with either socialism or capitalism as theoretical systems: they were interested solely in results. They approved the major objectives of the Labour Government, which had indeed become the major objectives of all parties, and they were not unduly disturbed because the achievement of these objectives called for some socialist measures. But they tended to be critical of any controls or restraints which appeared irrelevant or unnecessary and they evinced little enthusiasm for new nationalization proposals for which the Labour Party had failed to make out a really strong case.

That lack of enthusiasm was related to the fact that none of the industries nationalized between 1945 and 1949 had as yet provided a dramatic demonstration of the virtues of public ownership. No doubt, as the previous chapter suggested, it was unfair to expect them to do so in the short time available. However, the records of several of the nationalized industries indicated the need for extensive alterations in their managerial structure if they were to carry out the social and economic responsibilities laid upon them. Even some warm supporters of nationalization felt, for instance, that the administrative machinery provided by statute for the coal and transport industries was unduly rigid and over-centralized. In particular, it seemed, much needed to be done to give real substance to the provision made for workers' consultation and for representation of consumer interests in these and other publicly owned industries. Hence there was a good deal of support for the idea that existing nationalization schemes should be revised in the light of experience before further experiments were undertaken.[1]

By giving the Labour Party a majority in February 1950 the electorate insured against the risks of reaction: by making the majority barely effective, it secured a halt in the spate of legislation, some of it poorly digested, which had been poured out by the previous Parliament. The Labour Government could contrive for a time to maintain itself in office, provided its followers kept healthy and maintained strict party discipline: it could continue to control the administrative and financial machinery of the country; it could reap in the fields of foreign trade and industrial development some of the fruits of its previous toil. But

[1] See *The Political Quarterly*, April-June 1950, vol. XXI, No. 2.

it was in no position to undertake new legislation of a controversial nature. Willy-nilly, the Labour Party was forced to pause and reflect.

Thus the beginning of the 1950's saw Britain still on the road it had been following for some seventy years but enjoying a breather while its leaders checked their bearings. Moving gradually towards socialism it had reached the zone of a 'mixed economy' where it might continue to sojourn for a considerable period. Private enterprise, albeit subject to controls and compelled to accept many social responsibilities, continued to operate over a wide area. But key industries and services had passed into the hands of the State and major economic decisions were no longer made by the subconscious processes of the market or by boards of directors of giant corporations. Instead, the distribution of national resources between consumption and savings, and the division of savings between social and industrial investment, were now planned and directed by the Government on behalf of the people. Whether as the result of these changes Britain could be described as a socialist country was a matter for argument. But in the author's opinion it was certainly no longer possible to talk of the British capitalist system in anything like the sense in which that term was used in the late nineteenth century or even in the first three decades of the present one. That is why he has ventured to write not merely of the decline but of the fall of British capitalism.

BOOKS QUOTED AND CONSULTED

This is not a complete bibliography of the period covered by this work; it is merely a list of some of the books consulted by the author.

ADAMS, BROOKS, *America's Economic Supremacy*, with a new evaluation by Marquis W. Childs, Harper, New York, 1947.

ALLEN, G. C., *British Industries and Their Organization*, Longmans, Green, London, 1939.

ARNOT, R. PAGE, *The General Strike, 1926*, Labour Research Department, London, 1926.

ATTLEE, C. R., *The Labour Party in Perspective — And Twelve Years Later*, with an introduction by Francis Williams, Gollancz, London, 1949.

BAKER, CHARLES WHITING, *Government Control and Operation of Industry in Great Britain and the United States during the World War*, Oxford University Press, New York, 1921.

BELLAIRS, CHARLES E., *Conservative Social and Industrial Reform 1800-1945* (pamphlet), Conservative Political Centre, London, 1947.

BENHAM, FREDERIC, *Great Britain Under Protection*, Macmillan, 1941.

BETHMANN-HOLLWEG, THEOBALD VON, *Reflections on the World War* (Tr. by George Young), Thornton Butterworth, London, 1920.

BEVERIDGE, SIR WILLIAM H., *British Food Control*, Oxford University Press, London, 1928.

BEVERIDGE, SIR WILLIAM H., *Full Employment in a Free Society*, Allen & Unwin, London, 1944.

BEVERIDGE, SIR WILLIAM H., *Some Experiences of Economic Control in War-Time*, Oxford University Press, London, 1940.

BEVERIDGE, W. H., *Unemployment: A Problem of Industry*, Longmans, Green, London, 1930.

BEVERIDGE, LORD, *Voluntary Action*, Allen & Unwin, London, 1948.

BLATCHFORD, ROBERT, *Merrie England*, London, 1895.

BLUNT, WILFRED SCAWEN, *My Diaries*, London, 1921 (2 vols.).

BOLITHO, HECTOR, *The Reign of Queen Victoria*, Collins, London, 1949.

BOOTH, CHARLES, *Life and Labour of the People of London*, Macmillan, London, 1892.

BOWLEY, ARTHUR L., *Some Economic Consequences of the War*, Williams & Norgate, London, 1930.

BROWN, WILLIAM ADAMS, JR., *The International Gold Standard Reinterpreted 1914-1934*, National Bureau of Economic Research, New York, 1940.

BÜLOW, PRINCE VON, *Memoirs*, Putnam, London, 1931.

BOOKS QUOTED AND CONSULTED

CECIL, LADY GWENDOLEN, *Life of Robert, Marquis of Salisbury*, vol. IV, Hodder & Stoughton, London, 1932.

CHAMBERLAIN, SIR AUSTEN, *Down The Years*, Cassell, London, 1935.

CHURCHILL, WINSTON S., *The World Crisis; the Aftermath*, Thornton Butterworth, London, 1929.

CHURCHILL, WINSTON S., *Thoughts and Adventures*, Thornton Butterworth, 1932.

CHURCHILL, WINSTON S., *The Second World War*: vol. I, *The Gathering Storm*, Cassell, London, 1948.

CHURCHILL, WINSTON S., *Liberalism, and the Social Problem*, Hodder & Stoughton, London, 1909.

CHURCHILL, WINSTON S., *Lord Randolph Churchill*, Macmillan, London, 1906.

CHURCHILL, WINSTON S., *Sinews of Peace*, Cassell, London (Luxembourg printed), 1948.

CHURCHILL, WINSTON S., *The Second World War*: vol. II, *Their Finest Hour*, Cassell, London, 1949.

CHURCHILL, WINSTON S., *The World Crisis* (6 vols.), Thornton Butterworth, London, 1923-5; also 4 vols., 1911-18, Odhams Press, London, 1939.

CLAPHAM, J. H., *An Economic History of Modern Britain*, vol. III, Cambridge University Press, 1938.

CLARK, COLIN, *National Income and Outlay*, Macmillan, London, 1938.

COLE, G. D. H., *The World of Labour*, George Bell & Sons, London, 1913.

COLE, G. D. H., and POSTGATE, RAYMOND, *The Common People, 1746-1946*, Methuen, London, 1946.

COLE, MARGARET, *Makers of the Labour Movement*, Longmans, Green, London, 1940.

COLE, MARGARET, *Growing up into Revolution*, Longmans, Green, London, 1949.

COLLIER, JOHN, and LANG, IAIN, *Just the Other Day*, London, 1932.

CONNOLLY, JAMES, *Socialism Made Easy*, C. H. Kerr, Chicago, 1909.

CORNWALLIS-WEST, GEORGE F. M., *Edwardian Hey-Days*, Putnam, London, 1931.

DANGERFIELD, GEORGE, *The Strange Death of Liberal England*, Constable, London, 1936.

DUGDALE, BLANCHE E. C., *Arthur James Balfour, First Earl of Balfour*, vol. II, 1906-1930, London, 1937.

ECKARDSTEIN, BARON VON, *Ten Years at the Court of St. James, 1895-1905*, Thornton Butterworth, London, 1921.

ELTON, LORD, *Imperial Commonwealth*, London, 1946.

ENSOR, R. C. K., *England, 1870-1914*, Oxford University Press, 1936.

BOOKS QUOTED AND CONSULTED

ESCOTT, T. H. S., *England, Its People, Polity, and Pursuits,* Cassell, London, 1880.

ESCOTT, T. H. S., *Social Transformations of the Victorian Age,* Seeley, London, 1897.

FABIAN ESSAYS, *The Fabian Society,* London, 1885.

FEILING, KEITH, *The Life of Neville Chamberlain,* Macmillan, London, 1946.

FITZROY, SIR ALMERIC, *Memoirs,* Hutchinson, London, 1925.

GARDINER, A. G., *Life of Sir William Harcourt,* vol. II, London, 1922.

GARVIN, J. L., *The Life of Joseph Chamberlain,* Macmillan, London, 1932.

GLASIER, J. BRUCE, *William Morris and the Early Days of the Socialist Movement,* Longmans, Green, London, 1921.

GRETTON, R. H., *Modern History of the English People 1880-1922,* London, 1930.

HALDANE, RICHARD BURDON, *An Autobiography,* Hodder & Stoughton, London, 1929.

HALÉVY, ELIE, *History of the English People, Epilogue,* vol. I (1895-1905), Benn, London, 1929.

HALÉVY, ELIE, *History of the English People, Epilogue,* vol. II (1905-1915), Benn, London, 1934.

HALL, J. E. D., *Labour's First Year,* Penguin, London, 1947.

HAMILTON, MARY AGNES, *Arthur Henderson,* Heinemann, London, 1938.

HANCOCK, W. K., and GOWING, M. M., *British War Economy,* History of the Second World War, United Kingdom Civil Series, H. M. Stationery Office, London, 1949.

HAYES, CARLTON J. H., *British Social Politics,* Ginn, Boston, 1913.

HIRST, F. W., *The Consequences of the War to Great Britain,* Oxford University Press, 1934.

HIRST, F. W., *Early Life and Letters of John Morley,* vol. II, Macmillan, London, 1927.

HIRST, F. W., *The Political Economy of War,* J. M. Dent, London, 1915.

HOBSON, C. K., *The Export of Capital,* Constable, London, 1914.

HOFFMANN, ROSS, J. S., *Great Britain and the German Trade Rivalry,* University of Pennsylvania Press, Philadelphia, 1933.

HOGG, QUINTIN, *The Case for Conservatism,* Penguin, London, 1947.

HURWITZ, SAMUEL J., *State Intervention in Great Britain,* Columbia University Press, New York, 1949.

HUTCHISON, KEITH, *Rival Partners: America and Britain in the Postwar World,* Macmillan, New York, 1946.

HUTT, ALLEN, *The Condition of the Working Class in Britain,* Martin Lawrence, London, 1933.

331

HYNDMAN, H. M., *Record of an Adventurous Life*, Macmillan, London, 1911.

JEWKES, JOHN, *Ordeal by Planning*, Macmillan, London, 1948.

JOUVENEL, BERTRAND DE, *Problems of Socialist England*, London, 1949.

KAHN, ALFRED E., *Great Britain in the World Economy*, Columbia University Press, New York, 1946.

KEYNES, JOHN MAYNARD, *Economic Consequences of Mr. Churchill*, Hogarth Press, London, 1925.

KEYNES, JOHN MAYNARD, *The General Theory of Employment, Interest, and Money*, Macmillan, London, 1936.

KEYNES, JOHN MAYNARD, *Monetary Reform*, London, 1924.

LEWIS, ROY, AND MAUDE, ANGUS, *The English Middle Classes*, Phoenix House, London, 1949.

LLOYD GEORGE, DAVID, *War Memoirs*, Ivor Nicholson & Watson London, 1933-37 (6 vols.).

LYND, HELEN MERRELL, *England in the Eighteen-Eighties*, Oxford University Press, 1945.

MACKAIL, J. W., *Life of William Morris*, Longmans, Green, London, 1899.

MACPHERSON, WILLIAM CHARTERIS, *The Baronage and the Senate*, John Murray, London, 1893.

MACROSTY, HENRY W., *Trusts and the State*, Fabian Series No. 1, G. Richards, London, 1901.

MALLET, BERNARD C. B., *British Budgets, 1887-88 to 1912-13* Macmillan, London, 1913.

MALLET, SIR BERNARD, and GEORGE C. OSWALD, *British Budgets, 2nd Series, 1913-14 to 1920-21*, Macmillan, London, 1929.

MALLET, SIR BERNARD, and GEORGE C. OSWALD, *British Budgets, 3rd Series 1921-22 to 1932-33*, Macmillan, London, 1933.

MALLET, SIR CHARLES, *Mr. Lloyd George, A Study*, Benn, London, 1930.

MAUROIS, ANDRÉ, *The Edwardian Era*, London, 1933.

MONEY, L. CHIOZZA, *Riches and Poverty*, Methuen, London, 1911.

MORLEY, JOHN, *Life of Gladstone*, vol. III, Macmillan, London, 1903.

MORLEY, VISCOUNT JOHN, *Recollections*, vol. II, Macmillan, London, 1917.

MURPHY, J. T., *Labour's Big Three*, The Bodley Head, London, 1948.

NEWTON, LORD, *Lord Lansdowne, A Biography*, Macmillan, London, 1929.

NICOLSON, HAROLD, *Sir Arthur Nicolson, Bart., First Lord Carnock*, Constable, London, 1930.

OXFORD AND ASQUITH, EARL OF, *Fifty Years of British Parliament*, vol. II, London, 1926.

BOOKS QUOTED AND CONSULTED

OXFORD AND ASQUITH, EARL OF, *Memories and Reflections 1852-1927*, Little Brown, Boston, 1928.

PARKER, JOHN, *Labour Marches on*, Penguin, London, 1947.

PEASE, E. R., *History of the Fabian Society*, 2nd. Ed., Allen & Unwin, London, 1925.

P E P (POLITICAL AND ECONOMIC PLANNING), *Britain and World Trade, A Report by P E P*, Published by P E P, London, 1947.

PERRIS, G. H., *The Industrial History of Modern England*, Kegan, Paul, London, 1914.

POLANYI, KARL, *The Great Transformation*, Farrar & Rinehart, New York, 1944.

PONSONBY, ARTHUR, *Henry Ponsonby, Queen Victoria's Private Secretary*, Macmillan, London, 1942.

RAYMOND, E. T., *Mr. Lloyd George*, Collins, London, 1922.

ROBB, JANET HENDERSON, *The Primrose League 1883-1906*, Columbia University Press, New York, 1942.

ROBBINS, LIONEL, *The Economic Problem in Peace and War*, Macmillan, London, 1947.

ROSEBERY, LORD, *Lord Randolph Churchill*, London, 1906.

ROYAL INSTITUTE OF INTERNATIONAL AFFAIRS, *The Problem of International Investment*, Oxford University Press, 1937.

RUSSELL, G. W. E., *One Look Back*, London, 1912.

SALTER, SIR ARTHUR, *Recovery: The Second Effort*, London, 1932.

SHAW, GEORGE BERNARD, *The Early History of the Fabian Society*, Fabian Society, London, 1891.

SIDEBOTHAM, HERBERT, *Pillars of the State*, Nisbet, London, 1921.

SLATER, GILBERT, *The Growth of Modern England*, 2nd. edition revised, Constable, London, 1939.

SMELLIE, K. B., *A Hundred Years of English Government*, Duckworth, London, 1937.

SNOWDEN, PHILIP (Viscount), *An Autobiography*, Ivor Nicholson & Watson, London, 1934.

SNOWDEN, PHILIP, *Labour and the New World*, Cassell, London, 2nd edition revised, 1924.

SOMERVELL, D. C., *The Reign of King George V*, Faber, London, 1935.

SPENCER, HERBERT, *The Man Versus the State*, Williams & Norgate, London, 1884.

SPENDER, J. A., *The Public Life*, Cassell, London, 1925.

SPENDER, J. A., *A Short History of Our Own Time*, London, 1934.

STEWART, WILLIAM, *J. Keir Hardie, A Biography*, Keir Hardie Memorial Committee, London, 1924.

STRACHEY, RAY, '*The Cause*', *A Short History of the Women's Movement in Great Britain*, G. Bell & Sons, London, 1928.

BOOKS QUOTED AND CONSULTED

STRAUSS, PATRICIA, *Bevin and Co., The Leaders of British Labour*, London, 1941.

STRAUSS, PATRICIA, *Cripps, Advocate Extraordinary*, London, 1942.

TREVELYAN, G. M., *British History in the Nineteenth Century, 1782-1919*, Longmans, Green, London, 1931.

VILLIERS, BROUGHAM, *The Socialist Movement in England*, Unwin, London, 1910.

WEBB, BEATRICE, *My Apprenticeship*, Longmans, Green, London, 1926.

WEBB, BEATRICE, *Our Partnership*, Longmans, Green, London, 1948.

WEBB, SIDNEY and BEATRICE, *The History of Trade Unionism 1666-1920*, Longmans, Green, London, 1920.

WELLS, H. G., *Experiment in Autobiography*, Gollancz & Cresset, London, 1934.

WILLIAMS, FRANCIS, *Socialist Britain*, London, 1949.

WOOTTON, BARBARA, *Freedom Under Planning*, Allen & Unwin, London, 1945.

ZILLIACUS, KONNI, *I Choose Peace*, Penguin, London, 1949.

INDEX

INDEX

INDEX

Y*

INDEX

Crewe, Lord, on Lord Lansdowne's 'negotiated peace' memorandum, 177

Crimea, 151

Cripps, Sir Stafford, as Socialist League leader, 246; on sanctions under capitalism, 248; policies as Chancellor of Exchequer and Minister of Economic Planning, 305-6, devalues sterling, 306-7; on Labour Government's benefits to people, 312

Crooks, Will, elected Labour M.P., 116

Cumberland, 258

Cunard Co., rejection of shipping cartel plan, 95; Government loans to, 259

Cunliffe, Lord, Governor of Bank of England, 193

Cunliffe Report, gold standard restoration advocated by, 193-4; deflationary implications of, 194-5

Cunningham, Sir Graham, quoted, 322

Curzon of Kedleston, Lord, actions on Parliament Bill, 135-6; on Asquith Government (1915), 173; opposes extension of franchise, 183; as Foreign Secretary (1922-3), 221

Czechoslovakia, 'sold out' at Munich, 266; seizure by Hitler, 267

D'ABERNON, LORD, on A. J. Balfour, 99

Daily Chronicle (*The*), Fabian Society's influence on, 39

Daily Mail (*The*), urges 'business as usual' (1914), 163; anti-Labour, anti-Soviet views, 214-15; and 'Zinoviev Letter', 228-9

Daily News (*The*), on Ramsay MacDonald's diplomacy (1924), 227

Daily Telegraph (*The*), on wartime (1914) trade opportunities, 159; publishes 'Lansdowne Letter', 181

Daladier, as French Premier, 273

Dale, Rev. R. W., influence on Joseph Chamberlain, 33

Dalton, Hugh, as Churchill's Minister of Economic Warfare, 273; as Chancellor of Exchequer (1945-7), 303-5

Dangerfield, George (*The Strange Death of Liberal England*), quoted on House of Lords, 132; on spirit of revolt (1910-14), 139

Darmstädter und Nationalbank, failure(1931) deepens crisis, 242

Dardanelles (the), 173

Darkest England (General William Booth), 70

Dawes Plan (the), 199, 227

Defence of the Realm Act, 164

Deflation, 1870-1900, world-wide, influ-

enced by gold shortage, 22; effects on British economy, 22-3; promoted by 1921 Budget, 196-7; in 1931-2, 241-2; *see also Bank of England*, Cunliffe Report, Gold Standard

Delcassé, E., French Foreign Minister, 108

Democracy, political, Beatrice Webb on, 13; Britain transformed to, 41; Prof. W. Arthur Lewis on, 313; *see also* County Franchise Act, Parliament

Denmark, trade agreement with, 259; German invasion of, 273

Depression (1921), 196-7; (1929-33), 203-4, 238-9, 259

Derby, Earl of, directs National Service Campaign (1915), 175

Devonport, Lord, as Port of London Authority Chairman, 138; Food Controller (World War I), 166

Devonshire, Duke of, 80

Diamond Jubilee, 26, 27

Dilke, Sir Charles, 41

Dillon, John, criticism of Asquith, 129

'Dilution of Labour', 164

Disraeli, Benjamin (later Earl of Beaconsfield), 42; as 'Dizzy', 46, 51, 54, 76

Dock workers, London strike of (1889), 60-1, 65; Liverpool strike, 146; refuse to load munitions (1920), 211; win national minimum wage, 213

'Dockers' Tanner', 60

Dual Alliance of Russia and France, 105

Duckham, Sir Arthur, on coal industry unification, 212

Dugdale, Blanche E. C. (*Arthur James Balfour, First Earl of Balfour*), quoted, 118, 141-2, 169

Duke, J. B., his tobacco trust invades Britain, 94-5

Dunkirk, evacuation of, 273-4; spirit of, 294

EAST AFRICA, Fascist Armies in, 265

Eckardstein, Baron von (*Ten Years at the Court of St. James, 1895-1905*), on Joseph Chamberlain, 106

Economic Journal, cited, 87

Economist (*The*), on 'advance to State Socialism', 70; on cost of social reform, 74, 77; quoted, 286; criticism of Labour Government (1949), 308; on economic rigidities, 308-9, 314, 317, 322

Edelman, Maurice, M.P., on Socialism, 321

Eden, Anthony, pledges Tory Party to social reform, 285-6

341

INDEX

Free trade, Richard Cobden on, 29; discourages monopoly, 97; as political issue (1906), 99-100; in relation to British Empire, 104-5; Parliamentary majority for (1923), 223-4

French Congo, German request for, 148

French, Field Marshal Sir John, 173

Freud, 139

Gardiner, A. G., quoted, 81

Gardner, General Lynedoch, on demoralizing the poor, 70

'Gas and water socialism', 73-5

Gas-workers Union, 59-60

Gathering Storm (The), Winston S. Churchill, 272

Geddes, Sir Eric, chairman of Government economy committee, 198

General Strike, syndicalist hopes for (1914), 148; threat of (1920) in event of war against Russia, 210-11; miners press for (1921), 213-14

General Strike of 1926 (the), 203, 230-1; legislative consequences of, 231

Geneva, 264

George V, King, succeeds Edward VII, 134; role in Parliament Bill crisis, 135-6

George, C. Oswald, cited, 162

George, David Lloyd, opposes Boer War, 56, 86, 87; on inherited wealth, 88, 100; in Campbell-Bannerman Cabinet, 125-6; on House of Lords, 128, 132; his 'People's Budget' (1909), 128-34, 149; Coalition proposals (1910), 140-1; warns Germany, 148; opposes 'Big Navy', 149-50; war budgets (1914-15), 160; aids coal strike settlement (1915), 164, 171; hastens disintegration of Liberal Party, 171-2; opposition to war (July 1914), 172; Minister of Munitions, 174; cabal against Asquith, 175-6; as wartime Prime Minister, 176-7; his differences with Arthur Henderson on Russian revolution, 180-1; on war aims, 181-2; on franchise extension, 182-3, 186; his government's postwar problems, 192; election strategy (1918), 207-8; feud with the Asquithians, 208; postpones coal strike by appointing Royal Commission, 212-13; resignation (1922), 218; negotiates with Irish, 221; 1929 election programme, 234, 239, 241

George, Henry (*Progress and Poverty*), influence in England, 31-3, 131

Germany, industrial competition of, 19; interest in colonies, 28-9; foreign investments of, 89; naval ambitions, 101-2; economic rivalry with Britain, 103-4; J. Chamberlain's overtures to, 104-7; reactions to Anglo-French and Anglo-Russian agreements, 108-9; naval building programme, 110; suspected war plans disturb British Government, 148; naval race with Britain, 149-50; British press on menace of, 151; Grey's warnings to, 153; gambles on British neutrality, 153; financial panic (1914), 157; war weariness, 178; American investments in, 199; coal industry recaptures markets, 202; British demands for reparations, 207-8; consequences of Ruhr occupation, 221; negotiations on Dawes Plan and reparations, 227-8; banking crisis, 241-3; Hitler secures power, 247; successive violations of Versailles Treaty, 248-9, 263; annexes Austria and Czechoslovakia, 265-6; invades Poland, 271-2; offensive in West (1940), 273; *see also* Hitler, Nazism, Third Reich, William II

Gladstone, Herbert, as Home Secretary, 120-1, 125

Gladstone, William Ewart, 34, 40; and franchise reform, 42-3; splits Liberals by introducing Home Rule Bill, 44; character and career, 45-7; on transformation of Tories, 49, 56, 58, 69

Glasier, J. Bruce, cited, 36

Goebbels, 271

Gold, relative scarcity as deflationary influence (1875-1900), 21-2; effects of rising production after 1900, 88-9; free market in, reopened (1919), 195-6

Gold standard, growing adherence to, 22; Britain departs from during World War I, 191-2; Cunliffe Report urges restoration of, 192-4; moves toward restoration of, 197-8; re-establishment announced by Churchill (1925), 200; economic and social cost of, 201-2; second Labour Government's attempts to save, 204-5, 242-3; abandoned (1931), 245

Good Templars, 62

Gorst, John, 50

Goschen, G. J., quoted, 47; appointed Chancellor of Exchequer, 54; tax policies and debt conversion scheme, 79; criticism of Harcourt's death duties, 80-1

Gough, General, as Fifth Army Commander, 176

Gowing, M. M.; *see* Hancock, W. K.

INDEX

Graham, R. B. Cunninghame, imprisoned, 37
Graham, William, as President of Board of Trade, 242
Great Transformation (The), Karl Polanyi, cited, 69
Greece, 221; Bevin follows Churchill's policies in, 301
Greenwood, Arthur, as Health Minister, his housing and slum clearance measures, 238; attacks conscription (1939), 250; 'speaks for England', 271; joins war cabinet, 273
Grenfell, David, on intervention in Spain, 249
Grey, Sir Edward, as Foreign Minister, 108, 125; offers Germany 'non-aggression pact', 149, 152; exchange of notes with Cambon, 152-3; diplomatic ambiguity, 153, 172
Guardians, Boards of, 18; abolished, 232; *see also* Poor Law

HAGUE (THE), International Peace Conference, 110
Haldane, Richard Burdon (later Viscount Haldane of Cloan), 100; Secretary for War, 108; on trade-union law, 113; on Trade Disputes Bill (1906), 119, 125; reorganizes army, 149; victim of yellow press, 174; quoted on MacDonald Cabinet (1924), 226
Halévy, Elie (*History of the English People: Epilogue*), cited, 50, 124; quoted, 109, 110, 128
Halifax, Viscount (later Earl of), as Foreign Secretary turns against appeasement, 268
Halsbury, Earl of, leads fight against Parliament Bill, 136
Hamburg-America Line, 95
Hamilton, Mary Agnes (*Arthur Henderson, A Biography*), quoted on Wesleyanism, 34; cited, 180; on Labour M.P.s' discontent in 1930, 241; on break-up of Labour Government, 243
Hamilton, Mary Agnes (*Atlantic Monthly*, April, 1938), on Ramsay MacDonald, 240
Hancock, W. K., and Gowing, M. M. (*British War Economy*), quoted 280, 283; cited, 281
Harcourt, Sir William, as Whig, 40; as Leader of the House, 63; as Chancellor of Exchequer introduces 'Death Duties Budget', 80-1, 86
Hardie, James Keir, quoted, 56; opposes Boer War, 56; fight against Trades

Union Congress 'old guard', 59-60; as leader of Independent Labour Party, 61-2; early career, 62-3; howled down in Commons, 63-4; exclusion by Trades Union Congress, 64-5; elected at Merthyr, 66, 115; hopes for trade-union political action realized, 66-7; at first conference, Labour Representation Committee, 113-14, 117, 151; opposition to World War I, 172, 187
Health, Public, Birmingham water supply, 74; slums, 75-6
Health Insurance, National, 88, 120
Health Service, National, inaugurated by Labour Government (1948), 296; in relation to redistribution of wealth, 311; Conservatives promise to maintain, 323
Henderson, Arthur, as unemployed iron moulder, 17, 34; wins by-election (1903), 116; as political organizer, 118; on role of Labour Party (1906), 118; opposes Lloyd George's coalition proposals (1910), 123; joins wartime coalitions, 174, 176; opposes purge of Labour pacifists, 178; visit to Russia (1917), 180; supports Stockholm Socialist Conference and resigns from Government, 180-1; helps draft War Aims Memorandum, 181; plans reconstruction of Labour Party (1918), 185-6; on labour unrest, 206; defeated 1918 election, 209, 214; opposes Communist affiliation to Labour Party, 216; as Foreign Secretary, 236; discourages revolt against MacDonald, 241, 242
Herriot, E., French Premier, negotiations with MacDonald (1924), 227-8
Hicks-Beach, Sir Michael, as Chancellor of Exchequer, 80; introduces wheat duty, 98-9
Hill, Octavia, 70
Hills, J. W., M.P., on Tory opposition to social reform, 121
Hirst, F. W. (*The Consequences of the War to Great Britain*), cited, 177
Hitler, Adolph, 239n, 247, 249, 250, 262; denounces Locarno Treaty, orders Rhineland reoccupied, 263; successive coups of, 265-7; British appeasers fear overthrow of, 267-8; 'Sitzkrieg' strategy, 273
Hoare, Sir Samuel, Foreign Secretary, resigns after agreement with Laval on Ethiopia repudiated, 265-6
Hobson, C. K. (*The Export of Capital*, 1914), cited, 21
Hobson, J. A., quoted, 91

INDEX

Ireland, 218; 'Black and Tan' terror in, 221; *see also* Eire, Home Rule.

Irish Nationalist Party, holds balance of power (1885), 44, 50, 128; position after 1910 elections, 123; conditions for supporting 'People's Budget', 133-4; accepts Home Rule compromise, 142-3; arms embargo against, 143; smothered by Sinn Fein, 171; supports government in World War I, 172, 174

Irish Republican Army, 221

Iron and Steel Federation, British, 260

Iron and steel industry, tariff protection and cartelization, 260-1; Nationalization Act passed, 295; *see also* Steel

Italy, in Triple Alliance, 105, 174; conquers Ethiopia, 249; British attitude on sanctions, 264-5; Berlin-Rome Axis, 265

JAPAN, British alliance with, 101, 107; German trade captured by, 168; invasion of China leads to proposals of sanctions, 247-8; surrender (1945), 293

Jenkins, John, President of T.U.C., 64

Jews (the), blamed for war, 267, 271

Johannesburg, 29

Jouvenal, Bertrand de (*Problems of Socialist England*), quoted, 302

Joynes, J. L., 35

Jubilee Imperial Conference, rejects Empire customs union, 101

Justice, 39

Kapital, Das, quoted 12; first English translation, 31

Keate, John, flogs Gladstone, 46

Kenya, 28

Kerensky, 179

Keynes, John Maynard (*The Economic Consequences of Mr. Churchill*); quoted on theories of economic society, 191; on restoration of gold standard, 200-1; on adjusting wages and prices, 201-2

Keynes, John Maynard (later Lord), 240; on investment stimulation, 254; economic adviser to Treasury, 280

'Khaki Election', 66, 98-9; Labour candidates in, 115; won by Tories, 117

Kiel Canal, 110

Kimberley diamond field, 27-8

Kitchener, Lord, as World War I Secretary for War, 160, 173-4; death, 175

Korea, Russian designs against, 107, 313

Kreditanstalt, insolvency of, 242

Labour and the New Social Order, Labour Party's postwar reconstruction statement (1918), 184; election policy fashioned from, 186

Labour Electoral Association, 40, 58-9

Labour Government (1924), monetary policy, 199, 200; difficulties of minority position, 225; limited domestic achievements, 169-70; MacDonald's successful 'open diplomacy', 227-8; defeat of, 228; 'Zinoviev Letter' in 1924 election, 228-9

Labour Government (1929-31), leading members of, 236; early legislative programme, 237-8; failure to check mounting unemployment, 238-9; policies in financial crisis, 203-4, 241-3; break-up, 242-3

Labour Government (1945-50), 11, 13; election manifesto, 291-2; secures large majority, 292-3; faces grave postwar problems, 299-300; legislative record, 297-8; nationalization, 297; National Coal Board, 298-9; expansion of production and exports, 299; high cost of foreign policy, 300, 302-3; Anglo-Soviet relations, 300-1; sterling debts and convertibility, 302-3; economic policies of Cripps, 305-6; *The Economist's* criticisms, 308-9; full employment and industrial peace, 310-11; its equalitarian policies pose dilemma for Tories, 311-12

Labour Leader (weekly), 66

Labour, Ministry of, 176; in World War II, 274-6

Labour Party, 17, 40, 65, 66-7; position on tariff issue, 100-1; influence in Commons, 111, 112; emerges from Labour Representation Committee (1906), 117-18; forces rewriting of Trade Disputes Bill, 118-19; growth hindered by Osborne Case, 122-3; position after 1910 elections, 123, 130-1; supports women's suffrage, 146; position in World War I, 158-9, 176, 178; supports Stockholm Socialist Conference (1917), 180-1; War Aims Memorandum, 181; reorganization and postwar programme, 183-4; urges capital levy, 194, 203-5; becomes official opposition, 207; opposes intervention in Russia, 210-12, 214-15; bars Communist Party, 216; electoral progress (1910-18), 216; MacDonald's ascendancy, 216-17; 1922 election gains, 218-19; 1923 election, 223-5; restricted by Trades Disputes and Trade Unions

346

INDEX

Morris, William, on stirring up the workers, 31; as leader of S.D.F. and Socialist League, 35-7

Morrison, Herbert, opposes intervention in Russia (1919), 210; plan for London transport, 238; joins Churchill War Cabinet, 273, 320, 321

Moscow, 211, 271

Mosley, Sir Oswald, as member 2nd Labour Government, 238; resignation and organization of British Fascists, 239; follows Nazi line, 271

Munich Pact, 265, 267

Munitions Act, 165

Munitions, Ministry of (World War I), 164, Lloyd George appointed to, 174

Mussolini, 248, 265-7

NAPOLEON, PERIOD OF, World War I and aftermath compared with, 191-2

National Coal Board, 297-8

National debt, increase in World War I, 160-2; proposed reduction by capital levy, 194; burden increased by deflation, 198, 203-4

'National Democratic Party', 209

National Government (1931-40), inception of, 244; election tactics (1931), 245-6; appeasement policies of, 249-50, 262-8; Tory dominance of, 251; social and economic policies, 252-62; conduct of war (to May 1940), 271-3

National Government (1940-45), formation of, and leadership by Churchill, 273; secures total national mobilization, 273-7; economic and social policies, 276-82; postwar reconstruction plans, 282-6

National Liberals, in Parliament, 209, 255

National Review, cited, 91

National Union of Conservative Associations, 50

Nationalization of industry, 327-8; absence from Labour 1950 election programme, 320

Navigation Acts, 259

Navy, the British, cost of expansion as cause of 'Death Duties Budget' (1894), 79-80; in relation to French, Russian and German fleets, 101-3; advantage gained by dreadnought, 110-11; expansion (1909) causes controversy, 149-50; agreement with French Navy for wartime concentration, 151-3; Invergordon strike, 244

Nazi-Soviet Pact, 271

Nazism, 247, 250; British refusal to understand it, 262-3, 265; considered 'un-British', 267; new pogrom against Jews, 267; *see also* Germany, Hitler, Third Reich

Near East, peace in, 148, 221; British position in, 301

Nehru, 303

Nevill, Lady Dorothy, 73

New Deal, in U.S. compared with period 1906-11 in Britain, 120

'New Party', 239n

New Statesman and Nation, 321, 326

New Zealand, 256

Newcastle, Duke of, as Gladstone's political patron, 46

'Newcastle Programme', of Liberal Party, 39

Newfoundland fisheries, 107

News from Nowhere (William Morris), 36

Newton, Lord (*Lord Lansdowne: a Biography*), cited, 127, 148, 173

Nicolson, Sir Arthur (later Lord Carnock), as ambassador to Russia, 109

Nicolson, Harold (*Portrait of a Diplomatist*), quoted, 152

No Easy Way, 316

Norman, Montagu, Governor of Bank of England, 198, 204

North German Lloyd, 95

Northcliffe, Lord, his newspapers feature 'German menace', 151; Lloyd George's ally (1916), 175; post-Armistice propaganda, 207-8

Northcote, Sir Stafford, 50-3

Northumberland, Dukes of, value of properties enhanced by industrial growth, 49

Norway, German invasion of, 272-3

O'CONNOR, T. P., in *M.A.P.*, on Labour Party's influence on Commons, 111

Orr, Sir John Boyd, on malnutrition in Britain, 277

Osborne Case, decision in, blocks use of trade-union funds for political purposes, 111, 122-3

Osborne, W. V., 122 (*see* Osborne Case)

Ottawa agreement, on Empire tariffs, 255-6

Oxford and Asquith, Earl of, *see* Asquith, H. H.

Oxford Dictionary, admits 'unemployment', 18

PAKISTAN, granted independence, 296

Palestine, 301

Pall Mall Gazette, on capturing German trade (1914), 159

Pankhurst, Christabel, 145-6

349

INDEX

Pankhurst, Mrs. Emmeline, 145-6

Parliament, rural districts over-represented in, 41-2; passage and consequences of Third Reform Act, 42-3; businessmen in, 49-50; preoccupations of (1886-1900), 56; first trade union members of, 58-9; shocked by Hardie, 62-3; Labour Party's advent in, 117-18; becomes more representative (1906), 124; strain of Home Rule debates on, 138; character of (1918-22), 192, 209; composition of (1922), 218-19; (1923), 224; (1924), 229; (1929), 234; (1931), 246; (1945), 293

Parliament Act of 1911, struggle over, 133-4, 140, 141, 324; of 1949, 295-6

Parliamentarianism versus Revolution, Labour movement's debates on, 214-16

Parliamentary Labour Party, *see* Labour Party

Paupers, treatment of, 232

Pease, E. R. (*History of the Fabian Society*), cited, 38

Peel, Sir Robert, 140, 324

Pensions, Old Age, 72, 88, 120; Lansdowne on, 127; cost of, 130, 232

Pensions, Widows' and Orphans', 232-3

'People's Budget' (1909), approved by Cabinet, 130; details of, 130-1; as challenge to Lords, 132-3, 149

Perkin, Sir W. H., synthetic dye discoveries, 24

Perris, G. H. (*Industrial History of Modern England*), cited, 71, 76

Persia, Anglo-Russian agreement on, 109

Peterloo, massacre of, 192

Petrograd Council of Soldiers and Workers, 179-80

Playfair, Sir Lyon, 76

Plural Voting, bill to abolish, killed by Tory peers, 128

Poincaré, MacDonald's letters to, 227

Poland, at war with Soviet Union (1920), 210-11; German invasion of (1939), 271-2

Polanyi, Karl (*The Great Transformation*), cited, 69

Political Quarterly, The, on nationalization, 327

Ponsonby, Arthur (Lord Ponsonby of Shulbrede), (*Henry Ponsonby, Queen Victoria's Private Secretary*), cited, 45, 46, 47, 68, 70, 76; elected as Labour M.P. (1922), 219

Ponsonby, Sir Henry, 47; on socialism, 68, 70

Poor Law, 18; workhouse population at peak (1910), 87, 88, 232

Port Arthur, seized by Russia, 107

Postgate, Raymond, and G. D. H. Cole (*The British People, 1746-1946*), quoted 22; cited, 277*n*

Pound Sterling, *see* Devaluation, Gold standard, Inflation

Prest, A. R., cited, 87

Primrose League, organization and early history, 51-3

Progressives, in London County Council, 39-40

Property rights, wartime interference with, 169

Protectionism, Lord Randolph Churchill on, 20; as issue divides businessmen, 98; Baldwin fails to secure mandate for, 223-4; results of (1932-9), 254-62; *see also* Tariffs

Protestantism, 56

Prussia, 177, 302

'RADICAL PROGRAMME (THE)', on emergence of working class electoral majority, 41

Railroads, wartime government control of, 163

Railway Servants, Amalgamated Society of, and Taff Vale Case, 112-13; Osborne Case, 122

Railway workers, conditions of, 57, 113; Taff Vale strike leads to damage suit. 112-13; strikes of, 147, 213

Railwaymen, National Union of, in 'Triple Alliance', 148, 213-14

Rand goldfield, world monetary effect of output, 29, 49, 88; Chinese labour in, 117

Raymond, E. T. (*Mr. Lloyd George*), quoted, 209

Reconstruction Programme (1917-18), 182-3; in World War II, 282-303

Red Army, 211

Redistribution of electoral districts (1868), 41; (1884), 43

Redmond, John, 158, 172

Reform Act, Second (1867), 41, 45

Reform Act, Third (1884). *See* County Franchise Act

Rents, control and decontrol, 222-3

Representation of the People Act (1918), 182-3, 185-6, 207; (1948), 318

Rhodes, Cecil, 28, 104

Rhodesia, 28

Rhondda, Lord, as Food Controller (World War I), 166, 167

Right Road for Britain, 325

Ritchie, C. T., resigns as Balfour's Chancellor of Exchequer on tariff issue, 99

INDEX

Robb, Janet Henderson (*The Primrose League*, 1883-1906), cited, 52
Robbins, Prof. Lionel, on Britain's sterling debts, 302
Roberts, Field-Marshal Lord, 151
Rosebery, Earl of, on 'Khaki Election', 99, 100
Round Table (The), on 'social justice' in wartime, 167; on reconstruction, 182
Rowntree, B. Seebohm, study of poverty in York (1899), 75; on 'poverty line', in 1930's, 277
Royal Institute of International Affairs (*The Problem of International Investment*), cited, 90
Ruhr (the), French occupation of, 199, 218, 221, 227; coal exports of, 202
Runciman, Walter, as President Board of Trade, on human nature and profits, 163; on restoration of gold standard, 200
Russell, G. W. E. (*One Look Back*), cited, 146
Russia, 101; naval plans, 102; Asiatic expansion causes friction with Britain, 105-7; British agreement with, 109; 117, 148, 149; Balkan advances, 153; war debts of, 169, 172; 1917 Revolution, 179; Arthur Henderson's visit to, 180, 181, 194, 206; British intervention in, 210-11; *see also* Soviet Union
Russian Communist Party, 214-15
Russian Revolution, effects on British Labour movement, 179-80, 194, 210, 214-15

S.D.F. *See* Social Democratic Federation
St. Matthew, Guild of, 33
Salisbury, Robert, Marquis of, role in partition of Africa, 27-9, 43, 52; on composition of Tory Party, 53; on Socialist feeling, 54-5, 69; on social reform, 73; cautions Lords against rejecting 'Death Duties Budget', 80, 99; diplomacy of, 105-6, 121, 132, 152
Salt, E. S., 35
Salt Union, Ltd., 93
Salvation Army, 33
Samuel, Sir Herbert (later Viscount), report on coal industry (1926), 203; Liberal followers withdrawn from National Government, 251
Sankey, Sir John (later Lord), as chairman of Royal Commission on coal industry, favours nationalization, 212-13; as Lord Chancellor, 243

Sarajevo murders, 153
Schlieffen Plan, for invading France, 154
Scotland, as depressed area, 258
Serbia, 153
Sexton, James, 64
Shackleton, David, elected Labour M.P., 116
Shaw, George Bernard, Fabian Society activities, 38-9; and Boer War, 57; on John Burns, 125-6n
Shaw, Tom, Minister of Labour (1924), 227
Shinwell, Emanuel, Minister of Fuel and Power (1945-47), 304
Shipping industry, monopolistic tendencies in, 95; government control of (World War I), 165; subsidies to, 259
Siamese frontier, 107
Sidebotham, Herbert (*Pillars of the State*), on Lloyd George, 140
Simon, Sir John (later Viscount), resigns as protest against conscription (1915), 175, 245, 268
Single Tax, 32
Sinn Fein, displaces Irish Nationalist Party, 171; boycotts Parliament, 209
Smillie, Robert, 64, 178; as miners' representative on Royal Commission on Coal Industry (1919), 212
Smith, Adam, on price fixing, 93
Smith, F. E. (later Earl of Birkenhead), 139, 141, 146
Snowden, Philip (later Viscount), on Labour Representation Committee, 115, 130; on World War I financing, 161-2; opposition to war, 172, 170-9, 199, 204, 209; re-elected to Parliament, 219; his orthodox policies as Chancellor of Exchequer in first and second Labour Governments, 226, 239-41; opposes suspension of gold standard, 242-3, 244; attacks Labour Party, 245; resigns from National Government on tariff issue, 251
Social Democratic Federation (S.D.F.), unemployment rally produces rioting, 18; foundation, 34; Marxian principles, 36; as pioneer socialist body, 37-8, 40, 57; contrasted to Independent Labour Party, 61-2; sponsors study of London poverty, 71; relations with Labour Representation Committee, 113-14; merged in British Socialist Party, 215n
Social Democratic Party of Germany, 158
Social Democratic State, Quintin Hogg, M.P. on, 326

351

INDEX

Social Security, National Government's postwar plans for, 283-4; Labour Government provision for, 295-6, 311-12; Tory pledges on, 307-12; *see also* Beveridge Report, Health Insurance, Pensions, Unemployment Insurance

Socialism, advance of, 11-14; late nineteenth-century conceptions of, 68-9; social reform as antidote to, 73; Edwardian 'society' oblivious to, 86; non-committal attitude of Labour Party on, 113, 119-20, 121; wartime growth of, 158, 167; adopted as definite objective by Labour Party (1918), 183-4; major theme in Labour Party programme (1945), 291-2, 321, 326, 328

Socialist League, organized under leadership of William Morris, 36-7

Socialist League (of 1930's), 246-7

'Society', last fling of, 86

Somervell, D. C. (*The Reign of King George the Fifth*), quoted, 192

Soviet Union, Curzon and, 221; trade negotiations with, 228; MacDonald's protest to (on 'Zinoviev Letter'), 228-9; appeasers' fears of, 267; Hitler's pact with, and attack on, 272; Labour Government's relations with, 300-1, 311; *see also* Bolsheviks, Bolshevism, Russia

Spain, Franco's revolt, 249; Labour Party debates intervention, 249

Spencer, Herbert (*The Man Versus the State*), on individualism and socialism, 68-9; on 'the undeserving poor', 70, 72

Spender, J. A. (*The Public Life*), on political consequences of World War I, 171

Standard, The Evening, 326

Star (The), 'collared' by Fabians, 39

State (the), changing role of, 11-14; limited sphere of (before 1880), 44; Gladstone's distrust of, 46; growing responsibilities of, 69-72; enlarged costs of, 79-81, 94; economic role in World War I, 163-9, 222; National Government's victory reinstates capitalist control of, 251; economic intervention of (in 1930's), 258-61; control of labour and industry by (World War II), 272-8

State Socialism, Herbert Spencer on, 68-9; *The Economist* on, 70, 74

Statistical Abstract for the United Kingdom, cited, 91

Steel, British production compared to that of U.S. and Germany, 23-4; *see also* Iron and Steel Industry

Steel Sheet Makers Association, 94

Stock Exchanges, panic on outbreak of war (1914), 157-8; inflationary boom (1919-20), 196; liquidation on (1931), 241-4

Stockholm, International Socialist Congress in, 150-1

Strauss, G. R., M.P., and Steel Nationalization Bill of 1948, 261

Strikes, dockers (1889), 60-1; engineers (1897), 65-6; South Wales miners (1898), 66; between 1910 and 1914, 146-7; the Webbs and G. D. H. Cole on, 147; suspension of (1914), 158; South Wales miners (1915), 165; unofficial (1917), 179; coal industry, 197, 202-3, 213-14; railway workers (1919), 213; unofficial (1946-8), 310-11; *see also* General Strike, Taff Vale Case.

Suffrage, Women's, 138, 139, 144; militant campaign for, by Women's Social and Political Union, 145-6; role of National Union of Women's Suffrage Societies, 146, 158; partial enactment of, 183; extension of, 234

Syndicalism, 146-7, 210

T.U.C. *see* Trades Union Congress

Taff Vale Case, trade unions paralysed by, 91, 111-12, 115; Trade Disputes Act (1906) as sequel to, 119

Tariffs (Tariff Reform), political issue of, revived, 85; J. Chamberlain's campaign for, 97-9; Tory division on, 100; as cause of Anglo-German dissension, 101-2, 105; Baldwin unsuccessfully seeks mandate for (1925), 223-4; feature of National Government's recovery policies (1932), 234, 252-8; as method of economic planning, 258

Tariffs, foreign, extension of, hamper British trade, 19

Tate & Lyle, anti-nationalization campaign, 320*n*

Tawney, R. H., 234

Taxation, Randolph Churchill's plans for reform of, 54; Goschen's innovations (1889), 79; extended by 'Death Duties Budget' (1894), 80-1; of incomes increased, 98; provisions of 'People's Budget' (1909), 130-1; in World War I, 159-62; in postwar period, 194-6; of food, reduced by Snowden (1923), 226; increases in (1930), 239; (1931), 244; in World

352

INDEX